Politicized Economies

NUMBER FOURTEEN:
*Texas A&M University
Economics Series*

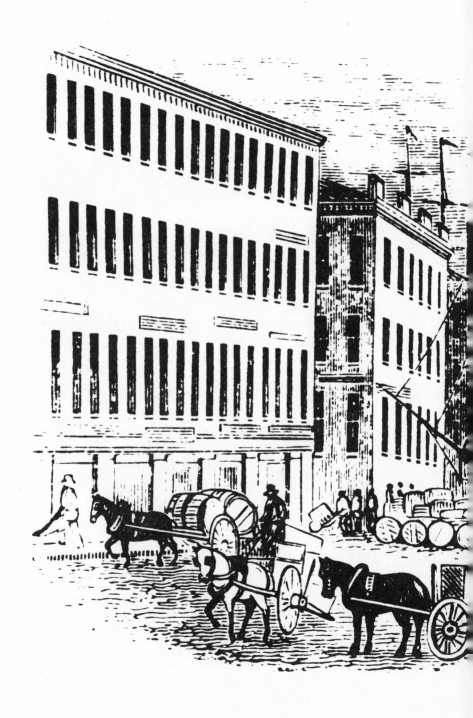

Politicized Economies

Monarchy, Monopoly, and Mercantilism

By Robert B. Ekelund, Jr.
and
Robert D. Tollison

Texas A&M University Press
College Station

The paper used in this book meets the minimum requirements
of the American National Standard for Permanence
of Paper for Printed Library Materials, Z39.48-1984.
Binding materials have been chosen for durability.

Library of Congress Cataloging-in-Publication Data

Ekelund, Robert B. (Robert Burton), 1940–
    Politicized economies : monarchy, monopoly, and mercantilism / by Robert B.
Ekelund, Jr. and Robert D. Tollison.
        p.   cm. — (Texas A&M University economics series ; 14)
    Includes bibliographical references and index.
    ISBN 0-89096-745-8
        1. Mercantile system—History. 2. International trade—History. 3. East
India Company—History. 4. Economic history—1600–1750.   I. Tollison,
Robert D. II. Title. III. Series.
HB91.E42   1997
382´.3´0940903—dc20   96-38971
                                                                  CIP

For Mark, with whom "the moon's a balloon"
                                        —R. B. E.

For James M. Buchannan
                            —R. D. T.

Contents

Preface

The sentiments of modern mercantilists could not be more apparent in the arena of world nations. Cyclical waves of internal and external regulation, protection, and political-bureaucratic provisions of all kinds continue to punctuate contemporary Western economies, just as they are features of third world developments. But these fin de siècle manifestations of "mercantilism" had their roots in policies and institutions of half a millennium ago.

More than a decade and a half has passed since our first foray into the questions posed by these institutions of "historical mercantilism." In our initial study—*Mercantilism as a Rent-Seeking Society: Economic Regulation in Historical Perspective* (1981)—we attempted to fill a void in the literature on the internal motivations of interest groups. Our aim was to establish a new and modern framework for evaluating changes in institutions (and institutional rigidities) over the high tide of mercantilism in England and France. In particular we sought to help "complete and establish a theory of policy and institutional change over the 'high time' of the mercantile age (1540–1640) in England, while simultaneously explaining the entrenchment of controls in the French economy." That theory used self-interested coalitions to explain changes in institutions, including political institutions, that affected economic growth. We proposed a new methodology for studying the economics of mercantile economies. Judging from the warm reception we received from this first effort, both supportive and critical, we met some success in our initial aims.

This present book builds upon and expands our initial treatment of historical mercantilism. We seek, in general terms, to place our ideas on mercantile institutions within the nexus of a neoclassical-neoinstitutional framework of analysis. Our first effort was clearly a part of that literature, as its reception has suggested. In the present work we make that connection more explicit and, in the process, provide a critique of older and more modern approaches to a theory of institutional development. Our view, which again focuses on orthodox traditions in property rights, rent seeking, and interest group analysis, is stubbornly neoclassical. This methodological orientation is developed throughout our study.

We adopt a two-step approach to the study of mercantile institutions. Chapters 3, 4, and 5 deal with mercantile institutions (primarily) within the economies of England, France, and Spain. Then, in chapters 6 and 7, these economy-wide studies are embellished with two chapters on a particular key institution of the period—the early companies. Our analysis of both England and France focuses on internal developments in institutions as a response to interest group and other pressures. The role of Sir Edward Coke in institutional change in England is now given full discussion in chapter 3. One source of the architecture of Spanish mercantilism is also addressed. Rent seeking through the mobile shepherding industry is the primary topic of chapter 5 on Spanish mercantilism, although other important factors which led to the stultification of Spain in the premodern and early modern worlds are discussed as well.

In chapters 6 and 7 we project our neoclassical-neoinstitutional analysis to the regulation of mercantilist foreign trade. Here we analyze the general economic organization of the mercantile companies and then focus on the economic inner workings of the East India Company. Some insight is thus obtained into the origins of the modern corporation and the effects of regulatory forms on the types of business organization that emerged to engage in foreign trade.

Both this work and our previous studies have greatly benefited from the comments of critics and friends. Those who have had less sympathy with our approach have been almost as valuable as supporters in provoking the present work. Among the latter, we must thank Professors Don Boudreaux, James Buchanan, Tyler Cowen, David Gay, Robin Grier, Robert Hebert, John Jackson, David Kaserman, David Laband, William Mitchell, Parth Shah, John Sophocleus, Mark Thornton, and Gordon Tullock who read and commented upon earlier draft portions of the manuscript. In particular we are deeply grateful to Professor Don Street, who was of critical assistance in developing our work on Spanish mercantilism, to Professors Gary Anderson and Robert McCormick, who assisted us in our study of the early companies, and to Professor Bill Shughart, who read and commented on the entire manuscript. In this regard we would also like to thank graduate student Luis Dopico and, for assistance in reading, preparing, and editing the manuscript we are most grateful to Paula Gant, Keith Reutter and, most especially, Frank Adams. Tom Saving, editor of the Texas A&M University economics series, has been extremely supportive of our project.

Portions of this work have drawn upon previously published papers and manuscripts. In particular some of the materials for chapters 3, 5, 6, and 7 draw upon the following papers: Gary M. Anderson and Robert D. Tollison, "Apologiae for Chartered Monopolies in Foreign Trade, 1600–1800," *History of Political Economy* (Winter 1983): 549–66; Gary M. Anderson, Robert D. McCormick, and Robert D. Tollison, "The Economic Organization of the English East India Company," *Journal of Economic Behavior and Organization* (December 1983): 221–38; Gary Anderson and Robert D. Tollison, "Barristers and Barriers: Sir Edward Coke and the Regulation of Trade," *Cato Journal* (Spring/Summer 1993): 46–67; Gary M. Anderson and Robert D. Tollison, "The Myth of the Corporation as a Creation of the State," *International Review of Law and Economics* (1983): 107–20; Robert B. Ekelund Jr., Donald R. Street, and R. D. Tollison, "Rent Seeking and Property Rights Assignments as a Process: The Mesta Cartel of Mercantile Spain," *Journal of European Economic History* (1996). Naturally, we are grateful to Gary Anderson, Bobby McCormick, and Don Street and to the publishers of these journals for allowing us to use these materials in this book.

Our overall purpose is to place historical mercantilism in a broader context of a theory of institutional change. How and why did these earlier economies emerge as they did? The interest group approach adopted herein does not completely answer all such issues, but we think that the reservoir of unexplained behavior in the mercantile economies is considerably emptier than it used to be.

Politicized Economies

Chapter One

Mercantilism, Rent Seeking, and Institutional Change

Natura non facit Saltum
—Frontispiece to Alfred Marshall's *Principles*

Enduring interest in mercantilism or the "mercantile period" by scholars from many disciplines requires no apologetics. Events over this period, ranging from 1500 to 1776 in some accounts, are pivotal with respect to the economic and social development of the modern world—our world. But a set of important questions has deviled economists and historians for many generations: What *is* mercantilism—a set of policies or doctrines that occurred over some discrete period of time? Is it the time period itself? Do the key institutional changes and the *process* by which these changes took place "define" mercantilism, making it understandable to social scientists? Is mercantilism—however defined—still with us? This book, as did the earlier effort upon which it builds (Ekelund and Tollison 1981), attempts to provide at least tentative answers to such questions, at least for economists interested in the impact of institutions and institutional change on economic growth and development.

The study of mercantilism, both as a system of ideas and as an actual episode in economic history, has long been considered a "black box," despite the serious attention by generations of economists and historiographers. The 1930s have often been regarded by scholars as the high period for the study of mercantilism. Over this period the classic studies of Heckscher (1934), Viner (1930, 1967), and Cole (1939) appeared and established the prevailing paradigm about mercantilism.[1] Within this paradigm there have been two traditions in what (if anything) is presently taught to economists about mercantilism.

The dominant tradition has been that propagated by historians of economic thought, such as Jacob Viner, who tended to view the history of economic theory as a progression from error to truth.[2] These writers, whose approach is derivative of Adam Smith's famous critique of the mercantilists, have concentrated on an exposé of the fallacies of the mercantilists as expressed by the "central tendencies" in the vast literature of the writers of the period (roughly dated from 1500 to 1776). Among the most often stressed tenets of the mercantilists are the equation of specie with wealth, regulation of the trade sector to produce specie inflow, and emphasis upon population growth and low wages.[3] These scholars emphasize the presence of grave errors in mercantilist logic, errors that were exposed by David Hume and the classical economists. The primary example of such faulty reasoning was, of course, the failure of the mercantilists to recognize the self-regulating nature of the internal and external economy that the "specie flow mechanism" imposed on the mercantilist objective of a perennial trade surplus.[4]

The tradition established for the study of mercantilism by scholars in the German Historical School and by their English disciples has been given far less emphasis over the twentieth century. These writers argued that mercantilist policies and ideas were very sensible for a period in history during which the attainment of state power was the overriding goal of the polity. This tradition in the study of mercantilism has greatly receded in popularity over the years, so that (until recently at least) the principal thing the present generation of economists learned concerning the mercantilists was not their historical relevance but their theoretical confusions. Recent work (North and Weingast 1989; North 1989; Root 1994; Weingast 1995), including our own (Ekelund and Tollison 1981), aimed at completing the positive-economic analysis of mercantile political economy hinted at by scholars in the German Historical tradition.

The central treatment in the literature on mercantilism, however, remains the classic study by Heckscher (1934), the one writer on mercantilism who spans both of the above traditions.[5] Heckscher's treatment, while historically comprehensive, was in clear need of a reassessment based on modern developments in economic theory, an analysis we provided in 1981. That work was an attempt to utilize contemporary insights into political choice (Buchanan and Tullock 1962), rent seeking (Tullock 1967), and economic regulation (Stigler 1971b; Peltzman 1976) in an attempt to reexamine the historians' analyses.

MERCANTILISM AND POLITICAL ECONOMY

Our initial application of what is now called neoinstitutionalist theory to mercantilism was a confrontation with all of the major students of the subject who organized their interpretations of the period around a paradigm that emphasized certain regulatory implications flowing from a balance-of-trade and specie-accumulation objective. The "utility of specie argument," linked to the process of creating and developing the nation state, appealed to these early and important scholars as logical and orderly. We argued that it was as if the process described by economic historians had been imposed by a benevolent dictator or central planner, whose primary goal was the development of a powerful and effective central state. We argued that causation in the historical paradigm was exactly reversed—that the balance-of-trade objective was nothing more than the by-product of the interplay of numerous self-interested parties who were seeking rents from monopolization in these early nation-states. And the literature defending the balance-of-trade objective was just so much propaganda to justify private interests.

The present work expands and extends our study of mercantilism in several directions while at the same time retaining our fundamental approach and our analysis of the mercantile economies of England and France. This work is motivated by the fact that economic theory has progressed since our initial examination of mercantilism. This is especially so concerning the elements of neoinstitutional economics upon which our earlier investigation was founded. In addition, the reception of our earlier efforts has led us to investigate whether the rent-seeking/property rights paradigm applies to other mercantile economies, Spain in particular. A key institution in both mercantile and modern worlds—the firm—is identified in much of the literature linking institutions to economic growth and development. The study of how certain property rights alterations created the prototype of the modern firm over the mercantile period is also examined in the present work.

The theoretical focus of the supply and demand for monopoly rights through the machinery of the state is again modeled as the essence of mercantilism. Clearly, the institutional settings in England, France, and Spain differed, but the general forces motivating the supply and demand of monopoly rights were similar. On the one hand, states found it efficient to seek revenues by selling monopoly and cartel (or guild) privileges. Such revenues supplemented, sometimes handsomely, the tax revenues available to the English and, especially, to the French and Spanish monarchs. During the administration of French Finance Minister Jean-Baptiste Colbert (1662–83), for example, the French state procured roughly one-half of its yearly revenues from the granting of extensive monopoly and cartel rights. The crown take in Spain from the cartelized sheepherding industry (through an organization called the Mesta) was at times substantial (see chapter 5). On the other hand, the demand side of the market for monopoly rights in these times was inspired by the familiar desire of individuals to procure the shelter of the state from competition and thereby to earn monopoly rents.

Our purpose is not to *evaluate* mercantilist ideas from the standpoint of modern economic theory. Rather, it is to *explain* mercantile political economy using positive-economic theory. We offer an explanation of mercantilism in terms of the costs and benefits that accrued to participants— interest groups and coalitions of self-interested participants in both private and political markets—in the processes of self-interested activity. Merchants, monarch, the courts and the public are thus featured as self-interested protagonists in institutional change. We focus on *specific examples* of such activity and on particular institutions (the firm) in mercantile England, France, and Spain, as well as upon the comparative institutional frameworks in these countries. With the model suggested by modern political economy we seek to explain with our theory: (a) why mercantilism declined in England while failing to be significantly reduced in France and Spain; (b) how an analysis of self-interested forces reacting to the shifting costs and benefits of rent seeking presents a more satisfying explanation for mercantilism and for its course in England, France, and Spain than the well-known alternative, which suggests that mercantilism was an irrational social order; and (c) how the interplay between crown monopoly and self-interested activity produced the genesis of the modern corporate firm. We chose, in our initial study, to designate these general activities of monopolization as *rent seeking*. But rent-seeking activity, which transfers property rights and alters the fundamental institutional structure of nations, is but part of a larger skein of activities that have been described under the rubric "neoinstitutional economics." In the present work we seek to refine our initial use of rent seeking to explain institutional change and to apply it in the context of this more inclusive study.

Mercantilism and Institutional Change

The study of mercantilism within the context of change in economic and political institutions is but part of a new and ongoing research prolegomenon within economics. A broad historical methodology featuring the impact of economic activity as creating particular social and economic institutions was not original with our initial study of mercantilism (1981). North and Thomas (1973), in an important book explaining the rise of Western institutions and economic growth, identified fiscal policy and alterations in population and property rights as causal factors in the emergence of efficient economic organization.[6] Their focus was on the relative growth of economies as a function of arrangements—rules of the game and organizations—that create incentives to undertake socially desirable activities.

Since this time, a veritable cottage industry in the "theory of institutions" has developed. While it is not our purpose here to develop and critically evaluate this still-evolving literature, it is important briefly to outline this area of research in relation to our current study of mercantilism. Neoinstitutional economics, the theoretical base we utilize in the present study, is the product of the application of modern microeconomic analysis to institutions and institutional change. It flows from the proposition that rational choice (under particular constraints) creates and alters institutions such as property rights structures, law, contracts, government forms, and regulation. These institutions and the "organizations" they help create provide incentives or establish costs and benefits that, for a time, govern economic activity and economic growth (which does not have to be of a "socially desirable" kind, of course). Intertemporally, however, institutions are themselves altered through economic activity either because of "feedback" mechanisms or because particular institutions create economic incentives for change.[7] Within such a model, of course, any change in an "exogenous" or "shock" variable could alter the configuration of property rights or costs and benefits, eliciting institutional change.[8] For example, laws surrounding marriage, all administrative regulatory institutions, and the form of religious and taxing institutions may all be analyzed using neoinstitutional economics so constituted.

The neoinstitutionalist paradigm, as it is presently constituted, includes the property rights approach to economics, expands the bare-bones Marshallian model to include positive transactions costs, and uses insights from the new industrial organization economics, law and economics, public choice, and from the rent-seeking literature.[9] In short, neoinstitutional economics seeks a theory of institutional change using a modified static theory of rational choice. Problems associated with fitting neoclassical theory (modern) to the analysis of institutions have created important dissenters.[10] An entirely *new* theory of economics relating to institutional change might well be forthcoming. But we maintain that particular problems related to the study of institutional change over the mercantile era can be informed and evaluated with a modified and modern *neoclassical* theory of micro-economic activity.[11]

Our initial approach to British mercantilism filled one gap in the study of institutions generally and the study of mercantilism in particular.[12] The political process through which rent-seeking and property rights transfers were accomplished were described in some detail. This was accomplished chiefly by describing (1) how jurisdictional problems, of a largely self-interested nature, between the "royal" court system and the common law courts created shifts in the locus of political power and economic authority between the monarch and democratic institutions (the Parliament), and (2) how agency problems between the monarch and enforcement mechanisms within the British economy (among the local sheriffs) led to the de facto internal deregulation. The sequence was that rent-seeking activity altered property rights through the political process; property rights changes created new incentives, which changed the direction of economic activities that had implications for growth and the nature of the economic and political system. Our analysis was conducted in the "polinomic method" suggested by Davis (1980) and broke new ground in considering the role of rent-seeking and property rights alterations as part and parcel of the process through which "competitive" institutions emerged within the changing political and economic environment of the mercantile era (Gay 1982; Anderson 1982; Hill 1983; Woodruff 1983; McCord 1983; Wolfe 1984; Bean 1984; Schwier 1994; Stoetzer 1984; Rider 1995). As such, we described the impact of economizing economic actors under a *given* set of institutions on *new* political and economic institutions, which transferred powers to Parliament, with less power to the monarch.[13] The result was a lessened ability of both monarch and Parliament to establish monopolies, a general movement towards political freedom, and the significant declension of mercantilism and a new thrust for laissez-faire in the British economy.[14]

This approach, with significant nuances and extensions, has been followed by a number of analysts. North and Weingast (1989), in one of the most significant recent essays on the era we considered, utilize the central elements of our argument and press on to "test" for the stability of "new" institutions in the post-Glorious Revolution (1688) phase. They focus, as we did, on the role of crown-Parliament competition to extract taxes and to create monopoly rights and on the role of the independent judiciary in providing credible commitments (1981, 46, 51–56) as key elements in institutional change over the seventeenth century. Their emphasis, however, is on the latter parts of the century, chiefly on fiscal developments after the civil war, Restoration (1660), and the Glorious Revolution. Our initial argument, upon which they build (1989, 817–18), was that the setting for institutional change was established somewhat earlier. In particular, the competition between "king's courts" and common law courts (such as Coke's Court of Common Pleas) over legal and monarchical jurisdiction was a late Tudor development that was finally resolved in the late seventeenth century.[15] We also argued that the inability of the crown to extract rents and wealth transfers through a system of internal regulation—and the economic activity that the attempt generated—was another factor in the declension of mercantilism and the economic ascendance of England at the time. North and Weingast significantly extend this argument, however, by providing a "test" of the new institutional structure of "the King in Parliament" together with an independent judiciary. They present an analysis of the post-1688 stock market and rates on long-term government loans as evidence of the stability of commitments made by the crown.[16] The important point is established that economic growth and incentive was fostered under the new institutions as investors gained confidence and certainty that monarchs could not capriciously "change the rules."

Root (1994) has also developed an argument concerning seventeenth-century British and French institutional change. Specifically, Root aimed to "bridge" economists' concerns for rational argumentation with the traditional historians' concern for demonstrations of connections between social structure, institutions, and culture (xiv). In order to accomplish this formidable task with respect to the political and economic markets of mercantile France and England, Root attempts to graph Fernand Braudel's tripartite distinction of "privilege" in Old Regime France with the model of rent seeking and competition described in our initial book and in North and Weingast. Whether Root's research will satisfy historians is problematical, but the theoretical structure of Root's argument does not diverge in any significant direction from that established earlier. In the British case, the competition for monopoly rights between crown and parliamentary interests (145), the role of unpaid justices of the peace vis-à-vis self-interested enforcement (151), and the reasons that competitive markets developed more fully in England than in France (156–59) closely follow our initial arguments. Root, however, adds filigree to the argument with interesting illustrations relating to post-Colbertian mercantile France.[17]

These studies, as well as our own, are examples or applications of the neoinstitutional economics.[18] They are also reminders that all such "ex-periments" using such tools are partial in nature. No one expects that the institutional structure of England over the mercantile period to be repli-cated in France and Spain. The neoinstitutional economics points up the reasons: the institutional base, and therefore the form of competition un-der certain "rules of the game"—along of course with exogenous forces or shocks to the system—guarantees that competitive or market conditions (and growth paths) will be different. Be it *"ad hocism"* or a problem in some nondefined path dependence, the neoinstitutional economics must adopt this method in studying any particular period or event. This "par-ticularized approach" was of necessity the thrust of our original discussion as it is in the present study, although we paid no explicit attention there to problems of path dependence. Precise tools or models containing a "path dependent" analysis of the mercantile or any other period are as yet un-available. We continue to use more standard tools of property rights and the modern theory of regulation and rent seeking in the present work.

Heckscher's Treatment of Mercantilism

The standard, traditional approach to mercantilism prior to our study was historiographic in nature. Eli Heckscher wrote the brilliant and still un-challenged historiographic treatment of the subject. But while Heckscher was highly regarded as a scholar, the important critics of his treatment of mercantilism pointed to the utter absence of economic actors in his chef d'oeuvre. Economic historians, in particular, were disturbed by his gener-alized treatment of economic policy and his excessive emphasis on the co-hesiveness of mercantilism as an economic doctrine and as a set of unifying policy prescriptions unaffected by actual economic events (Marshall 1935; Heaton 1937; Coleman 1957).[19] Specifically, the historians charged that Heckscher's treatment, embedded as it was in ideas, was practically inno-cent of all reference to the political process through which the so-called unifying mercantile policies were made. Coleman (1957, 24–25), for example, concluded that the term *mercantilism* as a label for economic policy "is not simply misleading but actively confusing, a red-herring of historiography. It seems to give a false unity to disparate events, to conceal the close up reality of particular times and circumstances, to blot out the vital intermix-ture of ideas and preconceptions, of interests and influences, political and economic, and of the personalities of men." Policy, in other words, could not be treated in a vacuum, nor could the role and interests of parties to the political process be ignored.

Coleman, however, rejects assessments of mercantilism as institutional policy changes guided by self-interested motives (1982, 332–23), noting that the elevation of that notion to a central position in explaining mercantile developments "is unlikely to convince historians." Modern economics, particularly that dealing with implicit markets and institutional change, is slowly but inexorably replacing historiography, which, in its most concatenated identification of elements and categories, asserts that "history happens" and neither explains nor seeks to explain events. Coleman is joined in this latter view by others (Myint 1983). Curiously, Coleman assessed and, in effect, rejected earlier economic approaches to mercantilism. Further he asserted (1969, 8) that "evidence is what historians need; theories are what economists make." He does not appear to understand that the accumulation of evidence to support a theory is the very essence of what modern economists "do." In the present case, anecdotal evidence, of a reasonably high quality (North and Weingast 1989; North 1989; Root 1994), has been brought to bear on questions of institutional change over the mercantile era. Historians, no doubt in their own self-interest, tend to reject such "evidence."

Herlitz (1964) noted that Cunningham (1968), Schmoller (1897), and Heckscher ignored Adam Smith's emphasis upon class interests as a dominant force in mercantilism. For these writers, according to Herlitz, "the driving force of mercantilism was the creation of states and the strivings of statesmen after power and authority" (107). Herlitz's general indictment is, no doubt, on the mark, and in this sense our analysis, both in our initial argument and in the present work, is a return to Smith's original emphasis. One of Smith's principal themes in the *Wealth of Nations* was that mercantilism was equivalent to the demand for regulation and rents by merchants and manufacturer (1937, 250, 403, 420, 425, 460–61, 695–96). Smith attributes mercantile restrictions of all kinds—colonization, restrictions designed for specie accumulation, and so forth—to the self-seeking interests of merchants. Typical of Smith's "capture theory" is the following: "It cannot be very difficult to determine who have been the contrivers of this whole mercantile system; not the consumers, we may believe, whose interest has been entirely neglected; but the producers, whose interest has been so carefully attended to; and among this latter class our merchants and manufacturers have been by far the principal architects" (626). Smith even extends the self-interest axiom to explain the Navigation Acts and colonial policy: "To found a great empire for the sole purpose of raising up a people of customers, may at first sight appear a project fit only for a nation of shopkeepers. It is, however, a project altogether unfit for a nation of shopkeepers; but extremely fit for a nation whose government is influenced by shopkeepers" (579). Although Smith featured the monarch as a rent seeker, he did not elaborate greatly upon the self-interested role of politicians, though he probably did so more than Stigler (1971a) believed. Smith, in other words, would not find the general lines of our argument very surprising. Indeed, he went on to become a creative regulator of the mercantile system (Anderson et al. 1985).

Heckscher may well have at some point sensed the necessity for providing a "transmission mechanism" (as will be evident in our discussions of his account of British mercantilism in chapter 3 and his position on the methodology of economic history in chapter 8). There is evidence, moreover, that there were some differences between his actual treatment of mercantilism and his vision of the role of theory and politics in economic history (see the discussion of Heckscher's method in the concluding chapter). But unlike Smith, he did not or was unable to provide a satisfactory bridge between ideas and events, on the one hand, and mercantile policies on the other. In the present work we show how economic theory relating to public choice, positive and normative rent seeking, interest group analysis, and property rights alterations, within a *generalized neoclassical theory of institutional change,* goes far in filling this important gap in Heckscher's discussion.

Our initial discussion readily acknowledged that other hypotheses may contain factors observationally equivalent to our "rent seeking, self interested" view of individual and group economic actors. It is clearly the case, moreover, that *no single model can yet explain all facets of the era.* But the question of the relative importance of factors affecting institutional change over the mercantile period can only be answered in a fair test of which theory—state power/ideas/ideology (or whatever) versus self-interested rent-seeking activity that alters "rules of the game," incentives and economic activity—performs best in explaining institutional change. It is the author's right to define his subject and approach. If it is the task of economic history, as North maintains (1981, 3) "to explain the structure and performance of economies through time," the neoinstitutional paradigm applied to activities within mercantile states appears to offer important and cohesive insights. After examination of the quality of alternatives proposed, we again adopt the rational self-interest approach to institutional change in the present work.[20] Those who demur from this approach are free to offer and evaluate alternative approaches to questions relating to mercantile developments, but our nod to "neighboring fields," unlike Root's treatment (1995), is minimal.

THE ROLE OF IDEAS AND IDEOLOGY IN NEOINSTITUTIONAL ECONOMICS

A good deal of criticism and confusion has surrounded the relation between ideas, institutional change, and the process of rent seeking and wealth transfers. Much of this criticism was manifest in the wake of our initial treatment of mercantilism. However ill-defined, ideas have a place, even an important position, in explaining particular policies and policy shifts under any given set of institutions. We maintained as much in our original treatment, although we argued there that the importance of ideas in creating policy changes was subordinate to compliant or supporting interest groups able to manipulate or influence the political process. This position, of course, does not mean that idea spinners or academics themselves necessarily *represent* those interests or that separate treatments must be accorded policy and doctrine (Wiles 1987, 149) as some have maintained.[21] It simply means that the study of ideas, their filiations between individuals (and nations), and their *specific* impact upon *specific* economic or political interest group activity is a necessary and valid accoutrement to the study of institutional change. However, singular reliance on ideas or values to characterize or explain the "mercantile order or period" has created more heat than light.[22]

There is another and very direct sense in which ideas mattered in the *post*mercantile period. By exposing and advertising error, writers such as Smith and Hume made it more costly to defend protectionist schemes. Thus, in one stroke, so to speak, they destroyed pre-Smithian capital in fallacious concepts by ever after raising the cost of protectionist arguments. This argument does not apply, however, to the preclassical ages. The generalized and widespread theory and "evidence" offered for the efficiency of unregulated markets was indeed a powerful force that was "sold" to self-interested groups of consumers and affected merchants who, with freer trade, were able to expropriate gains heretofore prohibited or limited by regulation. The case for interferences, both domestic and those related to foreign trade, was a harder "sell." But prior to the widespread acceptance of Smith and classical market theory—in a preclassical context—without central authority and general acceptance to point to, protectionists and rent-seeking interest groups had a far easier time selling regulations and protectionist schemes.

Many researchers, however, persist in defending two interrelated views suggesting that mercantilism was an irrational social and economic order founded on central tenants or ideas. The first, sponsored to a large extent by the historians, emphasizes mercantilism as a concerted policy of nationalism or state building, stressing an exogenously determined economic policy divorced from the endogenous interplay of self-interested forces. Trade restrictions such as taxing the import and subsidizing the export of finished goods is seen as a method of state building, of accumulating specie, or of promoting domestic employment, rather than as the simple product of rent maximization by parties to the resulting income distribution.[23] Mercantile policy, in this view, achieves a life of its own, and the underlying forces producing it (which are to us the important matter) remain unexplored and, worse, unexplained.

A second tactic of historians of thought in dealing with the mercantile era, not incompatible with the first view, has been to argue, at least implicitly, that the achievement of laissez-faire was the product of the subjective-philosophical forces of the times. Here we encounter "anticipatory" works on individualism and the natural ordering of economic phenomena, ranging from the writings of John Hales, Locke, Petty, and Cantillon, through those of Mandeville, Hume, and the Physiocrats. Indeed, most common references, following Heckscher's emphasis on "ideas," imply that the intellectual case for free trade (Smith, Ricardo, and earlier writers) made such an impression on effective decision makers that they quickly transformed the proposals of such authors into practice.

While the latter of these positions may possess some merit as an auxiliary, supporting explanation of the mercantile era, the former, in our view, clouds our understanding of the period and especially of the institutional evolution to laissez-faire in England. While neither position is inconsistent with our own, both of these ideational interpretations of mercantilism are incapable of explaining the movement to a free economy in England.[24] The problem is that in order to have an impact, ideas must find a market as George Stigler once noted (1982). Many, of course, found a market within the political arena, and institutions were changed as a result. But no clear explanation or evidence accompanies the allegations that "ideas changed events" over the period.

That the emergence of a philosophical defense of the domestic market economy occurred in the late sixteenth century, however tentative or piece-meal, is indisputable. In addition, the defense of free trade internally and simultaneous support of import or export controls is not inconsistent if both are of net benefit to the individual, group, or political party involved. It may well be that merchants increasingly focused on the necessity of export-import controls after they were constrained from demanding do-mestic regulation. The process was similar in both areas, although small-number situations and pressure groups may obtain more often among exporters and in export associations.[25] Merchants, in other words, had ev-ery reason to support protectionist devices under the guise of state build-ing or any other apologetic they could think of. We simply argue that profit maximization from rent seeking will occur whenever the net benefits of obtaining regulation are positive. Any explanation of the relative intensity of regulation in domestic or international spheres at any given time and under any set of institutional constraints in the mercantile era must pro-ceed along these lines.

The concept of "mercantilism" becomes an empty box when consid-ered as a collection of ideas, primarily because the concept of the *nature* of mercantilism must be decided beforehand. These arcane puzzles and con-fusions suffuse virtually all of the ideational research on mercantilism. Thus, A. W. Coats's essays (1973; 1985) on mercantilism have continued to express a quixotic attempt to identify the interests of intellectual history, which are, in his lexicon, "a matter of individual preference." These may, accord-ing to Coats, constitute a laundry list of different questions, which include "What did the authors actually say? What did they mean by their state-ments? Why did they hold those views? Were their statements internally consistent? Were their statements based on correct observation? What was the influence of their views on their own and on subsequent generations? What was the quality of their intellectual response, as judged by the stan-dards of later times?" (1973, 486). Unfortunately, this research program has yielded no cogent or consistent results if its aim has been a "definition" of mercantilism or an understanding of the period's events and institutional change. It is difficult to disagree with W. R. Allen's assessment (1973, 497) that "intellectual historiography (if not the intellectual historian) is some-thing of a mess." That "mess" is exemplified in historiographic "defini-tions" of mercantilism, such as that of Charles Wilson: "the mercantilist system was composed of all the devices, legislative, administrative, and regu-latory, by which *societies* still predominantly agrarian sought to transform themselves into trading and industrial societies" (1963, 26, emphasis added).

Societies do not transform themselves into anything. Rent-seeking coalitions operating within particular constitutional rules do.

The purpose of obtaining historiographical concepts or definitions is rarely if ever stated. Magnusson (1994) continues to search for this red herring of historiography by attempting to show that the evolution of mercantile writings gave us an economic vocabulary by the eighteenth century. Mercantile writers, in the early seventeenth century, were becoming more aware of the market mechanism, of holistic methods of analysis and of an economic order with an emphasis on the method of achieving national power and wealth. In essential repetition of earlier research (Chalk 1951; Grampp 1952), Magnusson concludes that mercantilism, at least as a set of ideas, was blossoming into the "science of trade" at the end of the seventeenth century.

This hypothesis is fundamentally that English intellectuals devised the case for a free economy and that their ideas had a great impact on public policy in England and, through exportation, in other European capitals (Kindleberger 1975).[26] While it is flattering to think that intellectuals affect public policy—and surely they do to the extent that they find an audience or "market"—it seems completely out of character for economists to think that intellectual arguments could affect real magnitudes so strongly. This is the problem with the conventional mercantilist paradigm. In this kind of historiographic research, where the only North cited is Dudley, the mercantilists are seen as irrational specie accumulators who were routed by David Hume's specie-flow mechanism and Adam Smith's *Wealth of Nations.* Our conclusion is that the train had already left the station by the time these and other great free-trade intellectuals systematized the principles and theories underlying a laissez-faire economy.[27] Ideas, ex post to be sure, have at least potential impact, but the strength and timing of their impact is determined by how well they fit into the individual and group interests that move the political process and create the impact. Ideas and self-interested activity, again depending upon how one defines ideas, are often complementary activities, although ideas do not always produce profits or material gain.

Ideology as the Causal Explanation
of "Unanswered Questions"

Emerging neoinstitutional theory has not yet placed the role of ideas or what historians call ideology within the context of change. Clearly, not all factors in a theory can be considered endogenous, a logical ploy that would make the neoclassical system of economizing, or any system, overdetermined or "reductionist."[28] Depending on the focus of the analysis and with appropriate specification of both endogenous and exogenous factors, institutions that have not traditionally been regarded as "economic" in character—religion, law, traditions, habits, tropisms, or particular forms of cuisine—may in fact be analyzed within the neoinstitutionalist framework.[29] Thus, the role of ideology (however that is conceived) might be considered as endogenous to institutional change—as when the pressure of events shapes ideas with feedback to events—or modeled as exogenous factors affecting events.[30]

The ideological rationalizations and acceptance of quickened market activity in the seventeenth century described by Appleby (1978) appear to be of this nature. Appleby argues that ideology and the ideas of pamphleteers may have played some (as yet undefined) role in the development of acceptance of the natural law apparatus in the emerging economic forms in the seventeenth century. However, she is incorrect when she implies that the markets "began" in that century (1978, 103–104). Economizing actors and coalitions in markets, characterized by both explicit and implicit exchange, existed from the beginning of civilization. As North has consistently emphasized, feudal relations were eroded and real per capita incomes rose as the result of relative price changes and property rights alterations propelled by system shocks. These institutional changes were, of course, the *result* of market activity.

Ideology may perhaps be considered a random shock in a model of institutional change, much as in the modern literature on macroeconomic theory and real business cycles. But the absence of any positive theory of idea formation or role for ideology leads us to support economizing activity as the primary explanation for institutional change. Indeed one of the perennial questions in political science is whether political representatives are true agents of constituents or whether representatives represent their own ideology ("delegation" versus "agency"). But whether (and how) ideology fits into a positive theory of institutional or "organizational" change is still problematical. Modern evidence on the role of ideology in legislation (Kau and Rubin 1979; Kalt and Zupan 1984) is equally inconclusive (Lott and Bronars 1993). It is not easily identified as a residual in a regression equation and it does not appear to be an independent factor—apart from economic interests—in explaining economic change.[31] Ideology itself, be it of the laissez-faire, free-market, or collectivist type, may usefully be thought of as a "habit of mind" originated and propelled by relative costs and benefits in an economizing process. As an explanation for events or policies, it is a grin without a cat.

The mercantile era was a period punctuated by rapidly evolving institutions, which happened to result in the transition to liberalism and greater reliance on free markets. Ideas—especially those relating to markets, labor, and the balance of payments—undoubtedly had consequences over this period. But ideas, like technological advance, changes in transactions costs, and innovations, must be "sold" through some economic or political process. They are shocks to a *given* system composed of a particular set of institutions. These shocks must work through institutions that are established and evolve through markets guided by self-interested activity.

New Assaults on the Self-Interest Axiom

Denial of the use of the self-interest and rational economizing axioms in analyzing economic institutions has been the primary critical response of many general economic historians, traditional economic historians (there really is not much difference), and some historians of economic thought who have taken refuge in historical-sociological approaches to particular historical episodes. In the modern theoretical world of comparative institutions and information costs, it is odd to see the self-interest axiom attacked so strongly by "economists."[32] Self-interest enters the discussion, if at all, only on a par with many other sociological-historiographic categories. In the most common form of the criticism, sometimes called "economism," self-interest is depicted as explaining too much and therefore nothing. The tautological form of the self-interest axiom is of course broken by framing hypotheses that provide testable alternatives.

The most subtle criticism of the neoinstitutional approach to economic theory has come from contemporary evolutionists. However "old" institutionalists of a modified Veblenian stripe appear as onlookers and apologists in the emerging paradigm (Rutherford 1994). The new/old institutionalists stress adaptive rationality (ostensibly of the type described in physiological terms by the philosopher William James) as associated with habit formation and institutional change. Presumably this builds on Veblen's theory, which because of some "lack of exactness" has permitted the survival of neoclassical maximizing models (Rutherford 1994, 78). The reason for the survival of neoclassical theorizing—as positively applied to markets *and institutions*—is that Veblen's theory, if indeed one can call it that, is constantly bested by evidence. Veblen's approach to institutions, framed in nontestable form and therefore irrefutable, is inchoate and incomprehensible.[33]

Veblen also thought that institutions emerged "out of the drift of things." But on the wings of such acute observations neither old nor new Veblenian economics is capable of answering important economic questions because it contains no unified theory of institutional change. Do institutions determine technical change or does technical change determine new institutions? The only way to settle or add light to such questions is with the methodology of Alfred Marshall. Cheers for the abandonment of the rationality postulate of modern neoclassical economics in the "new Veblenism" are as jejune as the belief that Veblen had a functional theory of institutional change.

Critiques of the self-interest postulate within the rent-seeking-neoinstitutionalist approach continue to punctuate some of the confused literature on mercantilism. In particular, the charge of tautology is a poison arrow that badly misses the mark. Coats directly criticized our initial approach by asking, "what evidence, if any, would constitute falsification of their theory, or what counter-examples, if any would persuade them to abandon it?" (1985, 31). The answer is that we would of course abandon the rent-seeking-neoinstitutionalist theory describing mercantilism and its decline if another theory better fit the essential facts of institutional change over that period. A rent-seeking-interest group analysis of mercantilism would be seriously challenged if critics could show that mercantile policies were passed by political representatives (solons?) who consistently increased the general welfare at the expense of particular interest groups. Our theory has the power of explaining real world events in terms of self-interest and political processes. It is based on economic foundations, not on the legerdemain of "ideas" and "ideology" typically invoked by historians to describe pieces of history.

THE RED HERRING OF "PATH DEPENDENCE" AND EXTRA-ECONOMIC PHENOMENA

As in Marshall's own era, but for other reasons, some modern economists are searching for a new theoretical basis to analyze institutions. Some (Williamson 1975) claim that rational choice cannot apply to problems where transactions costs and bounded rationality lead to nonmarket solutions. Allegedly, these problems together with the "path dependence" and "rule

following" associated with institutional change have led important and informed observers to call for the sacking of traditional microeconomics
entirely (Furubotn 1994) and for replacing it with a new theory. We acknowledge these in-progress concerns with the theory of institutional change
but believe that the neoinstitutionalist paradigm based on modern neoclassical economics is more than sufficient for *particular* preclassical analyses. None of these approaches—those asserting informational problems
or bounded rationality—have yet produced comparative analyses of preclassical institutional change, let alone ones superior to neoclassical-
oriented neoinstitutional economics.[34]

North (1990, 112) argues for a modification of static neoclassical theory
to accommodate the problem of path dependence. He maintains that "path
dependence is the key to an analytical understanding of long-run economic
change. The promise of this approach is that it extends the most construc-
tive building blocks of neoclassical theory—both the scarcity/competition
postulate and incentives as the driving force—but modifies that theory by
incorporating incomplete information and subjective models of *reality* and
the increasing returns characteristic of institutions." Formal analytical results—there are none yet produced within this paradigm, as North admits
(1990, 115)—would ostensibly attempt to bridge the gap between strict de-
terminism and randomness, producing a *variety* of possible solutions.
But would logical construction of such a theory be possible or useful in the
context of economic history?

There is growing evidence that path dependence—a critical aspect of
the so-called "new economics"—is a theoretically empty concept and a real
world unicorn. In a series of papers, Liebowitz and Margolis convincingly
debunk the most common forms of alleged path dependence and note that
(what they call) third-degree path dependence is the only kind that might
conflict with the neoclassical model of rational behavior and efficient outcomes. In their words, "*Third-degree pate dependence* occurs if an action is
ex ante path inefficient, which means that at some time t_0 there is an alternative action $a_1 \in A_0$ such that the discounted present value of the total
social benefit of selecting a_1 instead of a_0 are known to be greater than the
discounted present value of costs, yet the action a_0 is taken nonetheless"
(1995b, 211–12). Such path dependence implies market failure and lock-in by
historical events that were or are (presumably by government action) *reme-
diable*. An event (even a seemingly insignificant event), a choice of technology, or an institution *could* be subject to increasing returns. But, as Liebowitz
and Margolis show, third-degree path dependence requires restrictive in-

formational assumptions plus highly implausible and constrained market responses. There are *no* real world examples of path dependence.[35]

More important for our investigation, Liebowitz and Margolis address the problems raised for historical investigation. Rising to the allegations (Arthur 1989) that under increasing returns many historical outcomes are possible, including those that are inefficient from a neoclassical (optimizing behavioral) perspective, Liebowitz and Margolis provide a convincing argument that path dependence is demonstrably empty of content. We are in full agreement with the conclusion that such a view is entirely vacant insofar as it avoids the principal observation that important and frequent shocks do in fact take place over time so that "a knowledge of some initial endowment alone could never tell us very much about the eventual path of real economies over time" (Liebowitz and Margolis 1995b, 223). Further, they cleverly separate two views of history—one based on neoclassical purposive behavior and the other on path dependence:

> One [the neoclassical] holds that efficiency explanations are important and that economic history, at least, is the search for purpose in past actions. We find, where we can, explanations of events that are based on purposeful behavior: Technology responds to scarcities, technique responds to price, and so on. The other [the "new economics" of path dependence] holds that history is important only to the extent that, for one reason or another, agents do not successfully optimize. History then is the tool to understand what rationality and efficiency do not explain—that is, the random sequence of insignificant events that are not addressable by economic theory. (Liebowitz and Margolis 1995b, 223)

History, in our view at least, would not be very interesting or informative in explaining the growth or course of nations or institutions in the latter view even if a theory of the "new economics" could be developed.

North (1990, chap. 3) also highlights not only what he regards as the problems of modern neoclassical tools used in institutional analysis but the so-called failure of an economic view of human behavior to explain particular categories of human activities. North argues that

> The broad range of human actions characterized by such activities as the anonymous free donation of blood, the dedication to ideological causes such as communism, the deep commitment to religious precepts, or even the sacrificing of one's life for abstract causes could all be dismissed (as many neoclassical economists dismiss them) if they were isolated events.

But obviously they are not and they must be taken into account if we are to
advance our understanding of human behavior. (North 1990, 25–26)

In evaluating such comments we must remember "first principles." Economics is not, fundamentally, a science of wealth maximization. Rather it is
utility maximization, of which wealth maximization is a subset, that is the
tap root of economic science. That one is dedicated to ideological causes
such as communism may indeed represent some kind of philosophical maximization. It may also represent the calculation of one's prospects within
income distribution under communism. Contemporary research, moreover, continues to place many heretofore "noneconomic" phenomena within
the reach of economic analysis (for example, Becker 1981; Azzi and Ehrenberg
1975; Iannaccone 1995).

The suggestion, however, that rational self-interest is somehow a de-
fective premise for use in a theory of institutional change because of
informational problems (including bounded rationality, outcome uncertainty, and path dependence) must be dealt with directly. The fact is that
no one has yet produced a cogent and "testable" (either directly or anec-
dotally) theory of institutional change that includes nonrational elements
as central to the analysis. That other motives *might* be involved in such a
model or explanation is indisputable. But science demands a fair test of
their influence.[36]

THE POLITICAL ECONOMY
OF MERCANTILISM: PLAN OF THE BOOK

A neoinstitutionalist perspective, with primary emphasis on positive and
normative rent-seeking activity of individuals and coalitions, is applied to
the historical experience of *internal* economic regulation in mercantile
England, France, and Spain as well as to the origin and development of one
key institution—the modern firm—in the present work. Before we turn to
the formal plan of our book and to some of the highlights of our analysis,
consider, briefly, the historical scene of our study and the institutional base
(the "givens") upon which it builds.

A Synopsis of General Trends, 1600–1750

The period with which this "institutional episode" deals is one that historians commonly label a "transition period." The century and a half from

1600 to 1750 opens at the close of a period of trade expansion and early capitalistic developments and ends before the beginning of the Industrial Revolution, which heralded the beginnings of contemporary society. This period, which historians have only recently been studying for unifying themes (deVries 1976; Appleby 1978), was generally one of economic crisis and stagnation for most European nations, especially for Italy, Spain, and the largest European power, France, but it was also one of relative development and growth for northern and western Europe, especially for England.

The factors leading to the crisis are numerous, and specific influences are difficult to pinpoint. There were clear and stark population declines in the Mediterranean area and in central Europe over the seventeenth century (particularly in Spain), although the population of England, the rest of the British Isles, and Scandinavia rose by over 50 percent.[37] The latter development constituted a strong relative gain for northern Europe. Malthusian effects (for example, marriage postponement and epidemics), though probably not a Malthusian crisis, appear to explain these population trends. While a succession of civil disturbances in France, England, and Spain, the Thirty Years' War, and other military confrontations may also contribute to an explanation for general economic depression, they (along with monetary or specie disturbances) cannot constitute a general explanation for the crisis of the period.

Along with these broad developments, and perhaps as a result of them, the nexus of European commercial and political power shifted northward from the Mediterranean, specifically from Venice, and ultimately to England. The Dutch were an exception to the general rule of economic stagnation on the Continent over the early part of the period, but their seafaring hegemony and nascent capitalist preconditions failed to lead to an industrial revolution.[38]

Clearly the basic economic conditions in the individual mercantile nations must explain differences within countries and a large portion of specific historical events, but such forces have often been the deus ex machina of historians in place of explanations of how basic institutional arrangements gave rise to the observed economic conditions. It was our initial purpose to study a number of important institutions within these countries in order to add specific content to the often vague notion of institutional change. A cogent explanation for historical developments in the mercantile (or any other) period, in other words, requires specificity, organizing principles, and an appreciation that institutions matter for the course of economic history. Our studies of mercantilism and institutional change over the mercantile era (1600–1750), originating in *diverse given institutional settings,* attempt partially to fill that gap.

The Book in Brief

The analytical framework employed in the subsequent analysis is established in chapter 2. As noted above, we call this framework rent seeking, but we now explicitly place the concept within the broader context of institutions, property rights alterations, and interest group activity. We use this terminology to refer to the activities whereby individuals seek returns from state-sanctioned monopoly and cartel rights. Rent seeking as an analytical framework has both positive and normative elements, both of which are important parts of our analysis of mercantilism. As a form of positive-economic analysis, rent seeking is directed toward showing how individuals behave in seeking rents in alternative institutional settings. What difference does it make, for example, if protective legislation is provided by a unified, powerful monarchy rather than a diverse legislature with competing powerful interests? The normative aspect of rent seeking refers to the social costs of such activities to an economy. As we shall see, these costs will form part of the basis of a new explanation for a phenomenon that has long puzzled economic historians, namely, why France and Spain did not experience an industrial revolution comparable in time and intensity to that which occurred in England.

In chapter 3 we apply the rent-seeking framework to analyze economic regulation in mercantile England. The important aspect of this analysis concerns the development of an explanation of why internal regulation subsided in England, establishing a basically free economy. As emphasized above, credit is normally given to intellectuals for this transition, and there is certainly some truth to the adage that ideas matter and have consequences. But in the absence of some testable theory of how ideas and intellectuals affect the economizing activity through which critical institutions (political constraints, property rights, and so forth) are changed, that argument is like a "grin without a cat." We argue that poor regulatory design on the local level and competitive rent-seeking forces at the national level were the primary factors leading to the demise of economic regulation (and mercantilism) in England. This analysis features the struggle to capture the rents from economic regulation that emanated from the king, Parliament, and the mercantile judiciary. We argue that rent-seeking analysis provides a far richer understanding of the rise of a free economy in England than that offered by such historians as Heckscher, who resort to hero stories (for example, the common law jurists), to ideological explanations, or to great-men theories in explaining the same historical developments.

The rent-seeking framework is applied to internal regulation in France in chapter 4. Here, in contrast to events in England, we find a vast and very effective system of rent seeking, especially during the administration of Colbert. We show that the rent-seeking model offers a better explanation for some of the various puzzles of French economic development (among them, attacks on innovations and an emphasis on luxury productions at the expense of basic industries) than those offered by the historians, especially Cole's fatuous emphasis on the public-spiritedness of Colbert. Moreover, we argue that the rent-seeking paradigm provides a cogent explanation (namely, an explanation couched in terms of social costs) for the famous puzzle of why an industrial revolution was postponed in France.

Exact reasons for the decline in the fortunes of Spain over the period we cover has always provided a major challenge to economic historians. In chapter 5, we show how the close examination of one important economic institution from the perspective of public choice helps explain the ebbs and flows of economic development in medieval-mercantile Spain. Specifically, the regulation of internal commerce by the crown and through the legal and political system is characterized as a process of rent-seeking wealth transfers among local grazing, agricultural, and crown-cartel interests. The chief vehicle for redistributions (and an institution that also collected rents, as such competing with the crown) was the Mesta, a cartelized guild of sheepherders engaged in producing high-quality wool for export from the seasonal migration of sheep. This famous institution originated in twelfth-century Spain and became the concerted object of crown rent seeking during the high time of European mercantilism.

In chapter 6 mercantilist foreign-trade and industrial organization will be evaluated "in the large." In particular, we analyze the formation and evolution of the mercantile trading companies, especially those in England. Here the rent-seeking framework is pushed a stage further in order to analyze the cartel behavior of these early companies and their relation to the mercantile state. We also analyze an important controversy involving these early monopolies. Namely, were their monopoly charters justified by any public goods that they supplied (such as forts)?

In chapter 7, we present a detailed "micro" account of the operations of a prominent mercantile monopoly company—the English East India Company. We also illustrate the very "modern" principles upon which the company was organized. We seek to discover how share transferability in the early companies was a key factor that led to the invention of the corporate form of business organization. We also trace the evolution of the corporate form in England through the Bubble Act of 1720 and beyond.

A summary and conclusion of our analysis is offered in chapter 8. In addition to a summary of the major tenets of the analysis, several concluding points are stressed. First, we emphasize that the rent-seeking framework is not intended as a monolithic theory of all the historical events in the mercantile era. While our model performs very well in explaining certain fundamental changes in policies and institutions, it must be remembered that the policies and institutions we analyze are subsumed beneath a panoply of wars, revolutions, alliances, religious conflicts, colonization, emerging ideas, ideologies, science and technologies. *We are certainly not proposing the rent-seeking model, independently or as part of the emerging neoinstitutionalist paradigm, as an explanation for all events!* Rather, we view rent seeking and neoinstitutional economics as improved methods for scholars to analyze important developments in these (and possibly other) precapitalist economies. Second, for the sake of historical completeness, we briefly point to subsequent developments in England, France, and Spain that go beyond the rather arbitrary end point of our analysis.[39] While France basically returned to variants of mercantile institutions after the Revolution and Spain continued in tragic stagnation, England experienced an unparalleled era of free enterprise, with only intermittent outbreaks of rent seeking until the latter part of the nineteenth century. Third, and finally, we stress some of the lessons that our study can offer for modern concerns about the regulation and deregulation of industry and for the course of development in less developed nations of the world. England experienced a massive and unplanned deregulation of its economy, and it is important to try to understand if modern efforts to counteract rent-seeking and wealth-redistributing regulation may be improved from this experience.

Chapter Two

Rent-Seeking Theory and Its Application to Mercantilism

> *But let us be honest. How much more do we know*
> *about market process than Adam Smith knew*
> *that is of practical relevance?*
>
> —James M. Buchanan,
> *Toward a Theory of the Rent-Seeking Society*

Government, as all students of public choice know, is not free. Yet until very recently the cost of government intervention in the economy has been underestimated. The reason for this is that the economic theory underlying such analysis was incomplete. Gordon Tullock (1967) offered a more complete picture of the economic theory of the cost of government when he presented an analysis of what has come to be called the theory of rent seeking. Tullock's theory has both normative and positive aspects. As a normative theory, it allows a more accurate estimation of the costs of government intervention in the economy. As a positive theory, it allows the economic scientist to make predictive and explanatory statements about the form and content of government intervention. Both of these aspects of Tullock's analysis are crucial in applying the rent-seeking model to historical mercantilism. The early mercantile economies—lacking, as they did, countervailing constitutional constraints—were heavily regulated, so that the theory of rent seeking is important in reaching an understanding of why they were regulated and the impact of the regulation on the growth and evolution of these economies. Moreover, as will be discussed in the course of this book, these economies, especially that of England, later came to be deregulated to a modified form of laissez-faire capitalism. The posi-

tive rent-seeking model is also critical to understanding why, to a significant extent, the mercantile regulations in England came tumbling down.
The purpose of this chapter is to introduce the rent-seeking model and to
expand its relevance for advancing the positive and normative political
economy of mercantilism.

RENT SEEKING DEFINED

Rent seeking is the socially costly pursuit of wealth transfers. The concept
of rent seeking was introduced to the economics profession by Tullock
(1967). The early doctrinal development of the theory of rent seeking proceeded as follows. Krueger (1974) gave the field a name in her paper on
"The Political Economy of the Rent-Seeking Society." Although she presented some empirical estimates of the costs of rent seeking, Krueger's
paper was primarily theoretical in nature, showing how rent seeking can
lead to social costs in the adoption of policies to restrict international trade.
Posner (1975) wrote the first empirical paper concerning rent seeking. His
estimates suggested that the social costs of rent seeking in the regulated
sector of the U.S. economy could be substantial. Cowling and Mueller
(1978) presented estimates of the welfare loss from monopoly power in the
United States and United Kingdom, which included calculations of rent-
seeking types of costs. They found high social costs of monopoly in both
economies, emphasizing that their social cost estimates were, in contrast to
Posner, for private monopoly power. As will be discussed later, the empirical magnitude of rent-seeking costs is now a matter of some controversy in
the literature. Since these early papers, the literature on rent seeking has
grown rapidly (see Tollison 1987).

Tullock originally framed the theory of rent seeking in contrast to the
prevailing wisdom in the late 1950s and early 1960s that the deadweight
costs of monopoly and tariffs were empirically quite small. Harberger's
(1954) famous calculations on the extent of monopoly power in the United
States and the discussions of how little British economic welfare would be
increased if the United Kingdom joined the Common Market are good
examples of this type of thinking (Mundell 1962). Microeconomics was on
the verge of being trivialized. Tullock's insight in this context was to advance an argument that rectangles as well as triangles matter in the calculation of the social costs of such policies as tariffs and monopolies. Tullock
introduced, as it were, the concept of a trapezoidal society.

Tullock's point was simple, but full of potential pitfalls. He argued that expenditures made to capture a transfer were a form of social cost. The social cost arises because the resources used for transfer seeking have a positive opportunity cost elsewhere in the economy with respect to engaging in positive-sum activities. Transfer seeking is at best a zero-sum activity in that it simply shuffles dollars among people and groups and is probably negative-sum if traditional deadweight costs result as a by-product of such activities (Tullock 1980b). Social costs clearly arise in the process by which resources are shifted from positive-to-zero and negative-sum activities. Rent seeking thus embodies a social cost in terms of the foregone product of the resources employed in rent seeking.[1]

Several points should be kept in mind at this juncture. The theory of rent seeking does not condemn all types of profit seeking. As Buchanan (1980b) articulated clearly, traditional competitive profit seeking or entrepreneurship in the competitive model (seeking quasi-rents) does not qualify as rent seeking. Such profit seeking is productive; it creates value such as new products. Rent seeking is unproductive; it destroys value by wasting valuable resources.

Normally, the concept of rent seeking is applied to cases where governmental intervention in the economy leads to the creation of artificial or contrived rents. Seeking such returns leads to social costs because output is fixed by definition in, for example, a government regulation. Entrepreneurship in this setting can only be said to be negative; it will simply dissipate rents and lead to no increase in output. Nonetheless, it is quite possible to conceive of rent seeking as taking place in a nongovernmental setting. Buchanan (1983), for example, argued that the rivalry of siblings for an inheritance can lead to rent-seeking activities within families, and Frank (1986) has shown how certain labor markets involving competition for position (the rat race, tournaments) generate costly rent-seeking activities by participants.

Another point to keep in mind is that to the degree that the process of rent seeking involves the provision of utility or real income to participants in the process, these benefits should be netted out against the cost of rent seeking. As Congleton (1988) has argued, if the rent seeker takes the regulator out to dinner, the value that the regulator places on the dinner must be subtracted from the social costs of rent seeking.

A final definitional point to bear in mind is that bribes are technically not a rent-seeking cost. A bribe is a transfer, and as such, it represents a method of influencing governmental behavior that does not involve explicit rent-seeking costs. Recall that rent seeking involves the expenditure of costly resources to procure a transfer. Hiring a lawyer or a lobbyist to obtain a favorable law is rent seeking; bribing a legislator for the same law is not. The point is not intended as a moral defense of bribery; it is simply a useful analytical distinction.

Moving beyond bribes, however, once artificial rents have been created, it is hard to avoid the implication that rent seeking will occur along some margin. If a tax deduction is offered, tax shelters will be created and used. If civil servants are paid a wage in excess of their marginal revenue products, queues will develop for government jobs. All of these processes involve the use of scarce resources to seek transfers; the process is relentless.

THE THEORY OF RENT SEEKING

Any pool of rents will do for purposes of this preliminary analysis. Later, the argument will be applied specifically to the creation of monopoly power through law and regulation, a hallmark of the mercantile economies.

Let us assume a simple rent-seeking game (Posner 1975). The game is constant-cost, in which the probability of winning is proportional to investment, and there are risk-neutral bidders, a fixed prize, and a given number of bidders. Where, for example, the pool of rents equals $100,000, and there are 10 rent seekers, each bidder will offer or expend resources of $10,000 to capture the rents. In this model rent seeking is analogous to buying a lottery ticket with a 1 in 10 chance of being successful. Under such conditions rents are exactly dissipated; $100,000 is spent to capture $100,000.[2]

Posner's exact dissipation hypothesis is popular in the literature because it makes empirical work easier. A rectangle is a definite area whose value can be reasonably estimated. Moreover, Posner's model is robust with respect to the free entry and exit of bidders (Corcoran 1984; Higgins, Shughart, and Tollison 1985). That is, it naturally generalizes to a concept of a long-run equilibrium of bids and bidders. Rents are perfectly competed away with an endogenous number of bidders, and the prize to the winning rent seeker represents only a normal rate of return on his rent-seeking investment.

Two points concerning this exact-dissipation result should be kept in mind. First, it is important to understand that this is an equilibrium result under the postulated conditions. Government cannot simply put the regulatory favor or monopoly right up for rebidding and expect that bidders will not adjust their bids for such unexpected takings. If takings are expected, the original bids will reflect the relevant probabilities. Either way, instability in government policy comes to be reflected in a rent-seeking equilibrium outcome. Government cannot simply endlessly bid off regulatory favors. Second, the concept of an equilibrium in a rent-seeking contest does not mean that an incumbent possessor of a monopoly right will not make expenditures to defend and protect his or her monopoly. These investments will most likely show up as business expenses, which means that the observed rectangle for the monopolist is net of his rent-protection costs. This point goes to the symmetry of rent-seeking and rent-protecting expenditures; each is socially costly. It does not defeat the concept of an equilibrium in the original rent-seeking game; initial bids will be deflated to reflect the expected costs of defending the monopoly right.

The constant-cost rent-seeking game represents a popular equilibrium hypothesis. The exact dissipation model is like the model of perfect competition; it is a useful, though not necessarily descriptive, analytical construct for increasing understanding of how the world works. This does not mean, however, that all or even most rent-seeking contests are perfectly competitive in nature.

Tullock (1980a) presented classes of models where rent seeking is imperfectly competitive in the sense that the competitive process for rents leads to over- or under-dissipation of the available rents. That is, more or less than the value of the rents is expended to capture them. Rent seeking in these models does not take place under constant-cost conditions. These cases are interesting, and they are generated by assumptions about risk aversion, limitations on the number of bidders, imperfect information, and so on. They are not very popular, however, because imperfect dissipation makes the problem of deriving reduced-form equations with which to estimate rent-seeking costs much more difficult and case-specific (Fisher 1985). One can no longer simply estimate the area of a trapezoid; rather, the task is to estimate the area of something more or less than a trapezoid that is a function of behavior in the economy. This observation creates far more difficult modeling problems for the analyst.

As between Tullock's analysis of over- and under-dissipation possibilities, the over-dissipation possibility does not seem to be very plausible. In this case rent seekers are somehow led to bid more than the value of the prize. That is, they would be better off not playing the game in the first place. While this is perhaps possible once, through the distortion of information to rent seekers about their expected chances of winning, such behavior should not persist for long. The regulator/bureaucrat should be able to mislead only once. In the next round of rent seeking, bids will be adjusted to reflect "true" probabilities of winning; bureaucratic prospects will be properly discounted.

The best known version of a maximalist hypothesis about rent seeking is the black-hole tariff result of Magee, Brock, and Young (1989). They devise circumstances under which the rate of return to lobbying switches in a fashion so as to lead to huge (proportionately) amounts of the resources in an economy being devoted to lobbying. Indeed, in the black-hole case, almost 100 percent of the economy is devoted to lobbying. This result is driven by assumptions under which the returns to capital from lobbying (versus production) became magnified or arbitrarily large, so that it becomes rational for capital to invest nearly all its resources in redistributive competition. By symmetry, labor follows suit. The returns from lobbying are magnified because of the assumption that changes in product price have very large effects on factor prices. Lobbying consumes most of the productive activity in this stylized economy. This is an important result that deserves further study. A central issue in this regard will be the empirical relevance of the black-hole model. Economic historians may be able to find examples of such cases; the only one that comes immediately to mind is the case of certain hyperinflations. In general, however, over-dissipation results would seem to be rare, given the theoretical preconditions on which they are based.

Underbidding, where rent-seekers in the aggregate spend less than the value of the prize, is another matter. There are several plausible bases for underbidding equilibria, including risk aversion (Hillman and Katz 1984), comparative advantage among monopolizing inputs (Rogerson 1982), and game-theoretic considerations (Tullock 1980a; 1985). As stressed above, such considerations make the problem of analyzing the costs of rent seeking more difficult and case-specific, but be this as it may, under-dissipation seems an intuitively more plausible description of the real world. Even given the above point about rent-seeking costs being submerged into normal business costs, it is hard to think of many examples where rent-seeking expenditures bulk very large in relation to the expected rewards.

The minimalist hypothesis is that rent-seeking costs are approximately zero. Dougan and Snyder (1993) have argued that there are powerful and plausible incentives to convert rent-seeking costs into transfers. Something close to this same result seems to underlie Becker's (1983) work on pressure groups, though it is not explicit in his theory. The problem is complex. Obviously, recipients of transfers would prefer to receive them as money transfers. If not, rent seekers will find out what the recipients prefer and give it to them (fishing trips?). Dougan and Snyder argue this point well. They stress that transfers are endogenously determined, and so the social costs of transfers are minimized by successful interest groups. It will also be generally more efficient for rent seekers to deal in money transfers (bribes). Nonetheless, there is no competitive mechanism that guarantees such a result. If monopolizing inputs (for example, lawyers) are able, by acting as an interest group themselves, to control the processes of rent assignment, then bribes and auctions for regulatory and other governmental favors will be illegal, and the use of monopolizing inputs to compete for such favors will be pervasive. These inputs become, through their own influence, a necessary cost for doing business with the government, and the interest of the monopolizing inputs resides in maximizing the costs associated with transfers.

All this is to say that exact dissipation appears to be a useful general conjecture about equilibrium in rent-seeking contests, but this theory must be adapted to the circumstances of any particular case of rent-seeking. Like the model of perfect competition, the model of exactly dissipated rents is a vehicle and starting point for helping us to understand actual rent-seeking processes.

MEASUREMENT OF RENT-SEEKING COSTS

There are numerous empirical results on the social costs of rent seeking, depending on the methodology, coverage, and economy analyzed by the author. Krueger (1974) suggested that 7 percent of Indian GNP was wasted in rent seeking and 15 percent of Turkish GNP was lost because of rent seeking for import licenses. Posner (1975) estimated that as much as 3 percent of U.S. GNP was lost because of the social costs of monopolization through regulation. These are obviously substantial sums of money in any economy. Cowling and Mueller (1978) derived an estimate that the rent-seeking and deadweight costs of private monopoly in the United States was 13 percent of gross corporate product.[3]

Subsequent empirical work in this area has proceeded along a variety of routes. A reasonable amount of work has followed the lead of Krueger in seeking to examine the rent-seeking costs of trade intervention in various economies. In general, these works come up with higher numbers than Krueger. Magee, Brock, and Young (1989, chap. 15) provide a survey of this research. Ross (1984), for example, estimated that trade-related rent seeking accounted for 38 percent of GDP in Kenya.

Other work has attempted to estimate the costs of rent seeking for economies as a whole. This analysis has taken two general forms. First, there are the lawyer regressions. Various authors, including Laband and Sophocleus (1988), Magee, Brock, and Young (1989), and Murphy, Shleifer, and Vishny (1991), have added lawyers in various regression formats set up to explain GNP or rates of growth in GNP, both in the United States and across countries. The robust conclusion of this work is: more lawyers, lower growth, lower GNP.[4] Some of these admittedly simplistic regression estimates suggest that lawyers reduce aggregate income by as much as 45 percent.

Eschewing a regression-based approach, Laband and Sophocleus (1992) attempted an aggregate, sector-by-sector accounting of rent-seeking costs in the U.S. economy. They counted expenditures on such items as locks, insurance, police, and military expenditures as being driven by rent-seeking or rent-protecting incentives. On this basis they estimated that almost one-half of the U.S. GNP in 1985 was consumed by such costs.[5] Their approach will surely be controversial. A small sample of the categories that they treated as rent-seeking costs include crime prevention (Federal Bureau of Investigation), police (corrections), restraint of trade (Federal Trade Commission), residential investments (locks), commercial investments (guards), educational (library theft), property rights disputes (tort litigation), and government (defense, lobbyists, PACs). Following an accounting-like procedure, these authors go sector by sector to obtain their estimates of rent-seeking costs.

The results of the various studies are summarized in table 2.1. In one sense, the table shows the importance of the rent-seeking insight. No longer can the costs of tariffs, monopolies, and theft be called a trivial issue in virtually any economy. These are generally not small numbers.

Table 2.1
Estimates of the Costs of Rent Seeking

STUDY	ECONOMY	YEAR	RENT-SEEKING COSTS
Krueger	India	1964	7% GNP
Krueger	Turkey	1968	15% GNP (trade sector)
Posner	U.S.	Various Years	3% GNP (regulation)

Table 2.1 continued

STUDY	ECONOMY	YEAR	RENT-SEEKING COSTS
Cowling and Mueller	U.S.	1963–66	13% GCP* (private monopoly)
Cowling and Mueller	U.K.	1968–69	7% GCP* (private monopoly)
Ross	Kenya	1980	38% GDP (trade sector)
Mohammand and Whalley	India	1980–81	25–40% GNP
Laband and Sophocleus	U.S.	1992	50% GNP
Regression-Based Studies	Various Countries	Various Years	Up to 45% GNP

*Cowling and Mueller (1978) use gross corporate product as the basis of their calculation.

As with all empirical work, these various approaches are only as good as the theories and models upon which they are based. Several points are worth making here. One is that lawyers per se may not be the problem; the problem may be the nature of legal processes. The vast expansion of tort and plaintiff-driven litigation is not necessarily owing to the fact that lawyers lobby successfully for such changes in the law. Indeed, the use of the legal process to resolve conflicts may simply have been expanded in recent years because other forums for conflict resolution (the church, the family) have receded in effectiveness. Moreover, there is a quotient of trust in any economy. Buying a lock is a response to the security of property rights in a society. This security can be produced in a variety of ways, including moral exhortation, but in the face of the relevant probabilities, a lock can hardly be seen as an unproductive investment. Given the prevailing ethos, a lock protects property rights, and the protection of property rights enhances the productivity of resources over what they could produce without the lock. To argue that one can be wealthier without locks and lawyers implies that there are feasible reforms in behavior that will reduce such costs. This is certainly believable, but this is exactly the burden that estimators of the costs of rent seeking face. The lock and the lawyer are only wasteful to the extent that these resources can be feasibly reallocated to more productive uses. Alternatively, contributions to churches should be regarded as substitutes for locks.

In principle, the cost of rent seeking is simply the increase in GNP that would result if a feasible way to reallocate resources from locks and lawyers to more productive uses could be found by a political entrepreneur. This figure could be high or low, but it is probably low given the ability of rent-seeking inputs to resist such reallocations. And the mere resistance of the inputs is yet another reason not to waste resources attempting such a reallocation (Tollison and Wagner 1991).

RENT SEEKING AND THE RISE OF MERCANTILISM

Assume, for purposes of initial exposition, that monopolies are created by the rent-seeking activities of individuals rather than appearing spontaneously or being independently created by governmental authorities. At some time, competition emerges in the production of goods and services, and there exists a state or government having authority to order society as it chooses within the limits of feasible production possibilities (limits which include enforcement costs). In this context imagine individuals arising who perceive potential gains from procuring monopoly rights to produce particular goods and services. These individuals will attempt to subvert the forces of the market and to monopolize the production of goods and services by having the state limit production to themselves by fiat.[6] The process may be illustrated using figure 2.1.

The entire triangle, P_cPB, in figure 2.1 is a measure of consumer surplus in the case of a competitively organized market. Although this surplus accrues to consumers under competition, it is in general a surplus for which no one has a property right. The surplus exists because of technological conditions that preclude producers from perfect price discrimination. The entire area belongs to no one, yet consumers and producers may both attempt to claim it. From the point of view of the contenders for the surplus, the problem is not primarily one of economic efficiency. Incipient monopolists seek to achieve a position close to P_m, and consumer forces seek a position toward P_c. There are no principles in the theory of choice assigning preference to either position.

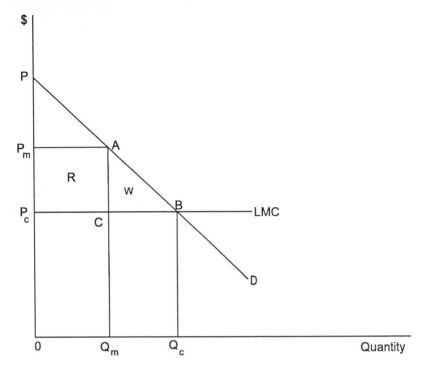

Figure 2.1. Rent-Seeking Model

The two parties will, in such matters, typically retain brokers (lobbyist-lawyers) to seek a favorable outcome, and each party will devote resources in their efforts to procure a favorable outcome. That producers are better able to organize and effect the P_m solution is well known, but this is no more undesirable (net of the welfare triangle) than the technological constraints precluding perfect price discrimination. The social waste of monopoly thus involves: (1) the traditional welfare triangle measuring the portion of consumers' surplus that is lost to society because some individuals refrain from purchasing the monopolized output at higher prices (area W in figure 2.1), and (2) the use of lobbyist-lawyer resources to effect a pure transfer (area R in figure 2.1). The latter social cost derives from the use of real resources to seek transfers. Such activities clearly add nothing to social product, and the social cost of using resources in this way is their opportunity cost elsewhere in the economy in arranging positive-sum agreements among individuals. Thus, lawyers could be writing contracts rather than lobbying for monopoly rights.

If an incipient monopolist is successful in his dealings with the state, he will be able to impose the classic monopoly solution of $P_m Q_m$ in figure 2.1, receiving a return on his rent-seeking investment of $P_m ACP_c$, less his lobbyist-lawyer expenditures. With the gain in monopoly rents so depicted, we expect several other features of the rent-seeking model to be present.

First, there is no fundamental reason to believe that only one individual will discover the gains from seeking monopoly rights sponsored by the state. We thus expect numerous aspiring monopolists to compete for these rights, and we assume for analytical convenience that in the long run this competition will drive the returns from using the state as source of profit to normal levels.

Also, as the above discussion intimates, we expect that those who stand to lose from the monopolization of an activity will have an interest in preventing such losses. Consumers stand to lose $P_m ACP_c$ figure 2.1, the rent gained by the successful monopolist, plus the deadweight welfare loss, ABC. In a costless world consumers would invest resources to retain this surplus, and there would be no monopolies because consumers stand to gain more from competitive organization than monopolists gain from monopolies. However, we will exclude such behavior here because of the well-known transaction costs involved in organizing consumer efforts to resist government action in raising prices.

But what about the remaining party in the rent-seeking model, the state authority holding the power to grant monopoly rights? The interests of the rent seekers are clear, but what are the interests of the suppliers of monopoly rights? In the historical context with which we are concerned, the state may be pictured as a unified, revenue-seeking leviathan, where fiscal needs (defense, court expenses, and so forth) prompted the sale of protective legislation. For example, to "the mercantilist politician, the state was more or less the leviathan, absolute and all powerful" (Heaton 1937, 392). In the rent-seeking model, this case corresponds to an absolute monarchy in which the royal authority possesses an unrivaled ability to grant monopoly rights. This type of institutional arrangement tilts the bargaining power in the market for monopoly rights in favor of the crown. If enforceable monopoly rights cannot be bought elsewhere in the dominion, most of the consumer surplus in figure 2.1 will end up in the king's treasury. To be worth anything, however, the king's monopoly rights must be enforced, and since enforcement is not costless, the royal authority will have to spend some of its monopoly revenues on enforcement. Moreover, to the extent that there is competition for positions of royal authority, the monarchy must expend resources to resist bids to take over the royal apparatus. As a part of a cost-minimization strategy for staying in power, it may be efficient for the king to take consumer interests into account to some degree. The absolute monarch is thus not "absolute" in these senses and does not make pure monopoly profits from the sale of monopoly rights.

The revenue-seeking view of mercantilism conforms closely to European history in the mercantilist era, as we shall develop more fully in the next two chapters. For example, one historian of the period characterizes mercantilism "as a negative and restrictive factor, which had its principal source, not in any deliberate plan of promoting economic progress, but in the fiscal exigencies of short-sighted and impecunious government" (Tawney 1958, lxiv). Heaton (1937, 375–76), reflecting on this appraisal, concurs, adding that "rarely in framing government policy did a government have the deplorable condition of the exchequer far out of mind, and every projector who presented a scheme to his ruler stressed the benefit that would directly or indirectly flow into the royal covers." Or, consider Heckscher's (1934, 1:178) view: "One of the most important features of economic policy, if not the most important of all. . . . The state, by its intervention, wanted to create large sources of revenue for itself. . . . The state exploited for its own ends the monopolistic advantages which the gilds had secured for their members or the owners of private privileges had secured for themselves."

In sum, then, we posit that the pursuit of special favor by individuals was the driving force behind the flourishing rent-seeking activities over the mercantile era. "The incentive rarely came from a whole class, for a class was too unwieldy, too class-unconscious, and too much torn by conflicting factors or interest to have one will or voice. Action came from individuals or compact groups who saw an opportunity to profit by protection or promotion" (Heaton 1937, 387). The ascension of mercantilism in the early part of the era is readily explained by the institutional setting facing the participants in the process of monopolization. Since the transaction costs required to seek rents were low with a unified state authority (the monarch), the flowering of mercantilism as an extensive system of monopolization and economic regulation of the economy may be easily explained. That is, since the cost of seeking monopolies was relatively low under absolute monarchy and since the monarchy found it efficient to seek revenues from the granting and enforcement of monopolies (for reasons to be explained in more detail in chapter 3), other things equal, more of this activity may be expected.

The theory of rent seeking, as noted in the introduction to this chapter, has both positive and normative elements. The normative economics of rent seeking refers to the elaboration of models with which to measure the social costs of rent seeking. The point of such exercises is clearly to suggest that these costs are high and could perhaps be lowered through policy interventions. The positive economics of rent seeking consists of using rent-seeking motivations to explain the pattern of government intervention in the economy. The theory of mercantilism presented here involves both positive and normative elements.

The positive element is obvious. The interplay among the monarch and various individuals and interest groups who sought her favor was driven by the prospect of economic gain by both sides of the political transaction.

The normative issue is how costly such practices were for the mercantile economies. At base, one suggests that they were not very costly. Neither the monarch nor the interest groups would have liked to see transfers competed away into costs; both would have simply preferred to receive transfers. Hence, there were clear incentives to minimize rent-seeking losses in the relevant political transaction. If this argument is correct, then it is easy to explain why monopolies proliferated during the mercantile era: the cost of providing monopoly was low. We would expect to see a large number of monopolies with a low social cost per monopoly. A tentative observation is that the English mercantile monopolies per se may not have greatly suppressed economic growth and development in that economy but that there were important differences between England, France, and Spain in this regard, which will be discussed below.[7] And there are important other themes in the story of the impact of normative rent seeking under "mercantile" conditions.

Rent-Seeking and the Neoinstitutional Perspective: Positive and Normative Aspects

Rent-seeking/interest group analysis is, as noted in chapter 1, part and parcel of the neoinstitutional approach to mercantilism. Self-interested competitions, in positive terms, were in the clear interests of particular protagonists. Mercantile (and premercantile) England witnessed competitive court systems and frustrated attempts to invoke internal regulations through, for example, the guild system. To the extent that such "rent seeking" was converted into transfers (or was conducted through outright bribery), the deleterious effects of monopoly were reduced (but with traditional deadweight costs attached).

A normative analysis of rent-seeking activity would have to include, however, the growth-reducing aspects of some property rights movements that underlie the activity of rent seeking. Coalitions and individuals are demanding control over property rights. When analyzed from a property rights perspective (Benson 1984), rent-seeking activity takes on normative implications, some of which are ominous. Nonpecuniary lobbying activity must be included in the net costs of rent seeking in addition to the pecuniary aspects of the dissipation.[8] But, in a parliamentary or legislative context, "a property rights approach to rent seeking provides predictions of a spiraling process of government growth since successful rent seeking by one interest group generally requires expansion of bureaucratic powers, while at the same time creating incentives for the formation of additional rent-seeking interest groups" (Benson 1994, 388). Thus, in the postconstitutional reform period in England and the ascendance of secure parliamentary checks on monarchical monopoly creation, rent-seeking coalitions and property rights alterations did not disappear. The nexus of power changed, but certain readjustments accompanied the change that initiated a process culminating in bureaucratic expansion and government growth in the nineteenth and twentieth centuries.

These features were not shared with the French and Spanish mercantile economies. The failure to develop significant constitutional constraints on monarchical/aristocratic elements in these economies led, we shall argue in chapters 4 and 5, to less significant decline in "mercantilism" in the French case and to actual "stagnation" in the case of Spain. High enforcement costs of direct monarchical and central enforcement of bureaucratic mercantilism was the only salvation—a small salvation—in both these economies. Constitutional checks and balances in England led to relatively secure property rights with important implications for economic incentives and long-term investments. Private market exchange was far less secure in France and Spain, with the inevitable consequences relating to economic growth and economy-wide development. Wars between these and other nations, colonial developments, monetary discoveries, and other "shocks" attended all of these nations over the period. But relative growth patterns depended upon property rights structures and their security and upon underlying rent-seeking coalitions within these economies. In some "static" sense, therefore, rent-seeking costs to an economy may be relatively low, but "dynamic" long-term costs of institutional paths of rent-seeking and property rights alterations may act as important restraints on economic growth.

Rent Seeking and the Distribution of Income

Before Tullock, the effect of monopoly on the distribution of income was clear: the monopolist got richer and consumers got poorer (Comanor and Smiley 1975); monopoly rents were simply transfers. In the rent-seeking approach, the impact of monopoly on income distribution is a more complicated issue. Of the original formulators of the theory, only Posner relates his analysis to the distribution of income. He states: "There is no reason to think that monopoly has a significant distributive effect. Consumers' wealth is not transferred to the shareholders of monopoly firms; it is dissipated in the purchase of inputs into the activity of becoming a monopolist" (1975, 821).

Posner's argument seems logical. Rent seeking dissipates monopoly rents, translating potential transfers into social costs. The effect of monopoly on the distribution of income in the rent-seeking society would thus appear to be nil. However, the argument needs to be scrutinized carefully.

Using the simple example employed by Posner, suppose that there are $1 million in rents to be captured and ten risk-neutral bidders for a monopoly right. Each bidder bids $100,000 for the franchise; $1 million is spent to capture $1 million; at a social level the monopoly rents are exactly wasted. The example, however, embodies a distributional consequence. Clearly, one of the ten bidders wins the competition, and receives a net return on his efforts of $900,000. Without more information, one cannot clearly say in this stylized example whether rent seeking increases or decreases the degree of inequality in the distribution of income. The most logical presumption, given that rent seekers earn normal rates of return on their investments in rent seeking, is that consumers (poor?) are worse off and rent seekers (rich?) are no better off than before. A type of low-level, wasteful inequality is thereby generated. It seems a little far-fetched, however, to think that rent seeking generally promotes a leveling or only a mild inequality in the income distribution. Set in a world of tradition, class, privilege, power, and differential organization costs, rent seeking most likely promotes more significant inequalities in the distribution of income.

Perhaps more realistically, there will not be an equal distribution of rent-seeking ability in a society. Thus, the mechanism by which rents are assigned is likely to affect the distribution of wealth to the extent that Ricardian rents are earned in rent seeking (Higgins and Tollison 1988). Consider a regulatory hearing mechanism for assigning rents, and suppose that some lawyers or economists earn inframarginal rents in rent seeking. On average, these individuals will be wealthier than their marginal competitors and wealthier than they would be without a rent-seeking mechanism of the particular type that rewards their skills. The choice of such a transfer mechanism increases the demand for lawyers above that which would hold with (say) an auction mechanism for assigning monopoly rents. So, first of all, the mechanism will alter the distribution of wealth by occupation. Moreover, if the requisite talents of the favored occupation cannot be reproduced at constant costs, the inequality of wealth in society may be further affected. For example, suppose the qualities of a good businessman/speculator are more fungible among the population than the qualities of a good lawyer. Then, inframarginal rents will accrue to the best of the legal profession in regulatory hearing cases, whereas with an auction no Ricardian rents would be earned. The distribution of wealth would differ between these two societies as a consequence.

Undoubtedly, rent seeking caused the distribution of income in the mercantile societies to be more unequal. In England, the king's fortune rose (unless he dissipated it in wars), and those interest groups and individuals who won the king's favor also gained wealth at the expense of less successful groups and individuals. In France, as will be discussed, the ability of French monarchs to rent seek virtually captured all of the rents in the private sector, in both output and input markets, at least until the post-Colbertian period (the eighteenth century). Hence, here, the state became wealthier at the expense of society in general. In Spain, the lack of any effective constitutional constraints on taxation and regulation created a highly controlled redistribution of income and wealth to monarchical and other aristocratic interests. The principal point is clear—rent seeking does not have a neutral effect on the distribution of income.

RENT SEEKING AND THE DECLINE OF MERCANTILISM IN ENGLAND

At the other extreme from the rent-seeking leviathan were the emerging institutions of representative democracy. The rise of democracy in England was embodied in a struggle over the power to supply legislation in a rent-seeking context. This struggle ultimately led to the demise of English mercantilism because of the profound changes taking place in the institutional environment. Under the assumption that self-interest is independent of time, we argue that an important source of the fall of mercantilism must be found in the changing cost-benefit structure facing potential rent seekers. We have thus far suggested that mercantilism rose because the relative costs of negotiating favored treatment with a state in which authority was vested in a central figure were low. Prior to the centralization of authority, rent seekers had to deal with a multitude of feudal rulers, which caused the costs of negotiating and enforcing exclusive rights to be relatively higher. The correlated rise of mercantilism and central monarchies was thus the result of changed cost conditions, and the fall of widespread mercantile activity in England may be explained as a manifestation of changes in the bargaining environment occurring as the result of political upheaval.

In seeking an explanation for the decline of English mercantilist policies within the rent-seeking paradigm, we follow Hayek (1960) when he notes that "it was finally in the dispute about the authority to legislate in which the contending parties reproached each other for acting arbitrarily— acting, that is, not in accordance with recognized general laws—that the cause of individual freedom was inadvertently advanced" (163). Throughout his discussion of the emergence of the rule of law in England, Hayek stresses that economic freedom came about as a by-product of a struggle for the power to supply legislation. This struggle embodied an effort by Parliament and the common law jurists not, as historians like Heckscher would have us believe, to invoke competition in England in a public-spirited gesture but rather to share in the monopoly rents being collected by the monarchy. In this struggle several important institutional changes, which dramatically affected relative rates of return to investments in rent seeking by both suppliers and demanders, were introduced unintentionally. Our explanation of the deregulation in mercantile England relies on these changes in costs and benefits.

As the power of the English monarchy declined, the movement to a form of representative democracy shifted the locus of rent-seeking activity to new forums, primarily to the legislature and the common law judiciary, with predictable implications for the decline of rent seeking. For example, with respect to the legislature, the costs of lobbying a representative body for monopoly charters are higher than the costs of lobbying a unified monarchy, because there are multiple decision makers unevenly distributed across legislative houses.[9] The rational rent seeker will reduce his bid for a monopoly right when lobbying costs rise. Moreover, the uncertainty cost facing the rent seeker will rise under representative government. Logrolling in the legislature will mask current votes to some extent, making current legislative outcomes more uncertain. Further, there will be turnover among politicians and uncertainty about the durability of legislation from session to session of the legislature. Also, by the time the English Parliament had asserted its power as the source of legislation, there was basically no prevailing administrative apparatus by which the central state could reinstitute and enforce an extensive system of monopoly rights in the economy. For these and other reasons to be discussed in chapter 3, the costs of seeking monopoly rights rose under early English representative democracy, and the decline of government interference in the economy was predictable because of these higher costs.

With respect to the mercantile judiciary in England, there was an important jurisdictional competition between the common law courts and those supporting the king's interests. The common law courts evolved a doctrine that held that royal monopoly and prerogative were illegal, while the special interests sanctioned by Parliament were legitimate. The king's courts naturally disagreed with this doctrine. The net result was a legal conflict in which one court system would rule that a monopoly right was valid and the other that it was invalid. Under these conditions there was, in effect, no legal basis for enforcing a universally valid monopoly right. This meant that even if a rent seeker could obtain a monopoly grant from the king or Parliament, he had no guarantee that it could be sustained against interlopers. Seeking monopoly through the shelter of the state was clearly going to be a less profitable activity under these circumstances.

As we shall see, a great struggle evolved in England between the king and Parliament and between the king's courts and the common law courts allied to parliamentary interests. This struggle, which had important religious and political themes, was also a struggle over who was to run and profit from the rent-seeking economy of English mercantilism. This conflict over the authority to legislate and to adjudicate legal disputes ultimately meant that the costs of seeking and enforcing monopoly protection from the state rose to exceed the potential benefits for rent seekers, and state interference in the economy consequently declined. A very different cost structure existed in mercantile France and, especially, in Spain, but the monopoly rent-seeking paradigm performs admirably in explaining developments there, as well, as we shall see in chapters 4 and 5.

CONCLUSION

The reader now has an outline of what rent seeking means and how we intend to use it in analyzing mercantilism. Our argument is that the rent-seeking model is more useful in explaining developments in the mercantile economies than the usual specie-accumulation interpretation. The rent-seeking model rationalizes the emergence and decline of the social order of mercantilism in England, France, and Spain in terms of individual behavior in the face of varying institutional constraints rather than in terms of the irrationality or error in the social order of mercantilism. The institutional architecture within these economies—particularly that relating to the political nexus and control of property rights over market development—is central to explaining the interplay of forces that either vivified economic institutions or mired them in long-term stultification.

Chapter Three

Economic Regulation and Rent Seeking in Mercantile England

It was finally in a dispute about the authority to legislate in which the contending parties reproached each other for acting arbitrarily—acting, that is, not in accordance with recognized general laws—that the cause of individual freedom was inadvertently advanced.

—Friedrich Hayek,
The Constitution of Liberty

No topic in the history of ideas or in economic history has received more attention than the critical period that preceded the Industrial Revolution and, subsequently, the modern world. Recent studies, including our own (1981), have focused on certain critical changes in political and economic institutions over the Tudor and Stuart periods of English history. Over this period, economic regulation was extensive and was instituted on both the local and national levels. Yet much of this regulation disappeared in the period after 1649. By applying the rent-seeking model to analyze the forces that drove local and national regulations, we can elucidate and improve the prevailing historical interpretation of the rise and fall of widespread government intervention in the economy of mercantile England.

Specifically, the present chapter analyzes Heckscher's discussion (1934, 1:221–325) of the rise of internal regulation in England in terms of how changing constraints redirected resource allocation into rent-seeking behavior by economic agents.[1] This part of Heckscher's argument is shown to be consistent in its basic elements with the modern theory of economic regulation (Stigler 1971b; Posner 1971; Peltzman 1976). The Elizabethan Statute of Artificers (and to a lesser extent the Poor Law), which was the centerpiece of the regulation of local industry and employment during the English mercantilist era, is also considered in detail. The main point of our discussion is to show that the provisions for enforcement of this regulation by unpaid justices of the peace and the existence of an unregulated sector (the countryside) of the economy had profound effects upon the pattern and durability of this monopoly-inspired system of local economic regulation.

Heckscher's treatment of the relationship between the mercantilist judiciary and the national monopolies created by royal grant is also reviewed and criticized in the present chapter. Specifically, we shall challenge his interpretation of two competing court systems in England prior to and during mercantile times: one (the common law courts) pliant to the special interests related to the Parliament, and one (represented by chancery and the court of the Star Chamber) pliant to the special interests related to the monarchy. Further, we consider how this jurisdictional competition ultimately led to a situation in which regulation to promote national monopoly was not feasible. Our argument contrasts markedly with that of Heckscher, who, incorrectly in our view, saw the common law courts as the repository of traditional free-trade sentiments.

The struggle for the power to supply monopoly rights through legislation is also examined in chapter 3. This struggle led to the Puritan Revolution and to the victory of parliamentary interests in regard to the supply of monopoly rights and sounded the death knell for the rent-seeking society of mercantile England.

After brief consideration of the issue of customs, some concluding remarks are offered on the relationship between our analysis and the conventional wisdom about mercantilism.

THE RISE OF INTERNAL REGULATION IN MERCANTILE ENGLAND

Heckscher is very explicit about the origin of economic regulation in England: "English municipalities pursued the same ends as the continental, and the forces they set up to achieve these ends were more fundamental than one might think. They bought their privileges, particularly the *gratia emendsiet vendendi*, that is, the power over the organization of the market and of industry in general, by monetary sacrifices to the king" (1934, 224).

There are some important differences in monarchical and democratic rent seeking, but, in a fundamental sense, the old and the modern mercantilism are the same phenomenon. ("Old mercantilism" may be distinguished from its modern variant by the bureaucratic administrative machinery that was attached to the latter in the first half of the nineteenth century in England.) Moreover, in a fully complementary sense local economic regulation served as a primitive manpower policy to forestall the migration of farm labor to the towns. The earliest charters by the Norman kings to boroughs include the power to establish the guild merchant, that is, to restrict entry to those already on the spot and in control. Public-interest arguments, such as the maintenance of quality, were advanced for such procedures, but the self-serving nature of the arguments is apparent.

Economic regulation took a familiar form in English mercantilism— licensing and the restriction of competition among suppliers—but it is important to understand certain critical differences between the conduct of local and national regulation and monopoly and the institutions surrounding them. Local regulation of trades, prices, and wage rates stemmed from the medieval guild system. Enforcement of these guild regulations in the Tudor period prior to Elizabeth was the responsibility of the guild bureaucracy, in combination with the town or shire administrative machinery. Elizabeth attempted to codify and strengthen these detailed regulations with the Statute of Artificers, which outlines the detailed enforcement duties of local justices of the peace, aldermen, and local administrators. Enforcers of local regulations were either unpaid or paid very little for these services, as we shall see, which led to local alignments of economic interests. We will argue that these cabals of interests ultimately rendered the local provision of monopoly rights ineffective.[2]

At the national level, on the other hand, industrial regulation was created by three means: (a) by statute of Parliament, (b) by royal proclamations and letters patent, and (c) by orders as decrees of the Privy Council or the king's court. Monarchical rent seeking led to monopoly rights in large numbers of national industries, such as those in gunpowder, saltpeter, salt, paper, mineral extraction, and others. The meshing of private interests of monarch and monopolist was firmly enshrined in English practice as early as the fourteenth century (see Power's [1941] analysis of the medieval wool trade). The nature of this alliance was underscored in debate on the issue of monopoly in the House of Commons in 1601: "First, let us consider the word Monopoly, what is it; *Monos* is *Unus,* and *Polis, Civitas.* So then, the Meaning of the Word is; a Restraint of any thing Publick, in a City or

Common-Wealth, to a Private Use. And the User called Monopolitan; *quasi, cujus privatum lucrum est urbis et orbis Commune Malum.* And we may well term this Man, The Whirlpool of the Princes Profits" (Tawney and Power 1924, 2:270). These revealing definitions of monopoly and the monopolitan (monopolist) remind us that the motives of economic actors are clearly recognizable and have not changed over the centuries. But, on at least two counts, analogies between the old and modern mercantilism within our analytical framework must be carefully drawn. The first caveat concerns the available forms of rent seeking, and the second relates to the supply side of the market for regulation between the two periods.

The question naturally arises as to why the sovereign did not use taxes rather than monopolies for revenue. In the first place there were some early consensual constraints on the English monarch's ability to tax. England's Parliament was already well established when France's first Estates General met in 1302. Maitland (1908, 179) reports that by 1297 Parliament had announced the principle that common consent of the realm was necessary for the imposition of all taxes, save ancient "aids, prizes, and customs." However, these elements of parliamentary consent were not absolute until the revolutionary period of the mid-seventeenth century, which was in large part engendered by a conflict between monarch and the House of Commons over the authority to collect rents to support armed struggles (see Wolfe 1972).

But beyond the consensual constraints, tax collection was a relatively inefficient means to raise revenue for the mercantile central state because the costs of monitoring and controlling tax evasion were high. Barter and nonmarket production were undoubtedly widespread in the agricultural economy of these times, and commercial record keeping was not highly developed for market production. Moreover, tax collectors were susceptible to bribery and not very vigorous because they did not receive the full marginal value of their efforts to collect taxes. These sorts of factors made tax collection an unattractive revenue alternative (at the margin) for the mercantile authorities. Indeed, since most trade off the manor took place in open markets until the end of the sixteenth century, the power to tax these transactions was not, after Magna Carta, within the reach of the sovereign.

Granting monopoly rights as a means to raise revenue did not suffer from the same deficiencies as taxation. Most important, competition among potential monopolists revealed to state authorities the worth of such privileges. There were no problems of evasion or guessing at taxable values in this case. Competition among aspiring monopolists yielded the necessary data for revenue purposes to the central authorities, and, unlike the tax collector, the monopolist had strong incentives to protect his monopoly right because he received the full marginal value of his efforts in this regard. Such a system, of course, would be sensitive to collusion among bidders, but there is no evidence that these monarchies acted in such a way (sealed bids, for example) as to make collusion easy for bidders. Indeed, much of the court intrigue of these times, which has a revered place in literary history, may be seen as the means by which the monarch promoted competition among aspiring monopolists.

A second point relates to the nature of the market for regulation. In a modern context Stigler (1971b, 3) has observed that "as a rule, regulation is acquired by the industry and is designed and operated primarily for its benefit." In both old and modern mercantilism the pursuit of economic regulation is inspired by prospect of a monopolistic privilege sheltered by the state, and, in this respect, the economic logic of both historical episodes is essentially the same.[3] Economic regulation may be seen as the result of a rivalrous process whereby economic interests actively seek the shelter of the state from competition. Modern examples of such regulation are abundant and well documented (Posner 1974). In the mercantile setting the relevant interest groups were local administrators, merchants and laborers in the towns, and, in part, monopoly interests engaged in national and international production and trade. But it would be a mistake to carry the comparison too far. Though the basic natures of the old and modern mercantilism are the same, there are important institutional differences in the constraints facing economic agents within the two rent-seeking environments. The most important difference for the purposes of the discussion here concerns the supply side of the market for regulatory legislation. The national mercantilism described by Heckscher was supplied by a monarchy, and a monarchy represents a uniquely low-cost environment for rent seeking, especially when compared with a modern democratic setting in which the power to supply and sustain regulatory legislation is dispersed among various governmental powers. The consolidation of national power under the mercantile monarchies thus provides a sensible explanation for the widespread rent seeking and economic regulation during this period of English history.

In the course of the discussion, we will see how the struggle between the sovereign and Parliament over the power to supply legislation, and Parliament's ultimate victory in this struggle, dramatically altered the costs and benefits to buyers and sellers of monopoly rights in such a way as to lead to a deterioration of English mercantilist regulation. Our analysis will stress that a free economy emerged in England as a by-product of this competition to supply legislation (Hayek [1960, 163] makes a similar argument). The emergence of English economic freedom is thus depicted as an unplanned, undeliberated, evolutionary result of rivalry for control of the legislative-regulatory apparatus. Few individuals, and least of all the common man, consciously conceived of the freely competitive economy as an alternative society for Englishmen prior to 1800. Certainly, Smith and others had a vision of a "system of natural liberty" prior to 1800, and they understood clearly how economic freedom increased the efficiency of aggregate production. We argue, however, that these visions were not the force behind institutional change, especially in the period preceding 1750. This change came about as an unintended consequence of a struggle to control the supply of government-protected monopoly rents.

THE ENFORCEMENT OF LOCAL MERCANTILE ECONOMIC REGULATION

The legal framework for the enforcement of mercantilist economic regulation on the local level was set out by the Elizabethan Statute of Artificers. The central issues in this section will concern the provisions in the Statute of Artificers for enforcing a nationally uniform system of regulation on the local level and how the means of enforcement affected the pattern and survival of local monopolies in mercantile England. Specifically, the adequacy of Heckscher's interpretations of two key points related to enforcement of the statute will be questioned: (a) that concerning the motives of the local justices of the peace (the chief enforcers) and (b) that associated with worker mobility, given the presence of unregulated sectors close to local regulated economies. Before turning to these issues, however, consider briefly the move to a national system of regulation.

The statute was an attempted codification of older rules for the regulation of industry, labor, and poor relief, with the important difference that such regulations were to be national rather than local in scope. The reason Heckscher gives for the move to national regulation was the enormous increase in wages after the Black Death. He argues that "from that date the regulation of wages ceased to be a local affair and became a national problem" (Heckscher 1934, 1:226). Heckscher, however, is being somewhat reckless with time. The Black Death decimated population in 1347–48, and the Statute of Artificers was enacted in 1563. It is thus very doubtful that much of a link exists between the two events. In our view the more immediate economic reason for the move to national regulation was the inability of the towns to restrict cheating on local cartel arrangements.[4] Towns, in other words, attempted to buy a nationally uniform system of regulation from the king, and local monopoly rights were to be protected against encroachment, especially by "foreigners."

The attempt by self-interested merchants and administrators of towns to regulate economic activity and to prevent "interlopers" on local franchises is evidenced in numerous Tudor documents. The City of London, especially, wished to restrict aliens and foreign technology as inhibitory of town profits.[5] The solution most often proffered was banishing to the countryside aliens or those workers who did not meet "legal" qualifications for trades. Moreover, according to several writers (for example, Plucknett 1948, 32), the royal courts took over the cases involving peasants and workers not because of the increase in wages owing to the Black Death but as an assertion of royal power over the manor courts. The evidence would thus seem to favor a rent-seeking interpretation of the evolution of a national system of economic regulation in mercantile England. At best the one-time increase in wages at the end of the fourteenth century was used as a pretext for state intervention on the local level.

Enforcement of the Statute by Unpaid Justices of the Peace

The nationally uniform system of local monopolies was to be enforced by the justices of the peace. As Heckscher notes, "the Justices of the Peace were the agents of unified industrial legislation" (1934, 1:246), and several aspects of this enforcement system are important. A primary feature of the system was that the justices of the peace were to be unpaid. Heckscher argues that no pay for the officials led to ineptitude and laziness on their part with respect to enforcement. We argue to the contrary that nonpayment or low pay for justices of the peace established a ripe setting for malfeasance and led to a self-interested pattern of enforcement, one suggesting both sub-rosa activities and selective cartel enforcement of industries in which the enforcers had economic interests.

Although Heckscher does allude to some evidence on corruption, his main conclusion is that there was an inept, rather than corrupt, pattern of enforcement of local cartels:

> Justices of the Peace were unpaid. It is not easy to say how far they recouped themselves by accepting bribes. Allegations to that effect were not

absent. Thus, in the year 1601 a speaker in the House of Commons stated: 'A justice of peace is a living Creature that for half a Dozen of Chickens will Dispense with a whole Dozen of Penal Statutes'; and there is divers other proof of their corruption. Still writers who have thoroughly gone into the conditions consider this fairly exceptional, particularly in rural districts. *The weakness of the system lay not so much in this as in their indifference and carelessness.* As early as the time of the first great manual to justices of the peace, first published by Lambarde in 1583 under the title of *Eirenarcha,* the complaint was made that justices were scarcely willing to devote even three hours of their time to the Quarter Sessions, where an innumerable number of county problems remained to be dealt with. It was more and more common for justices to meet in public-houses, enjoy an ample repast with alcoholic accompaniment and then carry on without any agenda whatever. Obviously the detailed control demanded by the industrial regulations could not be efficiently carried out in these conditions. (1934, 1:246–47; emphasis added)

Heckscher's use of the term *efficiently* is curious in light of modern economics. The behavior of the justices of the peace was quite efficient and predictable, given the constraints imposed by the Statute of Artificers (see Becker 1976). Indeed, modern economic theory leads us to *expect* malfeasance as the predictable response to low pay in situations where there is an element of trust inherent in the labor contract (Becker and Stigler 1974). This conclusion follows because the opportunity cost of being apprehended and fired is low. We contend, therefore, that the absence of pay for the justices of the peace led to malfeasance and a predictable pattern of enforcement of the local cartel regulations.

Heckscher may have sensed these points because the implicit pattern in his lengthy discussion of enforcement (1934, 1:246–63) is that the regulations were applied in such manner as to increase the net worth of the officials' holdings in regulated enterprises. A particular manifestation of this type of behavior involved the adage "set a thief to catch a thief." Many of the justices of the peace had interests in the industries they regulated, and this method of garnering income led to a pattern of cartel enforcement that favored the enforcers' holdings in firms. Heckscher put the matter in terms of industries rather than firms when he observed that, "as regards the control of industry itself, there were a large number of people among the controllers who were themselves interested in the particular industries, and of course not in the application of the legal regulations; and to appoint them controllers was to set a thief to catch a thief" (1934, 1:248).

There are clearly numerous ways in which the justices of the peace could increase the net worth of their holdings in the cartel system they enforced. We would expect that the general pattern of cartel enforcement by the enforcers would feature favoritism for the firms in which they had interests—for example, by allowing their firms to cheat on the cartel arrangement while preventing cheating by other cartel members. Consider a possible example offered by Heckscher: "The laws are very significant in so far as they indicate a sincere desire to call a halt to the exodus of industry from the towns and in general to prevent the formation of larger enterprises especially in rural areas. It is true that the resistance was weaker against those powerful urban 'merchants' who employed rural weavers; the law did not place such great obstacles in their way as it did in those cases where the urban masters had to be protected from extra-urban competition" (1934, 1:239).

Independent evidence from Tudor and other mercantile documents helps support the contention that unpaid justices of the peace were not merely indifferent participants in the process (Heckscher's conception) but actively and profitably subverted the system. First, let us consider their responsibilities. Though their duties are not spelled out in the "industrial program" endorsed by Parliament in 1559, the Statute of Artificers of 1563 (Tawney and Power 1924, 1:338–50) charges the justices of the peace with the conduct of price-and-wage controls in their jurisdictions (determined at regularly held meetings, in some cases twice a year). They were to issue public proclamations and to hear and adjudicate complaints concerning apprenticeship infractions, worker mobility, wage-price violations, illegal entry and exit by laborers and producers, and so forth (Holdsworth 1966, 1:285–98).[6] It appears, however, that the day-to-day enforcement was delegated to mayors, other city officials, and a "governour of Laborers" appointed in every town.[7]

Although day-to-day regulations were delegated to a degree, it is nonetheless clear that the justices of the peace were the final authority on adjudication and enforcement and that, early on, enforcement was something less than lackluster. Insinuations that justices' regulations and enforcement were working at cross-purposes to the statute may be found in a letter written by a justice (William Tyldesley) as early as 1561. Tyldesley wrote that enforcement of the statutes had been uneven in the shires, fearing that in the end "all will be as good as nothing." But in the matter of evaluating particular regulations, Tyldesley (possibly suggesting conflict of interest) wrote: "of Alehouses (which I do thynck to be the verey stake & staye of all false theves and vagobundes) yf one of ij Justices be Redye to put them downe that be to bad, by & by other Justices be Redye to sett them vpp agayne, yea, and that with stoutnesse, besyde more. So that in Alehouses, they ys littill hope of eny Amendment to be had." And of the wine market: "they that sell them by my lordes servands, or my masters servands, yea, or have suche kynd of Lycenses, & Lycens out of Lycens to them & ther Deputyes & assignesse & to the assignes of ther deputyes & assignes, that no dout off, yf they maye be allowed for good, they have Autoryte to gyve Lycens unto all men whom please them to sell wyne" (Tawney and Power 1924, 1:330–31).

There is plentiful evidence that the justices of the peace were at the very least ignoring their duties, as evidenced by a memorandum on the statute in 1573.[8] But, more important, the queen's council provided that high constables (of less authority than the justices of the peace) meet in "Statute sessions" to police them "so as nothinge be by them done therin contrary or repugnaunte to the said Acte" (Tawney and Power 1924, 1:363). It is, of course, most likely that mayors, constables, and aldermen also participated in the self-interested supply of regulation.

That the justices of the peace had acquired a power to seek rents by bribes and side payments was open knowledge by the time of James I. In most revealing testimony before Parliament in 1620 concerning the patent for inns and other local regulations, a member (Mr. Noye) in the Committee of Grievances noted:

> There are some patents that in themselves are good and lawful, but abused by the patentees in the execution of them, who perform not the trust reposed in them for his maj.; and of such a kind is the Patent for Inns, but those that have the execution abuse it by setting up Inns in forests and bye villages, only to harbour rogues and thieves; and such as the justices of peace of the shire, who best know where Inns are fittest to be, and who best deserve to have licenses for them, have suppressed from keeping of alehouses; *for none is now refused, that will make a good composition*. There are also some, who have gotten a power to dispense with the statute of Vagabonds, Rogues, &c. and so make themselves dispensers of the royalties only proper for the king himself.—The like patent is granted for toll, leets, warrens, markets, &c. and set up bills of it on posts, like new physicians that

are new come to town, making merchandises of it. (Corbbett 1966, 1:192–93; emphasis added)

Here the local administrators are singled out for rent seeking by the Parliament, with particular emphasis upon the justices of the peace. The issuing of licenses by the justices in return for a "good composition," meaning a good settlement or agreement, could mean nothing if not sub-rosa bribes or side payments.

But there is even clearer evidence supporting our view that low pay (or no pay) for enforcement led to a pattern of selective regulation that favored local justices' holdings in regulated enterprises. Consider the case of a grain-mill patent granted by Elizabeth to Bridgwater in 1585 (Bridgwater was the large port in southwestern England on the Bristol Channel). In the original letters patent:

a clause was inserted binding the mayor, recorder, and aldermen not to allow anyone to brew or sell any beer and ale in the town unless the malt and other grain had been ground at certain water-driven mills called Little Mills. These mills were owned partly by the crown and partly by the Earl of Hertford. Some twenty-five years later, in 1609 or 1610, a prominent citizen of the town named Robert Chute built a horse mill for grinding malt, for his "owne private gaine". Chute was mayor of the town and a justice of the peace, so his duty to uphold the brewing clause of the municipal charter was clear. Yet he not only permitted brewers and others to desert Little Mills for his horse mill, he brought pressure to bear on them to do so. He used the power of his office against some who did not. He had a part of the water supply diverted from Little Mills, and this prevented the two wheels there from turning steadily during dry summers. He had his wife talk with persons who took their grain to Little Mills. Mrs. Chute went to see the son and the maid of a Mrs. Newman who kept a fairly large stock of malt. According to the maid, the mayor's wife had said, "whie doe not your Dame grind her malt at my husbands horsemill. I hope you were well used [there]". Richard Newman, the son, testified that Mrs. Chute had been sharper and plainer with him. She had threatened that if his mother did not take her malt to the horse mill, "Mr. Maior would looke aboute". And, sure enough, he did. A week later Mrs. Newman was arrested and taken to prison. Her husband was fined 20s. at the next quarter sessions. When charges were brought in the court of exchequer against Chute for defying the brewing clause of the town charter, his witnesses defended him on the ground

that Little Mills had not a sufficient supply of water to grind all the malt
consumed in Bridgwater. As Chute had deprived Little Mills of part of its
supply, this was not surprising! Chute's witnesses also testified that the brewing clause had been inserted not for the general welfare of the townspeople,
but for the private advantage of John Courte, another prominent citizen,
now dead, who had held from the queen a lease for three lives of her part in
Little Mills when the town was granted its charter. Courte's son and widow
were still getting a profit from this part when Chute built his horse mill.
(Nef 1968, 52–53)

The incident, taken from the Exchequer Depositions of James I, clearly
illustrates the pattern of local enforcement. In the case described, the self-
interested justice of the peace succeeded in utilizing his regulatory power
in blatant subversion of the patent's charge.

Although it is difficult to find records of illegal transactions in any age,
testimony of contemporary observers seems to support a characterization
of an enforcement system of internal mercantile regulation in which the
chief enforcers were self-interested parties. On the evidence we find
Heckscher's claim unfounded that the essence of the pattern of enforcement of internal regulation was indifference and carelessness owing to lack
of pay. Rather the system of no pay for enforcement led to a pattern of self-
interested rent seeking and, by implication, to a pattern of regulation in
favor of firms in which the justices of the peace held interests. Heckscher's
implicit suggestions, together with independent evidence from mercantile
documents, corroborate this view. Indeed, in these ruder times what other
goal of regulation could there have been except unvarnished rent seeking?
To apply conceptions of the "public interest" to the historical context of
mercantile England requires a great stretch of the imagination.

Occupational Mobility and Local Regulation

There were factors other than unpaid justices of the peace that made the
Elizabethan system of local economic regulation difficult to sustain. A more
important reason was that it was possible to escape these regulations within
England at the time. While the regulations concerning mobility were clearly
set out by both the Statute of Artificers and by local justices of the peace,
there is evidence that the rules were blatantly unobserved.[9] For example,
the "decay, impoverishment and ruin of the cities" allegedly caused by
artificers' movement to the countryside was the subject of the remonstrance

issued by the queen's council in 1573 (see "Memorandum on the Statute of Artificers," Tawney and Power 1924, 1:353–65). Again, the justices of the peace were to be chief enforcers of the statute, but their actual enforcement was far different than the crown intended.

In effect, buyers and sellers could migrate to an unregulated sector in the suburbs and the countryside, and the existence of this unregulated sector created powerful incentives to destroy the local cartel arrangements in the towns.[10] Considering the difference in internal regulation in France and England, Heckscher (1934, 1:266) notes that "the most vital difference was that many important districts were set free from the application of the statutes in England, while in France nothing remained unregulated in principle, apart from purely accidental exceptions or subordinate points." The effect in England may be seen in the departure of handicraftsmen and industry from the regulated towns in order to produce and sell in the suburbs and the countryside. There is no evidence to suggest that the countryside was "set" free in any conscious, deliberate act of policy, but rather this form of avoiding local regulation seems to have been a response to the pattern of enforcement of local regulation pursued by the justices of the peace. Movement out of the towns was simply a way for some artisans and merchants to raise the costs of enforcement above the potential returns.

It should be kept in mind that these moves to escape local cartel regulations did not have to be distant. The suburbs of towns were filled with handicraftsmen who could not get into the town guilds or who wanted to escape their control. Various efforts to bring these cheaters on the local cartels under control proved futile (Heckscher 1934, 1:240–241).[11] It was simply not feasible to control chiseling on the cartel price in this mercantilist version of a widely dispersed flea market. Adam Smith illustrated this point nicely when he wrote: "If you would have your work tolerably executed, it must be done in the suburbs where the workmen, having no exclusive privilege, have nothing but their character to depend upon, and you must then smuggle it into town as well as you can" (Smith 1937, 313). Moreover, attempts to bring the activities of rural industry, which moved farther from town, under guild control predictably failed even more miserably (Heckscher 1934, 1:238–44). Cheating on the local cartels thus became the economic order of the day, and the state's lack of success in dealing with these problems is ample testimony to the inefficient nature of the Elizabethan cartel machinery.[12]

Other enforcers had more direct incentives in pursuing such matters as patent infringements, as Heckscher (1934, 1:253–56) outlines. For example, Elizabeth made a practice of granting court favorites the right to collect fines for violations of the regulatory code. Such farming out of tax and fine collections led to a regular pattern of enforcement, for the more lucrative fines came from local patent infringements and not from pursuing the entrepreneurs who fled from town regulation. Given the enforcement system adopted to promote mercantile regulation, then, it is easily seen that an optimal pattern of enforcement, even where there was a bounty system for violations, involved a substantial unregulated sector. The costs and benefits of such a system of enforcement are aptly summarized by Heckscher: "One of them for example wrote in 1618 with engaging frankness that 'having spent a great part of his means in soliciting and seeking after suits, he had at last hit upon one' in the supervision of English lead" (1934, 1:253).

The Demise of Local Regulation

A puzzling aspect of the demise of local economic regulation is why the guilds sought a system of regulation that had such poor enforcement provisions. The answer appears to be that the guilds imperfectly foresaw the difficulties of forestalling potential competition both without and within their cartel arrangements. The towns, which were typically synonymous with guild administration, bought their monopoly privileges from the king: "It was precisely these payments, in which the king had a special interest, that gave towns the opportunity of providing a privileged position for their taxpaying citizens and of treating all other people as foreigners" (Heckscher 1934, 1:224). The emphasis in local economic regulation, following the tradition of manorial control, was thus directly aimed at the immediate threat of outsiders, who were not to participate in the city's privileges. The subsequent evolution of effective means to chisel on the cartel, such as moving outside the reach of the enforcement authorities to the suburbs or the countryside, was not entirely foreseen at the time the cartels were established. Moreover, as Heckscher points out, the local guilds were organized in such a way that internal competition was not easily suppressed:

> Finally there were several specific features in the English gilds contributing to lessen their effectiveness. One of them was the association of the most varied crafts in one and the same organization—a very common occurrence in England. It is obvious that control could be of little value when entrusted to such corporations. Then there was the Custom of London

according to which the completion of apprenticeship in one craft gave the right to practice in any other. In London itself the municipal government attempted to exclude small crafts from making use of this right and succeeded to some extent; but no more than that, at the time of the great municipal reform in 1835, the Custom of London still persisted in more than half the number of cases reviewed. And despite its name, the Custom of London was to be found in a large number of provincial towns. A few examples will suffice to prove how varied the offshoots of this practice could be. A member of the goldsmiths' gild in London called a whole family of stone setters (paviors) to life, all of whom belonged to the goldsmiths' organization. In 1671 these "goldsmith-paviors" were thirty-nine in number, as against only fifty-two stone setters in their own gild. A confectioner who wished to become a freeman of Newcastle in 1685 was allowed to choose a gild, and like the London stone setters, he chose the goldsmiths. Thus the attempt to bind newly accepted apprentices to their own professional bodies was a failure. Above all, the chances of effective professional control [were] thereby rendered very difficult. (1934, 1:244–45)

This does not mean, of course, that the guild merchants, or anyone else in the England of these times, actively thought in terms of a freely competitive society as an alternative to the highly regulated world in which they lived. Since they had never known such a phenomenon, it is hardly likely that they would have conceptualized in this manner. Rather, we are arguing that the possible emergence of the competitive alternative, brought about by poor regulatory design, could have, at best, been only vaguely perceived by the local monopolists.

Specifically, at the time they bought their privileges from the king, the local guilds were only imperfectly aware of the difficulties of suppressing competition from outside and inside their cartels. Logically, their payments for these privileges would have reflected an estimate of these difficulties, that is, of the expected durability of their protection. As Landes and Posner (1975: 883–85) demonstrate in the context of judicial decision making (to be discussed further below), legislation protecting special interests may have significant present values, even where the probabilities of nullification are substantial. Thus, it was not irrational for the local guilds to have sought monopoly protection in the face of potential difficulties of enforcing this protection. Moreover, modern parallels abound. The railroads could hardly have foreseen the rise of intercity trucking, and the airlines provide a convenient example of a case where the industry sought a cartel arrangement that, for a variety of reasons (for example, nonprice competition), the government could not effectively enforce.

Our conclusion is that the Statute of Artificers embodied the means of its own destruction. The behavior of the unpaid justices of the peace and the ability of firms to escape regulation were the two major factors leading to its undoing. Heckscher appears to have sensed these points, but he did not examine their implications in terms of economic analysis.[13] We turn now to a consideration of the important part played by the mercantilist judiciary in the demise of national economic regulation.

THE MERCANTILIST JUDICIARY AND THE BREAKDOWN OF NATIONAL MONOPOLIES

In the case of national regulation, there were no unregulated sectors, such as the countryside, where competitive alternatives prevailed and undermined the stability of cartel arrangements. Rather, the factors that led to the undoing of national monopolies must be sought in the changing constraints facing economic actors in the rent-seeking economy of England at this time. In this section the role of mercantile judiciaries in the demise of the national monopolies will be examined, reserving for the next section the role played by the struggle between Parliament and the monarchy to control the supply of legislation. Before turning to Heckscher's interpretation of the mercantilist judiciary (and to our alternative hypothesis), a brief discussion of the historical development of the English court system is warranted. An understanding of these judicial institutions is all the more important since Heckscher stresses at the outset of his own discussion that "the greatest gap in the literature of the subject is the part dealing with the practice of the law courts" (1934, 1:224).[14]

Mercantile Court Systems

The development of the judiciary in England was a long, complex, and tortuous process. Basically, three common law courts evolved in the period between the Norman invasion and the mercantile era: the Court of King's Bench, the Court of Common Pleas, and the Exchequer. Matters before these courts were essentially civil in nature, and all were initially under the crown's direct control (with the king even rendering decisions in the early period). During the thirteenth through the fifteenth centuries, however, the courts became increasingly independent of the crown, although judges were appointed by the king, who could (at the outset, at least) remove them for any reason.

Although we are not concerned here with the origins and early developments of the common law courts, it is interesting to note that jurisdictional competition among the courts (meaning a direct competition not for litigants but for changes in their charters by government) was vigorous up to the time of the Tudors (Holdsworth 1966, 1:195, 253–55; Smith 1937, 697). This may be attributed to the facts that jurisdictions of the tripartite court system were ill-defined and that compensation of judges depended in part on court fee collections (the remainder paid by the crown). More importantly, for our purposes, the functional separation of the organs of government toward the end of the fourteenth century intensified the cleavage of interests between the king's council, the Court of King's Bench, and the Parliament.[15] The council became identified and allied with the executive branch of government (the monarch), King's Bench associated with the judiciary, and Parliament identified as a legislative body (although the latter retained some judicial powers; the House of Lords remains the highest appellate court in England). The separation of governmental functions brought with it a self-interested alignment of concerns between the common law courts and Parliament. Although there seems to have been some question over whether these courts would be attracted to the council (representing the king's authoritarian interests) or to Parliament, Holdsworth observes:

> Parliament they [the common law courts] recognized as the body whose consent was necessary to the making of the laws which they applied; while the Council sometimes did or attempted to do things which in their opinion went beyond both the statute and the common law. Common lawyers were an important element in the House of Commons; and the judges of the King's Bench and the Common Pleas were common lawyers similarly educated, similarly employed, often changing from one bench to the other. They were tending to fall apart from that large body of royal clerks who acted in the various departments of government controlled by king and council. It is not surprising, therefore, that the common lawyers came to think that errors in the King's Bench ought to be corrected in Parliament, and not by the Council. (Holdsworth 1966, 1:210–11)

Thus, it appears that the alliance between the common law courts and the Parliament began centuries before the mercantile period, by which time the common law courts had cartelized and established firm jurisdictions (and bureaucracies).[16] Equally significant for the matters at hand is the fact that this identity of interests intensified by 1550, owing principally to the presence of a competing legal system, the royal courts, which were most in evidence by the time of Elizabeth I. The competing judicial system, principally representing equity, was based upon a tradition in Roman law (*curia regis*) that crown powers were above normal legal jurisdictions, that is, outside the common law court system (Heckscher 1934, 1:299) . These royal courts were found in branches of the Royal Council, in its subordinate court—the court of the Star Chamber—and in other parts of the executive branch of government, the chancellor and the court of chancery. Most of the concilliar apparatus came to the foreground of English political institutions during the reign of Henry VIII (see Elton 1966).

Confrontation and competition between the common law and royal court systems ensued (Hanbury 1960, 99, 111, and 135).[17] Predictably, the intrusion by chancery and Star Chamber into common law jurisdictions via "legal fictions," "writs of errors," and other procedural devices was met by an aggressive response from the common law courts' "cartel." Holdsworth observes: "Towards the end of Elizabeth's reign the [royal] court was attacked by the courts of common law. We shall see that the courts of common law showed at this period a jealousy of all jurisdiction other than their own. They had . . . won a complete victory over the older local courts. They now attacked courts which had greater powers of resistance because they had sprung, like themselves, from the crown. Their theory was that a court could not be a legal court unless its jurisdiction was based either upon an Act of Parliament or upon prescription" (1966, 1:414). Maitland (1957, 115) reports that one of the courts of chancery (the court of requests) "perished under the persistent attack of the common lawyers." Clearly, then, the fight over jurisdiction was an important aspect of the struggle between the two court systems during the sixteenth century (Holdsworth 1966, 1:459–61; Plucknett 1948, 151). But along with this struggle came an intensified alliance between common law courts and Parliament. As Parliament's power developed relative to that of the crown, it needed support for its legal actions, a support the common law courts were eager to provide. Beyond being peopled by individuals of similar training and interests, the common law courts were also attracted to the interests of Parliament because they regarded Parliament as simply another common law court (the House of Commons could overturn any decision made by a court of common law). Parliament, moreover, could legislate jurisdictional boundaries and other aspects of the courts but was nevertheless dependent upon the courts for the permanence and security of its laws.[18] It is in this judicial environment that the issue of the power to institute national regulation must be considered.

Alternative Interpretations of Mercantile Judicial Competition

We now turn to Heckscher's interpretation of the complicated and unstable balance of forces within the executive, legislative, and judicial framework of mercantile England. To be sure, Heckscher acknowledges the dual nature of the mercantile judiciary. Further, he displays the common law courts as the repository of the wisdom of the past, operating under the famous premise that they could not create law, only interpret it, and that the law "grows" through such applications of old principles. But throughout his analysis, Heckscher stresses that these courts were the primal element in the cause for free enterprise and against the cause of restraint of trade, the reason being that restraint of trade was not part of the conventional wisdom that guided the common law jurists. Given this assumed free-trade emphasis of the common law courts, how could monopolies be established? In Heckscher's view, the king tried to avoid the common law courts by establishing a royal court system centered in the Privy Council (the court of the Star Chamber), which gave the crown an administrative elasticity to enforce grants of national monopoly. In the competitive struggle between the crown and the Parliament for the right to supply legislation, the common law courts were allied to parliamentary interests against the absolutist tendencies of the crown, and in Heckscher's study the common law jurists thereby emerge as the heroes of the rise of free trade in England.

Thus, Heckscher recognizes a long-standing bond between Parliament and the courts, arguing that "the absolutist tendencies [of the crown] were just as unwelcome to the professional interests of these lawyers as they were repugnant to the upholders of the powers of parliament" (1934, 1:279). But he assigns the high marks for the emergence of liberalism to the common law jurists, and especially Coke, for supplying Commons with the intellectual weapons for combating royal prerogative. While acknowledging that professional envy and the reduced derived demand for legal services might have prejudiced jurists against industrial regulation, Heckscher argues that "the sincere belief in an established legal code" largely contributed to that effect. Holdsworth, one of Heckscher's principal sources on these issues, espouses a very similar view, to the effect that grants by the crown simply got out of hand, becoming objects of personal profit. Common law and Parliament were thus representing the public interest by taking patent control from the crown (Holdsworth 1966, 4:346–48). There are many other similarities between Heckscher's and Holdsworth's treatments of the entire mercantile period, possibly because the latter relies exclusively upon the historians' (Ashley and Cunningham) "state power-specie accumulation" interpretation of the era, a position not very far from Heckscher's own main theme (see Holdsworth 1966, 4:315–16, 324–27).

Our view of the judicial situation in England at this time is substantially different. The main point of our alternative interpretation is that the mercantilist judiciary, whether the common law courts or the king's courts, was seeking to enforce monopoly rights in output markets and to rescind them in labor markets. Thus, there was vigorous rivalry between the two court systems to enforce monopoly rights, the object of each enforcer being to share in the rents from sustaining monopolies. Uncertainty over the durability of a monopoly right must have become immense in the presence of such judicial competition. Such an environment in fact leads to the condition that no monopoly is universally legal: one court could find that you held a legal monopoly right and the other the reverse.

Before expanding this interpretation of judicial competition in the mercantilist era, let us take a closer look at Heckscher's contention that the common law jurists were the philosophical agents of free trade. In evaluating this argument, the first crucial point to note is that most of this free-trade emphasis was on labor markets. Thus:

> The most important application of the discouragement of restraint of trade in private agreements in England was the struggle against journeymen associations, and later against trade unions, when they went on strike or in any way collectively came into conflict with the employers. . . . In England, the measures of the courts and the legislation against this form of restraint of trade were still further intensified by the application of the peculiar legal conception of conspiracy. According to this, a form of action which was considered socially harmful became a penal offense if exercised by a number of people in association, even though otherwise it was not punishable. . . . In England the trade unions could be penalized by common law under the legal category of restraint of trade, even after the statutes directed against them had been repealed. (Heckscher 1934, 1:281–82)

With respect to output markets the common law courts do not get such high marks in promoting free trade. Essentially, the common law courts and their allies in Parliament competed with the monarchy and its court system in the promotion of national monopoly rights. Thus, the pattern of national monopolies that existed was bifurcated, with some receiving legal sanction from the common law courts and some from the king's courts. This part of our argument requires further clarification, but the following reference to Heckscher will prove useful:

> The courts therefore usually held fast to more *constitutional* criteria; that is, they decided according to the legal title which the monopoly could claim and not according to its existence or to its economic character. This gave the common-law jurists greater opportunity of attacking the special interests of their opponents and of preserving the interests of their own associates. There is, however, no doubt that a kind of legal system developed, even though built up on rather formal foundations, and therefore, from the economic point of view, particularly arbitrary. The result was as follows.
>
> Monopolies based on royal privileges were considered invalid. From this followed the further fact that such regulations, issued by municipal authorities and professional associations, if grounded only in royal charters, were likewise rejected as soon as it was believed that they stood opposed to industrial freedom. But this, on the other hand, was far from meaning that unqualified freedom was maintained. First, monopolies created by Act of Parliament were respected; but they played a relatively small part as being rather scarce. Much more important was the second group. All kinds of local rights based on immemorial custom were also respected, and this influenced trade and handicrafts all over the country. . . . The system of royal privileges could not be upheld before the courts. This coincided not only with the political tendency of the common-law courts, but also with their fundamental conservatism. They themselves thought that they were the bearers of age-old legal traditions in the face of the monarchy's revolutionary tendencies. The cry *nolumus leges Angliae—mutari*—we will not allow the laws of England to be changed—is characteristic of this attitude. (Heckscher 1934, 1:284)

Monopoly founded on custom or by Parliament was held to be legitimate under the common law, while monopoly founded by royal grant was not. Heckscher sees this pattern of legal choice as an expression of tradition and conservatism rather than as a convenient prop for legal choice in a competitive legal environment.[19] The matter of monopoly, as such, was not at issue, except in labor markets, and except insofar as members of Parliament were able to convince their electors of the necessity of a "popular" (parliamentary) control over monopoly.[20] The relevant issues concerned the legality of certain monopoly rights and who had the legal right to supply these rights, Parliament or the crown.

Sir Edward Coke and Free Trade: A Digression

The case of Sir Edward Coke (1552–1634) is a telling example of the so-called "duplicity" with which common law jurists approached free trade. Coke, famed as one of the great defenders of personal and economic individualism, has long been regarded as a key figure in the emergence of free markets in England. Coke has a long career as attorney general of England (1594–1606), chief justice of the Court of Common Pleas (1606–1613), chief justice of the Court of King's Bench (1613–1616), and from 1620 leader of the parliamentary opposition to the crown in the House of Commons. That Coke was in fact a champion of legal and civil liberties for the individual is indisputable. But in the economic realm, Coke's is an extremely interesting case in that it pits the concept of "philosophical" or "ideological" motivations (so often ascribed to him by historians and others) against individual and group motivations that can, with evidence, be described as applying to behavior.

There is indeed weighty evidence against Coke's "public interest" motivations regarding the establishment of free trade. Coke may in fact be described as one of the biggest supporters of rent-generating entry barriers in the British legal profession. The judicial competition described above that motivated the shift of the power to grant monopolies to individuals from the crown to Parliament was well under way by Coke's time, and Coke consistently worked to expand the jurisdiction of the common law and the privileges of barristers. Simultaneously, of course, he restricted the jurisdiction of other courts and impeded the activities of nonbarrister lawyers. One of his principal interests throughout his writings concerned strengthening jurisdictional boundaries between courts, supposed because absence of such clear boundaries led to "excessive" and more costly lawsuits—although without explaining how this counterintuitive result could come to pass (White 1979, 50). He led the fight to limit the fees charged by lawyers in the Chancery court, which would have restricted the ability of that jurisdiction from competing with the common law (White 1979, 61–62). He fought to restrict the Chancery jurisdiction directly as well as other non-common law courts; these efforts were ultimately unsuccessful. Coke also worked to limit entry into the Inns of Court, that is, to the number of applicants accepted and the conditions for being admitted to the bar (Malament 1967, 1324).[21] He moved to reign in the jurisdictional competition of both the Admiralty and the Ecclesiastical courts in matters of commerce (asserted by Admiralty) and in lucrative testamentary cases (asserted by the Ecclesiastical courts) (Levack 1973, 79; Holdsworth 1966, 1:629).

The common law courts, as we have already emphasized, consistently fought for the privilege to allocate monopoly rents to be granted to the common law courts. Further, the common lawyers achieved a successful alliance with Parliament, and together those two groups sought and obtained a legal monopoly in the granting of monopoly privileges. The point to be made is that Coke was clearly a leader in these efforts in contrast to economic historians who have described Coke as having played a leading role in the fight against monopoly grants in the early seventeenth century.[22]

Eli Heckscher and other economic historians have tended to emphasize royal grants of monopoly as the prime examples of domestic restrictions on competition. But many important sources of restrictions rent were parliamentary in nature. For example, regulated and chartered companies gradually came under parliamentary control, although most had originally secured royal sanction (Holdsworth 1966, 4:320). Most important, economic regulation was statutory in nature and enacted by Parliament. For example, the following parliamentary acts were in force during the early seventeenth century (as discussed in Elton 1986, 231–50): domestic trade in grain was licensed; the prices of beer barrels were fixed; the number of taverns in towns was strictly limited, and their prices were fixed; the highly detailed Clothmaking Act of 1552 fixed standards of quality and specified regulations for the cloth industry; and a 1581 law prohibited iron-making within twenty-two miles of London.[23] Although some historians (Holdsworth 1966, 4:335) imply that such parliamentary regulation was aimed at promoting the "public interest," supposedly unlike the purely venal royal grants of monopoly, rent seeking by particular interest groups who expected to benefit from the passage of many such regulations was quite blatant and overt.

Neither Coke nor any of his fellow barristers opposed government economic regulations of the competitive process in principle. In fact, the common law courts consistently supported parliamentary regulation of all sorts.

On several occasions, the courts even extended the coverage of parliamentary regulations. Although Coke often railed against monopolies, he specifically approved of statutory, that is, legislative, restraints on trade (White 1979, 123).[24] According to Coke "liberty of trade" could lawfully be restricted by "common consent," that is, all parliamentary regulations, no matter how anticompetitive, were by definition lawful (White 1979, 122). Coke was also a strong proponent of the full panoply of mercantilist restrictions on foreign trade; by Tudor times, the bulk of such restrictions were statutory in origin (White 1979, 138).

Barristers and common law judges supported governmental restrictions on free competition in their own economic interests. "Lawyer welfare" was created through a successful alliance with Parliament in the form of supporting regulations that created work for barristers. Royal grants of monopoly to specific firms were not a primary source of demand, for example, for the Justices of the Peace whose jobs depended on the proliferation of statutory restrictions on market exchange. Most of the enforcement and adjudicatory officials were either barristers or members of one of the Inns of Court. The same went for the regulations creating and maintaining municipal corporations (Prest 1986, 238, 242). Barrister-M.P.s, estimated at between one-quarter and one-fifth of Parliament in Coke's time, also tended to dominate the design and drafting of legislation by virtue of their legal expertise. Barristers also had direct financial interests in regulated companies.

Two key events stand out in evaluating the effect of the common law courts in general, and Coke in particular, on the deregulation of trade in the early seventeenth century: the first being the *Darcy v. Allen* case (1603) and the second the Statute of Monopolies (1624, 21 James I, C. 3). The basic outline of *Darcy* (the "Case of Monopolies") is familiar. Darcy held a royal monopoly grant to the importation of playing cards. Allen imported the cards without asking Darcy for permission. Darcy sued Allen, and the court ruled that the monopoly grant was invalid (Donald 1961, 208–49; Pound and Plucknett 1927, 184–85). Since Coke wrote about this ruling, and placed great emphasis on its fundamental importance, some writers leave the impression that Coke was somehow partially responsible for this supposed challenge to monopoly grants.[25] But in fact, Coke was the attorney general at the time and was obliged to *defend* the contested patent in court, which he did. Moreover, the ruling itself simply did not claim all monopoly grants to be invalid. It only stated that trade must be left free except for "definite restrictions known to and recognized by common law" (Holdsworth 1966,

4:350). The common law recognized a bewildering array of restrictions on free trade, which shared no common thread in any economic sense. According to Barbara Malament (1967, 1354), Coke "again and again . . . distinguished between trade regulation and trade restriction" and provides numerous examples for this entirely arbitrary distinction-without-a-difference.[26]

This most peculiar feature of the seventeenth-century monopoly debate has been generally ignored: the common law jurists were adamantly opposed to royal grants of monopoly *dispensation* to parliamentary regulations. Many royal "patents of monopoly" were just grants of exemption to specific individuals from legislated restrictions on markets. The existence of such loopholes reduced the value of trade barriers produced by Parliament from the standpoint of their rent-seeking beneficiaries. However, most such dispensations surely enhanced economic efficiency and made a greater variety of goods available to consumers at lower prices. Nevertheless, in the case of the Penal Statutes (1605), the judges declared that such royal dispensations were the "scandal of justice and the offence of many" (Holdsworth 1966, 4:359). Although the issuance of such royal dispensations did not end until after the enactment of the Statute of Monopolies, their use declined following the 1605 ruling.

Coke has a more valid claim to another key event in seventeenth-century monopoly policy. In 1624, Parliament enacted the Statute of Monopolies, a sweeping reform bill that severely restricted the ability of the crown to issue monopoly grants to favored individuals. Coke was the leader of crown opposition and "the statute did very nearly embody Coke's views at the most radical stage of his career" (Malament 1967, 1351). His involvement with this legislation constitutes his primary claim to actual economic reforms.

While the statute did not eliminate monopolies, it did materially alter the political production of future legal entry barriers. Section 1 of the statute appeared to void all institutions granting exclusive control of any product. But some industries were allowed to continue as monopolies, including saltpeter, gunpowder, and other products "deemed essential to the realm." New production processes, old production processes new to England, companies with exclusive trading privileges, and city corporations were permitted to retain restrictions on competition within their boundaries.[27] Holdsworth (1966, 4:355) notes that the privileges of chartered companies, craft guilds, and boroughs "were recognized by the common law, and saved by the Act of 1624."[28]

Most critically, parliamentary regulations were automatically exempt in the statute regardless of the effect they might have on market competition. This most important feature of the statute had as its primary purpose the reallocation of regulatory authority from the monarch to Parliament. It *only* restricted the ability of the king to grant monopolies to favored individuals.[29]

Coke was personally in the thick of the operations of a number of important recipients of monopoly grants who benefited from the Statute of Monopolies, as he wrote it. He was intimately involved in the resolution of disputes between chartered companies and alleged interlopers while a member of the Privy Council after 1613, and was frequently retained by that body in earlier years for advice. After joining the Privy Council, Coke became involved in numerous disputes involving the exclusive privileges granted to companies and corporations. For a time, he was an enthusiastic supporter of the Project of Alderman Cockayne to obtain the monopoly right to import linen. He supported both the salt and the coal monopolies, and Coke's decisions in disputes over monopoly rights consistently tended to favor the monopolists.[30] Apparent exceptions even inspire suspicion, such as his opposition to the privileges of the Merchant Adventurers during the time he supported Cockayne, one of their principal rivals.

Coke, therefore, only consistently opposed royal grants of monopoly privileges to specific individuals. With equal consistency, he defended economic regulations enacted by Parliament, most of which generated entry barriers into markets that benefited specific interest groups, not individual persons. Coke's selective attacks on certain kinds of monopoly grants occurred as part of his consistent efforts to secure more valuable and better enforced monopoly privileges for himself and his fellow barristers. The purported enemy of legal monopoly grants worked diligently to defend and expand the legal monopoly jurisdiction of the common law, of which he was a lifetime practitioner. While the net impact of his diligent activities in fighting off jurisdictions other than the common law was to reduce the welfare of litigants, his defense of "monopoly in Parliament" ultimately created higher costs to obtaining, developing, and enforcing regulations. What often passes for (unexplained) "ideology" is sometimes partly or mainly (easily explainable) self-interest in disguise. Coke was no more and no less "duplicitous" than Adam Smith, whose free-trade principles did not enjoin a regulatory sinecure at the "custom's house" (Anderson, Shughart, and Tollison 1985).[31]

THE RENT-SEEKING PROCESS
IN ENGLAND: SOME EXAMPLES

The judiciary plays a special role in the modern interest-group theory of government. Landes and Posner (1975) envisage the independent judiciary as a means of enforcing long-term contracts between legislators and special interests.[32] Their basic point, which is highly relevant to mercantile England, is that monopoly rights must be durable to be worth anything to special interests. As we have seen, conditions prevailing in the English courts at this time led to great uncertainty over the enforceability of monopoly privileges. The existence of a two-court system, together with the cluster of interests surrounding them, was the underpinning of a very unstable cost-benefit configuration to would-be rent seekers. Grants of monopoly had a very predictable fate in this rent-seeking environment, and, as examples, we may consider medieval and Elizabethan examples of attempted monopolization, most of which failed to provide any rents to the crown.

The jurisdictional (court) competition was heightened for centuries before the execution of Charles I in 1649 by conflicts between Parliament and the crown. The conduct of the wool trade in fourteenth-century England provides a very clear example of this process, which, during the reign of the three Edwards, precipitated an earlier constitutional crisis presaging those of the seventeenth century. The first crisis was over the taxation of wool.

The Medieval Wool Trade

The wool trade of medieval England was characterized by a large number of competitively organized wool producers and by a smaller number of large-scale producers (largely monasteries), with an even smaller number of wool exporters. An export monopoly was fostered by the combined rent-seeking interests of large merchants and exporters in bilateral negotiation with the king. The mechanism through which these activities took place was an assembly of merchants called by the king as early as the late thirteenth century for the purpose of advice and consent on the matter of export and other taxation, especially on wool. This body, which rivaled the Parliament itself in functions, was willing to consent to taxation since monopoly and other privileges could be exacted from the crown. In short, merchants were willing to accept the costs of taxation and regulation so long as the benefits conferred by regulation exceeded them. In the words of Eileen Power:

What these interests were is as clear today as it was to men of the middle ages. There were first of all the merchants. All taxes on foreign trade were negotiated with them up to 1340, but they were affected by those taxes quite differently from the rest of the community. As long as the tax was not higher than "the traffic would bear," the merchants were of all classes least likely to suffer. They might even benefit from the tax if they could get a quid pro quo for granting it, such as the removal of an embargo, or the fixing of the staple somewhere where they wanted it to be, or the grant of a monopoly of export. (1941, 71).

The ability of merchants to shift the incidence of the wool tax both backward to wool growers, large and small, and forward to foreign consumers (depending, of course, upon elasticity of demand), forced a polarization of parliamentary interests, which came to recognize the deleterious effects of lower wool prices. This interest group was composed of lay and ecclesiastical magnates (the large wool producers) and the knights of the shire, who represented more than a million small freeholders in Commons. Parliament's fight for the abolition of the tax was thus premised upon their objection to the income (rent) reduction from the successful supply and demand for regulation on the part of the king (Edward I) and the wool merchants. Significant constitutional crises that occurred in the 1290s and 1330s resulted principally from a realignment and eventual commonality of interests between Parliament and the merchants. The costs of monarchical regulation (taxes) exceeded the benefits (entry-restricted monopoly) only so long as the king did not impose new taxes on the wool merchants. When he did in fact impose one, because of war and other pressures on the English fisc, wool merchants clearly recognized that the bilateral form of rent seeking was one-sided and unprofitable. Merchant voices thus joined those of Parliament calling for abolition of the tax.

The alienation of merchants was furthered when the king shifted his favor to a group of "rogue financiers" less than thirty in number, who advanced money to the crown on wool granted to him. Power (1941, 83) notes that the "king was . . . compelled to impose an embargo on general export for a time (sometimes a whole year) in order to enable his financiers to dispose of the wool on his behalf. And every time this happened a virtual monopoly of a financial group was established." The result was the dissolution of the larger group of merchant exporters, with those "shut out" becoming disposed (in their self interest) to urge Parliament to impose constraints on the king.

Though Parliament was unsuccessful in obtaining abolition of the periodically imposed ("extraordinary") wool tax ("maltote"), the increased demand of the sovereign for funds at the outbreak of the Hundred Years War (1337) was met by a tax, but with domestic price controls on wool as quid pro quo. At this point the wool merchants were still sanguine about the export monopoly franchise since the prospect of passing the tax forward still existed (Power 1941, 81). In 1350 Parliament finally gave up on the issue of abolishing the tax but got control over it and converted it into a parliamentary subsidy for specified time periods. A quasi-monopoly of the wool trade (the English Company of the Staple) remained, and, as Power reported, "it is by virtue of this monopoly alone that they were able to shoulder the subsidy" (85), the latter contingent on the will and consent of Parliament.[33]

The pattern and effects of mercantile monarchy, as developed in our theory of rent seeking, may be clearly discerned in the early history of the medieval wool trade. Again and again in the mercantile period—and most significantly in the sixteenth and seventeenth centuries—Parliament was strengthened to limit and oppose the ability of the crown to supply regulation. In England the rent-seeking proclivities of the crown were strengthened by a legislative constraint on its possible revenue. Extraordinary expenditures, which arose with ever-increasing frequency in order to conduct wars, meant that English monarchs were always in need of funds. (The French and Spanish monarchs were often similarly situated, but they did not face the same constraints, as we shall see in chapters 4 and 5.) The crown's reaction to this situation was initially to offer special favors, monopoly-entry control, to growing national industries (large exporters were often fewer in number, were organized with lower transactions costs, and were more easily controlled), who, in return, submitted to taxation.

Reactions to this state of affairs were twofold and eventually brought about the decline of monarchical rent seeking and an increase in costs to legislative supply of regulation. First, Parliament, which represented "society's" and, ultimately, merchants' interests, grew restive at the monarchical rent-seeking franchises. As the mercantile period wore on, this restiveness became more pronounced. Second, and more important perhaps, the absolutist aspects of the English monarchy were more and more eroded with the aid and action of the merchant classes themselves. A high degree of uncertainty crept in as merchants grew wary of the net benefits of a regulatory alliance with the king. Specifically, this uncertainty of benefits drove merchants to support the interests of Parliament, which reduced

the powers of the monarch in economic as well as legal and religious matters. In this manner it may be said that the caprice of monarchical power,
which led to uncertainty among merchants, landowners, and freeholders,
resulted in the emergent constitutional solution of the late sixteenth and
seventeenth centuries.

Later Examples of Rent Seeking

We must now amplify and further illustrate the pattern of rent seeking
discerned in the medieval wool trade and described by our theory. Here we
focus upon a "high period of mercantile monarchy," followed by its fall in
1640 or so. Roughly, our treatment extends from the reign of Elizabeth I,
the last Tudor monarch, through those of James I and Charles I, the first
two Stuarts.

The constraints on regulatory supply and demand between the death
of Henry VIII (1547) and the execution of Charles I (1649) were in kind
very much like those described for the earlier period. The monarch was still
dependent upon the consent of the taxed in order to obtain revenue. He
still depended, in other words, upon the good will and self-interest of the
wealthy gentry and landowners in order to function, especially when he
had to meet "extraordinary" expenses. Over this period, the three major
checks upon the crown's power and rent-seeking activities were (a) private
local interests composed of increasingly wealthy city merchants and magistrates, (b) common law courts, and (c) the House of Commons. The latter
two institutions were increasingly representative of and peopled by the
wealthy merchants from whom the king wished to extract rents.[34]

The actual means of rent seeking and the king's ability to enforce it
were likewise in transition, being eroded by self-interested forces and constitutional law. As indicated earlier in this chapter, the crown had to depend upon three means of imposing industrial regulation: (1) enactment of
regulation by statutes of Parliament, (2) royal proclamations and letters
patent, and (3) orders of privy council or decrees instituted by privy council
sitting in Star Chamber (the king's court). Developments of the period
1547–1640 may be characterized as leading to the practical supremacy of
Parliament in the imposition of regulation. The concept of the "crown in
council" as ultimate authority—the great Tudor contribution to administrative government—was also swept away by the events of these years,
though the conciliar form of executive administration survives and indeed
is enshrined in the forms of most contemporary representative govern-

ments (see Elton 1966). During this period, self-interested forces success-fully opposed every attempt of the crown to impose and enforce industrial regulation. We now turn to a few examples of these forces.

Elizabethan Rent Seeking

The reign of Elizabeth I (1558–1603) is regarded by many as the high time of successful mercantile policy. Historical facts do not appear to justify this view, however. To echo a modern directive, regulation should not be judged on the basis of its aim or intent, but on grounds of its effects (Stigler and Friedland 1962). The fact is that Elizabeth opened her reign with a great deal of patent granting and lusty rent seeking from industry but closed it meekly admitting that patent monopoly was a dangerous innovation con-trary to common law. Consider the following examples.

The queen claimed regalian rights to the manufacture of saltpeter and gunpowder (on grounds of national defense) and granted a monopoly to George and John Evlyn. The Evlyn family enjoyed lucrative benefits from the rent splitting for almost fifty years (until 1635).[35] But steady counter-action ensued on the part of merchants and the courts, dating from the initial award, which finally brought the monopoly restrictions down. Sub-sequently, the manufacture of both saltpeter and gunpowder became the object of open competition.

Examples of the attempts to monopolize other industries over the pe-riod and the failures of the state may be multiplied. The rights to royalties from the monopolization of ores other than gold and silver were shorn from the crown in a court decision of 1566, which limited regalian rights to gold and silver only (none in England). Self-interested officials charged with dealing with mining leases on royal lands were not above the lure of pecuniary aggrandizement. Thus, Nef notes: "Even in royal manors and forests, where the king or queen like any other landlord owned the miner-als and appointed special officials to deal with their mining lessees, these officials, like the justices of the peace and the sheriffs, were always local men who were frequently more mindful of the wishes of their rich neigh-bors with investments in the mines than of the interests of their royal mas-ters" (1968, 101).

Attempts by Elizabeth to duplicate the French king's successful and lucrative salt tax (the *gabelle*) were also doomed to failure. In 1564 she tried to establish a patent monopoly in salt, but the patentees gave up within five years, leaving huge salt pans rusting on the English coast. To rub salt in these wounds, private capitalists, sans grant, entered the industry and profitably produced and marketed salt over the next three decades in spite of repeated attempts by the crown to reestablish monopoly rights. A further example of the futile attempt of Elizabeth's councillors to grant monopolies to court favorites was the paper monopoly, originally granted to John Spilman in 1588. Spilman claimed to have a new process for producing white paper. In practice, patents issued to protect a new process or invention were ordinarily unopposed by Commons and the courts and were often extended to enable patentees to "engulf" closely related products. Such was the case with Spilman, who in 1597 was granted a monopoly over all kinds of paper. The monopoly privileges were not enforceable, however, and within six years Spilman had to rest content with "such a share of the expanding market for paper as the efficiency of his machinery, the skill of his workmen, and the situation of his mills enabled him to command" (Nef 1968, 106). Elizabeth's luckless adventures into monopoly-creating, rent-seeking activities ended in 1603 (the year of her death), when she personally declared with respect to a proposed monopoly on playing cards that such patents were contrary to common law.

Post-Elizabethan Rent Seeking

What was voiced opposition to crown attempts to monopolize during Elizabeth's era became shouts of protest, culminating in civil war, during the next forty years. As a general rule it may be said that after 1603—in spite of even more vigorous attempts by James I and Charles I to establish monopolies—no acts establishing national monopolies were enforceable if they interfered with the profits of merchants and the interests of those represented by Commons and the courts. Here we find the de facto end of monarchical mercantilism, when, in the context of expanding industries, the net benefit from no regulation outweighed the net benefit from crown protection. The demand for regulation may be said to have been reduced by rising franchise costs (taxes), together with the vicissitudes and uncertainties of crown supply of regulation. Potential competition for investment outlets and political pressures upon Commons by affected merchants must have greatly increased the uncertainty of gains from monarchially created monopoly.

Both James I and Charles I tried to revive Elizabeth's early policy of patent grants as sources of revenue, but both met with very limited success (principally in the cases of alum and soap manufacture). Meanwhile, Commons marshaled all of its strength to fight the king's prerogative to seek rents via monopolization. After a long struggle with James over the issue, Commons revived impeachment as a means of punishing monopolists in their midst and as a means of reminding the king of their total intolerance for his claimed prerogative to seek rents in this manner. Thus, in 1621, Commons (using impeachment for the first time in almost two hundred years) denounced Sir Giles Mompesson and Sir Francis Mitchell for "fraud and oppression committed as patentees for the exclusive manufacture of gold and silver thread, for the inspection of inns and hostelries, and for the licensing of ale houses" (Taylor 1898, 246). The House of Lords rendered the judgment and imposed fines and imprisonment on both men. Commons' objection to the crown's supposed right to supply regulation reached its zenith in 1624, when the famous act concerning monopolies legally stripped the king of all prerogative in patents and other means to monopolize industry.[36]

In 1625 Charles I came to the throne and promptly set about attempting to restore the principle of divine right of kings, which, of course, included a reassertion of right to grant monopoly via letters patent or by order of privy council. In doing so, Charles was led to a toe-to-toe confrontation with constitutionalists, a battle he ultimately lost, along with his head, in 1649. Together with his persuasive and powerful minister Francis Bacon, who supported the royal prerogative to supply regulation, Charles found a loophole in the 1624 statute: it did not apply to "corporations for benefit of trade" or to "companies of merchants."

Thus, after the repeated refusal of Parliament to fund the king's military adventures and the king's dissolution of Parliament in 1629, Charles tried to make deals with large producers in many industries. Alum and soap monopolies had been exempted from the 1624 act, but the king encouraged the formation of huge corporations in coal, salt, brickmaking, and others, to which monopoly protection was given (for fourteen years) in return for rents to the crown. Between 1629 and 1640 the alum patent brought in £126,000, with an additional revenue from soap (between 1630 and 1640) of £122,000, but the new rent seeking of Charles was doomed to failure (Nef 1968, 115). The circumstances of this failure should be, by now, very familiar. First, the king's monopoly protection and taxing arrangements were too costly for the merchants to continue to acquiesce to them. A competitive system in this period yielded them higher rents than could be obtained through legalized entry control, price fixing, and taxation. Thus, cartel arrangements broke down as participants blithely evaded price fixing when profitable. Second, as usual, these attempted new monopolies aroused the hostile and vociferous opposition of those merchants left out. The nonmerchant voices also joined these forces as they (correctly) perceived monopoly to be inimical to their interests (recall the wool-trade example).

Thus it was that the cartel breakdown and the more fundamental problems of enforcement brought on by the stringent objections of consumers and merchants left out combined to render the patents of Charles I ineffective three years after they were issued. Antimonopoly interests opposed to the king—reflected in self-interested inaction or adverse decisions by justices of the peace and by Commons—combined with those harboring legal and religious objections to the king's blatant and audacious assertion of supreme rights and signaled an end to his authority. In a crucial reassertion of rights, Parliament blocked, once and for all, the despotism of monarchy and established fundamental constitutional rights and the power of Parliament. Among these was the passage in 1640 of a statute putting an end to all but one of the exceptions in the statute of 1624.[37] Monarchical mercantilism was repulsed by wresting the ability of the king to supply regulation away from him. More important for understanding the course of constitutional history and regulation, the monarch lost his ability in large part because actual and potential demanders found the effects of these regulations of very uncertain and, most often, negative benefit, given the salubrious state of the competitive system in the English economy of the time. Franchises issued by the king were not durable.

Within our analytical framework these examples demonstrate that the returns from seeking national monopoly through the state fell drastically as the conflict between Parliament and the crown intensified in the sixteenth and early seventeenth centuries. This is not to argue by any means that the conflict was motivated primarily by monopoly policy, but rather that a conflict fueled by political and religious differences had important by-products in the rent seeking economy of England at the time.[38] We do not assert, moreover, that the public interest, whatever this may have been in these times, played no role in the classic decisions by which the common law courts transferred monopoly-granting powers to Parliament. But the institutional realities of the centuries-old alliance between the common law courts and Parliament, together with parliamentary control over jurisdictional disputes between the two court systems, all point to the likely existence of a self-interested economic entente between common law judges and Parliament. Heckscher merely hints at these forces and offers no analysis of their effects upon the fate of national regulation. We think that they carry much importance in any balanced interpretation of the period. The remaining issue concerns the question of why Parliament was unable to operate an effective special-interest economy, that is, to effect a powerful reinstitution of mercantilist policies, after it became the sole supplier of regulatory legislation.

THE RISE OF PARLIAMENT AND THE FALL OF MERCANTILISM

The focal point of the conflict between the crown and Parliament in the struggle to supply monopoly rights was in the area of patents. Parliament's interest lay in trying to set limits on the unlimited power of the crown to grant monopoly privileges. As we stressed in the last section, Heckscher, like most historians, tends to see the Parliament and its common-law-court allies jousting with the king over the matter of free trade. Thus:

> In the latter part of Elizabeth's reign a storm broke out against her unlimited grants of patents of monopoly as rewards to her favourites and servants. The old queen, however, understood how to quiet the minds of the people with such skill that parliament refrained from making any decision on the question. The queen referred the legality of the patents of monopoly to the decisions of the ordinary courts. The patent of her courtier, Darcy, for the production and import of playing-cards gave rise to the famous Case of Monopolies (*Darcy v. Allen* or *Allin* [or *Allein*] 1602/3). Without any qualification and without any attempt at prevarication, the decision declared the patent invalid. When James I again began to follow in Elizabeth's footsteps and grant patents, parliament once again returned to the attack. Its last and most remarkable piece of work was the Statute of Monopolies (1623/4). This memorable law introduced no essential innovations. It limited the crown's right to granting exclusive patents to investors of a trade which was new to the country. For future patents the validity of the patent thus granted was not to exceed fourteen years. The final break came when Charles I once again began granting patents, and the outcome was that the regulations laid down by the Statute of Monopolies were confirmed. (Heckscher 1934, 1:290)

Our interpretation of this struggle, which we feel is far more consistent with the economic environment of these times, is that both parties in the struggle sought to become the sole supplier of regulatory legislation. We have already detailed how common law interpretations supported Par-

liament's right to grant patents as opposed to that of the crown. But there
is a good deal of evidence demonstrating a direct confrontation between
members of Parliament and the crown on this matter. The debate over
monopolies was a debate not over free trade versus crown grants of patents
but rather over who would have the power to supply regulations. This facet
of rent seeking was somewhat apparent in a *Petition of the Commons to the
King, Complaining of divers Grievances,* presented to James I by the House
of Commons before the closing of Parliament in 1624. Within the petition
Commons claimed damage to public welfare from patents granted to apoth-
ecaries, fishermen, gold wire makers, gaolkeepers, and so forth, and re-
quested the right to grant regulation of these matters to Parliament. Of
particular interest was the patent for the Wintertonness Lights. Parliament
had originally issued a patent to erect and maintain the lighthouse to the
master of Trinity House, who was to charge "6d. for every 20 chaldron of
coals of ships passing that way." But meanwhile, one Sir John Meldrum
had petitioned James for a patent to the lighthouse and had received it.
The petition continues, arguing that

> though it were true, as sir John pretended, that he had petitioned to you
> maj. for erection of a light-house, before the said light-house of stone was
> erected, yet the said letters patent are void in law, for that they of the Trin-
> ity-House, having authority as is aforesaid by act of parl. did, before the
> said letters patent, erect a lighthouse as is aforesaid; where they of the Trin-
> ity did take but 6d. for every 20 chaldron of coals, the said sir John by
> colour of the said letters patent; for every 20 chaldron of coals, hath taken
> 3s4d. and will not suffer the ships to make their entries, or take cocquets,
> before they pay the said excessive duty of 3s4d. to the intolerable damage
> and loss of your subjects, he hath taken after the rate of 3s4d. of divers
> seafaring men, that sail not that way, nor in their course could take any
> benefit of the said light-house. Our humble Petition is, That your maj. will
> be pleased to publish the said letters patent to be void in law, and to com-
> mand that they be no more put in execution. (Corbbett 1966, 1492)

Though members of Parliament often cited public interest or public welfare as their rationale for wresting the patent-granting power from the crown,
it is much more plausible and consistent with economic incentives that
their intentions were simply to acquire the right to supply regulation themselves.

Parliament wrested these rights from the crown in numerous ways. One was, of course, to provide subsidies to the king only for a quid pro quo (which in some cases was a relinquishment of monopoly rights to the Parliament). Another was through the embarrassing exposé of blatant monarchical rent seeking. The latter occurred with increasing frequency during the reign of James I. In 1621 James's attorney general, Sir Henry Yelvington, was charged with and convicted of pocketing rents for himself and illegally attempting to restrain trade in the name of the king. Yelvington was receiving rents from a member of Parliament, Sir Giles Mompesson (who was impeached by Commons for illegal rent seeking with the crown's agent Yelvington), to enforce selectively legal complaints against hostelries licensees; of three thousand complaints Yelvington brought two to trial. A more serious matter occurred in 1623–1624, when Lionel, the earl of Middlesex—the lord treasurer of England—was impeached by Parliament (the House of Lords) for (among other abuses) revoking existing leases on the sugar trade and issuing them to two of his own servants in exchange for bribes and under-the-table payments. James, who (to no avail) defended Middlesex, was clearly acting under the correct assumption that parliamentary impeachments pertaining to these matters would shake the royal authority to supply rent-seeking privileges, placing that power instead in the hands of Parliament (Corbbett 1966, 1:1422, 1445–47, 1477–78).

Heckscher offers two interpretations of these developments. He first argues that "in actual fact there is nothing which would make it probable that there was any interest on the part of the administration to systematize the industrial code in one direction or another. Nothing is more significant regarding English development after 1688 than the absence of any sign of such activity in the central government" (1934, 1:295). In this view parliamentary interests were merely dormant after seizing legislative power from the crown. Yet Heckscher develops a second interpretation, which is consistent with our argument about the predispositions of the parliamentary agents and the difficulties they faced in rehabilitating the use of regulatory legislation for revenue.

> When authority was definitely transferred to parliament, this in itself meant
> no essential change in the political basis of industrial regulation. But it was
> a change in a negative direction, for it shut the door to administrative free-
> dom of action. This result of parliamentary government may seem unlikely,
> since there is in England to-day what the present Lord Chief Justice, Lord

Hewart, had called the "New Despotism," that is, the uncontrolled power
of the bureaucracy over statutes, which has shown itself to be perfectly
capable of an agreement with the constitutional preeminence of parliament.
But there was no question of delegating the legislative authority of parliament, on which the present-day position of the English central authority is
based, at a time when it had just won for itself its dominant position. Therefore the conditions for an all-embracing administrative power were not
present in England in the period between the Restoration and the Parliamentary Reform of 1832. And a system of interference in all spheres of social
life presupposes such a power. (1934, 1:295–96)

Parliament won the competition to be the sole supplier of legislation
but was unable to consolidate this power in a systematic way so as to be
able to continue to garner significant revenues from grants of monopoly.
Its inability to consolidate the power to pass and enforce special-interest
legislation resides primarily in the higher costs of democratic relative to
monarchial decision making in this respect. For example, as Heckscher
emphasizes in the above quotation, there was no administrative bureaucracy in England at this time to which the task of administering economic
regulation (cartel enforcement) could be delegated. Without the ability to
delegate authority in this way, we know that costs of decision making in the
legislature will tend to swamp the ability of legislators to monitor and control any regulatory measures they might pass (Ehrlich and Posner 1974;
McCormick and Tollison 1980). Much of the evidence that Heckscher cites
(1934, 1:294–325) on parliamentary attempts (failures) to seek profits through
legislation ("Parliamentary Colbertism") may be interpreted in this light.

Parliamentary interests struggled long and hard with the crown for the
right to operate the national system of economic regulation in England. In
the end, however, when Parliament had obtained this power, it found a
situation in which the costs of sustaining the bulk of the system were much
larger than the (pro rata) benefits. Mercantilism thus ultimately foundered,
and a significant deregulation of the internal English economy ensued. In
assessing the extent of this deregulation, it should be kept in mind that
Parliament was controlled by the landed class and that legislation favorable
to that class was characteristic of the period. It is also of importance to note
(as we do in the following section) that Parliament was in the thick, particularly after the civil war and Restoration, of laws respecting trade barriers and colonial policies to maximize the revenues of particular interest

groups. We thus characterize the deregulation of the English economy at this time as significant rather than massive. The great debate over the Corn Laws and their ultimate repeal in 1848 still lay some distance in the future.

Heckscher acknowledges this significant deregulation of the English internal economy in the post-Elizabethan period, especially after the dominance of Parliament and the common law courts was established in the post-Restoration period, after 1688 (Heckscher 1934, 1:294–97). Heckscher, however, characterizes it as an arbitrary and accidental dissolution of the old order (1:301) and attributes the decline in internal regulation solely to the inability of Parliament to delegate its authority (adherence to Locke's rule of *delegata protestas non potest delagari*). He entirely misses the point that the imposition of the *delegata* rule on Parliament simply increased the cost of supplying regulation. Policing, moreover, was very costly in this context, and it is significant that very few internal regulations actually granted in the post-Elizabethan period (such as those in the cloth industry) had to be administered by the industries themselves and enforced by the justices of the peace (Heckscher 1934, 1:296–97). Further, though Heckscher notes that legislative emphasis shifted largely (in the post-Elizabethan period) to trade restrictions and agrarian protection, he is at pains to explain the shift, changes that a public choice-regulatory perspective explain very well.

Naturally, these events had cataclysmic impact upon property rights, transactions costs, market exchange, and, ultimately, economic growth in the English economy. In particular, as North and Weingast emphasize (1989), the *stability* of property rights, especially given an independent judiciary and the "predictability of governmental decisions" (829), had enormous implications for long-term investments and capital accumulation. Focusing on the "triumph of parliamentary interests in the Glorious Revolution," North and Weingast argue, as we did (1981) for the immediately preceding period, that the struggle for control of the political, taxation, and regulatory apparatus created constraints on the monarch's rent-extracting abilities. They argue, further and with good evidence, that the stability created in financial markets by these institutional changes permitted a "financial revolution" enabling a growth in debt that was a necessary condition for England's successes in wars with France (including the one between 1703 and 1714).[39] Institutional change, particularly those relating to political power over tax and rent transfers, was absolutely prerequisite to these developments. The changes that culminated in the Glorious Revolution were afoot, as we have argued, more than a century before. The result was of course that England was poised to overtake France as the "growth-oriented economy" and primary site of the Industrial Revolution in Europe in the eighteenth and nineteenth centuries.[40]

CUSTOMS, COLONIZATION AND "DUALIST" INTERPRETATIONS OF MERCANTILISM

A number of writers have identified a dualism in mercantile writers' approach to domestic controls on the one hand and to protectionist and "state-building" mercantile policies on the other. Some of the apparent contradictions may be resolved by considering the mercantile period as one whose policies were guided by rent-seeking activities. These activities did not, of course, necessarily produce profits for interests involved. But in concluding the present chapter we look briefly at the issue of tariffs and quotas in the protection or encouragement of international competition and at the important policy of colonization in order to find unity in rent-seeking interpretations of mercantilism and mercantile policies.

Clearly, the nexus of power to levy customs duties ("tonnage and poundage") shifted often from the medieval period through the seventeenth century. Indeed, one of the major factors leading to the constitutional revolt in the reign of Charles I was exactly the matter of prerogative in the matter of customs duties. Charles claimed an "ancient right" to customs, but Parliament ultimately seized, in 1641, the exclusive power to set these duties. (Parliament later gave William and Mary customs and port duty for limited terms of four years, partially as a ploy to guarantee frequent parliaments [Taylor 1898, 419].) While Parliament was dissolved, however, an event took place that reveals that vested rent-seeking interests were operative in the matter of trade policy. In the interim over which Charles claimed absolute authority to levy taxes, merchant importers refused (in their own interests) to pay customs to the king, obeying a remonstrance of Parliament to refuse to pay duties not authorized by Parliament. The king ordered the seizure of goods, whereupon several merchants resisted and were brought before the privy council. One of them, Richard Chambers, declared that "merchants are in no part of the world so screwed as in England. In Turkey they have more encouragement" (Taylor 1898, 274). Imprisonment was the cost Chambers incurred for his flippancy.

This incident, small in itself, reveals that, while motives of unification and state power building may be pressed to explain macroeconomic protectionist trade policies, self-interested rent seeking was never far from the surface in shaping those policies that we regard as typically mercantile in nature. That is to say, there is a commonality about rent seeking whether its subject is international trade controls or domestic industrial regulation. Adam Smith made this point very emphatically:

> in the mercantile system, the interest of the consumer is almost constantly sacrificed to that of the producer; and it seems to consider production, and not consumption, as the ultimate end and object of all industry and commerce. . . . In the restraints upon the importation of all foreign commodities which can come into competition with those of our own growth, or manufacture, the interest of the home-consumer is evidently sacrificed to that of the producer. It is altogether for the benefit of the latter, that the former is obliged to pay that enhancement of price which this monopoly almost always occasions. (1937, 625)

Colonization policies (which we do not consider in detail) provide another important example of blatant rent seeking on the part of English economic interests, especially those of the crown. All of the great trading nations of Europe engaged in colonial pursuits between the fifteenth and eighteenth centuries. Such profit-creation led to great discoveries, including the modern discovery of the Americas. Economic motives of those who could at least *potentially* profit from exploration and development were, in virtually all cases, a driving force of colonization policy. Simple economics provides a ready explanation: Colonies provided the mother country with a cheap and ready source of resource inputs (and, in some cases, finished goods) and at the same time provided a new outlet for produced goods and services. In the process they became the lucrative object of monarchical and interest group returns.

Mercantile policies and practices, for example, had an enormous impact on U.S. history. In a world of economic freedom English and other immigrants to America would have been free to sell their wares to all demanders and to buy needed products from any willing sellers. However, as a legal extension of the English state, American colonists had to conform to trade, production, and price regulations set by the English monarch and later by the British Parliament. (As we will see, such policies did not always produce the results of perfect cartelization owing to enforcement and other problems). North American colonists, from practically the beginning, were shackled with regulations that created rents for English economic interests. The Stuart kings claimed "regalian rights" over the economic devel-

opment of the colonies and cut deals with, for example, the Virginia tobacco growers and merchants for a "take" in the form of taxes. Later, after
the Constitutional revolution (1650–1660) and the Restoration, amidst new
Parliamentary powers, both the monarchs and the Parliament determined
economic regulation of the colonies.

A small sample of such rules is illustrative. Under a series of Navigation
Acts (such as those passed in 1660, 1663, 1673, and 1696), colonists were
required to ship their exports in English-built ships. Particular exports of
the colonists were "enumerated," that is, required by Parliament to be
exported *only* to England or to English colonies. Tobacco, sugar, and in-
digo were on the list in 1660. The Navigation Act of 1663 went even further
to benefit English merchants. It stated that all European goods (with a few
exceptions that aided English merchants causes) going to the colonies must
be shipped from England and on English-built ships. This meant that the
monarch and other business and financial interests benefited by being able
to tax goods that were let through and by protecting certain British products altogether.

Later Acts gave customs officials in the colonies extraordinary powers
of search and seizure and voided all colonial laws contrary to the Acts.
Rent-seeking interests in England and by colonial governors and favored
merchants explains this kind of "mercantile" regulation. One example makes
clear the motives: the Hat Act passed Parliament in 1732 under pressures
from London felt makers. Already in fear of French competition, these
London businesses were fearful of the establishment of a hat industry in
the northern colonies. The Act prohibited the exportation of hats from
one colony to another, required colonists to have a seven-year apprenticeship before entering the trade, with apprentices limited to two per shop,
and barred the employment of Negroes in hatmaking altogether. A Mo-
lasses Act, passed the following year, had the same intent (Morris 1961,
510–14).

These kinds of mercantile policies naturally had to be enforced, and
distant enforcement was costly and often ineffective. Piracy, formal and
informal smuggling, and opportunistic behavior on the part of the colonial
"enforcement" was rampant. Walker (1993) advances a convincing case that
the attempts of James I and Charles I to rent-seek in the Virginian tobacco
market were, to even a large extent, unsuccessful. These monarchs were
unable to get the colonists to restrict production, to provide a high-quality
product, to eliminate contraband trade with other nations and in other

than English bottoms, or to sell at regulated prices. Taxes *were* collected, however, and rent-seeking policies do not prescribe or guarantee perfect monopoly profit maximization. Monarchs served multiple interests and interest balancing was an inextricable part of the process.[41] Indeed, economic harassment of the colonists was a central factor, perhaps *the* central factor, in the colonists' revolt.[42] We maintain simply that rent extraction was the concerted object of coalitions of aristocratic and (later) parliamentary interests in designing expansion policies and maintaining colonial interests.

Some writers have noted that the mercantile writers often defended free trade internally while simultaneously supporting external controls in international trade generally and tight economic control of the colonies specifically. An example described by Heckscher will illustrate this point: "From the end of the Middle Ages onwards, the import of wool cards into England was prohibited. They constituted an important means of production in the textile industry, which normally enjoyed greater favour than any other. A decree of 1630 went so far as to proscribe the sale of cards produced within the country from worn-out patterns. The maintenance of employment was given as the official motive for the measures, but in fact, at least as regards the latter prohibition, the object was to assist one of the oldest industrial joint-stock companies, the Mineral and Battery Works" (1934, 2:148). The point that this quotation illustrates is that the official motive for protectionist measures was, in all likelihood, seldom if ever the real motive for such measures.

Most writers on mercantilism identify some sort of "homogeneous" mercantile trade policy, employment policy, population policy, domestic policy, and so on, as if interests independent of those which drive economic man in all ages were responsible for the economic policy called mercantilism. We argue that there is no reason to expect that motives that operate on the demand or supply sides of monopoly protection in domestic industries are absent when it comes to another form of monopoly-creating device. Thus, one expects to observe some division of rents between manufacturing interests and the monarch when it is observed that mercantilists sought to establish a tariff-quota system in which the export of manufactures and the import of raw materials (and vice versa) was encouraged. We agree with Smith's assessment that mercantilism is but a tissue of protectionist fallacies supported by merchants, but we go further and argue that unvarnished rent seeking by merchants, monarch, and ultimately the masses represented by Parliament explains most economic intervention, as well as a good deal of political-legal change, over the period. A philosophical dualism may have existed as philosophers were converted to individualism (Locke) and natural law as a guide to economic conduct (Mandeville, Petty, Cantillon, Hume, and Smith). But as we have seen, the philosophical revolution was fostered by the conduct of rent seekers constrained by a particular form of polity. The form of that polity, moreover, underwent fundamental change under the impetus of the interplay of these self-interested economic forces. Mercantilist writers, Jacob Viner suggests, created "an elaborate system of confused and self-contradictory argument" (1967, 109). Our application to mercantilism of recent theory related to economic regulation suggests that the practitioners of mercantilism were anything but confused and self-contradictory. Through their actions, self-interested individuals ultimately altered the constraints within which rent-seeking activity could take place. In fact, our conclusion significantly amplifies Viner's belief that "pleas for special interest, whether open or disguised, constituted the bulk of the mercantilist literature. The disinterested patriot or philosopher played a minor part in the development of mercantilist doctrine" (1967, 115).

CONCLUSION

In the present chapter we have argued that important institutional changes in the rent-seeking economy of mercantilist England explain the rise of free trade in these times on both internal and external levels. This interpretation is more robust than the standard interpretation of English mercantilism in that it explains both the rise and the fall of mercantilism with the same model. Thus, we have argued that the conventional mercantilist paradigm of power versus plenty offers no convenient means of explaining the decline of state interference in England. Both the conventional interpretation and our own emphasize an inherent contradiction in the mercantile system. Specifically, both interpretations emphasize wealth destruction as the main feature of the system. In the conventional interpretation wealth is dissipated in a process of specie accumulation for state power building. The process is then adjudged to have been self-defeating and irrational, owing to the quantity theory of money and its international accoutrement, the price-specie flow mechanism.

In our interpretation, on the other hand, societal wealth is dissipated through monopoly creation and rent seeking at both local and national levels. Although the process was rational and efficient from the participants' point of view, economic growth was thwarted nonetheless. A major point of the rent-seeking interpretation, however, is that the process—including the enforcement apparatus of the local regulations—unintentionally helped bring about institutional changes that made rent seeking and internal regulation by the central government less feasible. Under the altered institutional structure liberalism and free trade became viable alternatives in England.

Chapter Four

Venality in French Mercantile Institutions

> Monseigneur:
> *The pains that you are lavishing to make commerce flourish in this kingdom have made me bold enough to offer to you this work, which I have entitled* The Complete Business Man. *I could dedicate it only to you, Monseigneur, since it is to your wise counsel that the public owes those beautiful regulations which have been made to repress disorders and to prevent misfortunes in matters of business.*
>
> —Jacques Savary to Jean-Baptiste Colbert,
> dedicatory preface to *Le Parfait Négociant*

> *In order to become the master, the politician poses as the servant.*
>
> —Charles de Gaulle

The French experience at rent seeking and the environment in which it took place contrast at almost every point with England's. Many writers (as noted in chapter 1) have treated mercantilism as a monolithic set of "principles" relating to political economy and more or less uniformly applied across countries. A mere perusal of French mercantile history, however, should convince historians that the French experience was markedly different than the English. In fact, if mercantilism means "a system of extensive economic controls employed under a monarch with absolute power," one could hardly find a better example than France from the sixteenth to eighteenth centuries. We develop separate treatments of French and (in chapter 5) Spanish mercantilism, although the analytical goals are quite the same as in our treatment of English developments. In the present chapter we develop a positive-economic theory of the internal regulation of industry in mercantile France and of the effects of this regulation upon the course of French economic development and industrialization.

The most important reason for a separate treatment of the French mercantile experience is that it permits us directly to confront the explanations of economic historians for the two most important features of the French economy of the time: (1) the repressive and controlled internal economic structure and (2) the very clear emphasis (bias?) upon luxury productions at the expense of basic manufactures, a characteristic of the French economy that is often said to have impeded an industrial revolution in France. To be sure there is some divergence of explanations among historians. Though his discussion differs from ours in many important respects, Heckscher came closest to a positive-economic view of French developments. The most celebrated historical interpretation of French mercantilism, however, that of Charles Woolsey Cole (1939; 1943), falls far short of providing a satisfying explanation of those two features of the French mercantile economy. Historians are often wont to lionize certain individuals, as Carlyle did, and Cole proves no exception as he features Jean-Baptiste Colbert, Louis XIV's indomitable finance minister, as the "great man" and prime mover of the French State for the seventeenth and eighteenth centuries. Further, Cole clearly and repeatedly expresses the view that Colbert's economic reforms were in the public interest, that is, made in the interests of the French people. Nation-state building was the objective for both the public interest and the glory of the monarch in Cole's scenario of French mercantilism.

While we do not dispute most of the details of these historical accounts of the French experience, we reject the "hero" and other major axioms of the historians and argue that positive-economic theory offers a more plausible account of these developments. We shall argue that the French political and economic environment was conducive to the self-interested supply of and demand for a massive system of economic regulation and that the success of this extensive intervention in the French economy greatly influenced French economic development up to the time of the Revolution. We shall argue further that the theory of economic regulation goes far in explaining aspects of French mercantilism that have long puzzled the historians, namely, the French mercantilists' response to innovations and their selective cartelization of industries. Thus, our interpretation is not a substitute for those of the historians but rather an attempt to provide the basic organizing principles for a more satisfying analysis of the major features of the period.[1]

A very general introduction to the "venal society," wherein official positions and favors were sold by the crown, is the first order of business in the present chapter. The rise of French mercantilism, like that of English mercantilism, is explained in terms of the relative efficiency of monopoly grants over taxation as a source of revenue for the French central state. The highly effective system of enforcing the consequent monopoly and cartel arrangements is then discussed. The usefulness of analyzing French mercantilism as an example of the theory of economic regulation and efficient rent seeking is illustrated in a section dealing with the efforts of the French administrators to restrict the introduction of printed calicos in the textile industry. Rather than a mindless attack on innovations, as Heckscher and other historians would have it, we explain this episode in terms of how printed calicos altered the French administrators' costs of enforcing the mercantile economic regulations. An economic explanation of why the French mercantilists stressed luxury-oriented cartels is then offered, as is an explanation for some episodes of economic regulation that would appear to escape the analytic power of the rent-seeking approach. The latter cases refer to the basically unregulated sectors of the French economy, such as wood and iron products. We offer a positive-economic theory capable of explaining these apparent contradictions, one that contributes to our understanding of the manner in which French economic development was "warped" for the next two hundred years or so. Finally, some of the roots of the demise of French mercantilism, which lie in the treatment of rural industry and in the competition among local officials for enforcement rents, are explored. Some concluding observations are offered contrasting Cole's interpretation of French mercantilism with our own.

FRANCE AS A VENAL SOCIETY: THE BACKGROUND

The English and French experiences over the mercantile period are dramatically different. Before turning to specific issues surrounding French mercantilism, an overview of the French experience and of uniquely French institutions is warranted. Subsequently in the chapter we shall return to many of the issues raised in the following overview.

Taxation and Venality

A chief source of the differences between how the mercantile age unfolded in England and in France lies with the absolutist property rights in taxation vested in the crown from 1439 through the French Revolution of the late eighteenth century. With minor alterations the tax system of the Old Regime continued that of the Renaissance and was characterized by institutionalized venality through the sale of tax exemptions. French monarchs shared the power to tax with the French aristocracy over the entire mercantile period, and the nobility and public office holders were typically exempt from taxation. Rent seeking by the monarch in the form of contracting to enterprises or to "tax farmers" was common as early as the thirteenth and fourteenth centuries (similar arrangements characterized the Spanish economy). A scholar of fiscal systems of the period aptly describes the situation: "the most important local revenues were 'farmed out' to enterprisers, who received the right to collect the *domaines* in return for lump sum payments. Amounts in excess of this sum became the revenue farmers' profits; and, if they collected less than the amounts paid, it was their loss—not the king's" (Wolfe 1972, 12. On this subject see also Hoselitz 1960.) Corruption permeated a gigantic fiscal bureaucracy, and, as in certain modern political systems, it became a way of life. Property rights shifted as the centuries passed, with tax farming and other "leases" becoming hereditary. Legal and judicial offices were sold by the crown, for example, and provide an interesting example of venality. There was great hypocrisy in the system: The oath of office in the case of justices and crown lawyers required a statement that they had not paid any money for their position. It has been observed that "for the whole sixteenth century the justices and royal lawyers began their careers with an act of perjury" (Wolfe 1972, 297).

Royal venality was of such magnitude, having grown throughout the period, that at the end of Louis XIII's reign (between 1636 and 1642) the French monarch was collecting between three and four times the amount of per capita taxes from his subjects as Charles I, who was then locked in a death battle with Parliament. The mercantile writer Gregory King estimated the "general income" of France in 1688 at £80,500,000 and that of England at £41,700,000, estimates rough in themselves but sufficient to indicate a much larger success of royal rent seeking in France over the mercantile period (Nef 1968, 128).

The Institutional Backdrop of Rent Seeking in France

The rent-seeking coalition of crown and aristocracy was facilitated in France by a number of institutional features stemming from and related to the absolute power to tax by the crown. There are the interrelated matters of (1) the enforcement of industrial regulation, (2) the degree of effective crown rent-seeking interference with old and new industries, and (3) the incidence of the tax structure and the incentives established thereby. After examination of each of these issues, it is clear that Heckscher's observations (1934, 1:145) regarding the design and implementation of industrial regulation in England and France is basically correct. That is, while English and French monarchs were equally zealous in establishing rent-seeking activity, the French system was far more effective at enforcement. We add to this the observation that not only was enforcement an underlying point of difference between the two systems, but an absence of other, countervailing forces in France permitted rampant venality by a royal-aristocratic coalition.

Enforcement

The guild system in France grew stronger from the time of the Middle Ages onward, in contrast to the English experience. At the opening of the sixteenth century most local industry was done by free craftsmen, but by the reign of Henry IV (1589–1610) the guild regime was dramatically strengthened. Two crown edicts (1581 and 1597) laid down uniform rules for the organization of handicrafts all over France and permitted master craftsmen who were not members of guilds to organize and obtain from royal officials all of the advantages of formal guild membership: regulated apprenticeships and entry, hours of work permitted, and so forth. Guild regulations, moreover, were confirmed by royal letters patent. The result of these activities was a massive extension of royal prerogative, superseding guild and local prerogative in the matter of decentralized royal control over industrial activity.[2] Entry control, the imposition of maximum wage rates upon journeymen, price controls, and the establishment of rent-seeking offices engendered by all this became a centralized crown prerogative, as we shall explain later in the chapter.

Although these developments set the stage for a venal society with centralized property rights, further developments significantly strengthened the control of the king's officers over municipal authority. *Intendants des provinces,* tried servants of the crown, were sent as commissioners to the provinces to establish administrative reforms. Gradually, under the aegis of Richelieu and Louis XIII, these well-paid *intendants* took over and consolidated most of the functions of earlier royal provincial administrators, thereby permitting crown ministers far greater assurance that the crown's policies would be undertaken. Adjudication of regulatory disputes at the local level was also more and more becoming the business of the crown courts, by invocation of the principle of *cas royaux*, whereby disputes over guild regulations and other industrial encumbrances could be tried in royal courts owing to "crown interests." Certainly Colbert, minister of France between 1661 and 1683, must have found these inherited institutions a great advantage in implementing the intensified rent seeking of Louis XIV.

Over this important period, then, the institutions of legislative and judicial enforcement over industry and trade were developing along sharply opposing lines in England and France. During the crucial century from 1540 to 1640, institutions that facilitated rent seeking by crown and aristocracy were greatly strengthened in France, while such enforcement institutions, legal and administrative, were becoming atrophied in England. The French crown did not have to brook the combined opposition of enforcers, those disgruntled by regulation, and the public in its quest for economic rents.

Industrial Rent Seeking and Economic Growth

The administrative machinery that served rent seekers vis-à-vis local handicraft regulation was duplicated over specific industries in a manner that could only be pitifully imitated by the English. Tight royal control over mines, saltpeter and gunpowder, and salt was greatly facilitated by decentralized local production with centralized control over rent-producing "franchises."

In the matter of saltpeter and gunpowder manufacture, the "grand master of the artillery" (the minister Sully served for a long while) was given exclusive management. In imitation of the tax-collection system, these rights were "farmed out" to commissioners who represented the grand master in granting or revoking rights to produce. Commissioners, in turn, exacted for themselves a split in the rents created.

Concession rights to the produce of mines were likewise farmed out to court favorites through an elaborate administrative machinery. Revenues in the form of lump-sum payments went to the crown, as did a regalian tax

on ores (*droit du dixième*). Entry, exit, and abandonment were all regulated to the mutual advantage of aristocratic franchise holders (*concession-
aires*) and the king.

The French crown, like its English counterpart, granted patents for
new inventions and, along with them, money subsidies and official salaried
help for inventors. But the French went further by determining the entire
direction of technology. By granting a large number of limited tax-exempt
concessions, kings from Henry IV and Louis XIII appear to have warped
technology by shifting emphasis toward new branches of artistic craftsmanship (cloth, glass, tapestries) and away from cost-reducing devices necessary for the introduction of quantity-oriented, large-scale production.
Though patents for the latter were not refused, crown advisors were establishing conditions that greatly favored the establishment of artistic productions. Such emphasis expanded into the well-known government studios
and art factories of Louis XIV and his royal successors. Indeed, the details
of this process—and the economic motives of the participants to it—constitute a major feature of our positive analysis of French mercantilism.

Taxes, Rent Seeking, and Economic Growth

Perhaps the single most successful application of venality by the French
crown related to the salt monopoly. Claiming regalian rights (which corresponded to the salt tribute of the imperial Roman state) in most of the
provinces of France, the crown imposed intricate regulations on salt producers, requiring them to sell all salt produced to royal storehouses at prices
fixed by the king's officers. Consumers were then forced to purchase salt
(with required quantities per parish) at rates four times as high as free-
market rates. Although there were infractions, monopoly conditions were
rigorously enforced, in large measure because of the effectiveness of royal
representatives at the local levels.

The *gabelle* and other taxes on salt became the single most important
revenue source next to the infamous *taille*. The *taille* was a tax levied on
the income and real property of peasants, shopkeepers, and craftsmen who
were not exempted by virtue of participation in royal manufactures. In real
terms receipts from the *gabelle* rose eight or ten times between 1523 and
1641 (Nef 1968, 83).

The imposition of both the *gabelle* and the *taille* had stark implications
for the distribution of income and economic growth. Both of these taxes
and the indirect taxes on commodities fell heavily upon the poor, discour-

aging capital formation. Unbridled taxing powers facilitated redistributions to the nobility and to the clergy, who utilized the wealth for "artistic consumptions."

Thus, institutionalized rent seeking had a number of implications for the form of the French mercantile state. Growth in real output lagged behind that in England over the seventeenth century because of a dearth of investment opportunities and, more important, a lack of incentive for capital formation.[3] Absolutism created much uncertainty in property rights, and high transaction costs were created by a bureaucratic inability to adapt to changing tastes and new technology.[4] Most of the best minds, as in all societies, were attracted to the areas of highest return. In France this meant that they sought a bureaucratic sinecure or purchased positions within the guilds, some of which could be passed on through hereditary rights. Only later, when cartel enforcement could not contain a growing competitive fringe challenge to guild dominance (Ekelund and Tollison 1981, 93–96; Root 1994, 127–29), did resources begin to flow to areas of high return and market developments begin to propel economic growth.

The certainty of absolute power and of an imposed system of rent seeking contrasted sharply with the uncertainty of private entrepreneurial returns in France. The high private returns of a relatively unfettered competitive system, which proved sufficient to bring down mercantile monarchy in the English case, were neither extant nor possible in France. The tradition of the venal system created there was so intense and the underpinnings so strong that the emergence of a liberal order was postponed until the late eighteenth century. With these introductory observations in mind, let us now turn to a more specific and microanalytic discussion of rent seeking in mercantile France.

A THEORY OF FRENCH MONARCHICAL RENT SEEKING

Heckscher (1934, 1:137) sets the stage for our analysis with his observation that "from the outset, the monarchy considered it one of its chief tasks to gather to itself those powers over handicraft and trade which had fallen into other hands during the confusion of the Middle Ages." This observation is, of course, quite consistent with historians' usual emphasis on mercantilism as a system featuring the enhancement of state power relative to the combination of particularism (the natural economy) and universalism (the church) prevailing in the medieval economic order. But we would like to interpret the development of the nation-state under the mercantilists in a different way.

Taxation Versus Monopolization

The French monarchy sought revenue to finance its expenditures, and the term that we apply to this behavior is *rent seeking*. In a fundamental sense the situation in France was the same as we discussed for England. There were basically two sources of revenue available to the French administrators—taxation and monopoly grants. Taxation was extensive in France at this time, and, as we saw above, this aspect of revenue seeking has been covered exhaustively by historians (Wolfe 1972). The extensive use of monopoly grants to raise revenue came about during the time of Colbert, who, under pressure to raise additional revenues for the king, found monopoly grants a more efficient form of rent seeking (at the margin) than taxation. Monopoly grants at the height of Colbert's administration thus became a major source of the French state's revenues.[5] Colbert's shift to monopoly grants forms the basis of our interpretation of French internal economic regulation, and the change in emphasis had profound implications for the course of French economic development. For the present, however, let us review the difficulties Colbert faced with taxation and then go on to analyze the relative efficiency of monopoly grants in the revenue-seeking context of Colbert's administration.

In the medieval and early mercantile period the difficulty of taxing in all economies was related to such factors as the absence of data on transactions and the general ease of tax evasion. Moreover, as noted in chapter 3, taxation places the burden on state authorities to ascertain taxable values and to collect tax revenues. Though difficulties of tax collection and assessment and the ease of tax evasion explain the emergence of rent-seeking behavior in the early French economy, the even greater reliance on monopoly creation as a means to raise revenue in the age of Colbert (the high time of French mercantilism) admits of further explanation. In addition to the continuing general technical difficulties of collection and assessment, Colbert in 1661 faced deeply entrenched interests of a fiscal bureaucracy and a fiendishly complex tax structure.[6] Colbert's hold on the king (Louis XIV) was a function of his ability to produce revenues, so that his first order of business (when he replaced Cardinal Mazarin as Louis's finance minister) was to attempt to circumvent an encrusted tax system born of feudal and medieval traditions. At this, and in spite of his very considerable intellectual powers and machinations, he was an abject failure, as Cole clearly documents.

After several dictatorial revenue-getting measures, which alienated a massive segment of the French financial community, Colbert attempted his great reform of the tax system.[7] First, Colbert attempted "reform" of the *taille réele,* a land tax that was the single largest revenue source of the state. But there were many, many exemptions based upon privilege, bribery, and tradition, so that Colbert's use of spies, seizures, and investigations of those claiming the exemptions were to no avail. Next, because of this failure, Colbert attempted to shift the incidence of taxation, reducing the *taille,* from which so many claimed exemption, and drastically raising the *aides,* which included an internal indirect tax on commodities at the wholesale and retail levels and tolls on river and road transportation, the collection of which was farmed. But so corrupt and intimidating were the farmers of the *taille* that Colbert was again thwarted and nullified (Cole 1939, 1:305–6).

Colbert's dilemma was thus the personal urgency of retaining the king's support in the face of an inability to increase revenues sufficiently via the tax system.[8] Vested interests, coupled with the exigencies of an opulent court and the 1672 war with the Dutch, drove Colbert to "new" and "extraordinary" methods of acquiring funds (Cole 1939, 1:307–12).

Colbert thus directed his rent-seeking efforts to the granting and enforcement of monopoly rights, and the French mercantile economy took on the form of a massive web of economic regulations administered by the central state. Monopoly creation was at the margin a more reliable source of state revenue than taxation, in which the state has to bear the costs of discovering taxable values and policing corruption among tax collectors, because aspiring monopolists will reveal the present value of monopolies to the authorities in their efforts to secure such grants from the state. State officials thus do not have to seek out estimates of the value of their enforcement services in the case of monopoly grants. Rather, monopoly seekers will come to them, and, so long as the bidding for monopoly privileges is competitive, they will reveal to state authorities the underlying value of the monopoly rights.[9] While these conditions did exist in England, in France they were magnified exponentially. For these underlying reasons, then, the French mercantile state found it efficient to raise revenue by creating a highly monopolized economy, and this argument is sufficient to explain the rise of the French nation-state as an extension and consolidation of monopoly power in the economy.

Our concern in the remainder of this chapter will be with showing how

this rent-seeking-through-monopolization interpretation of French mercantilism can be applied to offer a more appealing explanation of the main
features of French economic behavior and development over this period
than that offered by the historians. This is not to argue that the historians
have completely ignored the revenue-seeking aspect of French mercantilism (*fiscalisme*). There is ample evidence in Heckscher and other sources
about this aspect of French mercantilism: "It illustrates the tendency of the
monarchy to profit from the monopolies, and was turned into a regular
institution by Henry III's great edict of 1581 . . . The state had the sole aim
of continually forcing those within the industry to pay in order to exclude
competition" (1934, 1:179, 183). The historians, however, have tended to
treat rent seeking as a manifestation of some greater mercantile objective,
such as the balance of trade, rather than making it a central element in an
interpretation of the period. As we shall see, the French administrators
were very ingenious and intelligent rent seekers, and interpreting their behavior as a manifestation of efficient rent seeking offers a route to a fuller
understanding of the important episodes of economic regulation over the
period.

The Genesis of French Rent Seeking

Rent seeking is thus our basic model, and it might be well to begin our
analysis by sketching in general terms the monopolization process whereby
the French nation-state consolidated its power. We begin from a situation
in which monopoly power was extremely localized in the various town
economies and took the form of occupational licensing arrangements and
the control of access to town marketplaces. These local cartels were managed and enforced by guild officials. As in the case of England, the osten-
sible reason for central-state interference with the operation of the town
cartels was the increase in prices and wages that followed the pestilence of
the Black Death. The real aim of the monarchy, however, was a unified
system of economic regulation across the country, and it took essentially
two centuries to reach this goal (the famous edicts of 1581 and 1597).

Why did the monarchy intervene in the local cartel arrangements, and
what explains the desire for a uniform pattern of regulation? In the early
period the system of guilds and local monopolies was only weakly diffused
outside Paris. In most towns a majority of the trades were not organized
into monopolies (Heckscher 1934, 1:143–44). Clearly, there existed an op-

portunity for the monarchy to extend and enforce these local monopolies in such a way as to increase its revenues. The strengthening of the role of the French nation-state can best be explained in such simple rent-seeking terms. This interpretation makes Heckscher's repeated emphasis that the system of national regulation was fashioned on the model of the guilds much more understandable. The guild, of course, is the familiar model of economic regulation that features the usual monopoly provisions of licensed producers and restrictions on the degree of competition among license holders.

The desire for uniform national regulation in the context of the local cartels is fairly easy to understand since competition would have otherwise undermined the cartel arrangements in the towns. Uniformity in the pattern of regulated prices is thus a major aspect of the pattern of mercantile regulation in France, as it is in most systems of economic regulation. The differences that tend to appear are quite predictable in terms of a rent-seeking model. It is therefore not surprising that occupational masters who apprenticed in Paris could practice anywhere in the country they wished, while masters outside Paris did not receive the reciprocal benefit (Heckscher 1934, 1:146–47). In terms of a rent-seeking theory of government the Parisian masters were more densely populated and located closer to the source of monarchical fiat than their counterparts elsewhere in the country. They consequently faced lower organizational costs to lobby for crown protection, and they received a more inclusive monopoly as a result.[10] Other variations in regulatory uniformity appeared as a result of variation in enforcement practices, and we shall have more to say about these.

Monarchical rent seeking in France, therefore, is sufficient to explain the stress on the power of the nation-state in French mercantilism. There were rent-seeking opportunities for the central state, and economic regulation in the form of cartel expansion and enforcement ensued as a result. This rent-seeking competition took the form of a monopolist (the crown) providing cartel enforcement services, with the numerous "industries" throughout France bidding for these services. We surmise that, by presenting itself as the only agent in the process with an effective monopoly (of force), the French state was able to capture the bulk of the monopoly rents inherent in the regulation of the economy. As we shall see in the next section, these rents were not entirely "pure profits," as considerable sums had to be spent on the administration and enforcement of the economic regulations.

ENFORCEMENT OF
MONARCHICAL RENT SEEKING

The administrative machinery set up by the French to provide cartel-enforcement services is often admired as one of the greatest administrative accomplishments in the historical process of the development of nation-states. We view this administrative machinery as a natural expression of efficient rent seeking. That is, the enforcement system was an expression of a desire to maximize crown revenues from rent seeking.

As noted in our introduction, the primary means through which the French monarchy provided cartel enforcement services was through paid civil servants (the *intendants*).[11] The authority of the *intendants* under Louis XIV and Colbert was extensive. These officers of the crown were in charge of all the other authorities in their administrative district and formed the link with the central authority in the administration of cartel enforcement. They judged many cases presented by the crown, organized and superintended tax collections, inspected and regulated industry, directed public education, and controlled the police and administration of troops and municipalities (Boulenger 1967, 344).

The fact that they were paid is important. As discussed in chapter 3, higher pay is a means to control malfeasance in labor contracts in which an element of "trust" is involved. This follows from, for example, the fact that the official faces a greater opportunity cost from losing his position by accepting bribes. Paid enforcement agents, then, were primarily a means to control corruption and to ensure uniform cartel enforcement across the country. Without a guarantee of honest and even enforcement, the services of the monarchy in this respect would have been less valuable, and we can thus view the *intendants* as an efficient way to enforce the economic regulations of French mercantilism. This system of cartel enforcement contrasts dramatically with that of mercantile England where unpaid justices of the peace were relied upon as cartel-enforcement agents. English cartel administration was predictably lax, corrupt, uneven, and ultimately unstable, while exactly the opposite description applies to the French system of paid enforcers.

The nature of the regulations to be enforced by the *intendants* was also an expression of efficient rent-seeking policies. The monarchy not only set up uniform price-and-wage controls and restricted entry into the local cartels via the apprenticeship system, but it also sought to provide protection against competition from within the cartels. This latter condition is especially important in the enforcement of economic regulation because licensed sellers within the cartel will otherwise compete away excess profits through output expansion. Efficient rent seeking is thus a good working explanation for the incredibly detailed regulations governing cartel enforcement and outputs in mercantile France.

Consider the formal instructions given by Colbert and the king on August 13, 1669, to the newly appointed *commis,* or inspectors of manufactures. As cartel-enforcement provisions, they could hardly be surpassed. The inspectors were directly responsible to the *contrôleur-général* and were to secure meticulous observance of the industrial regulations laid down. The general articles of enforcement numbered sixty-five and were so detailed as to include monthly visits to workers' homes. Article 16, for example, required that "each month the wardens are to visit all the houses of workers. If the houses are located in distant villages or hamlets, the wardens may appoint sub-wardens to make the inspections and mark the goods. If the manufacture is considerable, the name of the village or hamlet is to be on the mark used by the sub-wardens" (Cole 1939, 2:420).

The general characteristics of the rules governing cartel outputs were also impressive. These regulations were incredibly detailed, on the order of a substantial planned economy, and the details were tailored to restrict the various means that cartel members could find to expand output from within the industry. Heckscher provides the following small example of the regulations.

Regulation followed the course of production. In the first place, it contained specifications regarding the handling of raw material, especially wool and the methods of dealing with it and went on to deal with all the subsequent stages of production, the most important of which were weaving and, especially, dyeing. Amongst numberless others, we will single out as an example of the weaving regulations a special *règlement* of 1718 for Burgundy and four neighbouring districts. As the *règlement* itself puts it, these districts produced woolen goods for the use of the soldiers and the general public, so that is was by no means a luxury industry. The dimensions of the cloths were specified in 18 articles for each place separately. We will confine ourselves to quoting the first five rules. The fabrics of Dijon and Selongey were to be put in reeds 1¾ ells wide, a warp was to contain 44 x 32 or 1408 threads including the selvedges, and when it came to the fulling-mill, the cloth was to be exactly one ell wide. Semur in Auxois, and Auxerre, Montbard, Avalon and Beaune were to have a warp of 43 x 32 or 1376 threads, the same width in the reed, and the same width of cloth when it left the fullinghammer. Saulieu was to have the same width with 42 x 32 or 1340

(really 1344) threads, but it seems that the white and the more finely spun
cloths were to have 74 x 32 or 2368 threads. Chatillon on the Seine and five
other places were to have 1216 threads in a width of 1-% ells with the same
variation for white cloths. The *sardis* fabric, which was produced in Bourg
en Bresse and various other towns was to have only 576 threads with reeds
of one ell and a width of half an ell after fulling, etc., etc. (1934, 1:160–61)

As we outlined above, the control of this system of economic regulation rested with paid agents of the monarchy, and their means of control
were extensive. There was widespread inspection of production, well-regu-
lated measurement of outputs, various marking procedures whereby outputs bore the name of the producer, town marks, and so forth. Penalties
for violating the regulations consisted of the confiscation and destruction
of "inferior" output, heavy fines, public mockery of the offender, and loss
of one's license to practice for continued offenses. The regulations, then,
formed an extensive system of output restriction. As Heckscher (1934, 1:162)
observes, "No measure of control was considered too severe where it served
to secure the greatest possible respect for the regulations." Indeed, Colbert
instituted a system of spies in each town who were to report cartel chiselers
to the local *intendant.* Another purpose of the spies appears to have been
to keep an eye on the *intendants,* who became less and less efficacious over
the period.

The French monarchy thus devised quite efficient means to enforce
economic regulation on a large scale. Paying the local enforcement agents
controlled malfeasance and unevenness in the application of the regulations, problems that would have reduced the returns from monarchical
rent seeking, and, moreover, the regulations governing cartel behavior appear to have provided an efficient system of output control on a massive
scale.

RENT SEEKING AS A USEFUL INTERPRETATION OF FRENCH MERCANTILISM

Evidence for the usefulness of the rent-seeking theory as the principal explanation of internal and external economic policy is plentiful, although
Heckscher and Cole ascribe such rent-seeking activity to other motives.
Cole, particularly, views mercantile developments, and especially those instituted by Colbert, as initiated to provide for a strong French state and
economy that would be of public benefit to the people and of glory to the
sovereign (for example, Cole 1939, 1:301, 307, 311–20, 329–30, and 2:141).

Nevertheless, both Heckscher and Cole in their historical descriptions provide a great deal of evidence for the rent-seeking interpretation.

Only an idiosyncratic reading of Cole's excellent historical accounts of Colbert and French mercantile development could leave an impression of Colbert as a lawgiver or quintessential public servant. What comes through an analysis of his life and works is that he was a calculating and hard-dealing agent of the king, without fear and without pity (Cole's own description), who best served himself by serving up huge sums of money to his monarch, Louis XIV, to conduct one of the most sumptuous courts in history.[12]

The General Dimensions of Rent Seeking Under Colbert

As evidence of Colbert's "public service," we might look briefly at some of the cartels formed during his administration. After several unsuccessful attempts, Colbert was able, in 1681, to form a tobacco monopoly that applied to the entire kingdom. The monopoly regulated all aspects of tobacco production, importation, manufacture, and sale. In spite of the heated opposition of consumers and retailers, revenues to the state multiplied rapidly—from 500,000 livres in 1681 and 600,000 in 1683 to an annual 30,000,000 livres in 1789. Colbert oversaw the conduct of the postal monopoly, which, after 1673, brought in 1,000,000 livres per year. United to the postal system in 1673, transport monopolies encouraged by Colbert (covering coaches and certain water transportation) brought in more than 5,500,000 livres per year by 1683. In 1674 Colbert forced all trades to form themselves into guilds, which then traded sums of money for statutes and regulations (Cole 1939, 1:307–9).

Cole reports that some of Colbert's intrusions met with "unhappy results." In 1674 he levied a tax in the form of a fee for the "inspection and making" of tin and pewterware. A great opposition developed, however, because such utensils were used almost exclusively by common people. Cole reports that

> taken in conjunction, the stamped-paper and tinware taxes, together with the tobacco monopoly, led to resistance that at times assumed the proportions of a revolt. At Bordeaux the people of the lower classes rose, when an attempt was made to collect the tinware fee in 1675. For a time in March the city was in the hands of the mob. The people were pacified at first by concessions and promises, but it was not until November that troops could be sent there in sufficient numbers to crush the rising, by executions and the presence of soldiers. In the same year and for similar reasons, a revolt flared

up in Brittany and had to be suppressed by troops, and parallel outbreaks
occurred in other parts of the country. (Cole 1939, 1:309)

A still more familiar rent-seeking expedient was employed by Colbert
when he farmed coinage rights to a syndicate of capitalists for 630,000
livres in 1674. Colbert's nephew, Desmarets, and his agent, Bellinzani (in
charge of managing the cartel), were bribed into silence by gifts, while the
monopolists struck off 26,000,000 four-*sous* pieces, far in excess of what
was permitted by contract, and reduced the fineness of coins by a twelfth.
Colbert ignored the enormous profits, however, since, as Cole reports (1939,
1:310), "the syndicate assisted him in certain financial operations." Only
after Colbert's death were Desmarets and Bellinzani brought to justice.
One eighteenth-century wag had it that Colbert began his regime with
bankruptcy and ended it by counterfeiting.

Examples of such cartelizing and monopoly-creating activity by Colbert
and other French administrators could be multiplied exponentially over
the mercantile period. Cole and other historians have maintained that
through all of Colbert's measures ran a "keynote of economy," that Colbert
"knew how hard it was to raise adequate funds, how necessary was money
for the glory of the king and the strength of the state" (1939, 1:311). The
modern economist has a better explanation. Aside from Colbert's own
motives, which were certainly not selfless, the best explanation for the economic structure of mercantile France is that its institutions permitted rent-
seeking behavior of a predictable type.

The Matter of Calicos

The superiority of a rent-seeking explanation, however, rests upon firmer
support, for it allows the interpretation of historical episodes that otherwise appear to be highly irrational. The outstanding example in this regard
concerns the attempt by the state to prevent the production, import, and
consumption of printed calicos and other cotton goods in France.

The implications drawn by the two leading mercantile historians of this
episode are noteworthy. Heckscher (1934, 1:170–75), terming the prohibitions an "attack on innovations," outlined the lengths to which cartel managers went to achieve these goals: "It is estimated that the economic
measures taken in this connection cost the lives of some 16000 people,
partly through executions and partly through armed affrays, without reck-

oning the unknown but certainly much larger number of people who were sent to the galleys, or punished in other ways. On one occasion in Valence, 77 were sentenced to be hanged, 58 were to be broken upon the wheel, 631 were sent to the galleys, one was set free and none were pardoned. But even this vigorous action did not help to attain the desired end" (1:173). Heckscher sees this episode as an irrational attempt by the administrators to stifle innovation. Cole, likewise, regards calico legislation as an "aberration of French policy" and as merely "one of a number of instances in which the French government tried to restrict or arrest the forces of technological, industrial or commercial change" (Cole 1943, 177).

The French textile industry (silk, linen, and wool productions) was the object of intense cartelization long before the time of Colbert, although Colbert cartelized these areas with renewed vigor (Cole 1939, 132–237). Private traders and the East India Company, which was created by Colbert in 1663–64 (See Pound and Plucknett 1927, 157–74), were responsible for the import of printed calicos into France. No attempt was made by Colbert (who died in 1683) or by his successor Seignelay (not Colbert's son, but 39 percent owner and president of the East India Company) to bring calicos under the umbrella of regulation. Before 1681, moreover, the Huguenots, already relegated to the role of second-class citizens, manufactured, within guilds, imitation calicos, which were consumed largely by the poor.

In 1681 a boom occurred in calico demand, causing guild leaders of the wool, cloth, silk, and linen industries to complain to local *intendants* of unfair competition and unemployment within their ranks.[13] The response, in spite of Seignelay's personal interests, was a ban in 1686 on both the domestic production and the import of calicos—a ban that may have adversely affected the cotton industry in France until the late nineteenth century. After the absolute ban in 1686 a number of "deals" took place whereby the king earned rents and the East India Company was permitted exclusive but very limited importation rights. Regulation of varying degrees of exclusiveness and severity took place between 1686 and 1700, with an absolute ban between 1700 and 1753, although a good deal of smuggling undoubtedly took place over the entire period, since the demand for calicos was strong and growing (Cole 1943, 164–77).

The question that economic historians have been at pains to answer concerning this episode concerns the extent of the enforcement and policing of the ban against printed calicos. Punishment was extreme, though perhaps less extreme than described by Heckscher.[14] Enforcement was extended after 1700 to a prohibition against the wearing of calicos in France.[15] But was this policy the result of irrational motives or a mindless attack on innovations, as Cole and Heckscher have argued?

These arguments simply fall short by failing to consider the implications of the calicos for the managers of French economic regulation. Two basic points are relevant in this regard. As noted above, the cartel managers had to contend with the reaction of the producers of substitute textile products (the wool, cloth, silk, and linen producers). Calico production would have encroached upon these markets, and it is no mystery why these producers would have sought to ban the production of calicos.[16]

The reaction of the producers of competing goods, however, does not explain why calicos were banned. Given the rents inherent in regulating the production of calicos, it seems reasonable to expect that the French administrators would have found a way to capture these rents and at the same time mollify the producers of substitutes (side payments?). The answer to this part of the puzzle lies in the fact that the management of economic regulation is less costly when the industry produces a homogeneous product. The price, entry, and output controls of French mercantilism could be more effectively implemented where cloth of uniform colors and sizes was produced. Indeed, uniformity was carried to the extreme in the previously described incredibly detailed regulation of the French textile industry (Cole 1939, 2:156–58 and 1943, 48).[17] The printed calicos thus presented a threat of no small importance to the French textile cartel—product differentiation. These colored cloths raised costs to the regulatory managers, because product differentiation opened the door to nonprice competition. Even where the cartel price was controlled and where there were extensive controls on entry from without and within, the introduction of the printed calicos would have meant that licensed calico firms could have competed for expanded market shares through quality (pattern and color) competition. Such nonprice competition would have dissipated excess profits within the cartel, an outcome that was in the interests of neither the regulatory managers nor the regulated firms (Stigler 1968; Douglas and Miller 1974).

When taken with the religious controversy, then, these two basic reasons—the reaction of producers of substitutes and the difficulty of regulating nonprice competition—show the response of the French mercantilists to calicos to be a highly rational expression of efficient rent seeking and not a mindless attack on innovation. Numerous other examples may be drawn from Cole, Heckscher, and various other sources to illustrate the usefulness of the rent-seeking theory in interpreting French internal regulations.[18] The example of printed calicos is sufficiently dramatic, however, to illustrate the usefulness of the theory.

LUXURY-ORIENTED CARTELS AND FRENCH ECONOMIC DEVELOPMENT

One of the most perplexing problems associated with French mercantile history is related to the very apparent encouragement of luxury industries through protective cartels and the clear neglect of certain basic industries such as iron and wood products.[19] (By neglect we simply mean a failure to cartelize, protect, and encourage.) This feature of French mercantile policy has figured prominently in historians' stock-in-trade explanation of the tardiness of industrialization in France. As one historian of the period put it: "Although the French boasted that their country was nearly self-sufficient because of its abundant natural riches, their governments . . . showed much more interest in expanding manufacturing and trade than in exploiting the land and its produce" (Mettam 1977, 230). Still another example is the French economic policy toward iron production. The managers of economic regulation offered no cartel services for this industry. Heckscher describes the situation: "There is no lack of contemporary statements to the effect that the usual type of French economic policy tended to obstruct the development of iron production. For instance, the head of an iron works wrote, 'Glass manufacturers, manufacturers of genuine porcelain and faience, cloth manufactures, embroidery concerns, silk and goldlace production, all enjoy every possible privilege and exemption; iron manufacturers alone have no advantages, and yet they cater for real needs while the others serve only luxury and comfort'" (1934, 1:198–99).

The important question, then, is why the French administrators sought rents primarily by cartelizing luxury industries. The traditional answers, which we will analyze, are distinctly unsatisfying, and we believe that positive-economic analysis offers a far better explanation.

Traditional Explanations

Consider two traditional explanations. First, there is the luxury consumption argument. In this case the French monarch and aristocracy are seen as the major demanders of luxury goods. They therefore had a direct interest in regulating the quality of their purchases. As examples, one could look at the tobacco monopoly already considered and at tapestry manufacture, the latter a good example of a totally state-directed cartel (Cole 1939, 2:287). This argument, though, ignores the facts that basic materials must also have been demanded by aristocrats (certainly indirectly as luxury items) and that cartel managers could have earned rents by cartelizing any industry, basic or otherwise.

A second line of reasoning, congruent with the luxury consumption argument, is that import substitution should be prevented for luxury productions. Indeed, most of the goods imported to France were luxury goods. As Cole describes the situation: "Royal letters of 1554, confirming the statutes of the workers in cloth of gold, cloth of silver, and silk in the city of Lyon, spoke of the establishment of such manufactures as the only way to prevent the export of money. In 1572 an edict evinced a desire on the part of the king that the French devote themselves to the manufacture and working up of wool, flax, hemp, and tow, which are produced abundantly in this kingdom . . . and from them make and get the profit that the foreigners (now) make, who come to buy them generally at a low price, export them, have them worked up, and then bring back the woolens and linens to sell at high prices" (1939, 1:9).

In this argument luxury cartels were formed to "expropriate" rents from foreigners. The lace industry provides a clear example of protectionist cant ("protect domestic employment") to support baser motives.[20] Certainly this could have been one of the reasons—especially when combined with the luxury-demand argument—for the establishment of luxury-directed cartels. It would give substance, moreover, to the so-called mercantile policy of importing raw materials and exporting finished goods, the "balance-of-labor" axiom of mercantilism. However, this latter argument ignores the fact that much, and in some cases (for example, tapestries) all, of the output of French luxury manufactures was consumed within France and not manufactured for export. However, it is not clear on the basis of the import-substitution argument why the directors of French mercantilism would not have wanted to be independent in all productions or why rents could not have been earned by cartelizing raw-materials production or other inputs, such as steel.

Rent-Seeking Explanations

The rent-seeking model provides the basis of a good explanation of this important aspect of French mercantilism, and three points are fundamental in this respect. First, certain basic production was not cartelized because the government itself was a major direct demander of industry output. For example, we find some interesting instructions regarding the supply of wood to the navy in a letter from Colbert to an official:

> The purchase of forests to be managed at the expense and under the care of His Majesty could never be advantageous, and there are grounds for astonishment that you should make such a proposition, which is subject to so many inconveniences which are so easy to see that it should not even be thought of.
>
> If there are forests for sale in Provence and Dauphine you must stimulate the merchants to purchase them, and make bargains with them to supply all sorts of wood to the navy at the best price possible. (Cole 1939, 1:350)

The government thus did not offer cartel services to certain basic industries—especially those involved in the production of public goods—but rather acted as a *monopsonist* in these cases, buying lumber and other basic inputs at the best terms available.[21]

Other rent-seeking schemes for the supply of public goods were used in France from medieval times. Competitive bidding by private entrepreneurs for the right to supply armaments, fortifications, canals, and so forth, was a distinct feature of the French fiscal superstructure (Hoselitz 1960; Ekelund and Hébert 1981). Demstez (1968) discusses a modern form of this system. In a rent-seeking context, however, we would not normally expect government to be concerned about efficiency in the production of publicly provided services by following, for example, the dictates of the Demsetz model. Nonetheless, in the case of the French mercantilists the state was a major buyer of certain commodities, and it therefore sought to capture rents in these situations through monopsonistic behavior. Iron and other basic inputs were consequently left unregulated. Moreover, to the extent that this monopsonistic behavior extracted rents from producers of basic commodities that would otherwise have been used for expansion or innovation, a linkage can be established between the rent-seeking theory and the retardation of French industrial growth.

A second reason for luxury-oriented cartels is that raw materials and basic industrial suppliers, located mainly in the countryside, were competitive suppliers of inputs to the cartelized luxury industries located in cities and towns. The crown was receiving regulatory rents from the latter industries, and in principle the crown's receipts would have been the same, regardless of whether the cartel tax was levied at the raw-material or finished-good stage of production. In other words, to cartelize basic suppliers and then force cartelized luxury-goods producers to pay cartel prices for inputs would have been redundant. Regulatory profits would have been the same had monopoly existed at any point in the production chain (Stigler 1951).

Consider the following stylized example.[22] Figure 4.1 illustrates the demand and cost functions for some luxury good—let us say fine furniture. Assume that both wood and furniture producers are constant-cost industries and that MC_F represents all the costs of producing furniture except lumber costs. Clearly, if both industries were competitively organized, assuming fixed proportions between inputs and outputs, the price and quantity of furniture would be OC and Q_c, a price representing the vertical addition of all furniture costs and a quantity determined at the intersection of average costs and the demand (average revenue) curve.

If furniture manufacturers were cartelized, they would face a competitive input price for wood of OA (per unit) and could produce Q_c at a selling price of OC. The cartel, however, acting as a single monopolist, will reduce the output of fine furniture—in the limit to Q_M at price OG. In this manner furniture cartel managers extract $CGHI$ in monopoly rents from consumers of fine furniture.

Consider the situation, however, if fine furniture manufacturers are competitively organized, but the wood input suppliers are organized into a cartel. (As a simplification, wood products are assumed to be used only for fine furniture.) How much would a producers' cartel now charge furniture makers? With full information wood producers would know that the monopoly rate on the final output of fine furniture was OG (per unit). They (the wood producers) would thus restrict the output of wood and charge furniture makers a rate OG, the monopoly price of fine furniture, minus OB, the average cost of producing furniture (less wood costs). The resulting per-unit rate for wood (BG in figure 4.1), when added to the furniture producers' costs (less OB, the cost of lumber), produces an average cost to the competitive furniture makers of OG per unit. A quantity, Q_M, of furniture is produced and sold at the "retail" level; furniture producers earn only "normal" competitive returns; and wood producers exact a cartel-monopoly rent (ultimately from consumers of the final product) of $CGHI$. To the French cartel manager, then, it would have made no difference in terms of regulatory profits where the cartel was located, assuming only that organization, policing, and enforcement costs were identical. This brings us to a third crucial point.

In general, a profitable cartel requires successful enforcement and po-

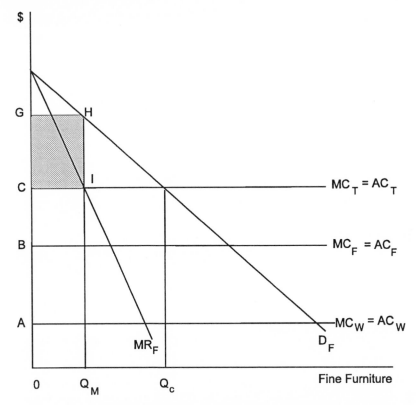

Figure 4.1. The Locus of French Rent Seeking

licing so that competition does not erode profits. But in mercantile France, nonluxury industries tended to be located away from towns, presenting the problem of rural regulatory enforcement. Rural economic regulation was difficult because the opportunities to cheat on cartel arrangements in a vast rural sector were numerous. By contrast regulation of a luxury industry agglomerated in cities was far less costly to the regulatory authorities. Organizational and enforcement costs influenced which industries would be cartelized since basic industry and raw-materials production were simply too costly to organize in this fashion.

Thus, monopsony, efficient rent seeking, and enforcement costs explain the so-called bias toward luxury cartels. Such a regulatory scheme was rational and readily understandable, given the economic incentives facing the French regulatory managers. It seems undeniable that such a pattern of rent seeking would dramatically affect the pattern and pace of French economic development. While we do not wish to become directly involved here in the heated discussion over whether French economic growth "stagnated" over the period or whether France ever went through an Industrial Revolution (see Roehl's [1976] proposed resolution of the matter, for instance), certain features of our cartel interpretation may be very relevant to this question. It seems clear, for instance, that the unwillingness to tamper with profitable cartels retarded the introduction of certain kinds of technology, but that, once they were introduced, the government tended to capture the rewards from innovation.[23] Looms, for example, were invented early in the seventeenth century, but they were principally used for producing silk stockings. When the technology began to be applied to the manufacture of woolen and linen goods, the reaction of the handknitters (an industry Colbert was fostering at the time) was entirely predictable. By decree in 1680 Colbert outlawed the use of looms on any article except silk. But the users of the new technology were powerful enough to pressure the government in 1684 to give them their own protective legislation, contravening the order of 1680. All sorts of offensive and defensive restrictions followed, with the government trying to take rents from both sides (Cole 1943, 177–79). Such activities within cartels must have taken a toll on the profitability of new technology, reducing the rewards for invention and innovation, with predictable effects upon economic growth. Still other kinds of cartels that must have suppressed creativity were Colbert's monopoly creations in the fine arts and academics, for example, in the teaching of arts and sciences (Cole 1939, 1:314–19). Doubtless, then, the cartel theory plays an important role in explaining French economic growth over this period, but a great deal more work is needed to assess this role quantitatively.

THE DEVOLUTION OF MERCANTILE REGULATIONS IN FRANCE

An exact date for the disappearance of mercantilism from France is very elusive, as it is in the case of England or any other mercantile country. Mercantile laws or edicts may be regarded as historical facts, whereas mercantilism as an operative system under which people live is dependent upon whether these laws are enforced or not. Mercantile laws, for instance, remained on the books in England long after they were enforced or enforceable; some remain still. In the present section we seek to present some arguments for the decline of centrally directed, monarchical mercantilism in France up to the Revolution of 1789. We do not attempt to date an absolute end of mercantilism in France, since it may be perfectly reasonable to argue that only the form of rent seeking changed under Napoleon after the Revolution. However, we do argue that two major institutional features of the French economic and political structure give us some insights into how the decline of traditional mercantilism took place. The first, which we discussed briefly in the previous section, deals with an emerging free-trade zone in the countryside, and the second concerns the competition between crown interests and local judicial interests for enforcement rents.

The Countryside as a Free-Trade Zone

Rural industry was a thorn in the side of the French regulatory managers, as it was in the comparable English case. This resulted primarily from the fact that it was not economically efficient for the administrators to attempt to effect a detailed control of rural production. Several aspects of this problem are of interest for the long-run fate of French mercantilism, however.

The original intent of the regulatory managers was quite clearly to cartelize the whole country on the model of the guilds. Heckscher puts the matter as follows:

> The most vital step was the great *règlements* of the time of Colbert. In principle, Colbert followed the line of policy formerly adhered to by the monarchy, in applying the industrial statutes over the whole country. This provision was intended to apply to the *règlements,* to which in theory there were to be no local or other exceptions. For rural industry this signified a theoretical right to exist. The *règlements* assisted the regulation of handicrafts outside the ambit of city politics. To this extent mercantilism took its programme seriously of creating unity within the state as a whole and thus paved the way for new social forces. On the other hand, the system of regulation brought into being rules for the practice of crafts which, while going into every detail of technical production, tried to fit it into a system created by the gilds and adapted to high-grade products. And this was particularly unwelcome to the rural industry of the old type, untrammelled as it was by regulations, arising here and there to cater for the needs of producers and consumers and confined in the main to coarse and simple brands, of which the latter, which counteracted rural industry, was undoubtedly the more important. (1934, 1:206)

As Heckscher senses here, the results of most legislation (or decrees) diverge considerably from the stated objectives. This is standard fare in the implementation of political programs. So it should come as no surprise that the regulatory managers in mercantile France ultimately found it un-economic to extend the guild model to the countryside. As Heckscher observes: "It may safely be said that not only did the attempt to create gilds in rural areas fail almost completely, but the inefficiency of the innumerable regulations diminished in proportion to the distance from towns which had gild organization. There is a sufficiency of official data to confirm this, especially in the 18th century. The rural population obstinately opposed all state encroachment, even to the extent of offering personal violence to agents of the administration" (1934, 1:210).

Other forces besides enforcement costs also pushed for lax enforce-ment of the regulations in the countryside. Perhaps the most important additional pressure came from certain municipal entrepreneurs who wanted to be able to procure the benefits of lower-cost, rural labor. Consider Heckscher (1934, 1:211) on this point: "This was partly due to the already mentioned antagonism between the municipal entrepreneurs and their workers inside the cities, because the state sided with the entrepreneurs in their endeavours to exploit the less 'class-conscious' rural population with its lower wage standards."

What we have, as a result of rising marginal costs of extending and enforcing the system of regulation and as a result of pressures from munici-pal entrepreneurs, is a more or less de facto free-trade zone in the French countryside. As in the English case, this unregulated sector checked the power of the monarchical cartel and created generalized pressures toward competition. However, the rural free-trade area did not have the same sig-nificant effect that it did in England. A possible explanation of this differ-ence is that the French government's greater but not complete police control was able to prevent large-scale but not small-scale developments in rural areas. For example, it was easier to police the production of luxuries, which of necessity had to be sold to a limited number of people and hence had to be retailed in places where they congregated. In general, however, we would agree with Heckscher, who concludes that "the French government did seek to apply the general rules to rural areas but they always had to yield to the impossibility of enforcing them" (1934, 1:212).

Root (1994, 127–33) elaborates on the growing threat to the guild sys-tem of the "informal sector" in the eighteenth century. The guilds initially (in the 1730s) responded to the unregulated sector by lobbying for Crown protection. The Crown provided them with edicts "demanding" new en-forcements, expanded coverage, and new enforcements of regulations re-garding apprenticeships and masterships. But by 1776, the guilds were abolished, at least nominally, through the efforts of individuals such as Turgot and other physiocrats. The "theories" of the Physiocrats were put into action long before they were ever penned owing to changing cost and benefit configuration facing market participants. The cracks in French mercantilism appeared long before in the enforcement problems encountered in attempts to corral the rurally dispersed textile manufactures and in the hostility and resistance that greeted the Crown regulators who tried to impose costly regulation on new entrants and potential entrants (Schaeper 1983, 165–66). Ultimately the Crown recognized the "unregulated sector" although the guilds did not disappear entirely, a result that could be predicted as costs and benefits to Crown support shifted through time.[24]

Parlements and the Decline of Monarchical Mercantilism

We have argued that the form of internal French mercantilism was well structured; it was essentially the cartelization and rent expropriation of industry based upon the guild model of restrictions. But we have oversimplified the process somewhat by failing to note that the power to rent seek at the provincial and local levels was, over the entire mercantile period, the object of competition between two opposing factions, the judiciary or *parlements* in cities and provinces and the crown and its agents—ministers, *contrôleurs,* and *intendants.* (Though the judicial system of France was more complex over the period, we adopt the term *parlements* as a simplification.) Our point is that competition for local administrative control of the cartel enforcement process and other rent-seeking activities led to situations wherein rent seeking was less feasible. Moreover, this competition for rent-seeking power may have been an additional factor precipitating the French Revolution.

First, let us look briefly at the development of the *parlements* prior to and during the high time of French mercantilism. The *parlement* of Paris was organized in 1302, with most others having been formed by mid-sixteenth century (Lough 1960, 119). They were originally established as sovereign courts of the provinces subservient only to the king, and it was through their legal authority that the monarch was able to tame the feudal aristocracy and to interpose sovereign power at the local level (Lough 1960, 128; Lefebvre 1947, 17). All local taxes after 1401, for example, required the approval of the king (Lewis 1968, 260). Judicial *parlements,* therefore, filled the lacuna left by the decline of monarchical subjugation of the feudal aristocracy.

As we have said, French mercantile policy was a massive attempt to cartelize industry along the lines of the guild system. Although we have treated rents from this system monolithically, they were actually of two different kinds: *sanction rents,* arising from the actual recognition, licensing, or franchising of cartels, and *enforcement rents,* those emerging from the day-to-day enforcement of the cartels at the local level. Sanction rents automatically went to the monarch, while enforcement rents could potentially be captured by local enforcement officials, for example, by the *intendants* and the officials of the *parlements.*

In the early French mercantile period the chief enforcers of crown regulations were the sovereign courts, but a number of features made them poor intermediaries in the receipt of enforcement rents for the crown. Boulenger (1967, 90) reports that the "independent nature" of judges, the hereditary (and blatantly venalized) judgeships, and the fact that pay came from local sources all combined to produce reduced levels of rents flowing to the monarch.

The crown therefore established a more reliable method of enforcement in the form of well-paid *intendants,* a system which reached its apogee under Louis XIV. Their efficiency has already been made evident. It is important to note, however, that *intendancies* were originally temporary, covering indeterminate territories, but that later under Colbert the officials became permanently ensconced, with specific geographic areas under their control. Indeed, Colbert's dream of enlarged powers for the central government involved a radical relocation of legal authority: "Colbert sought ever to strengthen the central government and to create unity and order. The power of the governors and of the Assembly of the Clergy was reduced. By firmness and by a judicious distribution of favors, the ancient prerogatives of the *parlements* were limited, and Colbert was delighted to see the humiliation of the legal folk for whom he had an intense dislike. In similar fashion the rights of the municipalities and of the provincial estates were gradually circumscribed. On the other hand the powers and influence of the intendants, and other bourgeois officials dependent directly on the king, were gradually strengthened" (Cole 1939, 1:313). Thus, the *intendants* were originally used to strip power from provincial, local, and *parlement* administrations, and under Louis XIV their powers were effective and vast. But gradually these enforcers became poorer rent collectors for the king and far better collectors for themselves as they engaged in what is now called "opportunistic behavior."

During the *intendants'* "introductory" period, after Louis XII, the *parlements* reacted with great hostility to their incursions. Some of their demands were that the *intendants* be abolished, that no new offices be created, that they have approval power over new taxes, and that a law of habeas corpus be enacted (Chambers 1974, 2:551). These demands, ignored at the time, very clearly did not represent a selfless opposition to absolutism and monarchy. Rather, they represented a means through which local enforcement rents could be captured by local officials themselves.

The *parlements'* fundamental political power was that of registering and remonstrating against the king's edicts, since edicts had no force of law until registered by *parlement*. This "veto power" was not absolute but was at times effective, though under Louis XIV these rights were abrogated, only to be reinstated after his death. (These powers were very influential in the ultimate destruction of French absolutism.)

The *parlements'* (ultimately successful) opposition to the crown was not the product of an attempt to support "the medieval aspects of the system," as Heckscher argued (1934, 1:156), but rather it was the inevitable result of the crown's expropriation of the *parlements'* enforcement rents.[25] During the eighteenth century, the *parlements* struggled with the crown for the privileges of the nobility and for "the exercise of political power in its interest" (Lough 1960, 129), and later in the century the *parlements* pushed for a return of the control of local administration. The attempt to have local powers restored simply reflects a desire to recoup enforcement rents, which, by the 1770s and 1780s, were being captured by the permanently entrenched *intendants,* who had lately become part of the "nobility" (Lefebvre 1947, 17).

We conclude that the conflicts engendered between crown and *parlements* over the power to seek enforcement rents had a great impact upon the decline of the monarchy and upon the manner of the Ancient Regime's end. Monarchical mercantilism in France declined contemporaneously with this struggle, but the struggle was not over the legitimacy of cartel formation or rent seeking. It was simply a contest over the locus of the rent-seeking power and in this respect is very analogous to the decline of English mercantilism.

CONCLUSION

We shall have more to say about the parallels and contrasts between English, French, and Spanish mercantilism in our concluding chapter. For now, we would like to compare our approach to French mercantilism with that of Cole, who along with Heckscher is the major prevailing scholar of French developments.

Cole presents a very misleading epitaph on French mercantilism when he notes that, since French mercantilism "was organized and administered by an officialdom which sought and aimed to serve the interests of the nation as a whole, under a monarch who was definitely not desirous of serving the bourgeois class more than others, it is probably incorrect to think of mercantilism in France as a class instrument or to attempt to interpret it as part of a class struggle, or to hold, even, that it sprang exclusively from the needs of the bourgeoisie, as a class" (1939, 2:554).

Cole thus attempts to counter the Marxian view of mercantilism as a class struggle by claiming that national unity was the basic aim of mercantile policies. But we argue that Cole is correct for the wrong reasons. The Marxist argument is very weak exactly because of the neutral nature of the struggle to acquire the regulatory apparatus: "Capital" does not use the State to exploit "Labor." As we have seen, labor may be just as likely to use the regulatory apparatus to further its own interests (for example, in the Statute of Artificers) at the expense of other interests. At times, one group captures the apparatus; at other times, another. Thus, the rent-seeking theory of economic regulation is not a Marxian theory, but, rather, it permits an explanation of why and when certain interests tend to dominate the mercantile landscape.

Cole, moreover, in his protracted quest to characterize mercantilism as a coherent group of policies, theories, and practices, presents a basically "supply-driven" definition of French mercantilism. "Mercantilism in France means that group of theories, policies, and practices arising from the traditions of the country and the conditions of the time, and upheld and applied by Jean-Baptiste Colbert during his years in office, 1661–83, in his efforts to secure for the nation, and for the king who symbolized it, power, wealth, and prosperity" (Cole 1939, 2:558, italicized in original). In contrasting English and French mercantilism, Cole further serves up the following figure of speech: "the English business interests were a batch of squalling children crying for candy and getting it from a somewhat inattentive mother, Parliament. The French business interests, less vocal though no less childlike, were made to behave in a manner which a more attentive mother— the royal government—believed to be for the best interests of all concerned" (1939, 2:533). We simply wish to emphasize that regulation, policies, and practices in both countries over the mercantile age were driven by very adult supply and demand forces. There is small evidence, further, for interpreting Colbert's massive supply of regulation as oriented to the public interest.[26] Colbert was simply a superb rent seeker for the king and for himself. And moreover, there is a great deal of evidence—much of it provided by Cole himself—that rents were shared with business interests, which demanded and acquired cartel privileges. This system, despite some progress toward economic liberty in the eighteenth century, survived the Revolution and helped determine the course of institutions in nineteenth- and twentieth-century France.

Chapter Five

Internal Regulation in the Spanish Mercantile Economy

There is a tide in the affairs of men,
Which, taken at the flood, leads on to fortune;
Omitted, all the voyage of their life
Is bound in shallows and in miseries.
—Shakespeare, *Julius Caesar*

The "tragedy" of economic developments in the late medieval and early mercantile economy of Spain is an old story. Economic growth, colonial expansion, and a seemingly unlimited horizon characterized Spain prior to the mid-sixteenth century. After that time the death grip of stagnation, including a Malthusian population crisis, took hold of the economy, lasting until well into the modern period. While there are certain similarities in the experience of France, the Spanish economy's plunge into stagnation and decline over the period is unique in that it was a clear reversal of developments in England, the Netherlands, and France. If the terms "sluggish growth" are aptly applied to France after the Revolution, "total stagnation" or "decline" are not.

The overwhelming analytical response of economists and economic historians to this unhappy but acknowledged state of affairs in mercantile Spain has been "doctrinal" in nature. That tradition, certainly in English language sources, has been fueled in this century with important "discoveries" of prescient mercantile observers on the scene from Gerónimo de Uztáriz to Sancho de Moncada (Castillo 1980), with special emphasis on the monetary difficulties and problems inherent to a "parasitic culture"

(Perrotta 1993). Spanish Enlightenment thinkers have not been neglected within this literature either. They followed a doctrinal path similar to the "liberal" precursors of Adam Smith in England and the physiocrats in France. Much in this literature, especially in the latter category, is informative and interesting.[1]

This chapter, as those on England and France preceding it, adopts a neoinstitutional approach to the medieval-mercantile economy of Spain. In particular and also in common with our earlier treatments, we focus on internal institutions with only peripheral attention paid to some larger and important questions such as those related to trade and colonization. Our attention is drawn to the regulation of internal commerce by the Crown through the legal and political system of medieval-mercantile Spain. A chief, though not the only, vehicle for internal redistribution was the Mesta, a cartelized guild of sheepherders engaged in producing high-quality Merino wool from the seasonal migration of sheep—a system called *transhumance*. This guild became the concerted object of Crown rent seeking from the thirteenth through the eighteenth centuries with, as we will see, varying degrees of success. This chapter focuses on the structure and conduct of the Mesta and on the property-rights alterations that occurred in the wake of actively competing interests affecting it.

The Mesta as a key institution affecting Spanish economic development is clearly anticipated in recent literature dealing with Spanish economic development. Indeed, our analysis of the Mesta rests on these accounts as well as those of the historians.[2] North and Thomas (1973, 85–86, 128–29) and North (1981, 150–52) suggest the key position of the Mesta as a "cash cow" of Spanish monarchs, especially of Ferdinand and Isabella and their successors. They also indicate that the skewing of rights in the direction of short-term property rights in *transhumance* and against longer-term sedentary agricultural interests was a significant and negative factor in explaining economic growth in Spain after the sixteenth century. Nugent and Sanchez (1989) provide a dissenting view by concluding that, in the absence of a low-cost means of fencing, monarchical control of the Mesta through edict and regulation contributed to economic efficiency in resource allocation over time.[3]

We have no fundamental disagreement with either of these general approaches to internal regulation or to the institutional implications it had within Spain. However, we believe that the received interpretation should be supplemented to emphasize some of the determinants of the *process* of property rights *alterations* in herding and agricultural interests over the centuries of the Mesta.[4] In our view the interplay of property rights, political expressions of rent-seeking behavior, and exogenous institutional change such as population growth and changing international demands for wool are all critical elements in understanding the role of the cartel in Spanish economic development. Anecdotal and empirical evidence (Ruiz Martín 1974; Le Flem 1972) strongly suggests the existence of an ever-changing characterization of property rights between the thirteenth and eighteenth centuries in Spain—a perspective that, of course, cannot be captured in a static model.

Our discussion opens with a brief discussion of general economic institutions and developments in Spain over the period we consider. We then turn to the structure of the Mesta and to its primary functions within the context of the political economy of Spain. Next we attempt to explain *how* the Mesta functioned as a monopoly and how and why it assumed varying importance to the Spanish crown as the bargaining strength, property rights of parties to distribution, opportunistic behavior, and rent flows changed through time. In a concluding section of the chapter we comment upon the status of our understanding of institutional change and Spanish economic development.

GENERAL DEVELOPMENTS
IN THE SPANISH ECONOMY

Early institutional developments undoubtedly explain much of the course of later developments in the Spanish economy—the period of unmatched growth and prosperity among European nations up to the time of the Catholic monarchs as well as the tragic decline afterwards. The Roman rule of Spain began in the third century B.C. (when the Carthaginians lost their Spanish possessions), and many later institutions, particularly tax institutions, find their origins over the period. High tributes of many kinds were required, including a general property tax, land and inheritance taxes, excise taxes on goods sold (the *alcabala*), road tolls and customs duties on both imports and exports (*portoría*). The Germanic tribes, occupying the Peninsula for several centuries prior to the Moors in the eighth century, found a denuded and depopulated country—owing principally to the tax exactions of the Romans. While the Visigoths attempted to address "externality" problems related to land division between grazing and sedentary agriculture and to the harvesting of trees, they also implanted a "feudal system" of land enclosures and a hereditary system of nobility based on land ownership (Castillo 1980, 6–7).

A period of high prosperity was opened up and lasted over the entire Middle Ages—from the eighth century through the monarchy of Ferdinand and Isabella—by the occupation of Spain by the Arabian Moslem tribes (later waves were African in origin). Sober and industrious, the Moors husbanded and developed natural and human resources by most accounts, including those in agriculture, manufactures, and commerce. New plants and trees were introduced, irrigation systems were developed, herding was carried on in a manner consistent with agriculture, mining flourished, and the weaving of silk (introduced by the Moors from the Orient) and wool was celebrated all over the Western world. An active international trade developed, contributing to the prosperity as did the Moorish provision of "infrastructure." Of greatest importance for the future development of Europe was the propagation and defense of learning, especially relating to mathematics, science, and architecture, by the Moors.

Perhaps the capstone of the Moorish occupation was the general religious tolerance of both Christians and Jews and the relatively low import tariffs and mild restrictions on trade (customs duties were charged for revenue purposes only). This put Spanish industry and trade at an advantage over the prohibitive systems of the Hanse and the Italian city-states. The Jews were free to pursue financial innovations and to become the most successful businessmen of medieval Spain.

Internal taxes, such as progressive head taxes, land taxes, and discriminatory taxes on profits (Jews and Christians paid higher percentages on profits than Moslems) and on towns (those resisting Moorish rule paid more), footed the bill for public goods. However, taxes were relatively low—certainly as a function of GDP and economic activity—throughout the Moors' tenure in Spain.

Three institutional developments, perhaps more than others, contributed to the "tragedy" of the mercantile and postmercantile periods: the reconquest or "Christianization" of Spain, the development of new and expanded taxing institutions, and the recognition of the rent-seeking possibilities in domestic regulation. While each of these elements deserves book-length treatment in any analysis of institutional underpinnings of mercantile Spain, our focus is reduced to a thumbnail sketch of the first two and an elaboration of the third in the remainder of the chapter.

The *theocratic elements* of the Christian reconquest are fairly well known and understood. The monopolistic Roman Catholic Church was attempting to spread its dominance around the world, but especially throughout Europe. Part of that dominance was the suppression of "heresy" and any rival sellers of the Church's primary product, "assurance of eternal salvation." Heretics included Moors and Jews. Relatively free commerce and exchange along with low taxes left with the progressive purges of the Moors. Slavery returned and manual labor and domestic service were the slaves' principal occupations (Castillo 1980, 13). Henceforth, such labor was considered beneath the dignity of free men and the exclusive province of slaves or of the lower classes. Territory reconquered from the Moors was divided between Christian princes, nobles, and the Church (including ecclesiastical Church "orders" such as Franciscans and Dominicans). The feudal system of land restrictions predominated, agriculture languished and was the almost exclusive pursuit of the serf as did industry and the industrial arts where personal freedom (nascent laissez-faire?) was nipped in the bud. Price and wage controls on agricultural goods and in labor markets, invoked by Christian lords and civil authorities, were common. Canonist teachings on usury, "just price," regulation "for the public good," and generalized support of the exclusionary practices of guilds, created as much drag on institutions facilitating trade as they did in other parts of Europe.[5]

Some seventeenth-century estimates, such as those of Sancho De Moncada, place the number of clergy, ecclesiastics, and hermits as high as one-fourth or one-third of the total population at various times over the Christian period. The religious bigotry and rent-seeking by the Roman Catholic Church produced a theocratic stultification of Spanish society and especially severe penalties for the Jews.[6] An edict of expulsion was issued on March 31, 1492, giving Jews until the end of July to convert, emigrate, or be put to death. Efforts by Ferdinand and Isabella's Jewish finance minister, Isaac Abrabanel, to have the edict rescinded proved futile and, at this time alone, 50,000 Jews converted to Christianity (*conversos*) and 150,000 left.[7] (Some returned later to "convert.") The latter development gutted the financial, medical and scientific sectors of the Spanish economy, over the protests of certain areas and cities of Spain such as Seville, Toledo, and Barcelona. It is difficult to find anything but negative factors in the banishment of Moorish and Jewish human capital from Spain—a movement that was all but complete by the late fifteenth century. The social and cultural repressions of the Inquisition lasted through the first third of the *nineteenth* century.

A second major institutional factor over the period of Christian reconquest was the growth and development of a *system of taxation and protection* that would have been the envy of any French bureaucrat. Catholic monarchs extended and greatly expanded the system of taxation established under the Moors. Many of the omnipresent taxes in various regions of the country were imposed for particular purposes and "self-destructed" in the Gladstonian manner. Others were particularly onerous and destructive of industry.

Consider only a sample of the taxes from the labyrinthine structure of medieval-mercantile Spain. Some taxes (for example, the *facendera*) was a personal tax requiring physical labor on roads and bridges (similar to the *courvées* of France). The *montazgo*, the importance of which will be discussed later in the chapter, was a tax paid by migratory flock owners to pass into seasonal grazing lands. Taxes were levied by the Papacy and by civil authorities to finance the ongoing wars against the Moors. Poll taxes, consumption taxes, taxes on iron and salt works, land taxes paid by the towns under the Catholic monarchs, taxes paid by towns where "murder" was committed, manor taxes on the death of vassals, taxes paid by towns during royal weddings were all revenue-producing devices at local, regional, and national levels. Some of the most important and destructive taxes were, however, the road tolls (*portazgos*), the taxes on Moors and Jews (*capitación de los moros y judíos*), and the extremely regressive and destructive general sales tax—the *alcabala*. Customs duties (*aduanas*), including both import and export tariffs, were always a lucrative "royal prerogative" (as they were in England and France). Opportunistic behavior riddled the collection of such taxes. Castillo (1980, 58) reports that the trade-restricting *alcabala* required more than 150,000 collectors and "tax farmers," which greatly restricted the amount of revenue to the crown along with the impediment to exchange. Class warfare, an incredible bureaucracy at regional and, later, at the national levels, a death grip on trade and exchange increasingly characterized the Spanish economy.

It is impossible to present or analyze these complex developments and their interrelationships in any brief treatment. Many other factors are critical to the story. However, it is important to note that, in the area of taxation, institutional constraints on the crown were either weak or ineffective, certainly when compared to the English Parliament's early grip on monarchical taxation. It is important to remember that in England wool merchants "purchased" legislative influence as a quid pro quo for submitting to crown taxation (Power 1941). These developments were not repeated in

Spain. North (1990) reports that the Cortes (legislative body) in Aragón were somewhat effective, representing the interests of merchants and playing an important role in civil administration. This was in contrast to the Cortes of Castile, which were seldom called, but which were embroiled in internal baronial strife and in competition with both crown interests and church interests. According to North (1990, 114), Isabella took control within fifteen years of unification and, while the Cortes exhibited some influence, "there was a centralized monarchy and bureaucracy in Castile, and it was Castile that defined the institutional evolution of . . . [Spain]." In many cases, the Cortes were merely a replication of the interests of the crown and its aristocratic supporters. Representative government in the form of an effective legislative body was, therefore, much less significant in forming a constraint to the spending proclivities of the monarchs in Spain and France. This factor, perhaps more than any other, is central to understanding the institutional evolution of the Spanish economy and its status over the mercantile era.

POLITICAL ECONOMY AND THE MESTA

A major ingredient in understanding the institutional structure of the Spanish economy—in addition to theocracy, taxing institutions, monetary and other elements—was the discovery of the revenue possibilities that inured to monopolization of domestic markets by the Catholic monarchs. A key industry, and the primary topic of this chapter, was the Mesta, a cartelized guild of sheepherders engaged in producing high-quality Merino wool from the seasonal migration of sheep *(serranos transhumantes).*[8] The Mesta (circa 1273–1836) provides an especially interesting object of study in the context of public choice and organization theory. In contrast to the typical objects of internal monopolization and rent seeking by English and French monarchs (for example, tapestries and other "luxury" consumptions in France, playing cards in England), Spanish monarchs directed major efforts toward a *nonsedentary* product (Merino wool) in a *geographically dispersed* pastoral setting.[9] Constant battles between rent-seeking interests over legal jurisdictions, property rights, tax jurisdictions, and the direction of wealth distribution occurred throughout the life of the Mesta. These interests included local organizational units, local and regional Church interests and episcopates, sedentary agricultural interests, the geographically dispersed and mobile Mesta and its sheepherder members, and crown interests of all sorts.

Industrial Organization of the Mesta

The *Honrado Concejo de la Mesta* was chartered on a national basis in Castile by Alfonso el Sabio (Alfonso X) in 1273. The features of the national Mesta were based on those of various local mestas that have evolved over time. One of the central functions of the local mestas was the allocation or assignment of stray sheep and the disposal of funds from the unassigned strays (called *mesteños*). It was, in part, these strays to which the national Mesta laid claim. The national Mesta—the name of the unified national cartel organization—was essentially represented by the organizational features described in figure 5.1.

The object of the Mesta's activities and the source of its earnings was a geographically dispersed Merino shepherding industry (Laguna Sanz 1986). The Merino sheep was developed from breeding stocks imported from North Africa and not raised elsewhere during the early centuries of the cartel. Migrations of the adaptable Merino sheep took place semi-annually,

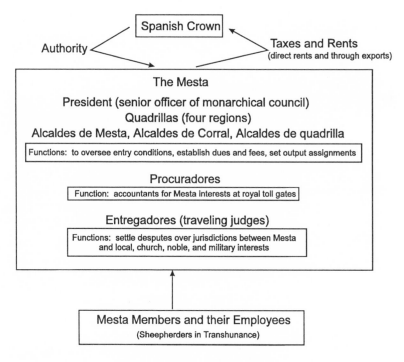

Figure 5.1. The Mesta Organization

which helped to produce kinky wool of superior quality through use of preferred grazing patterns. Clearly, the migration was necessary to produce wool of high quality. Also, the wool of the *transhumantes* was favored by Spanish aristocrats and in the import trade as compared to the local *churro* or soft-curled wool produced in sedentary conditions.[10] Such luxury or quality productions, of low-demand elasticity both within Spain and in the international market, were the natural "monopolies of choice" for rent seekers and monarchs in most emerging nation states. In terms of the Spanish agrarian economy of the thirteenth and fourteenth centuries, this meant that wool industry development (for export and as a tax source from both domestic and international sales) was to become a crown-favored activity in preference to many other agricultural interests in the ensuing centuries.

The national Mesta's functions were in part determined by the migratory nature of the herdsmen (and herdswomen, since there was no sexual discrimination at the basic levels of production). These functions were also constrained by the political and property rights structures the Mesta encountered and wished to modify or supersede. One of its primary tasks was to acquire sheep highways (or *cañadas*) for the migratory flocks. Included in this function was procurement of en route and temporary grazing rights to spring and winter quarters, protection against banditry, and protection against local tax collectors in towns and against church interferences.[11] Most important, the Mesta established facilities for shearing and exclusive marketing of the wool, collected "dues" from Mesta members, and monitored and controlled sheep supply by branding and registering all animals at border crossings. Last but not least, members of the national Mesta (numbering as many as two hundred at times) repatriated, through taxes and other means, a portion of the rents earned from the monopoly to monarchs, whose protection and approbation permitted the Mesta to exist with legal status.

Rent-Seeking Officials and Practices

The industrial organization of the Mesta was intertwined with that of various institutions in the rest of the Spanish economy. The national *cañadas* were institutionalized by the crown into three royal routes, the western, central, and eastern.[12] Extensive efforts to deter encroachment on rights of way by owners of sedentary flocks and uncontrolled supply were characteristic of the migrant pattern. Branding and registering sheep at counting stations along the way supported the deterrent function. Further, international competition in Merino wool production was prevented by absolute prohibitions on sheep export.

Continuous jurisdictional disputes arose after the national cartel organization took over the profitable role of stray sheep disposal in the municipalities. Towns had long provided the privilege. The national Mesta appointed officers with administrative power called *alcaldes de Mesta, alcaldes de corral,* and *alcaldes de quadrilla* to serve in the four *quadrillas*—districts with jurisdiction over all strays found in the migratory herds (Klein 1964, 13). These *alcaldes* (see figure 5.1) were the rule-makers of the monopoly, who set entry conditions, imposed district output assignments set at semi-annual national Mesta meetings, and established quality control.

Conflicts also arose between the Mesta and its interests and the lords who had royal seignorial privileges to revenues from stray sheep, along with the Roman Church and military orders, which had similar privileges. Successful cartel implementation thus required a legal arbiter and an enforcement arm. The nature of *transhumance* and the "road system" required the services of an *entregador,* or traveling judge, with extensive powers of adjudication and enforcement.[13] One of the main functions of the *entregadores* was to protect the rights of way, but they held enforcement rights over essentially all facets of the migratory industry.[14] As in the case of English urban guild regulations and Colbert's industrial regulations, the details relating to sheep production were tailored to restrict the various methods that Mesta members could find to cheat or expand output illegally.

Fiscal rules of the Mesta required accountants. Operating dues were assessed by the national Mesta assembly to sheep owners (who often hired herdsmen or herdswomen to tend their flocks) in proportion to the number of sheep owned. This number was monitored by *procuradores* placed at royal toll gates, a convenient control device for the entire industry. Clipping stations and wool warehouses (called *lonjas*) were located at convenient ports along the roads. The great fairs, such as the one at Medina del Campo, were used as central marketing points to facilitate domestic and export sale and distribution of the wool.[15] The *entregadores, alcaldes de Mesta,* and the *procuradores* were the nucleus of government in promoting the interests of the Mesta monopoly, and they were apparently paid well over the entire course of cartel operations (Le Flem 1972, 62–63). The functions of these officials would entail the procurement of privileges and exemptions at all levels in the national economy of medieval-mercantile Spain.

The Mesta as a Rent-Seeking Process

Economic rents—those above the opportunity cost of quasi-fixed resources—are fully capitalized, that is, "competed away" through entry and
exit in *static* competitive equilibrium. This useful concept hides the dynamic rent-seeking activity inherent in the system over time. The introduction of monopoly, as in the form of monarchical grants of property rights,
raises the possibility that rents are not simply pure transfers (as we discussed in chapter 2). Scarce resources may be expended as rent-seeking
dissipations to capture a pure transfer, and the value of these resources
must be added to the standard welfare-triangle (deadweight) loss associated with monopoly in order to properly calculate the social costs of state-
created monopolies or artificial scarcities.[16]

Questions posed by the process of rent seeking during the Spanish
medieval-mercantile era are both positive and normative. From the perspective of positive analysis, our evaluation seeks to discover the actual factors determining the presence, nature, and impact of rent-seeking activities
in the Spanish economy. Normatively, we wish to gauge the tentative impact of such activities on economic growth or on the possibility of significant retardation of the actual social product when compared with its potential
over time.

In order better to visualize this process, consider the Mesta in simplified terms as a loosely integrated monopoly institution where Mesta and
crown-aristocratic interests capture larger or smaller portions of upstream
rents using carefully placed output restrictions on exported wool.[17] In figure 5.2, rents would be created in the amount *PABT* through successful
monopolization of *transhumance* in the Spanish economy. Assuming, for
convenience, that marginal costs of sheep production and those related to
policing, enforcement, and marketing are constant (and labeled Marketing
[Mesta] in figure 5.2), export price—joint profit-maximizing price—would
equal *OP.* This price would depend upon demand elasticity and upon the
marginal costs of Mesta operations. Given that positive costs of managing
the cartel (*MM'* in figure 5.2) must be added to marketing costs under
competitive conditions (*OM'*), true competitive output would be represented by *Qc* rather than *Qm'* in figure 5.2.

The size of Mesta rents (static rents) under any *given* set of institutional
constraints on *property rights* and enforcement costs, therefore, depended
upon the interplay between the size and elasticity of export demand, domestic production costs, and the costs of Mesta operation. At a maximum,
rents in the amount *PABT* were available to be split between the Spanish

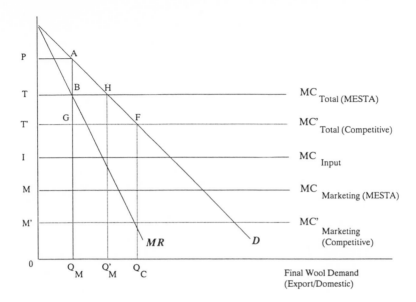

Figure 5.2. The Mesta Monopoly

crown (through tax collections, "loans," and subsidies from the Mesta organization) and monopoly interests within the Mesta cartel. The existence
of the rents was dependent on the ability of the cartel to restrict output and
on the extent of foreign demand for Spanish wool. The actual nature of the
rent split at any one time depended upon relative bargaining power of the
crown and the cartel operators, and upon the temporally determined structure of property rights of crown Mesta interests vis-à-vis regional and local
interests (towns, monasteries, the *ganadería estantes,* or sedentary estate
herds and agricultural interests).[18]

Policing and upstream enforcement costs also altered the size of the
rents created through time. Deadweight social losses, moreover, were produced by the establishment and conduct of the monopoly cartel. If monopoly operations are considered as costs of producing and marketing the
product that would be avoided under competitive conditions, deadweight
losses would be represented by triangle *AGF* (rather than *ABH*) in figure
5.2. In addition to these losses, however, the resource costs of developing
and maintaining the monopoly through time must be added to the traditional social loss. Intertemporal institutional rigidities, exogenous "shocks,"
and changing cost-benefit configurations emerged, which clearly changed
rent-seeking costs to participants in Mesta functioning, as reported in anecdotal historical evidence (Ruiz Martín 1974). From a longer-run perspec-

tive, opportunity costs to the Spanish economy in terms of foregone encouragement of alternative productions may have meant that the Mesta
monopoly had a significant impact on Spanish economic development.

Dynamics of Mesta Functioning

These dynamic elements of Mesta operations and monopoly rent production may be more finely delineated with the simple observation that
property rights are not fixed over time. Some given set of property rights
implies a set of costs and benefits and some form and direction of economizing behavior. Shifts in property rights will take place owing to the changing strengths of interest groups at both production and political levels
engaging in such economizing behavior. These shifting production and
political influences were able to skew property rights over time in sedentary agriculture and in the moveable sheep industry.[19] Factors that change
relative demands for the exported wool and the domestically consumed
foodstuffs, for example, created new configurations of property rights and
rent-seeking interests at the basic food-production/migratory-herding levels. Population changes in the Spanish economy (which were very significant in explaining historical directions of institutions) as well as changing
import elasticities in Spanish wool importing countries are examples of
such factors.

This admittedly highly stylized scenario of property-related institutions
is summarized in figure 5.3. Competing interests determine the property
rights system as it evolved over time. At the basic level of conflict are the
agricultural interests—desiring stable, secure, and enforceable property rights
in *sedentary* herding and farming—and Mesta interests. The Mesta found
primary political representation from the Spanish crown, although, as we
shall see, rent division between Mesta and crown interests became a question after the Mesta was established. The crown generally regarded the
Mesta as a "cash cow," which, in return for secure geographic and other
property rights, was a lucrative source of revenues.

The principal, but not the exclusive, political representation of Spanish
separatist, decentralized, and traditional agricultural interests were the Cortes
of the various regions of Spain—legislative bodies of varying powers and
influence through time.[20] (Regional and local governmental units and ecclesiastical interests were also supporters of sedentary agriculture). The Cortes
and court systems were, in effect, adjudicatory institutions between crown-
Mesta interests, on the one hand, and sedentary agricultural and church

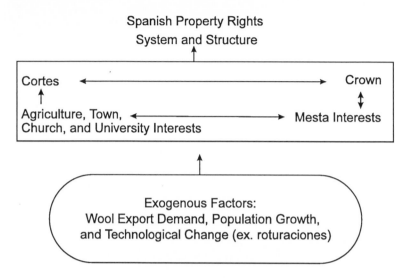

Figure 5.3. *Competing Interests*

interests on the other (monasteries were also important production units, especially in sedentary herding). Cortes and court interventions on the part of *large* agricultural interests were very much in evidence between the thirteenth and eighteenth centuries, as an interest group-public choice model would predict.

We argue that it was the *relative* strengths of these competing interests that vivified and explained property rights shifts and structural economic change in Spain over the period of Mesta cartel functioning. At times the Crown could grant *secure* property rights to Mesta interests, but not at others. At times, the Cortes could successfully intervene in the rent-seeking/property-rights granting activities of the crown and Mesta, but not at others. Part, perhaps a large part, of the prosperity and decline of both sedentary agriculture and the Mesta as well as the fortunes of the Spanish economy itself ultimately is to be explained within the process. In a "moving equilibrium," such institutional changes as population growth, degree of urbanization, wool and other exports and their prices, religious repressions, colonial discoveries and their monetary implications, agricultural technology and relative power divisions between crown and Cortes combine to explain the distribution of property rights at any given point in time. In the remainder of this chapter we focus on aspects of the rent-seeking competitions through which relative property rights were determined and on evidence of the ever-changing nature of the process.

THE RENT EXTRACTION PROCESS

Crown sponsorship of the Mesta cartel was little different from modern input cartels. The Spanish crown used the Mesta as its agent to collect rents from shepherds, towns, local and regional nobility, church interests, and both domestic and international wool purchasers. The appeal to maintaining the "quality of the product," made by Mesta officials and the crown, is a familiar ploy to justify monopoly.[21] In a world of high transactions and information costs, especially in terms of communications and transportation, Mesta cartel management required highly elaborate enforcement mechanisms, some of which we discussed above. This meant that property rights alterations, sometimes radical in nature, accompanied the establishment and maintenance of the Mesta.

Rent Transfers, Taxes, and Property Rights: An Overview

Sheep taxes reach back at least to Roman times, and they were levied in Spain by the Moors at local levels. They were retained at the local level after Christian knights fought and successfully regained large parts of Spain over the thirteenth century. The Muslim strongholds of the island of Majorca and the towns of Córdoba, Valencia, Murcia, and Seville were ultimately returned to Christian domination over the early part of the thirteenth century, although firm control of the Straits of Gibraltar was not achieved until 1344 and Granada was in Muslim hands until 1492. Klein (1964, 256) in his account of the origin of crown rights to these taxes, relates how Alfonso X got a *servicio de ganados* tax on migratory flocks to help replenish depleted treasury from reconquests of the previous fifty years. Spoils of victory had to be shared with the military orders, loyal towns, and nobles. The Cortes granted the extraordinary subsidy at the same time the sheep owners were organizing the national Mesta under the patronage of the King. This sheep tax became a "normal" source of revenue to the Castillian monarchs and did not require renewal by a special vote of the Cortes (as did the *ordinary servicio*, or general sales tax described earlier in the chapter).

The official charter of the Mesta guild of 1273 does not mention taxes or any other compensation, but Klein thought it clear that it was the quid pro quo for crown approbation and protection of the guild monopoly. The primary interest of the regional Cortes, including the Castillian Cortes, was in protecting the local nonmigratory *estantes* from taxes, but they were often unsuccessful. Also the crown was at times constrained by traditional (feudal) regional interests and by pressures from church episcopates. Naturally, the primary interests of the monarch and his royal council and chancellery—so long as expropriable rents were high enough to justify legal and enforcement support of the Mesta monopoly—were in defending and defining the rights of the national Mesta against all claims and challenges to the rents. According to Klein (1964, 260), "from about 1350 onward the accepted definition of a *transhumante* or a Mesta member became 'one who paid the royal *servicio*.'"

The original *servicio de ganados* soon was expanded as the power of the central government grew. Specifically, the crown expropriated the sheep tolls of the towns under Castillian control (the *montazgos*) and called (in 1343) the merged tax the *servicio de montazgos,* taxes levied on sheepherders as they entered seasonal grazing lands, which became the combined royal income from migratory sheep. Between 1350 and 1390 the towns tried to revive the *montazgos* and the period was characterized by a good deal of bartering between crown and towns for tax privileges with political and military support in the balance. Powerful cities and monasteries bought back these lost *montazgo* rights. Reassertion of separatism during the second half of the fourteenth century rolled back much of Alfonso XI's rent-seeking attempts to build up the *servicio y montazgo*. Civil disorders caused crown sheep tax revenues to decline over this period. This development clearly had implications for the security of local property rights in sedentary agriculture even in a period of civil unrest.[22]

There was a general reassertion by crown interests in the *servicio y montazgos* in the fifteenth century. In 1442 Alvaro promulgated reassertion and put down rivals in the nobility, most of whom were either important members of the Mesta or the possessors of long-cherished sheep tax privileges of their own. Alvaro did it by "discretely placed leases of the servicio" and a "few ostentatious bestowals of exemptions from the tax upon certain grandees and rich monasteries whose support was highly useful to him" (Klein 1964, 264–65). Under the weakling Henry IV (1454–74) title to the royal *servicio* went to two sordid courtiers (the Count of Ledesma and the Marquis of Villena), and the tax was farmed and recodified on a far more complex scale. Rent-seeking attempts by the crown and tax farmers took the form of "selling exemptions."[23] There was a major breakdown of control and enforcement of the Mesta cartel over this period. The Catholic clergy claimed exemption from assessments of the sheep *servicio*, which threatened the *servicio y montazgo* since the monasteries were among the largest sheep owners of Castile. Lawlessness and disorder wrought havoc with Mesta flocks—"robber barons" accosted the shepherds and demanded payments with sheep tax "leases" from venal tax farmers (such as Ledesma and Villena). As in the reassertion of local and other interests in the earlier period, the power shift must have had implications for the security of property rights of sedentary agriculture vis-à-vis the migratory sheep industry.

The Heyday of Mesta Functioning

Ferdinand and Isabella, recognizing the possibilities in the Mesta cartel, took control of royal rent seeking in the Castillian economy with much gusto. Indeed, their reign corresponded to the only real apogee of Mesta functioning. The Catholic monarchs soon regained possession of the whole of the *servicio y montazgo* and again made it a royal tax (*derecho real*). Upstream cheating was severely reduced as was the number of official toll gates at which the tax could be collected. They came down hard on fraudulent collectors. In 1480 Ferdinand and Isabella called the Cortes of Toledo and demanded repatriation of *juros* (30,000,000 *maravedíes*)—lost income from families who had illegally collected taxes. Each town, church, or private individual claiming a right to a split of the *servicio* had to produce evidence of a claim within ninety days. Anyone collecting taxes outside the eleven toll gates without authorization would be put to death. Under Ferdinand and Isabella, town interests and those of private persons were attacked and suppressed by invoking old and severely restrictive laws and regulations, but there was a very rapid rise in royal income (Klein 1964, 274 n. 2) from the Mesta cartel.

Ferdinand and Isabella, squeezing the cartel with new enforcement devices and with the suppression of agricultural property rights, set the stage for the sixteenth-century operations of the Hapsburgs. During the Austrian (Hapsburg) monarchy (1516–1700) and later under the Bourbons (1700–1836), the Mesta was even more severely pressed to pay for the world empire Spain was trying to build and for the maladministration of the financing required for such adventures (García Martín 1988). The well-known Spanish hegemony over Europe opened the century with huge increases in revenues, from the Italian possessions (Naples and Milan) and from the Low Countries (the Netherlands) until their independence later in the century. Colonies were acquired right and left, with the largest of them, Portugal, annexed in 1580. Huge expenditures, however, accompanied the expansions with the maintenance of the premier army and navy of Europe over the sixteenth century (under Charles V and Philip II). New World treasure hunts were less and less fruitful in producing gold and silver. Despite new crown efforts to extract rents in the form of monopoly privileges and ever-higher rates of taxation, as North observes (1981, 151), bankruptcies occurred in 1557, 1575, 1596, 1607, 1627, and 1647. The Bourbon Kings invoked a policy of selling *juros* "or annuities" to nobles and to the church based on alienated future crown revenues on the sheep taxes. Significantly, new toll stations were set up to increase exactions. Sheep "taxes" became less of a *servicio* and more of a direct subsidy to the crown. (At times over this period, the Mesta even turned to the Cortes for redress, although the Cortes continued to support the *estantes* and to protect the tradition of Spanish separatism.)

Under the Hapsburgs, Mesta rent payments to the crown rose in 1538 to more than three times what they had been in 1513 as a percentage of Mesta revenues (Le Flem 1972, 83). In 1518 Charles demanded a "loan" from the Mesta of 3,500,000 *maravedíes* and the following year demanded a direct subsidy, confiscating Mesta revenue records. Despite cartel protests, the Mesta acceded to these demands by invoking extra assessments on the flocks at the *puertos*. Amidst general financial incompetence, the Hapsburgs turned Mesta collections over to the Fuggers (a family of bankers) and further alienated future revenues with short-term leases. These events created new insecurities in property rights assignments for the Mesta in the seventeenth century.

Mesta-Crown Conflicts over Rents: Some Empirical Evidence

The historical record and virtually all other anecdotal evidence on the Mesta suggests that—at least over many segments of its history—the respective interests of the crown and the Mesta were in serious conflict. Other things equal, the higher the rents extracted from the cartel by the crown for any year, the lower the returns to the central administration of the cartel and to members of the cartel at all levels. The incentive of cartel members and directors would be to "hide" profits in order to avoid future (continuing and extraordinary) demands on its returns. These incentives would have been especially operative under the intense pressure created by the Hapsburgs over the sixteenth century.

The excellent statistical work of Jean Paul Le Flem on the budget and accounting records of the Mesta between 1510 and 1709 (between 1569–82 and 1664–83) are revealing as regards the rent-seeking and rent-division

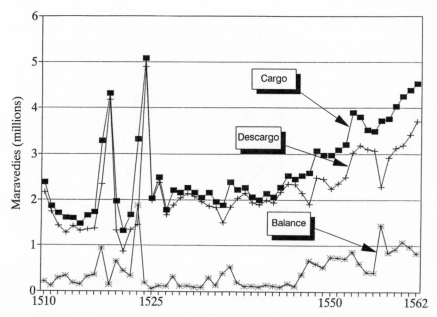

Figure 5.4. Receipts and Expenses of the Mesta, 1510–62

process. Le Flem's data on the receipts (*cargo*), expenses (*descargo*), and
the difference (*balance*) are depicted graphically in figure 5.4 for a portion
of the period (1510–62).

As Le Flem's data suggest, the official fortunes of the Mesta cartel varied widely over the sixteenth and seventeenth centuries. Mesta receipts
were a function of many variables: strength of the legal enforcement of its
interests (property rights enforcement), market power, wool export demands, and population growth. In general, however, expenses were the
"control variables" of the cartel. At times the Mesta assumed the role of
fiscal agent of the crown, but at others the cartel was subjected to revenue
seizures by the crown. From the beginning of the sixteenth century, new
pressures were placed on the Mesta. These took the form of more rigorous
enforcement and collection of the *servicio y montazgo*, on the legal status of
the *entregador* judges within the Mesta vis-à-vis crown courts (Klein 1964,
113), and on the requirements of loans and subsidies from the profits of the
cartel. A principal means through which the Mesta could protect itself from
such confiscations was to inflate its expenses in response to higher taxes or
enforcement and other extractions by the crown. This could be accomplished through a number of means: (a) within the cartel by bureaucratic
expansion of personnel; (b) by shirking and/or self-imposed reductions in

productivity or cheating on the part of cartel members, or (c) by "doctoring" the books.

Fortunately Le Flem's statistical research permits an informal test of the rent division conflict between Mesta and crown. Le Flem provides, in *maravedíes,* the amount of the *servicio y montazgo* actually *withdrawn* by the crown from the cartel between 1510 and 1562 (Le Flem 1972, Appendix 5B, p. 83). While the *servicio y montazgo* was nominally and in part (the *servicio*) a "head tax" on sheep, the crown's rent extraction from the Mesta would vary with the degree of legal enforcement, with the prevention of shirking, with the number of toll stations, and with extra, direct assessments ("loans and subsidies") from the Mesta treasury. Indeed, evidence from Klein (1964, 227–53) tells of a growing autocracy over the period with attempted crown dominance over the judicial arm of the Mesta and the legal powers of town officials. Increasingly, moreover, legal uncertainties were built into Mesta interests (Klein 1964, 235), as crown agents played town-agriculture interests against the Mesta in order to maximize revenues.

If the Mesta cartel was attempting to protect itself from new crown pressures for rents, accounting costs would be inflated in response to higher tax values of the *servicio y montazgo* both contemporaneously and in view of past Crown behavior. A simple model of such rent division may be expressed in equation [1]:

$$E_t = a_1 + a_2 SM_t + a_3 SM_{t-1} + \ldots + a_n SM_{t-n} + TIME[1]$$

where E are reported Mesta expenses, SM is the *servicio y montazgo* and $TIME$ (year + 1) is a time trend. In this distributed lag model, the value of a_2 is expected to be positive and, if expenses are adjusted consistently to the levels of past taxation, the coefficients are expected to be of alternating signs. The time trend tests for whether a common trend in the two variables (expenses and *servicio y montazgo*) account for any statistical significance found in the test.

The empirical results of a distributed lag model (up to four periods) with 53 observations fitting data to equation [1] is given in table 5.1. Tests for years between 1510 and 1553 using contemporaneous values (model 1) and lags up to four years (models 2 through 5) strongly support the hypothesis that rent-seeking conflicts between the Mesta and the crown took the predicted direction of expense inflation on the part of the cartel.[24] The coefficient of SM_t is positive and highly significant at the 1 percent level in all regressions. Separate regressions were run for each additional year's lag up to four years. The alternating signs of the lagged independent variables in each regression indicates adaptation on the part of the Mesta's managers and members to rent-seeking pressures by the monarchy. In model 5, for example, steady state equilibrium indicates that every dollar of tax increase by the crown inflated Mesta expenses by approximately 76 cents.[25] In all, both anecdotal and informal empirical evidence supports the fact that a part of the process of Mesta operations included rent-seeking conflicts between the authoritarian grantor of special rights (the crown) and cartel recipients of property rights and other legal advantages.

Table 5.1

Adaptation of Mesta Expenses to Crown Rent Seeking, 1510–63

Independent Variables	\multicolumn{5}{c}{*Dependent Variable: Mesta Expenses, 1510–63*}
	Model 1	Model 2	Model 3	Model 4	Model 5
Intercept	−42097092	−40362918	−41227716	−39976743	−41073664
	(−4.28)	(−4.72)	(−5.03)	(−4.99)	(−5.48)
SM(t)	1.014658	0.770651	0.659153	0.646795	0.807649
	(4.02)	(3.41)	(2.95)	(2.89)	(3.84)
SM(t–1)		0.908347	1.068224	1.076530	0.959154
		(4.08)	(4.71)	(4.64)	(4.47)
SM(t–2)			−0.472917	−0.499823	−0.606542
			(−2.14)	(−2.15)	(−2.84)
SM(t–3)				0.074114	0.290133
				(0.33)	(1.36)
SM(t–4)					−0.682649
					(−3.25)
Time	28346	26930	27675	26848	27779
	(4.43)	(4.86)	(5.18)	(5.13)	(5.68)
DW	2.200	1.968	1.942	1.885	2.036
R²	0.4466	0.5959	0.6341	0.6417	0.7083
F	18.562	22.118	19.062	15.762	16.998

Source: Jean Paul le Flem 1972, appendix 4B (El Presupuesto de la Mesta), p. 72; appendix 5B (El Servicio y Montazgo: Importe annual y relacio con el cargo total de la Mesta), p, 83.

Opportunistic Behavior Within the Cartel

The elaborate system of controls set up by the Mesta and the crown were required for successful rent seeking because of the migratory nature of the cartelized product. But these very systems set up opportunities for cheating and malfeasance. The system permitted cartel cheating against the crown, but it also created ripe situations for rent seeking on the part of individuals against the cartel. Both internal and external pressures on Mesta functioning guided the institutional process. Internal pressures were heightened by cartel enforcers such as the *entregadores* and the *alcaldes*, whereas property rights disputes between local and Crown interests—highlighted in legal procedures and pronouncements—formed the chief external constraints on Mesta functioning.

In the earliest days of the national Mesta, the crown essentially collected all of the profits of the *entregadores*, who were paid a salary. Later, during the administration of Ferdinand and Isabella, the Mesta received one-third of the share of the proceeds from the total receipts of the *entregadores*—a fact that suggests opportunities for rent diversion and/or other forms of malfeasance on their part. Incentives clearly mattered for these cartel enforcers. Over some periods, entregadores enriched themselves with one-third of the fines they collected for infractions on enclosures of common property. At other times and in some places they also profited from selling illegal licenses for enclosures (Klein 1964, 93–95) and by legal pronouncements on matters unrelated to the sheep roads, the right-of-way of which they were charged with maintaining. These legal pronouncements, according to Klein (1964, 104–105), enriched Mesta members, and in particular the *entregadores*, by depriving local officials of income sources. Given the rural and seriously unintegrated nature of the Spanish economy, such self-interested rent taking by internal officers of the cartel was understandable. Indeed, there is parallel evidence that English and French cartel enforcers were as opportunistic (see chapters 3 and 4).

Strong evidence, however, supports the fact that *entregadores* dissipated rents in an expanded "enforcement" bureaucracy. For example, increased pressures for rents placed on the Mesta cartel by the Hapsburg monarchs led to tighter enforcement criteria. The costs of the staffs of the *entregadores* purportedly amounted to more than a hundred million *maravedíes* in 1587 (Klein 1964, 107), a very significant amount for enforcement and integration of the cartel. When profits could not be internalized, *entre-*

gadores' rents were dissipated through expanded staff and high bureaucratic costs.

The *alcaldes* "or cartel rule makers" administered entry conditions,
output assignments, quality controls, and jurisdiction over stray sheep in
the four districts described in figure 5.2. As in the case of *entregadores,* there
was plenty of room for malfeasance by these officials who were elected
within the Mesta to four-year terms. Other than membership dues, the
Mesta's income was composed of fines from outside violators levied by
entregadores, sales of stray sheep, fines of members, and, at times, investments. In this regard the *alcaldes de quadrilla* farmed out rights to collect
fines, in common with the French (and Dutch) mercantile practice of tax
farming (see chapter 4). But the practice was a clear window to abuse and
internal rent seeking as was the right of *alcaldes* to sell the stray sheep. The
alcaldes, in the latter role, overstepped their authority by attempting to
supersede the rights of towns over the strays. Further, Klein reports (1964,
55) that appellate actions were allowed in the Mesta for member complaints
against *alcalde* decisions illustrating their attempts at self-aggrandizement.
Part of these costs contributed to the expense inflation of the cartel, and
part of the rents were dissipated in cheating, unproductive cartel labor, and
side payments.

RENT SEEKING AND
PROPERTY RIGHTS ALTERATIONS

Without question, property rights alterations *are* the key element for understanding the tragedies awaiting the Spanish economy in the late sixteenth century and beyond. While arguments might differ concerning the
more ultimate or exogenous cause or causes of these changes, virtually all
modern neoinstitutional observers recognize the proximate and critical
role of property rights (North 1981; Nugent and Sanchez 1989) in Spanish
economic growth (or lack thereof). A general assignment to the Mesta as
thwarting sedentary agricultural production and providing a stable and
growing food supply is also maintained in the literature. We agree, but
add that the story of the Mesta's role in Spanish economic development
is not as simple as it is often portrayed. Property rights for all participants
varied over time, and there was a high degree of uncertainty at any given
time created by rent seeking through interest-groups. While there was
a general preponderance of crown-Mesta interests, the relative uncertain-

ties were not distributed in the same manner throughout the period of interest.

Jurisdictions, for example, were most uncertain. The relative and fluctuating power of the crown vis-à-vis local towns and nobles determined both the site of jurisdictions and the probability of secure property rights. The Mesta stood between and "tested" these conflicting interests. Within the nexus of judicial decisions the Mesta had to expend resources in order to establish (at least at times) an effective lobby to support and enforce the integration of the organization.[26] Clearly, as Nugent and Sanchez suggest, secure property rights were required to avoid enclosures so that sheep could migrate unhampered.[27] But rent seeking in the form of internecine struggles between closely competing interests, and high transactions and enforcement costs made rights only *relatively* secure over most of Mesta history.[28]

Disputes between towns nobles, the church, and the universities were striking, with implications for property rights in agriculture versus *transhumance*. Threatened or actual excommunication was often used in competing struggles over property rights among the Mesta, church, and university jurisdictions. For example, the church was subdued by the Royal Council in 1540, causing the archbishop of Toledo to withdraw excommunication of an *entregador* who had allowed encroachment on church lands. Further, the universities and ecclesiastical judges used "religious" instruments in their challenges to the Mesta's jurisdiction in the seventeenth century by threatening to have excommunicated any *entregador* who opposed them. The gradual loss of power of the *entregadores* after the 1640s removed some of their impact in jurisdictional disputes.

Property rights favoring the *transhumantes* as opposed to sedentary herding and agricultural interests that were necessary for successful capture of cartel rents could not have been "optimal" over the entire period of Mesta functioning. Observers such as Ruiz Martín (1974, 276–84) have clearly emphasized the emergence of the latter interests, especially between 1527 and 1602, as effective counterpoints to Mesta interests in property rights conflicts. The Cortes, moreover, acted with increasing frequency and success in battles against the crown's council and against *entregadores'* attempts to trespass on and tax agricultural interests (Klein 1964, 113). These observations suggest that shifting and uncertain property rights characterized the sixteenth and seventeenth centuries (cf. Gerbert 1982). The assignments and divisions, moreover, were as complex and variable as the rent-seeking interests that determined them.

Longer-run exogenous factors were of critical importance as well. The size of the total rents on the "supply side" were naturally a function of the crown's willingness to suppress the property rights of the towns and sedentary agriculture and of the efficiency of cartel organization. But exogenous variables, chiefly on the "demand side," came into play as well. In particular, Spanish wool export demand and indigenous population changes were critical factors in the Mesta's ability successfully to generate rents.[29] Export demand for Spanish wool fell off sharply in 1550 (Phillips 1982, 778)—lasting for more than a century—and that ability suffered. Further, Spanish population growth quickened dramatically over the sixteenth century. Nadal (1986, 74–75) estimates the increase in total population to have been from 4,698,000 in 1530 to 6,632,000 in 1591 or a compounded growth of 57 percent. Increases of this magnitude clearly put significant pressure on agricultural production (Anes 1981). Emerging rents on existing agricultural lands suggest an increased ability of the town-agricultural-sedentary herding interests successfully to compete against the Mesta for property rights of fertile land at the margin. These higher rents, appropriable only through fencing, must have also given encouragement to enclosures even when fencing was "costly." The *roturaciones* movement encompassing better agricultural technology was also a part of these developments.

Direct and indirect evidence from the eighteenth and nineteenth centuries illustrates the continuing property rights pressures of Mesta and agricultural interests. The growth of population in the last half of the eighteenth century put more pressure on agricultural products because of inefficient allocation of resources brought on by the Mesta (Marín Barriguete 1990b). "Enlightened" ministers such as Jovellanos and Campomanes helped to ameliorate the misallocations in favor of agriculture in free trade movements (Anes 1981; García Martín and Sánchez Benito 1986). Some property rights regulations, instituted in earlier periods, were destined to become inefficient and ignored, if possible, over time. The institution of *posesión*, which fixed the price of pasture rents (until it was essentially abolished by Campomanes), was an impediment to the free movement of resources from pastoral to agricultural interests made more profitable through cyclical population growth. The concept, in effect since 1501, did not take dynamic demand elements into account, which would have, at times of high population growth, favored agriculture (Laguna Sanz 1986, 81; García Martín 1988). The infamous "food riots" in 1766 were, in part, a manifestation of misallocations in favor of the Mesta and against agricultural food production to provide subsistence to the masses.[30] Some methods by "progressives" in Spanish government to improve Mesta efficiency, such as the attempted elimination of payments to bounty hunters, backfired.[31]

The crown had to skew property rights or adapt enforcement in the direction of economically successful interests based on ultimate exogenous forces such as wool export demand and population in order to collect rents successfully. Opposing exogenous forces—apart from the ability of the cartel to generate rents through organizational monopoly—made long-term secure or even relatively secure assignment of property rights to Mesta interests impossible. A zoning authority, except at some specific points in time, could not assign secure property rights in the face of growing implicit and rising actual rents in agriculture. Attempts to do so would create nonoptimal adjustments to constantly altered exogenous conditions. Such adjustments ultimately would be achieved but at higher costs to society than if more fluid property rights systems were in place. The central point is that rent-seeking pressures of interest groups working through the political system on coercive authorities were the means through which property rights alterations were made in the Spanish economy. These rights were neither "constant" nor certain, and this fact has implications for internal economic activity and for relative productivity in the different branches of Spanish agriculture.

CONCLUSION: INSTITUTIONAL CHANGE AND SPANISH DEVELOPMENT

The analysis of Spanish institutional change over the medieval-mercantile period presents a primary challenge to economic historians. On many issues, all agree. The character of "received" Spanish institutions was fundamentally different from those of other major European powers. Constraints were plainly different from those that existed in England, France, and the Netherlands. Early constitutional legal and parliamentary checks on monarchical taxation and monopoly franchising developed in England but not in France or Spain.[32] But France and Spain are not exactly comparable either. The medieval-mercantile Spanish economy was far less integrated than the French with a greater and more powerful tradition of regional and local interests. Transactions costs created by Spanish institutional constraints also meant that rent seeking in a pastoral economy with a moveable product was costlier than in "controlled" urban environments wherein playing card or tapestry manufacture could more easily be monopolized.

A second major point upon which modern "institutionalists" and economic historians (with the emphasis on the adjective) appear to agree is that institutions affecting property rights, exchange, and long-term investment are the primary determinant of economic growth. In this context, a preliminary assessment of the relative progress of the English, Dutch, French, and Spanish economies is certainly possible. The development of relatively certain property rights fostered long-term investments and innovations in market and political institutions in the English and Dutch cases. Mercantile developments that created the preconditions for the great leap in these countries are seen as having been "path dependent" on earlier constraints on crown taxing powers. In the cases of France and Spain, another path— one with significantly fewer such constraints—was followed with the implication that vast uncertainties developed in property rights and exchange. With important filigree and elaborations, this is the story of North and other neoinstitutionalists.

The primary puzzle with respect to an explanation of Spanish underdevelopment after the mid-sixteenth century is to explain the *exact* determinants of property rights insecurity, their relative importance, and the nature of the negative path (actually a spiral) taken by the economy. We have emphasized interest-group/rent-seeking conflicts with respect to the Mesta cartel as being a major factor, but ours is only a preliminary and suggestive assessment. We have not, for example, broached the following critical questions. What role, *quantitatively*, did the cyclical fortunes of the Mesta play in Spanish economic development and in the overall (quantitative) scheme of taxation and regulation? *Quantitatively*, what was the impact of the Mesta on long-term contracting, investment, and per capita real income change in the sixteenth century and beyond?

Such questions have not found answers and they cannot be answered unless one simultaneously considers other major contributing factors to Spanish underdevelopment. There is no shortage of candidates in the latter realm, and any full and complete analysis of Spanish mercantilism and its relation to economic development must include them. Uncertainty in exchange would certainly be related to price inflation (or deflation). Therefore, specie inflows from the New World, and their abrupt interruptions in the sixteenth century, must have had an important impact on Spanish internal markets. The Spanish were unable to hold onto some possessions (the Dutch Republics were lost to Spain in the sixteenth centuries), which also reduced crown income. Problems relating to trade and foreign policy may, indeed, have been the key development leading to Spanish stagnation into the modern age.[33] The conduct of war and the radical price changes it engendered were clearly important factors in development in the seventeenth and eighteenth centuries (Hamilton 1947). Other matters relating to colonial expansion and military adventures, especially the new requirements of military technology, unquestionably created problems for development.

The well-known confiscatory tax system and the institutional changes the system itself engendered—changes, for example, in customs and mores concerning work and leisure—had enormous implications for the development of commerce and growth-enhancing market exchange. At times, the tax demands of monarchs in the sixteenth and seventeenth centuries led to outright venality in the sale of "patents of nobility" purchased for tax avoidance and/or distinction.[34] This practice dovetailed with institutionalized contempt for work and commerce and with the "bureaucratization" of the Spanish economy, so well described by North as a utility maximizing response.[35] Socially productive investment was discouraged, and fraud, corruption, and rent dissipation characterized market activity.

There was, in the face of these events, no dearth of advice from pamphleteers, government functionaries and bureaucrats, and, especially, Church scholastics whose "clerical perspective" virtually dominated Spanish education over the mercantile period. These sixteenth- through eighteenth- (and even nineteenth-) century writings ran the gamut, as they did in England and elsewhere, from "mercantile" advice based in protection, "industrial policy," and import substitution to more liberal and enlightened policy recommendations. In the former camp, names such as Sancho de Moncada (*Restauración Política de España y Deseos Públicos* [1619], composed of eight speeches), Pedro Fernández Navarrete (*Discursos* [1921]), Francisco Martínez de la Mata (publishing six "*discursos*" on depopulation in 1650), and Geronimo Uztariz (1670–1732) are typical and are of interest in the history of economic thought (Schumpeter 1954, 168–70; Castillo 1980).

The flood of "mercantile" advice on protection, monetary matters, and domestic and other obstacles to trade was matched by a countercurrent of enlightened liberalism in the eighteenth and early nineteenth centuries. These latter forces, whose bravery in the face of the Spanish Inquisition and whose achievements are only now being brought to full light, railed against the feudal arrangements in landholding, were advocates of free trade and offered very prescient practical reform proposals relating to economic sociology and economic education. Carefully crafted and sometimes anonymous *cartas* (pamphlets rather than "letters") pushed a reform agenda, and even these would not have been possible without support from the "enlightened despots" (chiefly Charles III [1759–88] and Charles IV [1788–1808]) who found support for the state in promoting the welfare of the individual, and who opposed the theocratic elements of the church.[36] Much of this literature, moreover, especially that penned by Campomanes and his contemporaries, pinpointed the critical observation that economic welfare would not be improved in Spain without a thoroughgoing reform of property rights. Literature reviews are obviously important, but there is no evidence that any of this literature, "mercantile" or "liberal," had even a "blip" in effect on economic growth in Spain. To equate Spanish mercantilism or its decline with "doctrine," with policy attribution, or with particular characteristics of the economy is not only wrongheaded, it is counterproductive. In much of the commentary on Spanish "mercantilism," for example, the tail wags the dog.[37]

Doctrinal approaches to the policies of Spanish mercantilism, including the theories of Spanish "mercantilists," have been clear failures in promoting understanding of critical questions of economic development. And contemporary neoinstitutional analysis *does* permit the painting of a broadbrush picture of Spanish mercantilism in which, we have argued, the Mesta organization played a major role. But a neoinstitutional approach, wherein particular institutional changes are explained with economizing actors, interest groups, and coalitions in some kind of path-dependent mode of analysis, demands more than an outline. A finer calibrated and integrated theory of institutional change is needed to answer critical questions related to Spanish development, and no such model yet exists (North 1990, 115). Particular exogenous and endogenous variables must be identified with an endogenous political sector in order to reduce the "ad hoc" character of most discussions, including our own. The trick is to isolate critical factors and to try to understand with a model of Spanish development and supporting evidence how property rights changed and to discover how these changes affected—promoted or restricted—market exchange.

Research is only beginning to point toward a cogent explanation, and taxing institutions and other factors will be a part of an integrated institutional model of the Spanish case. We, along with others, believe that the

Mesta cartel is a major picture in this gallery of institutions that *help* tell a story of the tragedy of underdevelopment in the Spanish economy of the sixteenth century. A rent-seeking/interest-group approach, along with neoinstitutional principles focusing on property rights, contributes to this overall enterprise.

Chapter Six

Economic Organization and Functions of the Mercantile Chartered Companies

A monopoly granted either to an individual or to a trading
company has the same effect as a secret in trade or manufacturers.
—Adam Smith, *The Wealth of Nations*

A positive-economic theory of mercantilism has been developed in this book—one that helps complete the historical record with an explanation of the course of state intervention in the English, French, and Spanish mercantile economies. The explanation is couched in terms of modern contributions to the theory of economic regulation and is based upon the costs and benefits facing individual economic agents in the mercantile historical context as they sought to use the power of the state to increase their wealth.

The purpose of this and the following chapter is twofold: to analyze the "aggregate" aspects of the mercantile companies and, then, to focus upon the economic inner workings of a particular company and to model the lines along which the modern corporation evolved. First, in chapter 6, we extend our analysis to consider the regulation of mercantilist foreign trade. A particular interest in analyzing the regulation of international trade in these early economies is in developing a plausible linkage between the various forms that this regulation took and the types of business organizations that emerged to engage in foreign trade. We begin with a simple cartel theory of the early English foreign-trading firms (the "regulated companies"), in which various aspects of cartel arrangements are discussed. We proceed to analyze the comparative economic performance of the trading companies in the various mercantile economies, which is viewed as a manifestation of the differing institutional environments within which the companies operated. The Dutch companies' efficiency, for example, resulted from the difficulties of suppressing competition among the Dutch towns, while the Portuguese, Spanish, and French companies exhibited the predictable inefficiency resulting from public control and operation of enterprise. We then consider a specific and controversial issue about the early companies—the argument concerning whether the monopoly grants to companies were justified by the public goods they provided (such as forts).

Chapter 7 examines the operations of the English East India Company in some detail, both to illustrate how these early companies functioned and to argue that the early companies faced many of the same economic problems as modern firms and hence can be seen as clear precursors of modern corporate organizations. We then use the experience of the early companies to develop a new hypothesis about the origin of the English joint-stock company, a forerunner of the modern corporation.

A CARTEL EXPLANATION OF THE EARLY ENGLISH TRADING COMPANIES

The general pattern observable in the early English trading companies is that of the formation, by local merchants, of national cartels to engage in international trade. As Heckscher points out: "The work of unification in foreign trade was fairly easy, in so far as the medieval municipal economic system in all its local exclusiveness could not possibly be applied to foreign trade. Apart from the powerful North Italian cities, with towns and provinces under their direct control, it was on the whole impossible for the towns to exclude the competition of merchants from other towns in foreign markets. So the tendency towards common organization of a number of towns or their merchants came into being, and was accentuated by other specific phenomena" (1934, 1:326). Thus, the historians' interpretation of mercantilism is as a process of unification and development of nation-states, emanating, in the area of foreign trade, from the desire to suppress competition. In fact, combinations of towns represented nothing more than combinations of various local cartel arrangements, such as those enforced under the Statute of Artificers. The unification of nation-states—a primary theme of students of mercantilism—may then be interpreted as an extension of monopoly power from the local to the national level.

For the most part, in the mercantile period the English national cartels were formed by private initiative. Thus, "the English companies, it might . . . appear, were just as much a product of the state or of the monarchy as were the French; but in fact it was not so at all. The English companies owed their rise as well as their capital to private initiative. The king's good-will was manifested only in the attempt to share in the profits as far as possible, without making any contribution" (Heckscher 1934, 1:439). But the hand of the state was never very far behind private initiative. Often, the monarch made active investments. There is evidence that in the 1550s several very profitable, though nonmonopolized, partnerships were formed for the Africa trade. Scott (1951, 2:5) reports that the great gains from African expeditions could not be concealed, whereupon Elizabeth was brought into the partnerships in 1561. She provided capital in the form of four ships and provisions and was to receive a full one-third of the profits. When the Levant Company—formed to deal in the Mediterranean trade—was established in 1581, Elizabeth granted exclusive privileges to twenty merchants and invested or lent as much as half of the capital as partner (Scott 1951, 2:83–85).

Other forms of rent seeking via the sale of cartel restrictions were common. To take a specific example,

> The corporative business arrangements in the regulated companies are thus chiefly interesting as a proof that it was a short step, from a theoretical point of view, from the medieval corporations to the associations of capital. The interest in this relationship is not however entirely theoretical, for it is possible to trace an influence upon actual developments: e.g., Elizabeth (1560 and also later) on Gresham's advice, distrained on the outgoing fleets of the Merchant Adventurers and seized their cargoes of cloth, so as to force a loan from them which would cover the crown's debts on the continent and influence the exchanges in England's favour. The loan was considered one from the company itself, to be assessed upon its members. (Heckscher 1934, 1:384)

In such a case the state stayed in the background and collected rents through "loans." Consequently, these companies fit into the rent-seeking predispositions of the times, whereby governments raised revenue by granting and enforcing monopoly privileges. This is, of course, not very different from the idea that firms granted Webb-Pomerene status might make large campaign contributions ("loans") to aspiring politicians. As we shall see, however, the form of state participation (franchising versus direct state control) had an important influence on the productive efficiency of the trading companies.

Cartels, then as now, were associations of firms (towns) maximizing joint profits via monopoly pricing, output restriction, and market allocations. The well-known problem with such business arrangements, once formed, relates to the matter of policing adherence to the agreement by the members. Since each cartel member faces a more elastic demand curve for its output with secret price reductions, cartel arrangements are often made unstable by a tendency of members to cheat on the agreement (Stigler 1964). Thus, once organized, the main task facing the foreign-trading cartels was to detect and sanction cheating on a joint price-output agreement. The various manifestations of this cartel-enforcement activity are interesting in their own right and, moreover, are illustrative of how cartels were organized and enforced in an era without antitrust sanctions against monopoly. Consider the cartel-enforcement activities of the English regulated companies.

Cartel Enforcement

It was quite common for the merchant associations to have agents in the foreign markets that were important centers of exchange. The point of such activity seems basically to have been to observe the buying and selling activities of one's merchant colleagues in the cartel. Thus:

> The English associations of merchants, on the other hand, had even their centre of activity abroad. In the years 1391 to 1408 a series of charters for various English corporations engaged in foreign trade were issued, and they described the merchants concerned as "sojourners" (commorantes, commorantes et conversantes respectively) in the foreign countries in question. The most important of these corporations was the famous Fellowship of Merchant(s) Adventurers or Merchant(s) Adventurers Company. It was governed from its Mart Town, that is, from its foreign office, down to its disappearance in Napoleonic times. . . . The second surviving medieval company in England was the Eastland Merchants or the Eastland Company. It is true that their centre was in London, not on the continent; but their continental office was allowed wide powers. When a less-known association trading with Andalusia obtained its charter in 1530, it referred to four Spanish cities as possible places for their meetings. The tradition therefore is clear. (Heckscher 1934, 1:327–28)

Clearly, then, each cartel member stationed observers in the major markets through which cartel output flowed. In such a way enforcement of the cartel followed the course of trade, and the costs of violating the agreement for short-run gains were uniformly raised to all members.[1]

CARTEL FACTORS

Cartel monitoring through agents or "factors" in foreign markets was not always wholly successful, as the experience of the Russia Company, a joint-stock association chartered by the crown in 1555, reveals. By 1568 there were allegations that "the factors were badly paid and that some of them embezzled the company's funds, others engaged in private trade, and a few even intrigued with the Dutch or interloping English merchants against the body that employed them" (Scott 1951, 2:42). As the earlier analysis in this book suggests, we expect malfeasance where agents are poorly paid, and the corruption of cartel agents was likely responsible for the early failures of the company. This situation added fuel to a later parliamentary assault on the company's exclusive privileges, but, in general, agent-monitors in foreign-trading centers appear to have been a very effective means of cartel enforcement.

SOCIAL CODES

Another manifestation of cartel-enforcement activity by the English foreign-trade companies was their strong social codes. Heckscher's description of the situation is informative:

> From an economic point of view, the meticulous regulation of the lives of the merchants, their agents and apprentices is of minor importance, but throws light on the spirit of the system and expresses the striving after a supra-personal organization, embracing the whole individuality of its members. The members were never described as anything but "brethren," their wives were "sisters"; the "brethren" were to go together to church, to assist at weddings and burials. A whole chapter in the by-laws of the Merchant Adventurers is given up to punishments for indecent language, quarrels between brethren, fighting, drunkenness, card-playing, immorality, keeping of hunting dogs and so on. It was also unlawful to enter the porter's lodge on the arrival of the post—instead, letters were to be received at his window outside the lodge; further no one was to carry through the streets any more than could be decently held under the arm or in the sleeve—

infringements of any of these carrying fines of different severity. The same rules are to be found in the sister organization, though typically enough masters were excepted from the prohibition against "undecent speeches or words of reproach or discredit" when they upbraided their apprentices and paid servants. Apprentices were the children of the large family and were treated as such. (1934, 1:380)

Although these codes could have been motivated by general social or religious considerations, their function seems to have been to make it virtually impossible for cartel members to have an opportunity to cheat on the agreement. Why else, for example, would mail be monitored within these associations, as Heckscher indicates, if not to check for violations of the cartel agreement? Thus, from the point of view of cartel enforcement, the detailed regulation of the lives of cartel members was not of minor economic importance, as Heckscher seems to think. The social codes of these trading associations were implicit cartel-monitoring devices dispersing the costs of enforcement over all the cartel members and their families.

MEMBERSHIP RESTRICTIONS

Another interesting manifestation of cartel-enforcement activity in the early companies was the severe membership restrictions on former retailers. Heckscher describes these restrictions: "The new state of affairs was given clear expression in the fact that members of the regulated companies were prohibited from devoting themselves to retail trading. In exceptionally strict cases it was even forbidden to accept people as members who had at any time been retailers. It became a rule that the members had to be 'mere merchants'" (1934, 1:378). In the case of the London merchants, Heckscher continues,

> Any person who had once been a retailer had to declare in writing one year before his admission to the organization, that he wished to renounce retail trading or shopkeeping, and he was not allowed to return to it within five years; all this on pain of heavy fines for infringement. The 1605 charter for the Levant Company and the 1611 charter for merchants trading with France went even farther. For a member to be a retailer was made to be as much a crime as "offences and the practices of evil demeanour", the punishment for which was expulsion. The rules had to be considerably toned down for the provincial cities; but the endeavour to erect a barrier between wholesale and above all maritime trade on the one hand and handicraft and retail

trade on the other dominated the regulated companies throughout their existence, and was, for instance, intensified in the Merchant Adventurers by governmental ordinances of 1634 and 1643. (1934, 1:379)

Heckscher offers no explanation for the separation of retailers from merchants, but it is clear that such separation was a device for controlling incentives to cheat on the cartel. A former retailer would have had numerous market contacts from his previous sales experience and would have been in a relatively advantageous position to make "illicit" sales. A ban on former retailers made perfectly good economic sense from the point of view of cartel management.

CENTRAL PORT SHIPPING

A final manifestation of cartel enforcement concerns the cartel policy of common shipping through and the general dominance of London as a port. The nature of the provisions for common shipping are clear in the following quotation from Heckscher:

> The rights of the local branches to ship independently were, even in other ways, most curiously treated in the Merchant Adventurers' by-laws. It is true that the clauses did not prohibit the use of other ports than London, and Newcastle even enjoyed special facilities for its goods, which differed somewhat from those of the London branch. But with this exception, the clauses were occupied almost exclusively with shipping from the London office. The codification of 1608 expressly stipulated that no prescriptions relating to shipping could be allowed without the advice of the London members. On the ground that decisions on the freighting of common ships must be kept under strict control of officials, members "of whatsoever place or port of England" were also forbidden to remove a commodity from London or the surrounding district, once they had brought it in. In the words of Wheeler (1601) who was the force behind the codification, "the most part of the commodities which the Merchants Adventurers carry out of the Realm, being shipped in appointed ships at London." In other words, the common shipping of the company in his day played a large part in its affairs. There was thus an unmistakable desire on the part of the Merchant Adventurers to concentrate trade and shipping in London. (1934, 1:427)

Common shipping was still another means of controlling cheating on the cartel arrangement, and such a policy lowered the costs to cartel managers of policing cartel transactions.[2] The focus on London as a central port for cartel management, moreover, must have been owing to lower costs of cartel operations there. Heckscher, though generally confusing the issue of London's dominance by viewing the issue in broad social and political terms, hints at our analysis in the following passage:

> The twofold origin of the animosity and the jealousy towards London, displayed from the start by the merchants and shipowners of the "outports," complicates the survey of the situation. On the one hand the unorganized traders, the provincial "interlopers," tried their utmost to make life unpleasant for their officially favoured competitors in London. On the other hand, there was the opposition between the provincial and the metropolitan members of the organizations themselves. This distinction is frequently overlooked; but the very fact that it could be overlooked arouses the suspicion that the interest of London was largely a company interest, in other words that the companies' advantage as such involved the favouring of London at the expense of the provinces. At the same time it must not be assumed that no distinction was made between these two kinds of opposition, and in fact the organized merchants in the provinces sometimes explicitly distinguished between their fight with the directors of their own company in London and the interlopers' fight with the companies as such. (1934, 1:418)

Heckscher seems to argue that there was something akin to a regional-development fight surrounding the matter of London's dominance as a port. Heckscher's view is certainly partially correct, but the economic basis of the dominance of London was more likely the lower costs of centralizing cartel operations in that city.

All of these aspects of cartel enforcement are obvious manifestations of cartel agreements. The point is that policing these agreements, which also means policing the cartel, is costly but efficient from the cartel's point of view. The internally efficient cartel will use efficient policing devices out of the whole array of possible devices.

Output Assignment in the Cartel

A problem plaguing any cartel is how to allocate production among members. The problem is especially difficult when member firms have different costs of production. Heckscher aptly characterizes the nature of the output-assignment problem in the early trading cartels: "On the whole, however, the system was rather more refined, and one of its usual tenets was the limitation of the total number of merchants and their sales, and the division of the total sales among various merchants by limiting the amounts which any merchant might ship, so that 'the rich' might not 'eat out the poor.' It was just this which was usually named 'stint,' and with the Merchant Adventurers it played a specially important role" (1934, 1:381).

The provision that "the rich might not eat out the poor" seems to be nothing more than an output-assignment rule in trading cartels. By analogy, the "rich" correspond to low-cost firms and the "poor" to high-cost firms. While a fully rationalized cartel would allocate the profit-maximizing output according to the marginal costs of its members, these early cartels evidently had as much trouble achieving full rationalization as do modern cartels. The difficulty was (is) perhaps owing to the fact that the prospect of shutting down—if one happens to be a relatively high-cost producer—is the functional equivalent to unilateral disarmament. Where the costs of reentry are high, the probability of being double-crossed by the low-cost firms that would remain in production becomes substantial. Most cartels thus have rules whereby all firms continue to produce. Rich (low-cost) firms do not eat out the poor (high-cost) firms, albeit cartel profits are not strictly maximized as a result.[3]

Cartel Formation: Summary

We have, in a way, put the cart before the horse by focusing first on the various ways in which the early companies enforced their cartel agreements and allocated production among members, rather than on the difficulties of forming the cartel. There is a good reason for this order of discussion, however, since there is no documentation of negotiations among various town merchants forming these early cartels. We do know, in general, that the associations of town merchants devised a very efficient form of collusion—the common selling agency. Coupled with various devices to control cheating on agreements discussed above, a common sales agency is an extremely effective means of private cartel management.[4] Heckscher understood this basic point quite clearly: "They sometimes took over the products of their members and put credits to their accounts, obliging the traders to deliver their goods only to the corporation warehouses, corresponding roughly to the arrangement in a modern cartel with a common selling syndicate" (1934, 1:383). We might also note that the general efficiency of collusive arrangements in this period was to be expected in a setting where cartels were not only legal but were actively encouraged by state authorities who stood to gain revenues from the creation of monopoly rents.

Heckscher's interests in recounting the history of the early companies were substantially broader, in general, than our interest in their cartel activities. Heckscher gave a starring role to the grand theme of mercantilism as a unifying force that created the nation-state. In this context Heckscher studied the impact of the early companies on unification and was not concerned with an interpretation from the standpoint of positive-economic theory. We view the history of the early English companies in a somewhat different light. The movement to unified trading companies was monopolistically inspired, and the various details of social history that followed the formation of these companies were manifestations of cartel activity.

COMPARATIVE ECONOMIC PERFORMANCE OF THE FOREIGN-TRADING COMPANIES

The comparative economic performance of the foreign-trading companies in several of the mercantile economies is surveyed by Heckscher. His interest in this subject is, again, not in the positive-economic aspects of this problem but in its relation to broader issues of the mercantilist era. Our interest is in the economic explanations for the observable differences in the operations of companies in the various countries.

Our argument essentially is that the economic performance of the trading companies in the mercantile economies was directly related to the degree of state involvement in the affairs of these enterprises. The efficiency of the Dutch companies was widely admired and rested on the private and competitive nature of these enterprises. The Portuguese and Spanish companies were notoriously inefficient, and they will be characterized as either public enterprises or as massive sole proprietorships owned solely by the king and queen. The (mainly government-owned) French companies were organized for political objectives. The English cartels seemed to operate on an efficient compromise. The crown granted the relevant monopoly trading privilege in return for what amounted to a monopoly-franchise fee from the companies in the form of loans, but the companies (cartels) were organized and operated by private initiative.

The Dutch Companies

Heckscher characterizes the Dutch companies as paradoxical. In his words, "the Netherlands were the most hated, and yet the most admired and envied commercial nation of the 17th century." The Dutch were, by far, the most efficient seafarers and cargo transporters of that century. Nonetheless, while the Netherlands were the seeming ideal of all mercantilists, they "were yet at the same time less affected by mercantilist tendencies than most other countries" (1934, 1:351). Heckscher attempts to dismiss this paradoxical observation on the grounds of "the national characteristics of the people" (1934, 1:353). While the personal initiative of the Dutch people is undoubtedly an important reason for the efficiency of their trading companies, we do not think that this a satisfactory economic explanation for the paradox that Heckscher poses.

Rather, we see the efficiency of the Dutch companies as stemming from two basic sources. First, in the early period of the trading companies, the Dutch towns experienced great difficulties in organizing a national cartel for the purpose of dealing in foreign trade. These difficulties seemed to be typical of those normally associated with cartel formation. Thus, "the 'directions' were all purely local institutions set up by the towns. The hostility between the 'directions' of various cities was often very keen, although certain attempts were made to induce them to co-operate. It is true that the extent of this hostility was greatly limited in practice by the overwhelming preponderance of Amsterdam both in the sea trade and in the shipping of the Netherlands. But it illustrated the ineradicable particularism, which had hardly been attacked at all seriously, in the conglomeration of cities and territories comprehended in the sometimes almost ironical name of the United Provinces—a particularism which scorned all mercantilist efforts at unification" (Heckscher 1934, 1:355).

Dutch particularism and local hostilities noted by Heckscher can here be interpreted as enhancing competition, in the sense that they made cartel formation more difficult, while, at the same time, making competition more prevalent among the merchants in the Dutch towns. While these hostilities and difficulties were certainly embedded in the characteristics of the Dutch peoples, it seems sensible as an economic hypothesis to ascribe the efficiency of the Dutch companies to the costs of cartel formation and to the consequent persistence of competitive pressures. Thus, for example, Heckscher's (1934, 1:352) discussion of the ability of the early Dutch companies to make do with fewer and simpler organizations than the comparable companies in other countries probably reflects the discipline of competition more than anything else. Also, purely technological explanations of superior Dutch efficiencies (for example, the well-known fact that they built lower-cost ships) can be seen as a manifestation of competitive pressures.

Dutch towns eventually overcame difficulties of cartel formation and united into a national trading company. Again, Heckscher describes this process:

> The various authorities, both municipal and provincial, as well as the States General were extremely perturbed by this competition in their East India trade, partly because they saw in it a danger for the very existence of this trade, but also for political and military reasons, since it prevented a united front being formed against the king of Spain, who at that time was also king of Portugal and thus master of the East Indian waters. Repeated attempts were made to unite the various interests. An amalgamation of the six companies which had their seats in Amsterdam also came into being, but it was of little avail, for the Zeeland merchants, who were always suspicious of the Holland merchants, kept themselves aloof and united in opposition to the Holland enterprises. Such being the situation, it was only the States General which could help. The work of unification was thrown on to the shoulders of the foremost Dutch statesman of the time, Oldenbarnevelt. After involved negotiations, promoted by the States General, all the existing enterprises were, with one negligible exception, amalgamated to form the "united" East India Company in 1602, eight years after the birth of the first company. One of the most powerful forces in the colonial history of Europe for the next two centuries was thus created. (1934, 1:356)

Thus, the East India Company was formed with some aid from the state, and, as documented by Heckscher and others, it became one of the most efficient national trading companies of the mercantile era. A second basic consideration, therefore, in understanding the effectiveness of the Dutch companies over this period concerns how the efficiency of the precartel Dutch companies was carried over to the East India Company.

An uncomplicated answer is that the forces of distrust and competitiveness among the precartel companies inhered in the national cartel arrangement of the Dutch, and these forces put considerable pressure on the various local units in the cartel to behave efficiently. For example, consider the great interest manifested in sharing schemes for cartel costs and returns in the following quotation:

> Functioning as the principal organs of the company and with far-reaching authority were six chambers, as they were called, organized on a purely

local basis. The greatest and by far the most important of them all was that of Amsterdam, the next that of the province Zeeland, and the remaining four those of Maas and the towns of the "northern quarter," Delft, Rotterdam, Hoorn and Enkhuizen. From the outset these chambers had each contributed a definite part of the company's capital and later too had to arrange for the distribution of dividends to the various shareholders. They had to bear a definite proportionate share of all the costs (one-half, one-quarter and one-sixteenth respectively, Art. 1 of the charter). For example, when it was arranged that the management in India receive annually eight legger of Rhine wine, the chambers had to contribute eight, four and one legger each, respectively. The equipment of the ships and the procuring of cargoes, provisions and arms, as well as actual building of the ships all devolved upon the individual chambers. The ships had eventually to return to those chambers from which they had departed (Art. 12). They had to bring back "returns," that is Indian products, for the chamber which had equipped the ship as well for the others. The orders for these "returns" were distributed among the chambers, and they each had to sell the goods received, but all on the common account of the company. The administration in India belonged indeed to the company as a whole, but, with the exception of the chief officials, it was recruited by nomination, made independently by the individual chambers whose hands were tied only in certain matters of secondary importance, and which moreover often treated with indifference the few legal limitations that had been laid down. (Heckscher 1934, 1:362)

The concern, illustrated here, about schemes for the allocation of costs and returns within the cartel was presumably a reflection of the distrust among former competitors. Such apprehensions about business colleagues led to investments in the careful monitoring of co-partners' behavior. These apprehensions, moreover, established a cartel administrative system that made cheating on the cartel costly and that appears to have tailored cartel output to each local unit's marginal cost ("the ships had eventually to return to those chambers from which they had departed"). Distrust among former competitors, in other words, serves as an explanation of the efficiency of the Dutch foreign-trading cartel.

A little hostility went a long way, as it were, in promoting economic efficiency in Dutch foreign trade in this era. If such competitiveness is a characteristic of the Dutch people, we hold that it is also a normal characteristic of most people. Our analysis of the impact of competition on economic organization thus offers a more familiar and useful route to the understanding of the commercial success of the mercantile Dutch than that offered by Heckscher.

The Portuguese and Spanish Companies

The state-owned-and-operated trading companies of Portugal and Spain reflect the opposite extreme from the Dutch experience. In these cases the crown completely financed the companies and was the sole residual claimant in the returns of their trading adventures. In effect, the trading companies of Portugal and Spain may be characterized in two ways.

First, they may be seen as monopolistically inspired public enterprises. When viewed as public enterprises, the results are entirely predictable. For example,

> On the return to Portugal the goods were then sold to merchants. This rule, though stringent in theory, was widely infringed in fact, through the private trade carried on by officials and the ship's crew. Such private trade was originally permitted to a small extent in accordance with the practice of former times, but it came to such a pass that eventually whole vessels were on occasions laden with the captain's own goods. The officials always took good care that their own private and illicit trading in India and at home should take precedence over the lawful trade. The work of Sir William Hunter, in fact, based on official English transcriptions of the materials in Portuguese archives, gives the impression that the illicit trade was even greater than that of the state. . . . This, the most far-reaching attempt of all to institute pure state trading, did not encourage imitation. (Heckscher 1934, 1:342)

As illustrated here, managerial shirking abounded in the Portuguese companies, a result that would come as no surprise to the modern economist familiar with the property-rights theory of the firm (Alchian and Demsetz 1972). Such behavior flows naturally from the absence of market competition and from the absence of well-defined and exchangeable property rights in public enterprises (Davies 1971). Production without property rights characterized the Portuguese and Spanish state trading companies, and general inefficiency in these firms followed as a direct economic consequence.

There is yet another, and perhaps more accurate, manner in which the Portuguese and Spanish companies may be characterized. Instead of being seen as public enterprises—owned by everyone and hence by no one—the companies might be viewed as large monopolies operated as sole proprietorships. The sole proprietor in this case was the monarchy. Under such an interpretation, the inefficiencies observed would be seen to have emerged for classical economic reasons. Where the king and queen were both the sole residual claimants and monopolists, span of control and managerial diseconomies would have been massive and would have led to large-firm inefficiencies. Either characterization of the Spanish and Portuguese enterprises predicts the results described by mercantile writers in this area.

The French Companies

The French were as poor at international rent seeking as they were expert in maintaining incredibly efficient internal regulations. As mentioned earlier, the Dutch were the undisputed masters of the "carrying trade" throughout the first three-quarters of the seventeenth century. Dutch hegemony included the European trade with Russia, a vast carrying trade between the Baltic nations and Spain and Portugal, and trade with the West Indies (at least for a time), not to mention the establishment of Amsterdam as the credit and money-market center of Europe. Both the English and the French attempted to contain the Dutch, but, from an economic point of view at least, sponsored efforts in this area were extremely costly. Most of the French experience in international "company formation" may be interpreted as an aggressive policy to teach the Dutch a lesson and to restrict their international influence. Rightly or wrongly, it seems, the French viewed the Dutch as responsible for long-term stagnation in the French economy. Brief examination of two of Colbert's major constructions in this area, the French West India Company and the Company of the North, yields some insights into the nature of French foreign-trading companies.

The East India and West India companies were linked with French colonization efforts, while the Company of the North was not. Nonetheless, all appear to have been financial disasters, supported in large measure by the treasury of Louis XIV and France. The West India Company was formed to oust the Dutch from the carrying trade in the French island possessions in the West Indies. Colbert envisioned great economies from a French monopoly over this trade, especially with regard to the large sugar trade with France and to the marketing of French linen in the new world. Thus, Colbert sought to set up, under one monopoly organization, trade with the West Indies, South America, Canada, and West Africa, subsequently buying out most of the private proprietors granted monopoly rights before 1665. Stock subscriptions were solicited between 1664 and 1669, with over five and one-half million livres collected for capital. But with 54 percent contributed by the king and with most of the rest pledged by government officials and not merchants, the "corporation" was more a government monopoly than a mercantile enterprise. As in the Spanish and Portuguese companies, this form of enterprise, because of the lack of clearly defined property rights within the firm, is the root explanation for the subsequent and costly inefficiencies of the French companies.

The West India Company was a debacle from the beginning. In 1664 a royal decree excluded the Dutch from trading in the French colonies, but because of the irregularities of supplies and high prices, the French colonists hated the company, on occasion rioting against it, and wanted the Dutch to return. Financial problems also beset the company, which was kept in business by treasury advances authorized by Colbert. In 1666 island wars with England, together with huge losses of ships, cargo, and trade unconnected with the English disputes, led Colbert gradually to abandon the company.

Several aspects of the West India Company's fate are interesting. Colbert had set up the company to be run by a stockholding chamber of directors in Paris and by decentralized boards of directors and governors in France and in the colonies (see Cole 1939, 1:3–5, for details). But there is some evidence of profit taking and shirking by those in control. When it became apparent that the company could not handle the basic requisites of trade to the colonies, especially during wartime in 1666, private French traders (and sometimes the Dutch as well) were let in, but with passports granted to the private firms by the company itself. Clearly, this opened the door to rent seeking by company officials, and there is evidence of such behavior: Colbert himself took over the right to grant licenses to private traders in an effort to prevent favoritism by the company.

Moreover, while Colbert gradually encouraged private French merchants to take over the West Indies trade, he did attempt to reorganize the company along more efficient lines in 1669. In the reorganization proceedings, each member of the board of directors was given specific duties and told to work on company business between 4 and 7 P.M. four days a week. However, since returns of company directors were not directly linked to their efforts on behalf of the company and since returns were not based upon performance (a stockholders' dividend out of the royal treasury was declared in January 1669, to solicit new investments), free riding and rent seeking by the directors was to be expected.

Another feature of the West India trade made its continuation precarious. Though the West Indies Company was a huge investment, the French were unwilling or unable to expend enough resources to contain the interloping of private traders and Dutch slave and livestock trade. Since the services of the company were notoriously inefficient and did not satisfy the colonists, the situation was ripe for outright avoidance of the law (smuggling) and for malfeasance by island officials and even by members of the company. At bottom, the French did in fact significantly displace Dutch trade in the French West Indies, but the displacement appears to have been largely by private traders. Whatever impact the West India Company had on this (largely) political feat, France paid dearly in terms of wasted resources.

Another (but non-colony-related) attempt to "get the Dutch" was the French attempt to move in on the Dutch carrying trade (of mainly French products) to northern Europe. But at this the French were utterly inept. Colbert tried to rouse businessmen's interests in the project, and the Company of the North was founded with monopoly privileges in 1669. Again, a central board of directors was appointed, with local boards in the trading cities, and the king invested well over one-third of the capital, together with escorts and naval protection for the company's ships. This time, however, trade was to be partly subsidized by government demand for naval supplies and by reciprocal exports of French goods and goods from the West Indies. But by 1671 Dutch competition was fierce, trade restrictions and counter-restrictions were invoked in Franco-Dutch political confrontations, and the company had spent all of its capital and had to be rescued by the royal treasury. The French could not get a foothold on the Dutch carrying trade between Spain and Portugal and the Baltic, and the entire experiment collapsed when open war broke out between the French and the Dutch in 1672. The Company of the North was liquidated, de facto at least, between 1673 and 1677, to become another example of disastrous political and economic warfare with the Dutch, who simply outcompeted the French. As we have stressed in this section, the reason for this result resides primarily in the competitive atmosphere and private-ownership structure of the Dutch companies compared with the state financing and state direction of the French companies.

The English Companies

Our final case for comparative analysis is the "regulated" trading companies in England, introduced earlier in this chapter. These may have been the most interesting of the foreign-trading companies, in terms of the institutional arrangements under which they operated. As pointed out previously, these cartels were formed by private initiative under the auspices of a monopoly grant from the crown, and the state sought to share in the consequent monopoly rents through what was the functional equivalent of monopoly franchising. In fact, the English-regulated companies appear to represent an historical example relevant to a modern theoretical argument about monopoly franchising (Demsetz 1968). Before turning to the details of the analysis, however, let us examine how Heckscher describes the institutional milieu of the English companies:

> The formal relationship between the companies and the state consisted in this, that the state paid for the advantages it received from the companies by issuing charters. But the actual profit derived from the company charters was twofold, and there was an important difference between the two.
>
> One part of the benefit was made up of a monopoly, in the usual sense of the word—exclusive rights granted to the companies in their various fields of activity. The monopoly, of course, was employed by its owner to demand higher prices than he would otherwise have been able to get, which meant, in effect, that the customers paid for the credit which the state had secured through the companies. The system thus involved an indirect taxation of consumers' goods in the financial interests of the state. It was indirect taxation of consumption by means of a monopoly, not in the hands of the state but wielded by private individuals . . . The second aspect was of a totally different kind, consisting as it did in the right to corporative status. It might appear as though the state in this case granted a favour costing nothing at all and as though the companies gained something for which no one had to pay; but that is a mistake. Where the actual advantage lay was in the fact that the arrangement was not extended to everybody. The state could demand payment in return for its permission to form corporative associations, simply because it withheld the same privilege from all the other concerns which could have made use of it. In reality these privileges, too, were exploited as private monopolies by the state for fiscal ends. The general effect on economic life and on the consumers was that the other non-

corporative undertakings did not provide the public with as good a service
as they might have done had they been allowed a corporative status; and
consequently the privileged enterprises made the public pay not only for
their specific privileges, but also for their more suitable organization. For
this reason they were prepared to pay the Crown for these advantages by
allowing it favourable terms for loans. (1934, 1:441–42)

The system under which the foreign-trading cartels operated in mercantile England was quite similar to Demsetz's (1968) proposal for franchising natural monopolies. Demsetz suggested that the formal regulation
of natural monopolies might be rendered unnecessary were government to
allow "rivalrous competitors" to bid for the exclusive right to supply the
good or service over some indefinite "contract" period. The existence of
natural monopoly does not imply a monopoly price and output in this
system, assuming an elastic supply of potential bidders and prohibitive collusion costs on the part of potential suppliers.[5] Rather, the result of the
Demsetz bidding scheme is that the firm with the lowest average-cost curve
will win the contract and will supply the market at an average-cost price.
The state is involved in this process only to the minimal extent of running
the franchising or contracting procedure. Direct regulation of the natural
monopoly to seek to get the firm to charge an average-cost price, with all
its incumbent problems, is avoided. Moreover, the Demsetz result does
not rely on the existence of a natural monopoly; it can be applied regardless of the cost conditions that are present among the firms bidding for the
contract.

Returning to the English trading companies, the analogy to monopoly
franchising is clear. Groups of merchants bought their monopoly privileges
by making "loans" to the state. So long as this process of selling monopoly
rights was reasonably competitive, and the historical accounts of court intrigues and cabals during this era suggest that it was, this system of establishing foreign-trading companies would have had a wholesome impact on
enterprise efficiency, as predicted by the Demsetz model.[6] Moreover, the
state was not involved in a direct way in the operation of these firms, as it
was in the Portuguese and Spanish cases (and somewhat in the French
case), and the fact that the monopoly rights were auctioned off tended to
ensure that the most efficient "monopolist" (collection of merchants) won
the bidding competition for the monopoly right. This system of "competition for the field" thus maximized the franchise fees received by the state
and enhanced the economic efficiency of the English trading companies.

Because of the interesting nature of the English companies, the next chapter will be devoted to a case study of the organization and operations of the English East India Company.

The Trading Companies: Summary

Across the mercantile economies the following pattern of enterprise efficiency in foreign-trading companies emerges. The Dutch developed more competitive and efficient trading companies. Moreover, that there was apparently little state involvement further enhanced the effectiveness of their operations. When the Dutch formed a national trading cartel (the East India Company), competitive pressures continued to manifest themselves in the promotion of an efficient cartel operation. The Portuguese and Spanish adopted pure state trading companies or very large "single proprietorships" sponsored by royal authorities, resulting in the predictable enterprise inefficiencies that come about as the result of production without property or ownership rights and the lack of competitive pressures. Some of these similar pressures appear to have been operative in the French experience with foreign-trading companies, which were only very nominally private in character. Finally, the English happened upon an efficient compromise, wherein private interests formed the trading cartels and bid for the pertinent monopoly right from the crown. The crown captured the monopoly rents, and the most efficient firm won the "contract" to operate the trading company.

CHARTERED MONOPOLIES AND PUBLIC GOODS

In defense of monopoly grants to the foreign trading companies in the mercantile era, a substantial body of apologiae emerged concentrating on the theme that a public-goods problem (mostly involving expenditures for forts) justified the award of monopoly rights to the chartered companies. In this argument, competition in foreign trade would have allowed free-riding on the provision of forts by the companies and hence would have resulted in a reduction in the level of trade (or even prevent the trade from developing at all). The apologists were commonly employees of a chartered company and were paid by the company for their pamphleteering services.

It might at first seem that these rationalizations were public-relations verbiage, interesting only as historical curiosa. However, the rationale for

monopoly privilege adduced by writers of the period has been picked up by
some leading recent historians of economic thought and dressed in the
clothes of modern economic jargon. These historians (notably W. R. Scott
and E. G. West) argue, following the essential points laid down three
hundred years ago by various pamphleteers, that grants of monopoly to
foreign-trading companies were justified because the public-goods problem associated with the necessary foreign-trading infrastructure created
conditions of natural monopoly.

Even a cursory examination of the relevant facts reveals serious difficulties with this argument. Most important, forts may have represented not
public goods but public bads in the form of cartel enforcement devices,
designed to operate as coercive entry barriers that reduced the level of
trade while protecting the monopoly rents of their owner-operators. Further, there were articulate contemporary critics of the defense of monopoly
privileges who enunciated the cartel-enforcement interpretation and who
have been largely ignored by modern writers.

Alternative Modern Hypotheses

The primary economic rationale offered at the time for the monopoly rights
of the chartered companies hinged on the alleged requirement for foreign-
trading infrastructure. In modern terms, the investment in trading infrastructure involved high and indivisible fixed costs and sizable economies of
scale. The crucial feature of the infrastructure was its alleged publicness.
For example, forts and garrisons, which figure prominently in discussions
of infrastructure during this period, were said to provide protection not
only for the agents of the companies who built them but also for "interlopers," or unlicensed competitors. Since it was not feasible to charge user fees
for infrastructure services, the combination of substantial economies of
scale and nonexcludability created what today would be termed a free-
rider problem. The companies and their proponents argued that in the
absence of monopoly charters for trading in particular areas, the free-rider
problem would cause a suboptimal level of investment in infrastructure, in
turn causing a reduced level of trade or in some cases reducing the level of
trade to zero. An argument along these general lines was the typical defense of the state-supported trading cartels against critics. For example, in
1696 Thomas Papillon (an employee of the English East India Company)
wrote in a pamphlet:

If the Trade be left open, will not all the Privileges and Immunities purchased [at] great expense by the East India-Company, be either lost, or else rendered void and insignificant? When every man is left to shift for himself, it will be, as to the National Interest, according to the Proverb, that which is every mans business, will be no mans business; when there is none by particular obligation of place, duty, and interest, engaged to mind the general security and privilege of the English-Trade, but every one minds only his own private concern, the National Honour and Interest will decline. (1696, 15)

In 1681 a pamphleteer claimed that capital outlays by the East India Company for infrastructure maintenance had amounted to over £300,000. By 1698 another writer claimed that fixed-capital expenditures by the Company had risen to £1,000,000 annually (Barber 1975, 49). Members of the Royal Muscovy Company frequently bemoaned free-riding by interlopers on the trading privileges they had purchased from the Russian Czar (Cawston and Keane 1968, 30). Similarly, the East India Company tended to attribute the slow development of its trade with China to free-riding by interlopers, whom the Chinese were alleged to be unable to distinguish from Company members. In 1669 Josiah Child (later the Director of the East India Company, at this time employed by its London office) wrote: "Were it not for the East India Company, we should be at the mercy of the Dutch traders; we should lose the protection secured for the country by the employment of so many stout ships and mariners" (Hurd 1921, 99). Commenting upon this body of contemporary economic rationalizations for the granting of monopoly charters, Holdsworth (1966, 8:210) concludes: "In fact, the maintenance of fortifications, when this was necessary or possible, or the maintenance of consular agents, was the sole excuse for the continued existence of these companies."

This argument is more than a historical curiosity. Economists who have examined the early foreign-trading companies have to a remarkable degree restated the arguments of the contemporary apologists for monopoly rights in modern terms. For example, the eminent historian of the early companies, W. R. Scott, wrote:

In the foreign trades under discussion concessions had to be purchased (giving right of entry into the country), while forts and other defensive appliances were judged necessary. The private trader obtained the benefit of this outlay by the Company; and therefore irrespective of the quality of the

management, he could carry on his business on a much lower capital outlay
. . . the private trader in competition . . . would have a distinct advantage,
through the appropriation of the fruits of others. (1951, 1:452–53)

Immediately following this statement, Scott refers to the investment by the
chartered companies in trading rights and forts, claiming: "When such large
expenditure had to be incurred, it was reasonable that the benefits, resulting from it, should be confined to those persons who had provided the
capital. This was the justification of the monopolies for foreign trade in
equity" (Scott 1951, 1:452–53). More recently, E. G. West writes: "Interlopers, therefore, in escaping such expenses, acted as free-riders enjoying public (collective) goods for which they were not obliged to pay . . . Certainly
the monopoly element might be reflected in the price of the license, but it
could still be regarded as a contribution towards the 'public good'—the
fortifications and garrisons" (West 1977, 8–9). Also, Barber (1975, 52) be-
lieves that the requirement for foreign-trading infrastructure implied a
public-goods problem. He argues, however, that governmental provision
of these public goods would have been feasible, and would have allowed
free entry into the trade (although he does not explain whether provision
of the public goods in this manner would be covered by user fees, and if so,
how these would be determined and collected).

Modern investigators into the problems of pre-nineteenth-century
foreign-trading companies have ignored or taken lightly a substantial body
of criticism of the natural monopoly, public goods argument for foreign-
trading monopolies, an argument that grew up contemporaneously with
the companies. Although the foreign-trading cartels had numerous critics
(particularly in England), a small but prominent minority of them stood
out as directly challenging and rejecting the rationalizations for these privileges based on the public-goods argument.

Adam Smith's View

Most prominent among these critics was Adam Smith (with whose position Scott was sparring in the above passage). In *The Wealth of Nations*
Smith admitted that a public-goods problem might sometimes arise and
might justify temporary grants of monopoly privilege (1937, 712). Yet he was
in general highly skeptical of the public-goods character of forts and garrisons as typically claimed by the chartered companies. Although conceding
the probable need for forts in the case of the African trade, "to defend
them [the merchants] from barbarous natives," he thought the alleged

necessity of the far larger and more numerous forts and garrisons in India (particularly those maintained by the English East India Company) was a decidedly more dubious proposition. He writes: "The disorders in the government of Indostan have been supposed to render a like precaution necessary even among the mild and gentle people; and it was under pretense of securing their persons and property from violence that both the English and the French East India Companies were allowed to erect the first forts which they possessed in that country" (1937, 690). Smith elaborates further upon his skepticism later in *Wealth*: "With the right of possessing forts and garrisons in distant and barbarous countries, is necessarily connected the right of making peace and war in those countries. . . . How unjustly, how capriciously, how cruelly they [the chartered companies] have commonly exercised it, is too well known from recent experience" (1937, 712).

In the case of the African Company he describes its forts as a necessary business expense but denies that they functioned as public goods (1937, 700).[7] In his discussion of the forts and garrisons of the East India Company, he argues that these investments did not appear to be necessary for trading operations and were in fact incompatible with voluntary exchange and served to function as means for the extortion of the native population.

In Smith's discussion, there is a hint of a further step beyond the mere criticism of the public-goods character of forts and garrisons. At one point, he argues that the Royal African Company on occasion used violent means to suppress interlopers, implying that the maintenance of garrisons at trading stations was at least in part for cartel-enforcement purposes.

This argument was made much more forcefully by Josiah Tucker writing in 1759.[8] Although he also thought that forts and garrisons functioned as tools of bureaucratic imperialism, offering the opportunity for increased patronage on the part of chartered-company directors (as well as tending to increase the salaries of overseas governors which were correlated with the size of the overseas organization), his main argument appears to have been that forts and garrisons functioned primarily as cartel-enforcement mechanisms. He argued that if private adventurers could not, as alleged, successfully trade without the advantages of forts and would not contribute toward the costs of such facilities, then the company in question should simply exclude them from the use of its facilities. Tucker implied that this was the way the chartered monopoly companies behaved in any event. In effect, Tucker rejected the nonexcludability argument regarding forts. Continuing, he wrote: "Therefore what need is there of any further exclusion, since this circumstance itself will effectively exclude them? And why so much pains taken to deny the poor adventurer the liberty of a Free Trade, when, after all, he could not use this Liberty, were it granted him?" (Schuyler 1931, 144). Unfortunately, Tucker, who throughout his writings has the tendency to state his opinions in the form of rhetorical questions, stops just short of killing the goose and stating outright that forts and garrisons were primarily cartel-enforcement devices (although this point is strongly implied).

There existed, then, at least as early as 1722, a critical response to the public-goods argument for monopoly rights that can be distilled to two major counter-propositions.[9] First, the provision of trading infrastructure, particularly in the form of forts and garrisons, did not represent a public-goods problem because interlopers could be efficiently excluded from the relevant benefit stream and in fact typically were. Second, an important function of the investments typically described as necessary prerequisites for trade, and perhaps the primary function, was that of enforcing cartel restrictions on competitive entry into the regional trade.[10]

In order to shed some light on the competing hypotheses involved in this debate, an examination of the available empirical evidence is in order. Modern writers (Scott, West, and Barber) seem to have accepted the public-goods conclusions of one side of the earlier debate without a careful examination of the facts regarding the actual nature and functioning of the supposed public goods.

WERE THE COMPANIES SUPPLYING PUBLIC GOODS?: SOME EVIDENCE

Writers during this period developed their public-goods defense along three main lines: (1) the need for forts and garrisons for protection against native depredations; (2) the need for naval power for protection from aggression by the forces of other European nations; and (3) the need for treaties with native rulers. These three major categories of investment were alleged to represent necessary trading infrastructure and to exhibit the characteristic of nonexcludability.

Forts and Garrisons

To hear the story the way contemporary spokesmen for the chartered companies told it, one imagines that the forts under discussion were massive affairs, capable of withstanding the most formidable attacks and vulnerable only to the longest and most painstaking siege by a huge opposing force. But this image is practically laughable in its inaccuracy. The largest company forts tended to be in India, and probably the largest and most powerful of these was Fort St. William, maintained by the English East India Company at Calcutta. In 1756 this fort was simply overrun by the forces of the Nawab Siraj-ud-daulla, despite ample warning of the impending attack. Apparently, the company had maintained the fort in a thoroughly decrepit condition (Fuller 1955, 2:221).[11]

In practice, the threat perceived by the (English) Royal African Company from the local populace must also have been quite minor. The company's African forts were so minuscule and haphazard in construction that they would hardly have even delayed an assault by rampaging natives. The leading authority on the company's operations, Davies, writes (1975, 246): "In principle and intention, forts were permanent settlements, defended by earth and sometimes by stone-works, and garrisoned by between 8 and 20 men. In fact . . . the occupation of such forts as Kommenda and Sekondi was not seldom interrupted."

The proposition that forts were established in India for the defense of traders against barbarous natives is also dubious. The "disorders" Adam Smith alludes to (1937, 690) as providing the pretense for protective fortifications were what Cipolla refers to as "the state of anarchy into which India was plunged after the death of Aurangzeb in 1707 and the defeat of the Marathas at the hands of the Afghans" (1965, 146). Prior to 1707, governmental administrators within Aurangzeb's empire (and the reigns of his predecessors) had been quite efficient at maintaining civil order within India, and there were apparently no cases in which the Indian governments subservient to the Emperor initiated aggressive acts directed at Europeans. It is, of course, from the seventeenth century that the bulk of the pamphlets defending the English East India Company's forts and garrisons as bulwarks against rampaging natives date.

There is additional evidence that forts in India and elsewhere throughout Asia were not designed with defense against native attacks in mind. Forts at this time were essentially reinforced walls with firing ports, and their most important piece of defensive apparatus was the cannon. Also, the cannon was the only really effective means available of reducing a fort before a successful attack; the attacker would literally attempt to blow down the walls of the fort before an infantry assault. This, in fact, was the principal use assigned to early cannon on land prior to about 1500. Moreover, the Europeans were considerably more advanced in the technology of cannon building than any of the Asian nations (Cipolla 1965, 105–6).

It would certainly seem odd, then, if the same trading companies that were advertising the supposed necessity for the provision of forts to defend against rampaging natives were simultaneously supplying the natives with the most effective means available of overcoming forts (cannons). But this is exactly what was occurring on a wide scale. As Cipolla writes (1965, 10–11): "Inevitably, an armament race developed. Cannon became a highly coveted commodity; a much sought after and well rewarded object of trade, the perfect gift for obtaining favors from a local ruler, the precious jewel of a princely dowry. There was nothing that cannon could not buy—in fact as well as fancy." Elsewhere, Cipolla adds (1965, 109 n. 60) that "the instances of guns presented to local rulers in order to obtain special permissions or privileges are so numerous that one can hardly cite even a small portion of all known cases." Early in the seventeenth century, the Dutch bastion of Batavia actually installed a cannon foundry outside the fort; later it was moved inside, not to afford it added protection against a native threat, but "to keep the art [of cannon-making] secret," thereby protecting the source of a valuable monopoly quasi-rent to the Company (Cipolla 1965, 111).

If there is strong evidence suggesting that the chartered companies in Asia prior to 1700 were not maintaining forts and garrisons for the purpose of the defense of the peaceful trading activities of fellow countrymen, or even just their own, there is also evidence suggesting that the principal utility these companies gained from such devices was in terms of cartel enforcement. Forts and garrisons were producing an input (cartel enforcement) for the protection of monopoly rents.[12]

The exclusive charters granted to these companies imposed legal entry restrictions on the trade; competitors with the companies became interlopers or illicit traders. In the case of the English East India Company, these protective agreements were periodically renewed. For example, in 1681 the king issued a royal proclamation forbidding anyone except the East India Company and persons who traded by their license to trade within the limits of their charter, punishment being the forfeiture and loss of ships and goods (Payne 1930, 44). The English chartered foreign-trading companies in general had the power to seize interlopers, their ships, and their goods.

The garrisons the company maintained at their establishments were expected to patrol against interlopers attempting to trade in the area. Without exception it was company policy (and this would apply to the French and Dutch as well as the English East India companies) to forbid interlopers to trade within the boundaries of company operations; sometimes (for example, in the case of the English settlement of Madras or the Dutch settlement of Bencoolen), this was an area of several thousand square miles. Forts built to command the harbor approaches were seen as an effective means of discouraging interloping ships from trading in the vicinity.[13]

Naval Power

Owing basically to the prohibitively high cost of transporting and maintaining large military forces at great distances from home countries, the primary means of projecting military force from Europe to Asia during this period was naval power. Naval force was a much more cost-effective means of both offense and defense. Fuller (1955, 216–18) explains the nature of this efficiency in India:

> In 1740, on the outbreak of the War of the Austrian Succession, Madras and Pondicherry were the chief trading posts of the English and French on the Coromandel coast. . . . Each was fortified, and as all were on the coast they could be supplied and reinforced from overseas . . . [this] meant that whichever of the two main trading powers—English or French—held command of the Indian seas, it could starve out its competitor. Sea power was, therefore, the key to the colonial problem. . . . Although nothing was accomplished by the First Carnatic War, much had been learnt, above all that whoever commanded the sea could in time control the land.

The English East India Company's spokesmen in the seventeenth century consistently implied that the Company's major expenses in its Indian operations involved the construction and maintenance of forts, but one of the leading authorities on British military matters, Fortescue (1899, 2:180), writes that the Company's Directors had always been relatively neglectful of fixed land defenses, keeping them too small to withstand all but the most minor European naval assaults until at least 1746, and before this, "relied on the British fleet and upon that alone" for protection.

There was much discussion in England of the prospective benefits to be derived from the state undertaking to maintain the forts and garrisons, mainly the benefit of making unrestricted entry into the trade feasible. Barber (1975, 52) summarizes this general line of argument when he notes that "the overhead costs might be 'nationalized' with the state assuming responsibility for all capital charges associated with the commerce. The

trade itself could then be genuinely open to all who might be interested."
A famous early pamphlet, attributed to Petyt, entitled *Britannia Languens,*
or a Discourse of Trade (1680), argued for this kind of reform (McCulloch
1970, 334). A century later so did Adam Smith (1937, 754). This situation
prompted Josiah Tucker to remark in apparent disgust that "in times of
peace, our exclusive Companies impose the very worst, and most detrimental taxes on their Fellow-Subjects, that any Nation can suffer; and in
Time of War they are so far from assisting us, that they do not defend
themselves, and expect that we should do it for them" (Schuyler 1931, 144).

What the state was providing in these cases was not national naval defense, in the sense the reformers assumed was necessary, but rather cartel-
enforcement services. Naval power was the most effective means for
preventing competition by other national companies based outside a given
area. As a by-product, it also provided a relatively effective means for pa-
trolling against interlopers of whatever nationality. The Royal Navy captains who seized vessels engaged in illegal trade shared a portion of the
auctioned value of the seized ship and its cargo with the chartered company. Indeed, the British Fleet's primary day-to-day business in Indian waters
was its patrol to check for "illegal practices" (Wilbur 1945, 255).

Trade Treaties

Scott (1951, 453) appended to his argument that interlopers were free-riders
the following proposition: "Further, there may be added the necessary
additional outlay, in the purchase of the right of trading from native rulers." The free-rider problem allegedly lay in the inability of native rulers to
distinguish one European from another. For example, the English East
India Company's Select Committee at Canton wrote to the directors in
1781, bemoaning "whether it be their policy or really incomprehensible to
their strict notions of subordination, they will not allow themselves to believe that every Englishman who comes here is not under the control of the
Chief, though every day's experience might have convinced them to the
contrary" (Eames 1970, 101).

"Treaties" ordinarily were interpreted by the various national companies as cartel rights and pursued for this reason. Willan (1968a, 195) explains:
"Sixteenth-century companies engaged in foreign trade were always faced
with the problem of getting and maintaining privileges in the countries
with which they traded. Such privileges often depended on the caprice of
despotic rulers as in Turkey or Morocco or Russia. They usually involved

the grant of trading rights to members of the company and the exclusion from such rights of those who were not members."

Tucker thought that the "treaties of trade," particularly those in India, were actually negotiated cartel privileges designed to exclude interlopers. The companies were eager to add the coercive power of native regimes to their own cartel enforcement activities, which were less than completely effective. In a discussion of the supposed need for treaties and their actual function in 1754, Tucker wrote: "In short, the real Fear, of the exclusive Company is this,—Not that the private Traders would be ruined, [by the absence of trade treaties] but that the Indians would prefer dealing with them, rather than with the Agents of the Company: For they know very well, that the Indians, in such a case, would both buy their goods upon better terms, and be better treated. And then their Governors might reign over the naked Walls of their empty Forts and Castles, without Trade, and without Inhabitants" (Schuyler 1931, 153).

We have examined evidence indicating that the military expenditures by the foreign-trading companies were not for public goods, as economic historians have commonly supposed, but were for cartel-enforcement purposes. One might ask in this regard why the companies and not the state provided cartel enforcement services. As argued in chapter 2, it is commonly accepted that groups of merchants in this period in effect bought their monopoly privileges by making loans to the state. This was a principal means of state finance in this period (see Heckscher 1955, 1:178; Tawney 1958, lxiv).

A problem confronted the monarch in this connection, however. The trade to which the monopoly rights were being auctioned off was highly heterogeneous, and its value was difficult to predict ex ante. This provided the monarch with an incentive to establish arrangements whereby he could meter and capture the monopoly rents accruing to the company over time. Basically, the monarch accomplished this objective by controlling the cartel-enforcement services provided for the companies. In such a way he was positioned to monitor and expropriate changes in the level of monopoly rents over time. As an example of this system in operation, at one point in the 1680s, Child and the Directors of the East India Company voted the king a present of £10,000 in order for the company to receive better protection against interlopers (Barber 1975, 49).

Of course, the King's appropriation of monopoly rents in this manner provided a company with an incentive to adjust its operations in a manner that reduced the efficiency of the monarch's metering system. In particular, if the company provided a substantial proportion of its cartel enforce-ment services, it would be in a stronger bargaining position over the dispo-sition of monopoly returns relative to the king. This incentive basically explains some of the dual enforcement systems observed over this period (for example, the Bombay Marine).

CONCLUDING REMARKS

In the present chapter we have argued that business organization in the mercantile age was complex and evolutionary. Competitive organization began to characterize many English internal markets (as we say in chap-ter 3), as it did, to some extent, French basic industry (chapter 4), while foreign-trading companies demanded and were supplied cartelization. The Spanish and Portuguese companies, by contrast, were of the nature of public enterprises. The form and characteristics of such cartels as well as the inevi-table cartel-enforcement problems were much the same as those encoun-tered in the modern age. But from the viewpoint of rent seeking, the mercantilists behaved very rationally in the search for monopoly through regulation of both internal and external trade.

For there to be a public-goods problem, there must first be a public good. This tautology has apparently been overlooked by recent writers who have studied the early chartered trading companies. They have of-fered a rationale for the grant of monopoly rights to these companies based on the supposed need to overcome the problem of competing traders free-riding on trading infrastructure (forts, garrisons, and so forth) supplied by the companies. This argument falls flat for a very simple reason; the forts and garrisons were actually being used to restrict entry into the trade by those same competitors. The public goods involved would be better termed public bads.

Certain insightful contemporary critics of the monopoly companies (in-cluding Adam Smith) questioned the public-goods character of chartered company military investments. But modern scholars have mostly ignored the critics, and instead have adopted the rationalizations of the companies' hired apologists. Our intention here has simply been to analyze the con-trasting positions. Like Coase (1974), we suggest that a public good may sometimes only be a stalking-horse.

Chapter Seven

The English East India Company and the Mercantile Origins of the Modern Corporation

The functioning of the corporate system has not to date been adequately explained. . . . one who reflects on the properties or characteristics of this system cannot help asking why it works and whether it will continue to work.
—E. S. Mason, *The Corporation in Modern Society*

The study of the "microanalytics" of individual mercantile monopoly companies is useful in its own right. Such research allows us to explicate clearly how these companies operated and how they resolved certain basic and timeless economic problems in their organizational forms. It also permits comparison of modern forms of economic organization with the forms adopted by the early companies. There are fundamental similarities in the economic problems faced by both the early and more modern companies, and hence a similarity in their organizational formats as well. Within the process of firm adaptation to transactions costs and external forces is the long, and often tentative, beginnings of the modern (limited liability) form of the corporation. The vital nature of the firm and corporation as the foundation for economic progress in all societies needs no rationale, of course. But historical research and economic logic gives us greater insight into the political economy of mercantilism and into the economic nature of the early companies.

Chandler (1966; 1977) and Williamson (1975) argue that the invention of the multidivisional firm in the United States in the 1920s was an organizational breakthrough in business history. It is our purpose in this chapter to challenge this claim. We believe that Williamson's account of the nature and functions of the multidivisional firm offers a useful analytical tool for explaining the organization of a least one firm in the seventeenth and eighteenth centuries that would seem to have almost nothing in common with General Motors or Dupont—the English East India Company.[1] There is considerable evidence that this early joint-stock firm displayed all of the essential characteristics of a multidivisional organization, which developed in response to economically analogous problems faced by firms that adopted the same organizational form in the twentieth century.

Our studies of the microanalytic aspects of the firm are extended in this chapter to some details of the evolution of the modern firm. The contemporary corporate form of business organization evolved over many centuries, and despite a large body of historical research its origins and the reasons it took hold and spread are still obscure. Why was the corporation invented? The early joint-stock companies in England embodied an important change in contractual form. Scholars have hypothesized that these corporations evolved in response to an exogenous increase in the demand for capital by the early foreign-trading companies. Our complementary, supply-side hypothesis stresses the advantages that more readily transferable property rights held for the owner-managers of these early companies. These two hypotheses and the historical evidence on their relative importance will help us explain the emergence of the corporate form of economic organization.

THE MULTIDIVISIONAL FIRM THESIS

Chandler and Williamson focused on the history of American business firms, and on this basis they argued that prior to the late 1800s firms were primarily organized as peer groups or simple hierarchies. Firms with more complex organizations in this period were characterized by an inside contracting system, in which the functional parts of the enterprise were loosely bound together through formal relationships (factory space, for example, was rented to subcontractors). A so-called employment relation across all stages is seen as a later development, one that emerged in the late 1800s. At this time, as Chandler (1977) documents, large enterprises organized along functional lines (production, sales, finance) began to emerge. These firms, which stressed specialization by function, permitted a more efficient division of labor within the firm, provided that control of the parts by the center could be effectively maintained. This control, however, tended to break down.

Chandler and Williamson argue that these problems were overcome to a large extent by the multidivisional firm. This innovation came to the fore in the early 1920s at General Motors and Dupont. Williamson (1975, 137) summarizes the characteristics of the multidivisional firm in this way:

(1) The responsibility for operating decisions is assigned to (essentially self-contained) operating divisions or quasi-firms.

(2) The elite staff attached to the general office performs both advisory and auditing functions. Both have the effect of securing greater control over operating division behavior.

(3) The general office is principally concerned with strategic decisions, involving planning, appraisal, and control, including the allocation of resources among the (competing) operating divisions.

(4) The separation of the general office from operations provides general office executives with the psychological commitment to be concerned with the overall performance of the organization rather than become absorbed in the affairs of the functional parts.

In Williamson's approach, divisional organization reduces costs in the firm. Information problems and the potential for opportunistic behavior are delimited in this organizational framework. Operating decisions are made at the divisional level, where managers possess the requisite information to make day-to-day decisions. Strategic decisions are made in a central office, which embodies a planning-coordination mechanism for resource allocation within the firm. This central office has access, moreover, to an internal auditing and control system that allows it to monitor and evaluate the performance of the various operating units.

It is important to note that decentralization of decision making in the enterprise is not sufficient by itself to increase the effectiveness with which the firm operates. Lower-level managers may possess more information with which to make operating decisions, but unless they have sufficient incentives to act upon this information, decentralization does not guarantee a more efficient outcome for the firm. If decentralized entrepreneurship is to be achieved within the firm, involving creative adaptation to changing economic conditions, some incentive scheme such as decentralized profit-sharing is implied. Profit-sharing allows the decentralized decision maker to appropriate monetary gain or loss from well-conceived decisions, and thereby provides an incentive for efforts in this regard. Thus, if the manager at the divisional level in the firm has economic interests that rise or fall with the corresponding rise or fall of the value of the firm, an incentive for the provision of services leading to the former end has been provided.

The Chandler-Williamson studies of economic organization are drawn primarily from American business history. In this chapter we seek to demonstrate that the English East India Company, one of the largest and most far-flung business organizations in history prior to the nineteenth century, is also an example of a complex multidivisional organization from its very founding in 1600. Based on Williamson's criteria, the English East India Company was a multidivisional enterprise antedating the modern appearance of this organizational form by more than two hundred years. Our argument will not be that the East India Company and General Motors are comparable with respect to lines of business or scales of operation. We will argue that the economic substance of the organizational forms adopted by the two companies was functionally the same, and more important, that the East India Company's organization evolved in response to the same type of economic problems that confronted more modern firms who have turned to multidivisional operations.

THE EAST INDIA COMPANY

In the charter of the London East India Company (1600), two important aspects of the company's organization were set out.[2] These were the Court of Committees, composed of twenty-four members of the company, and the General Court, composed of all shareholders. The Court of Committees consisted of a governor, a deputy, and "ordinary" members, and served as the main executive organ of the company.[3] The General Court exercised a supervisory role in policy making, and possessed final control in that it could either ratify or alter policy through majority voting. The members of the Court of Committees were city merchants, who were directly engaged in sales at home or re-export of company commodities to foreign countries. The General Court was composed of individuals who had invested in the company but did not actively participate in its trading operations.

The Court of Directors was elected annually by voting members of the Court of Proprietors from a list of their fellow proprietors who owned at least £2000 of stock. The Court of Directors essentially combined the functions of the board of directors and upper-echelon management in a modern corporation; the Governor of the Company was equivalent to a modern chief executive officer (Furber 1970, 11–12).

As is characteristic of modern corporations, the company had what was, for all intents and purposes, a full-time staff of managerial executives in London. Each week, the Court of Directors met at least once and often three times. Final decisions regarding the reports of subcommittees and the contents of dispatches to India were made as the result of a ballot (a quorum of thirteen directors was required). As many as forty or fifty ballots were taken at a normal meeting (Philips 1940, 8). In the eighteenth century a complicated system of committees of directors was maintained in order to facilitate an efficient division of labor in policy making; each committee had its chief, who in turn had a staff of officers (all full-time employees) to conduct committee business. In 1784, the regular officers employed at the India House numbered about 150 (Philips 1940, 16).

The Court of Directors, usually in the form of the various committees, was chiefly responsible for strategic decision making in the firm. For example, the directors decided where new factories in Asia were to be developed, and whether already established factories were to be maintained or expanded. The court determined the general pattern of investment to be undertaken by the presidencies in Asia, for example, whether a particular presidency should expand investment in cloth goods or procure agriculture exports of a certain kind, and allocated capital to the presidencies in Asia in the form of specie for operating expenses and goods for trading capital. The directors also allocated military protection and decided policy in response to threats from Asian competitors. Basically, the Court of Directors was responsible for evaluating operational decision making by the presidencies, but did not run the operations in Asia on a day-by-day basis.

Beginning in 1683, the directors organized a Secret Committee (usually composed of three or four members) to deal with "extraordinary political matters" (Philips 1940, 9). These included the direction of the company's naval and military operations in time of war with native rulers or other European trading powers, the conduct of negotiations with Indian powers, and the representation of the company in its dealings with ministers of the British government. The Secret Committee was in charge of the negotiations for the Treaty of Paris in 1763 at the conclusion of the Seven Years' War insofar as it concerned the company's Indian interests.

In other words, a considerable proportion of the strategic decision making undertaken by the Court of Directors involved the planning and conduct of military operations—that is, strategy in its original and literal sense. The value of centralized policy making in this domain is obvious; a coherent strategic plan is a most important ingredient of success in war.[4] But it is also clear that the conduct of military policy—itself only one as-

pect, albeit an important one, of firm-wide strategic planning by the directors—required a separate specialized committee that engaged in little else.
The Company's Court of Directors quite simply lacked the time to engage
in operational decision making, even if the long communication lag
with India had been overcome, say, by the early invention of long-range
telegraphy.

The company's factors in Asia were its trading representatives. They
managed the sale of export goods in Asia as well as the purchase of return
cargo for homeward-bound ships. The compensation arrangements for these
factors evolved over time from a pure salaried status to arrangements involving both salary and profit-sharing provisions—provisions that undoubtedly addressed agency problems. They were encouraged to invest in the
company, and apparently did so on a moderate scale. Moreover, the granting of freedom to engage in private trade on one's own account came to be
a principal attraction of a career in the Indies for senior factors.

The Central Office in London exercised considerable control over the
activities of the factories in India (Chaudhuri 1968, 86). It would be a mistake, however, to interpret such control as implying that the internal organization of the company relative to the factors was a simple hierarchy. The
Central Office was too far removed from the Indies to do much more than
endorse decisions already made by its chief factors or to sanction decisions
of which it disapproved. The slowness of communication and the distances
involved necessitated the factors being manager-entrepreneurs. As an example of the type of entrepreneurial decision making undertaken by factors, the original extension of the company's trade into Persia was initiated
by the head of the Surat factory, Aldworth, who obtained approval from
London but was not directed in his activities by the Central Office (Chaudhuri 1968, 51; Scott 1951, 1:60–61).

Early in the company's history, its system of joint-stock ownership and
finance was based not on a permanent stock but on separate *terminable
stocks,* which were only in effect for a specified period of years. Of principal
interest here is the additional organizational complexity of the firm owing
to this form of ownership finance. Separate voyages were separately financed,
and at times several such undertakings coexisted with different groups of
shareholders. A centralized marketing system in London was combined
with as many as five independent ventures. Scott (1951, 1:109–13) argued
that this system created a considerable amount of administrative confusion
in London owing to the common marketing of goods from separate voy-

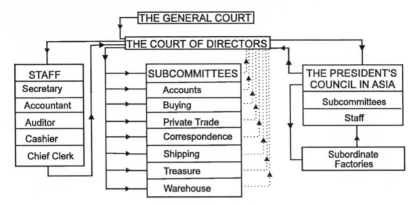

Figure 7.1. Organization of the English East India Company

ages and the consequent problems in allocating profits back to each individual voyage, a problem that still intrigues accountants. The potential for opportunistic behavior (which we argue later in this chapter) posed by the terminable joint stocks, combined with a centrally controlled marketing system, offers an explanation for the use of a vertically integrated firm rather than other contractual arrangements by the holders of the monopoly charter for the India trade.

For the reader's inspection the company's organizational chart over this period, as described by Chaudhuri (1978, 26), is given in figure 7.1. The sophistication of the company's organization is apparent. The central management was divorced from the day-to-day operations of the presidencies (discussed below), and was provided with ample staff support to carry out a planning-control mission for the company.

THE EAST INDIA COMPANY AS A MULTIDIVISIONAL FIRM

In analyzing the economic organization of the East India Company, we follow Williamson's definitional criteria for a multidivisional firm. First, we demonstrate that the company was divisionalized.

Divisionalization

In the early history of the company, the two principal factories in the Indies trade, Surat and Bantam, functioned as separate competing divisions. Shipping and cash flow were allocated between the factories by the Court of Committees in London according to their relative expected profits.

Beginning in 1653, the overseas administration of the company was divided into three presidencies, those at Bengal, Madras, and Bombay, as well as a trading establishment in China (Gardner 1972, 42). Each presidency administered a number of separate factories. The separate presidencies corresponded directly with the Court of Directors in London, as well as developed their own military forces and their own corps of employees (Furber 1976, 199). Each presidency in India was allowed to direct its country trading independently.

The Court of Directors made strategic decisions for the firm, including the establishment of long-term goals, administrative organization, and capital allocation among the presidencies. However, operational decisions concerning trading operations remained the responsibility of the presidencies. Decisions concerning specific investments in Asia of capital allocated by London were also made on the presidency level. The London India House was able to advise the Indian operations concerning future general investment strategies but essentially restricted itself to evaluating ex post the specific investment decisions undertaken by the presidencies (see letters from Court of Directors, 19 December 1755 and 11 February 1756, for example; Datta 1958, 129 and 141).

Gains and losses of particular presidencies were carefully separated in the company's accounts, and the performance of the presidencies was evaluated according to their profitability (Chaudhuri 1978, 57–59). The type of goods ordered by the London office usually allowed a presidency significant discretion as to the precise quality of the goods involved. The actual operation of the country trade was not controlled by the Court of Directors. Day-to-day operations were left for the separate divisions to manage autonomously (Chaudhuri 1978, 208).[5]

In sum, the Court of Directors was not concerned with day-to-day operating decisions but with establishing a set of consistent decision rules within which its servants in India could operate and with making long-term strategic decisions. The presidencies were not merely providing functionally distinct inputs into a single output process but were generating separable outputs on a profit-center basis. In short, the separate presidencies functioned as separate divisions within the firm subject to an internal control apparatus maintained by the central management in London.

Incentive Machinery

The East India Company's factors in Asia were the company's trading representatives. One possible means to provide the necessary incentive for these servants to pursue the Company's interests was to provide them with a salary, which included a rent payment over and above their opportunity cost (Becker and Stigler 1974). In this approach factor shirking would be constrained by the risk of loss of rents through dismissal. Basically, however, the company never pursued this course. Even as late as the 1750s, the company's servants were paid very low salaries (Datta 1958, xx).

The primary inducement offered factors was the freedom to engage in private trade. Private trading was a means to solve an information-incentive problem in the company. The company's agents in India possessed information regarding local exchanges and other company activities, and private trading represented a system of decentralized property rights, whereby the agents could be induced to act effectively on the basis of this information.

The system of private trading was simple in design. The Court of Directors in London would allocate additional shipping and trading capital to Indian factories, which showed relatively high rates of return. This allowed the trading operations of the factory to expand. In step with this expansion of trading operations was an expansion in the private opportunities available to the company's agents. The company would allocate space aboard East Indiamen on a priority basis to servants as a reward for effective efforts on the company's behalf, and would reduce the allocation of those whose efforts had proven less effective. In such a way a system of decentralized property rights evolved, and under this system the company was able to tailor rewards more closely to the productivity of its agents in India.

Internal Control

Bookkeeping for the company was centralized through an "account current, London," made up from books annually sent from overseas, allowing for an extensive central audit. The company employed accountants who examined the books sent home. Foster (1924), Stevens (1967), and Watts and Zimmerman (1981) detail the auditing procedures used by the company in its early years. Auditors, for example, were appointed at each session of the General Court (the shareholders' meeting).

There are numerous other examples of the working of the auditing and internal control processes in the company. On March 9, 1720, Mr. J. Fletcher wrote from the East India House in London to the governor and council at Bombay: "your Bombay journal and leger, letter Q, are the worst and most erroneously copied that ever the company received from any part of India . . . If we had the time to have copied them we would have sent them back to you to let you see what shameful pair of books they are. Pray let the same persons copy us over another pair" (Furber 1976, 200).

In the future they were directed to submit books that showed "the charges and losses of every particular factory amount" (Furber 1976, 200). As a further illustration, the company wrote to the Bombay Council in 1737: "The calculate of quick stock which we have ordered annually to be sent is not only to show us what remains for the use (of) the ensuing Investment, but likewise, that we may form a true judgement of our Estate, consisting of Cash, Goods, in the warehouse, stores and good debts. . . . You must therefore draw it out in the most accurate manner accordingly" (Chaudhuri 1978, 60).

The internal auditing process was not solely dependent upon the precision and honesty of record keeping by the various presidencies and factories. The central management in London attempted to extend the range of its sources, introducing a considerable amount of redundancy into the system and in effect making the net guarding against managerial opportunism more finely woven. Senior servants were encouraged to report on a wide range of subjects. The same events were often featured simultaneously in the letters of the officials from Bombay, Madras, or Calcutta. This duplication in correspondence allowed the Subcommittee of Correspondence to increase its monitoring efficiency. Discrepancies between two accounts of the same event by different officials were watched for closely and investigated further. This process allowed the company to isolate mistakes or inaccuracies in accounts by senior servants (Chaudhuri 1978, 78).

Of course, identified inaccuracies might or might not result from attempts to distort the facts on the part of company servants. As a result, the company had further information sources in the form of an extensive system of private correspondence (Chaudhuri 1978, 31). Monitoring was thus not entirely undertaken through the vehicle of the internal audit by accountants but was supplemented by a variety of other devices.[6]

As we stressed previously, the Directors in London allocated resources to the Asian presidencies to support the commercial plans of the various factories. The Subcommittee of Correspondence made the detailed calculations necessary for this operation, using the record books sent from India, correspondence and other sources of information, as well as information on the relative profitability of sales from the particular presidencies. For example, in 1681 the company announced that its investment in Bengal was about to be increased substantially, and the reason offered was that the goods sent to London from this region were higher quality and lower cost than those sent from other regions (Chaudhuri 1978, 72). In 1724, an extensive internal audit of the Bombay presidency's books, which went beyond the annual audit, was conducted by the Court in London, and this resulted in a stern warning to cut costs and run a tighter ship or else. Continuing inefficiency in the Bombay presidency resulted in the decline of cash investment there by the central office and also in a diminished shipping allocation (Chaudhuri 1978, 65–66).

Resource allocation in the form of cash investment as well as shipping provision was not merely dependent on the evaluation of the relative efficiency of the various factories and presidencies but was also determined by the expected demand for the imported goods, which would not arrive for approximately two years. Thus, not only recent profit performance but efficiency and expected future demands for particular goods all influenced strategic decisions by the Directors in London pertaining to resource allocation to the factories in Asia.

In sum, the mass of the evidence suggests to us that the day-to-day operations of the East India Company were much the same as any modern multidivisional company, although on a much smaller scale. Albert Sloan or Harold Geneen would have felt right at home at the helm of the English East India Company.

WHY DID THE EAST INDIA COMPANY MAINTAIN A DECENTRALIZED INTERNAL ORGANIZATION?

In this section we propose an explanation for the economic organization of the East India Company. There were two primary aspects of the company's organization, which, as we shall argue, were interrelated.[7] First, the company held a monopoly charter for the Indian trade. This meant that the East India Company was the only English Company licensed to do business in India and to sell Indian goods in England. The company did not possess a monopoly in its re-export business to the Continent, nor in its port-to-port trade in Asia. In both these spheres the company competed with other national trading companies, especially the Dutch, and to some degree with interlopers and smugglers. Second, the company was vertically integrated in the following sense. Company trading operations in India were conducted through a factory system in which company agents purchased goods with bullion for shipment to England. These agents were the first stage of the company's internal operations. The goods were transported to England in company ships, built by the company and manned by company employees, and sold at auction at the East India House in London. These auctions represented the upper end of the company's vertical operations. In other words, the company was integrated from the purchase of goods in India to their sale in London.

The first clue to understanding the organization of the company resides in its chartered monopoly status. In effect, the monopoly charter stimulated the emergence of a large vertically integrated firm, which otherwise might not have existed. Without a monopoly companies would have perhaps consisted of single ships; with a monopoly the development of separate, specialized, and competing firms was made more costly. Vertical integration of purchase, shipping, and sales in the case of East India Company did not represent an efficient adaptation to free market forces but would appear to have resulted from a legal obstruction to these forces.[8] In all probability the English East India Company as a multidivisional firm was an artifact of government regulation.

Within this interpretation of the company's organization, there remains the issue of why other seemingly viable alternatives for exploiting its monopoly status were not employed. In particular, why could not the owners of the trading rights have collected their monopoly rents through a system of franchising voyages or licensing importers? After first establishing the link between the company's organization and its monopoly charter, we return to this issue and consider why franchising or licensing was not a viable way for the owners of the company to collect monopoly rents.

Consider the conditions under which the company operated. Central management in London was basically two years away from its operatives in India and on ships in between. These distances represented a significant span of control problem. The incentive to act rested with residual claimants in London; the information to act rested with company operatives in the field. Resolving this divergence of incentives and information was the organizational problem facing the company. As we noted above, this problem would probably not have arisen without the monopoly status of the firm in the context of poorly developed Asian markets. Otherwise, decentralized ownership in the form of separate firms specializing in the Asian trade would likely have prevailed. The degree of vertical integration fostered by these difficulties required the East India Company to solve a complex organizational problem.

Consider the issue in terms of the example of shipping between London and India. Ship captains were not owner-operators. Had they been, the fact that they were out of touch with London for eight months or more would have been immaterial. Being residual claimants, the decisions they made during the course of a voyage—should they turn back in the face of a storm, work their crews harder, and so on—would have been profit-maximizing decisions. There would have been no divergence of incentives and information to act. But as a company employee, the ship captain posed a control problem for the firm.

As we stressed in our discussion of the factors, one alternative was to offer ship captains a wage in excess of their opportunity cost with the implication being that dismissal on grounds of incompetence would constitute an opportunity loss of rents for captains. This solution works fine for gross acts of malfeasance, but not so well in other circumstances. For example, how are the captain's decisions in the face of uncertainty (did he choose the best route given weather conditions) to be evaluated? A competent, alert captain might experience delays owing to chance circumstances beyond his control (the converse of this proposition is also true). Simple monitoring can insure formal compliance with regulations, but cannot distinguish reliably between competent, dedicated effort and its absence. As a result, self-monitoring by the employee is more efficient, but requires an incentive structure based on residual claimancy or some form of self-enforcing contract. To generate effective entrepreneurship on the part of the ship's captain, it was necessary for him to experience either profit or loss as the result of the quality of his efforts.

In the case of shipping there developed a system of trading in which the company and the captain had a mutuality of interests. This developed in the form of the privilege trade: the captain of an East Indiaman was allotted fifty-six tons (at most twenty feet of deck space) for his private cargo, which was sold at the company auction in London.[9]

This is not to argue that decentralized property rights led to a perfect solution of the company's organizational problem. It was not technically feasible to provide factors and ship captains with information pertaining to current prices in London, the fortunes of other ships in transit, and so forth. It must also be noted that illicit trade by factors was a continuing problem for the company, and there were various conflicts of interest over the years between the company's business and the private trade of factors. Gradually, after the middle of the seventeenth century factors became increasingly involved in local Indian trading operations to the point that purchases and sales for the company sometimes suffered. The company was by no means able to resolve its information-incentive problem in a comprehensive manner. Rather the company evolved a workable system of decentralized property rights, which mitigated some of the more important costs in the agent-principal problem that it faced. Our purpose is not to offer a normative evaluation of these arrangements, but to suggest the economic forces that led to their adoption by the company.

We note that there are additional possible explanations for the emergence of the East India Company into a vertically-integrated form, which are related to our argument that the company's monopoly charter was important for its organization and which merit further research. First, there is the issue of the security of the firm's monopoly right. While the monarchy had a clear incentive not to renege on sales of such rights because of the loss of revenue on future sales, such behavior was not totally implausible. By forming a large firm with many powerful merchants as investors and managers, the company clearly strengthened its political effectiveness relative to what it might have been under alternative, more independent arrangements. Second, it may seem far-fetched, but there is the possibility that the company designed its organizational arrangements such that if its monopoly status was ever revoked, it would continue to maintain a dominant position in the industry.

A final point is that the vertically integrated nature of the East India Company cannot be taken for granted in terms of economic analysis. In particular, why did the firm not evolve in the direction of some other set of contractual arrangements such as franchising (Rubin 1978) or import licenses? The chartered monopoly of the company may not provide a complete answer to this question, because other chartered monopolies over this era developed a franchise form of organization (the Mines Royal, for example, the domestic mining monopoly in England; see Cawston and Keane 1968).[10]

In the case of the East India Company, the development of parallel interests of factors in Asia is an example of a franchise form. The factors were technically salaried employees, but they participated through private trading and other means in profit sharing. It is interesting to note that according to Furber (1976, 195), "At the close of his career a captain expected to have the disposal of his command, so that he could 'sell' it for £6000 or more to one of the many mates who hoped to apply the profits of private trade to acquiring such an opportunity."

We are not arguing that these examples serve as evidence of full-fledged franchise contracts. The main reason for the interpretation of the company as a vertically integrated firm is that the marketing of output was centrally directed at the company's London auction.[11] To understand our argument on this point, consider the evolution of company practices over time.

The case can be made that the system of terminable joint stocks, which characterized the Old East India Company until the amalgamation with the New Company at the beginning of the eighteenth century, also had franchise characteristics. The different joint stocks represented different trading bodies within the company, each of which had its own separate factors in Asia who competed with each other for the country-trade (Scott 1951, 1:109). To quote Scott (1:462), "It follows that, while from the legal point of view, there was only one company, from the financial standpoint there had been many."[12]

We hypothesize that given its legal monopoly on marketing, the company was in a position to appropriate quasi-rents from the participants in the franchise-like terminable joint stocks. The economic forces that undermined the argument for franchising can be described in the following manner. The holders of the monopoly charter could have authorized individual firms to go to India and obtain goods for trade. Monopoly profits could have been collected by pricing franchises appropriately or by putting a tax on the right to sell at the London auction. Why was this organizational course not pursued? One hypothesis is that franchising was not a viable organizational option for the company owing to the potential for opportunistic behavior by the holders of the monopoly charter. An example of such behavior would have been selling the franchisee's goods for a low price at auction in the face of a high franchise fee. In fact, much of the discussion in the literature about the difficulties of keeping track of the returns at auction to the various members of the terminable joint stocks suggests the potential for opportunistic behavior of this type (Scott 1951, 1:109–13).

Thus, the Old Company's legally chartered competitor in the 1690s, the "New East India Company," was organized on the basis of a body of permanent stockholders, and grew rapidly while the Old Company stagnated. After the two companies were merged into the United East India Company, the separate terminable joint stock system was permanently abandoned, suggesting a competitive constraint on the appropriation of quasi-rents through the company's marketing monopoly.

However, we hasten to add that the potential for opportunistic behavior is not a general explanation of behavior in a repeat purchase, continuous dealing environment. As Klein, Crawford, and Alchian (1978) argued, the expected loss of rents on future business acts as a bonding device against the appropriation of quasi-rents. This is not to say that the capture of quasi-rents does not occur. It does, and the potential for rent appropriation may be a satisfactory explanation for the vertical integration of the East India Company. We simply do not know the relevant data with respect to individual discount rates, the annual flow of voyages, the probability of return voyages, and so forth. It could well have been the case that the quasi-rents and the relevant probabilities influencing behavior became such as to swamp the bonding value of repetitive dealing. Our point is simply that the rent appropriation argument is not a general explanation for the vertical integration of the company.[13]

Another explanation for the absence of franchise contracts in this case is the cost of contracting. With monopoly, efficient vertical disintegration requires that the monopoly right be exercised with respect to final output demand. To prevent distortion of factor proportions it may have been necessary to write complicated franchise contracts, which owing to the nature of the business in this case (ships at sea) would have been difficult to enforce. The franchise fee, for example, would have caused the shipping firms' minimum average cost to shift up and to the right and resulted in larger ships and more frequent trips than optimal. Presumably, the costs of writing and enforcing a contract to prevent this type of input distortion among franchisors were prohibitive. Vertical integration could thus have been adopted over franchising on rent-maximizing grounds.[14]

Both the rent-appropriation and the cost of contracting arguments provide possible explanations of the vertical integration of the company. Moreover, the evidence noted above that other contemporary monopolists successfully employed franchise contracts may mean that the East India Company was a comparatively inefficient firm that was somehow shielded from takeover. Such competing explanations provide grist for future research on the evolution on this and other early companies. In any event the East India Company evolved in the face of such problems into a multidivisional firm with a vertically integrated structure.[15]

The plain truth is that we do not have enough information to reject any of these explanations for the organization of the company. We do observe this, however. Many modern firms have chosen to exploit monopoly rights, such as patents, through vertical integration and production in the marketplace rather than through licensing or franchising. While we do not know all the reasons that some firms behave this way, we do know that the behavior of the East India Company, for whatever reasons, was analogous.

Summary: The Multidivisional Firm

The foregoing discussion represents the basis of an explanation for the emergence of the principles of a multidivisional firm in the East India Company. In essence, the organizational form of the East India Company was an anachronism. By virtue of its trading monopoly, the company was necessarily large in a time when the costs of communication, organization, and control dictated that efficient firm size be small. This point is bolstered by the fact that the company's shareholder-to-director ratio was incredibly small by modern standards. For example, in 1600 there were 24 directors out of 103 shareholders or a ratio of 4.3:1 (Stevens 1967, 58–63). Compare this with virtually any large modern firm. General Motors, for example, as of December 31, 1978, had 1,248,814 common stockholders and 24 directors, or a ratio of approximately 52,000:1. Presumably, the low ratio of the East India Company was necessitated by the very high organization costs and the need to monitor the affairs of the firm closely and frequently.

It is worth reiterating that we are *not* claiming that the differences between the East India Company and modern multidivisional corporations are trivial. We are arguing that the East India Company shared the most essential economic characteristics of the multidivisional firm with more modern and familiar examples, and that it turned to this organizational format in an effort to resolve economic problems that are not all that much different, if at all, from those faced by the modern, large-scale, multidivisional enterprise.

MERCANTILE ORIGINS OF THE CORPORATION

The resolution of economic problems in the early companies is also the raison d'être for a critical phase of firm-corporate development. Why and how was the modern corporate form of business organization invented?

How did it evolve? The remainder of this chapter is devoted to these overarching questions.

Our argument proceeds in two phases. First, we discuss the origins of the corporate form of business organization. The basic economic problems that were solved by share transferability and by the corporate form are introduced and discussed. We proceed secondly to show how the corporate form evolved and came into common usage in England. Here, the key issue is whether the joint-stock company was a creation of government, made possible by enabling legislation, or whether it was a contractual device that was invented through trial and error by private parties, in other words, a Hayekian invention. The two issues are distinct. The first involves the question of why the corporate form first came about. The second takes the corporate form as a given and known contractual alternative and asks how did it spread.

Mercantile Origins: The Conventional Wisdom

The foreign-trading companies in England were merchant cartels that had received monopoly charters from the crown to engage in trade with specified countries, as we detailed earlier in this chapter. The rules devised to govern these cartels were extensive and detailed, and they were thus designated as regulated companies. The early public joint-stock companies in England (circa 1553) were, predictably, little different in substance from the regulated companies. The standard hypothesis explaining the rise of joint-stock companies in England is that contractual provisions of these companies, especially limited liability, enabled them to raise capital more readily than the regulated companies. This argument was taken as a given by the classical writers, as it is by contemporary economic historians (Clough and Rapp 1975, 152; Tuma 1971, 297). To J. S. Mill for example, the capital-accumulative aspect was of primary importance: "Production on a large scale is greatly promoted by the practice of forming a large capital by the combination of many small contributions; or, in other words, by the formation of joint stock companies. The advantages of the joint stock principle are numerous and important. In the first place, many undertakings require an amount of capital beyond the means of the richest individual or private partnership" (1965, 137). Further, in a classic work on the mercantile companies, W. R. Scott (1951) argues that "the joint-stock company was no more than the ready means for improving production by arranging for the ready inflow of capital" (1:442; see also Scott's chap. 21).

The analytical basis for Scott's hypothesis was an exogenous increase in demand for capital by the regulated companies, which could only be accommodated by a change in legal form. There is certainly some truth to the argument that the trading companies' demand for capital increased over time. The early expeditions by the trading companies were essentially hand-to-mouth affairs. Each expedition was financed independently, to be decomposed into returns at the voyage's end. It is quite reasonable for writers to argue that these companies required a certain amount of infrastructure to carry on foreign trade on an ongoing basis as trade routes and business practices became more regular over the period. For example, warehouses became necessary to manage inventories at home and abroad.

There is thus nothing inherently incorrect in the "classical" view that as the trading companies grew their demand for capital also grew. To us, however, this cannot be the whole story of the evolution of the corporate form. The primary shortcoming is that it is a purely demand-driven explanation, and, as such, it excludes some important supply-side considerations. Moreover, as a single explanatory hypothesis, the demand-for-capital argument neglects some crucial market functions. For example, with respect to debt capital (and in these closely held companies this appears to have been the major method of raising capital), market forces would have been working to negate the capital-raising argument. A change in legal form from a closely held company, wherein the wealth of partners was mutually liable, to a joint-stock company with limited liability would not have dramatically affected the supply side of the loan market, that is, the terms on which companies could borrow (see Meiners, Mofsky, and Tollison 1979). The early joint-stock companies were still closely held; partner-stockholders put up the same loan collateral (for example, personal assets) as before or faced higher interest rates. Thus, the cost of capital to the early companies should have been roughly the same under either contractual arrangement.

Corporate Primogeniture: Property Rights in the Early Companies

The English-regulated companies, as we have stressed, were associations of merchants who colluded to restrict competition among the towns in international trade. These cartels, legally sanctioned and encouraged by state authorities, generally operated with great effectiveness.[16] However, one

aspect of their operations was troublesome: sustaining the economic organization over time as cartel owner-managers retired or otherwise sought to
leave the organization. The regulated companies solved this problem in
the way that most family firms solve it—by passing on cartel rights within
the family. Heckscher offers some of the flavor of this process:

> The companies could not possibly remain open to everyone, quite irrespec-
> tive of whether they admitted merchants from every city or not. This fol-
> lowed from its principle of limiting competition which was inherent in its
> medieval origins. Many facts can be adduced to substantiate the point. The
> fine was often extortionate. In the Merchant Adventurers' Company, ac-
> cording to its codified by-laws of 1608, it was no less than £200 sterling for
> "redemptioners," i.e. those who were not sons or apprentices of members.
> (1934, 1:387)

Primarily, of course, the apprenticeship system was designed to restrict
entry and create monopoly rents for cartel members. But submerged in the
background of this process was the issue of ensuring the continuity and
efficiency of the firm's operation over time. As we see it, this issue tele-
scopes to a question of the transferability of property rights in these cartels.[17] In the early regulated companies, and the African trade provides an
excellent example (Scott 1951, 2:5–8), the property rights of owner-managers were difficult to transfer. There was no active capital market where such
rights could be traded, and, moreover, there was the usual difficulty associated with partnerships—a partner's exit from the firm was restricted by the
requirement that a new partner be satisfactory to those partners remaining
in the firm. A partner thus maintained his stake in the cartel by staying in
the firm or by keeping the relevant property rights in the family. The lack
of easily transferable property rights made it efficient for the owner-managers to retain their cartel rights within their families.[18]

Corporate primogeniture, however, led to an economic problem for
the cartel, for there was no guarantee that sons, grandsons, or nephews (in
the case of no male issue) would constitute the most effective set of cartel
owner-managers. Thus, if these rights could be more readily traded, cartel
profitability would be enhanced over the long run. That important point
follows because the salable cartel rights would then flow to their highest-
valued uses, that is, to those who had a comparative advantage in cartel
management. Our basic hypothesis about the invention of the corporation
is straightforward. The cartel owner-managers had wealth-maximizing in-

centives to seek the development of a legal form of organization under which they could more easily trade their property rights in these firms. Such a system promoted greater efficiency in the market for the managers of state-chartered monopoly rights.

There are several related advantages of more readily tradable property rights that could have been important in the adaptation of economic organization to the joint-stock form. First, cartel management in the early companies may be viewed as a team-production process (Alchian and Demsetz 1972). Some device must be found in this setting to control incentives for cartel managers to shirk and free-ride off the managerial efforts of their colleagues. Market competition by alternative managers provided an obvious source of discipline, but such forces were attenuated by the monopolistic and closely held charter of these companies. Alternatively, these firms could have developed profit-sharing arrangements that tailored rewards to managerial productivity. However, where cartel managerial efforts are a team-production process and separate managerial inputs cannot be easily disentangled, such a profit-sharing scheme would not be easy to devise. A capital market, however, which went hand-in-hand with the joint-stock form, wherein firms' shares could be more easily traded, provided a mechanism external to the firm through which the behavior of the cartel owner-managers could be disciplined and monitored. Thus, an auxiliary and supporting explanation for the emergence of the corporation, also emanating from the supply side, is that more easily tradable property rights in the early companies provided an external system of discipline for cartel management. Second, a general argument developed by Demsetz (1967) and Jensen and Meckling (1976)—quite similar in spirit to our own—is that the advantage of a limited-liability provision is not that it exposes the investor to less risk but that it reduces certain relevant transaction costs for the investor (such as monitoring the course of co-partners' net wealth and their commitments on behalf of the firm). Rather than bear these costs, investors pay a higher interest rate in a regime of limited liability in which it is relatively easier to exchange shares. Finally, share transferability also permitted owners and managers to specialize. Whether this functional separation (and the incentive structure it creates) increases or decreases firm efficiency remains, of course, a matter of debate (see the appendix to this chapter). Limited liability, however, may be seen as a contractual device designed to mitigate any consequent divergence of interest between owners and managers.

The Historical Case for the Property-Rights Argument

Most accounts of the early companies by historians emphasize the demand-for-capital explanation of the rise of the joint-stock form. As we have pointed out, the property-rights argument that we advance does not contradict the capital-raising argument. There is, however, a question of the emphasis to be given to each argument. In this section we present some evidence on the relative importance of the two approaches in explaining the invention of the joint-stock corporation.

In assessing the importance of the demand-for-capital argument, we must keep in mind that the organization of early joint-stock companies was almost identical to that of the regulated companies. Both types of firms existed coincidentally; both were state-chartered monopolies; both were closely held firms. Heckscher makes this point quite clearly:

> This connection was also expressed in the fact that the pronounced medieval character of the trading bodies was not merely confined to the regulated companies, but was also extended to the capital associations. A pamphlet published as late as 1702 emphasized that "the general intent and end of all civil incorporations is for better government, either general or special," i.e. the same argument as that commonly adduced for the legality of the guilds; and to illustrate the point, its author quoted indiscriminately from municipal charters on the one hand and trading charters and various other sources on the other. In the joint stock companies, too, the members were "brethren," those accepted were "free of the company" or "freemen," just like the members of the innumerable medieval corporations, including the municipalities, which abounded throughout the country. Thus the East India Company, like the regulated companies, levied a special fee of admission from new members, without regard to the fact that the latter had purchased their share from a previous member. In other matters, too, the recruitment of new members corresponded to the principles prevailing in the regulated companies, with only such differences as were inevitable. Above all, new members were to be trained and brought up within the corporation and were not to be accepted haphazardly on a "capitalist" and impersonal basis. (1934, 1:397)

Is it conceivable that incorporation and limited liability would have affected the terms on which an early joint-stock company could borrow? To pose the issue in this manner reveals the weakness of the capital-raising argument. Bargaining in capital markets typically takes the form of negotiated, face-to-face transactions so that the cost of bargaining is independent of the liability provisions. The interest rate is not an impersonally established price in a (Coasian) world wherein instruments are personally negotiated. The capital market will pierce the veil of limited liability in such a way as to internalize the cost of capital to a given firm. The important and predictable point is that these closely held, early joint-stock firms would have faced the same cost of capital function as the contemporaneous regulated firms. Posting of personal collateral would have been required, or the loan rate would have risen. The capital-attraction argument for the invention of the corporation is thus an inherently weak economic argument.

The scale of capital requirements does not seem to have been a barrier to the formation of early regulated companies such as the English Merchant Adventurers, the Eastland, the Levant, and the Muscovy companies. It was out of companies such as these, however, that the joint-stock form grew. The East India Company (chartered in 1600) was launched "by men who had had experience with a regulated company—the Levant Company—and the first minutes of the company were kept in the books of the Levant enterprise" (Clough and Rapp 1975, 152), although the Levant Company itself at times took on some of the characteristics of a joint-stock association (Scott 1951, 2:83–92). The Dutch East India Company, formed two years later, grew out of multiple partnerships and "temporary" joint-stock associations, such as the English regulated companies did. Indeed, Adam Smith's mild defense of one joint-stock company, the Hudson Bay Company, was on the grounds that such a company, "consisting of a small number of proprietors, with a moderate capital, approaches very nearly to the nature of a private copartnery, and may be capable of nearly the same degree of diligence and attention" (1937, 702).

A final point (which was discussed extensively in chapter 6) that does not fit well with the capital-raising explanation concerns the ease with which the monopoly rights of the early firms were invaded. The demand for more capital thus essentially came from the desire to suppress competition, and it is important to note that it was relatively easy for the interlopers to operate profitably in the same sphere as the joint-stock companies.

The property-rights argument explaining the evolution of the corporation suggests that the enhanced wealth provided by transferable ownership claims should have affected relative growth rates of organizational forms in these times.[19] Scott's emphasis upon the early and significant success of the joint-stock companies is very revealing in this respect. He estimates (1951, 1:439) that by 1720 joint-stock enterprises produced about 13 percent of English national income. While mainly attributing the growth of the joint-stock form to the necessity for capital attraction, Scott touches upon the property-rights hypothesis when he notes the benefits of specialization that the transferability of shares permitted. He relates this point to maritime progress: "During the first half century of existence, the joint-stock company was the organization which, at each successive step, provided the requisites for the obtaining both sea-power and colonial possessions. The bravery of the privateersman and the endurance of the explorer are gratefully remembered; but, at the same time, the faith of the gentlemen and merchants, who provided the necessary capital, should not be forgotten, nor the system which had worked so smoothly on the whole and that made the co-operation of the man of action and the man of wealth possible" (1951, 1:440).

So while the two hypotheses are not mutually exclusive, the property-rights argument seems to be a more important force behind the evolution of the corporate form of business organization than the traditional demand-for-capital argument. Consequently, our point is that the demand-for-capital argument is not sufficient to explain the evolution of firms from regulated partnerships to joint-stock companies. Rather the benefits of share transferability within the mercantile cartels, expressed in terms of increased efficiency and profitability in the market for cartel management, created the necessary incentive for the emergence of the joint-stock firm and, ultimately, the modern corporation.

The legal evolution of the modern corporate form of business organization was clearly the product of centuries of adaptations. As discussed below, private-firm limited liability did not receive full and liberal statutory sanction in England or the United States until well into the nineteenth century.[20] We have argued, however, that the corporation as an actual and conceptual entity had its origin in the mercantilist period. Further, our hypothesis is that share transferability as a property-rights response to profit and efficiency incentives provides an explanation superior to the traditional argument. We should like to emphasize, however, that our property-rights argument applies only at the margin. Evidence in Scott and other sources is clear that the early joint-stock companies were sometimes subject to early dissolution because of problems of managerial succession. However, the joint-stock form took root and grew relative to other forms of business organization. The evolution toward the efficiencies and increased wealth represented by tradable shares took time to work its course, and our argument is not that salable shares solved all the early joint-stock companies' problems of managerial turnover.[21] Rather we have argued that a supply-side explanation of the origin of the corporation has been ignored. Inclusion of the supply side both completes and makes more forceful the explanation of circumstances surrounding the nascence of the modern corporation.

THE EVOLUTION OF THE CORPORATION

We now turn to the issue of how the corporate form evolved after its invention. In the schema commonly advanced by economic and legal historians regarding the evolution of the corporate form of business organization, legislative enactment of general limited liability provisions plays a key role. Prior to parliamentary passage of limited liability legislation in 1844 and 1855 and the passage of similar measures by American state legislatures at various times over the mid-nineteenth century, the development and expansion of the corporate form was allegedly hampered by the fact that unincorporated firms were legally regarded as partnerships and treated accordingly—which included the refusal of courts to recognize limited liability for shareholders. Moreover, incorporation was a costly procedure over this period, pursued by seeking special charters from the legislature or monarch. As stressed above, most historians argue that limited liability legislation significantly reduced the costs of raising capital for corporations by reducing the risk of stockholding; investment and growth in such firms were thereby fostered. In short, the evolution of the modern corporate form is believed to have been crucially dependent on legislation favoring this type of business organization. Therefore, the corporation was a creature born of government intervention.

We advance the alternative thesis here that the corporate form developed and spread as an efficient market innovation that preceded legislative enactments by a long margin. Moreover, as argued above, limited liability (usually held to be the sine qua non of the corporation) was not a necessary or even an important feature in the early evolution of the corporation. Careful scrutiny of pre-nineteenth-century business history demonstrates that the modern corporation developed and spread due to its superior economic efficiency as an organizational form, in spite of, not because of, governmental interference in the free market.

Early Development of the Corporation

There are two sides to the orthodox view of early corporate development promulgated by legal historians: (1) The corporate form required special legal dispensation for its effective operation, and (2) corporate status was a privilege that could be extended or restricted at the discretion of government. In other words, the superior *economic efficiency* of the corporate contract was not a primary reason for its emergence and spread; to flourish it first required governmental sanction and support.

This argument conflates the characteristics of corporateness (share transferability, limited liability, the separation of management from ownership, and so on) with incorporation. It is generally recognized that unincorporated joint-stock firms arose in considerable numbers prior to 1720 but that "abuses" caused by its unregulated development led Parliament to ban such firms in the Bubble Act of 1720. After 1720, corporate characteristics were only available to a firm that had first petitioned for a corporate charter from Parliament. The Act, according to Scott (1951, 1:438), stopped the development of the joint-stock system dead in its tracks: "It became both difficult and costly to obtain the necessary legal authorization for the starting of a new enterprise needing a large capital. In one that might have been established with a moderate outlay, which for any reason it was desirable to collect from a large number of persons, the trouble and cost proved prohibitive. Therefore, for upwards of a century, industry was deprived of the advantages of a certain amount of capital which would otherwise have been available."

We believe that this view is misleading. The corporate form developed in the face of various legal impediments during the eighteenth century and was well established by the time the supposedly crucial appropriate legal framework was in place. The corporation as an institution developed in its modern outlines in a legal environment that was at worst hostile and at best uncertain. This implies that the corporation represented a superior economic efficiency instrument and emerged for this reason.

Corporateness Without Incorporation

It is usually assumed that parliamentary incorporation was eagerly sought by firms in the eighteenth century for the same reasons that firms would seek the characteristics of the corporate form today—the advantages of a separable and distinct corporate identity, the ability to issue transferable shares of stock, and limited liability for shareholders. Technically, while firms could organize on a joint-stock basis without incorporating, they were still legally considered to be partnerships. As such, they possessed none of the advantages of the corporation. They could not establish distinct legal identities, their proprietors were subject to unlimited liability, and share transferability was contingent upon the approval of all partners. The Bubble Act (1720) provided that such unincorporated enterprises "were prohibited under very heavy penalties," (Shannon 1931, 267). These penalties included forfeiture of all lands, goods, and chattels, as well as imprisonment for life for the convicted undertakers of such a company.[22] This legal environment is alleged to have seriously retarded "the rise of joint-stock enterprise" (Evans 1936, 1).

This appears to be a case where legal scholars have been overimpressed with the impact of law on economic development. Despite these severe legal impediments, unincorporated joint-stock companies were increasingly numerous in England after 1720 (DuBois 1971, 266). Precise numbers of these firms are very difficult to establish. They were unregistered, and unless they became involved with government or unless their records survived by chance, all trace of them would have disappeared if they ceased business operations. However, in his comprehensive compilation of (approximately 180) recorded joint-stock enterprises in the eighteenth century (after 1720), DuBois (1971, 473–95) found that approximately half of these firms were unincorporated joint-stock companies. This is an impressive statistic when one considers that a significantly higher proportion of incorporated than unincorporated joint-stock firms would presumably have had surviving records.

A parliamentary charter was not necessary to secure the substance of corporate characteristics. However, the unincorporated joint-stock firm was a "step-child of the law," leaving "serious legal difficulties to surmount" (DuBois 1971, 217). Technically, they were subject to partnership law, meaning that every member must join in the conveyance of shares and in the bringing and defending of legal actions, and that the death of a member necessitated a reorganization of the enterprise (therefore granting minority interests in the firm a dominant strategic position).

The most frequently utilized means for the circumvention of these problems was the trustee device. Trustees were selected by the company's stockholders, usually from among their own number. All the stock in the firm would be vested in a trust overseen by the trustees. When an individual shareowner wished to sell or otherwise transfer a portion of his shares, the articles of association of the firm mandated that he had first to notify the trustees of this decision; the actual transaction would then be effected through the trustees. Unincorporated firms did not have corporate charters that functioned as legally binding company constitutions. They commonly created articles of association, a common law device that accomplished the same end. These articles of association were drawn up to include a stipulation requiring stock to be legally held by the trustees of the firm (while still owned by the stock purchaser). The sale of a share of stock was actually a package that included a contract with the buyer to assign the share to the legal trust established by the firm. Thus, the transfer of stock was unrestricted and did not require the prior approval of other members of the firm.

The organization's real and personal property were also placed in the names of trustees, evading the problem posed by the absence of a legally distinct corporate identity (available only by means of charter) and effectively allowing the firm to own and dispose of property. The trustees were authorized by the articles of association to act on the company's behalf. The trustees were in fact often the managers of the company, who could make binding decisions in company matters and legally commit the company to contracts as the result of their trustee status.

An example of the trustee device in practice is the scheme devised in 1749 for the (unincorporated) Cornfactors of London. The property on which the Corn Exchange was built was conveyed to three trustees by lease for five hundred years in trust for the proprietors. The trustees were to "receive the rents and disburse the surplus under the direction of the general meetings of the proprietors" (DuBois 1971, 218). The proprietors agreed with the trustees that the latter would hold all stock legally in trust. The trustee device allowed for a significant reduction in the transaction costs associated with investment by the firm on a number of occasions.

Greater difficulty was encountered by the unincorporated joint-stock company in the bringing and defending of suits. The market adapted to this problem. Private arbitrators were used extensively both by unincorporated companies and those doing business with them. Clauses were commonly inserted in articles of association by which all disputes of the members were pledged to be decided by arbitration. Problems related to inducing the parties to a dispute to use arbitration were apparently uncommon (DuBois 1971, 221). The community reputation for business integrity of individuals and firms represented capital that might rapidly depreciate in value in the face of unscrupulous strategic behavior.

Finally, incorporation was not necessary in order for a firm to acquire limited liability status. Unincorporated firms had access to limited liability in the form of customary restricted liability established in articles of association that were generally legally secure and recognized. We examine this matter in greater detail below.

All of this leaves the discussion in something of a quandary with respect to the Bubble Act, which contained severe penalties for undertaking a joint-stock firm without a parliamentary charter. The answer is simple; the act was ignored. It was not merely poorly enforced but unenforceable. As Shannon (1931, 269) explains: "This Act, in regulating a commercial matter, outlined the offense in almost unintelligible language and attached to it the gravest penalty known to English law. It seemed phrased to stultify itself. And except for a minor prosecution in 1723, it remained a dead letter until 1808."

The Decision to Incorporate

This is not to argue that it was costless to exercise corporate characteristics without the formality of incorporation. An example was access to the Court of Chancery for the settlement of business suits. Unincorporated firms were generally disallowed from pleading in these courts (which incorporated firms could do without fee), requiring the engagement of an arbitrator's services. Also, there were likely to be costs associated with devices for legal evasion such as trustees. On the whole these adaptations seem to have worked well, and the costs were probably quite small.

But neither was incorporation a costless procedure. Corporate charters before 1844 were not awarded routinely but represented extraordinary privileges. At the bare minimum the firm bore a paperwork burden in the form of a formal submission to Parliament of a Petition for Incorporation. This was a highly detailed legal document that had to include a full proposed corporate constitution. Under corrupt conditions companies would bid for incorporated status, by investing resources in bribes, or more indirectly by granting loans to the government at a discounted rate, or by some other device.

The incorporation process also involved important indirect costs. By incorporating, a firm was effectively announcing its existence to the regulatory authorities, who would otherwise most probably have ignored it. Information regarding the operations (or even the existence) of a firm was costly to obtain by government in the eighteenth century. Obviously, firms engaged in illicit business (for example, smuggling) were unlikely to seek incorporation. However, firms engaged in legal and mundane lines of business also had an incentive to evade regulations, which could potentially impose substantial costs on a firm's operations. By providing authorities with information pertaining to their existence, firms reduced the feasibility of evading costly regulations.

It is clear, then, that although there were positive costs associated with organizing a joint-stock enterprise as an incorporated or as an unincorporated firm, the costs associated with the former were generally greater. Companies did continue to petition Parliament for incorporation over the eighteenth century, but these were cases of firms seeking monopoly rights.

Limited Liability, Again

As argued previously, among legal scholars limited liability is the hallmark of the corporation. The legal privilege of distinct corporate identity, allowing the firm to contract debts in its own name, absolves shareholders of responsibility for those debts and thereby arguably confers a ("costless") capital market advantage on joint-stock firms. This is a free lunch argument that ignores certain costs of incorporation.

It is also commonly accepted among legal historians that this boon to the growth of the corporation originated in enlightened legislative enactment only in the nineteenth century in a form generally and routinely available to joint-stock firms (Shannon 1931). Prior to this time, limited liability was supposed to be available only to incorporated firms. In England prior to 1844, "the great prize offered by incorporation was legal personality" (Campbell 1967, 140) because this feature conferred limited liability on shareholders.

Many historians assume that the economic environment faced by unincorporated joint-stock firms changed radically after 1720. The only clear and widely acknowledged implication of the Bubble Act among lawyers and jurists was that unincorporated "corporations" were not entities legally distinct from their shareholders; they were partnerships albeit with peculiar organizational characteristics. Typically, observers have leapt to the false conclusion that limited liability status was unavailable to these firms. This was not the case. An unincorporated company could establish limited liability for its shareholders in several ways.

The company might include a clause in its articles of association stipulating that the company's shareholders had limited liability for debts incurred by the trustee managers of the firm. This was the case, for example, with the unincorporated General Bank of India, organized in 1786 (English commercial law being in force in India at the time). There is apparently no record of clauses of this sort being challenged in court (DuBois 1971, 224). Another way in which an unincorporated firm could formalize limited liability arrangements was by including clauses to this effect in contracts as a routine matter. This practice was utilized by unincorporated mining companies in Cornwall, Derby, and Wales (DuBois 1971, 223). More often than either of these two devices, limited liability for debt was established as a matter of custom. Informal contracts between the unincorporated joint-stock company and its creditors minimized the transactions costs associated with the provision of this type of shareholder protection in situations where continuing business relationships created a high degree of mutual reliance.

The other major contention of the historians, that limited liability somehow lowered the cost of capital to early firms, is analytically misleading. We have argued this point previously. Credit markets are a Coasian world of face-to-face transactions. Real interest rates negotiated by lenders and borrowers in this setting accurately reflect the underlying risk-return relationship posed by the firm. Firms cannot hide behind the veil of limited liability. If they choose limited liability and thereby offer less collateral to the lender, the borrowing rate will rise. It only takes a simple hypothesis about the efficiency of the capital market to see that limited liability would not have altered the real cost of capital to early joint-stock firms, incorporated or otherwise.

This—as well as the fact that liability for torts, which inspires so much contemporary controversy, was unheard of in the eighteenth century in relation to the operations of firms—may explain why, in spite of the availability to unincorporated firms of limited liability features at low cost, relatively few firms bothered with such arrangements.[23] In fact, in a number of cases unincorporated firms inserted in their articles of association clauses that expressly provided for the complete liability of shareholders for the company's debt. The Cheadle Brass Company formed in 1734, the Banking Company of Aberdeen formed in 1767, and numerous other firms utilized such clauses (DuBois 1971, 216). Some unincorporated firms went so far as to advertise the express full liability of their shareholders.[24]

By inserting such clauses in their articles of association, firms facilitated creditor court actions designed to collect debt (in the event of company insolvency) from shareholders, and thereby increased the effective amount of loan collateral available to the firm. The incentive for bearing the additional risk associated with ownership of this stock was the expected higher rate of return (dividends) owing to the availability of lower interest loans to the firm.

The economically relevant difference between the unincorporated firms, which offered their subscribers limited liability, and those that intentionally avoided this feature, may have been in terms of firm size. The examples cited above of firms with complete liability clauses were small organizations whose stockholders were apparently situated locally (the Cheadle Brass Company, for example, had six proprietors). The cost of information about managerial behavior and firm performance in such a setting would have been quite low. For example, it would have been easy for local shareholders, perhaps of the same family, to keep track of commitments made by managers and other partners on behalf of the firm. The risk confronting subscribers would have tended to be relatively low even in the absence of limited liability, and it would have been efficient for such a small firm to take advantage of the lower interest rates available by offering the maximum available collateral by means of complete liability clauses. Information costs confronting subscribers in large firms would have made these arrangements inefficient because of the higher risk associated with holding shares and not knowing what sort of commitments others were making in the name of the firm (especially when stockholders were geographically dispersed, considering the state of eighteenth-century communications). Hence, larger firms would offer limited liability clauses to potential investors as a way to economize on the transaction costs of keeping up with the activities of managers and other investors in the firm. This would explain why the larger chartered and unincorporated joint-stock firms usually offered this feature to investors.[25]

Limited liability is a form of investor asset insurance that, because of transaction costs, is usually more efficient for the firm to provide than for individual investors to provide themselves.[26] The market provided such insurance efficiently long before government made it generally available. In those cases where firms refrained from adopting limited liability provisions contractually, individual shareholders perceived that the cost of this insurance exceeded its benefits.

CONCLUSION: MULTIDIVISIONAL FIRMS AND THE ORIGINS OF THE CORPORATION

The modern firm evolved within the nexus of complex and interrelated forces. The M-form typical of many modern corporations was the result of the problems encountered in the administration of the monopoly companies—the English East India Company in the case discussed here. The form of the multidivisional firm emerged as a reaction to problems of agency, moral hazard, and the transactions and information costs so prevalent in a mercantile context. In short, the forces of competition and the drive to efficiency imposed by the profit motive in the East India Company led to its adoption of a variety of devices to stem opportunism and other problems. We have also argued that government regulation is, most likely, a primary reason for its organization form as a vertically integrated multidivisional enterprise.

A critical point is also worth remembering: *The emergence and spread of the corporate form did not depend on legislation.* The contractual characteristics that defined the joint-stock company evolved from the interplay of market forces as a response to the organizational difficulties posed by the partnership. The corporation emerged because it was an efficiency instrument. The history of unincorporated joint-stock companies in England during the eighteenth century (after the Bubble Act in 1720) offers ample testimony for this argument. Moreover, although the corporation is often defined with reference to its limited liability features and the legislation making these features generally available in the nineteenth century, limited liability was available (though not often utilized for rational economic reasons) under common law and without special charter much earlier. The advantages sought by the early unincorporated joint-stock companies resided in more basic economic benefits derivable from such features as share transferability.

We have *not* argued that the legal impediments to the corporate form made no difference. Evasion of the law was feasible, but it was not costless. Firms that chose to remain unincorporated prior to 1825 probably would have chosen otherwise if the process of incorporation had not been highly expensive and uncertain. In short, government policies with respect to the corporation over this period unquestionably had a detrimental effect on economic efficiency. The incentives behind the government's pursuit of an economically inefficient policy in this case are fairly clear. By restricting access to corporate status, the government sought to maximize its revenue from the sale of corporate rights that were usually associated with a grant of monopoly.

The question remains, why did government policy change in the nineteenth century? In 1825, Parliament repealed the Bubble Act; in 1844, Parliament made available incorporation by simple registration. Much of the reason probably lies in the fact that by the early to mid-nineteenth century unincorporated corporations were a highly successful and widespread form of business organization. Almost a thousand of these firms (not even counting banks) were already in existence in England at the time of the passage of the 1844 Act (Hunt 1935b). The legislative availability of cheap and simple incorporation was not the stimulus to the expansion of the corporate form but merely a response to previous developments. In effect, corporate chartering was deregulated because it was no longer feasible to regulate it.

Finally, the shift from partnership to corporation was gradual, occurring along relevant margins. There was no Corporate Revolution which turned on limited liability legislation or any other basis. Early joint-stock firms were only marginally different from partnerships and did not represent some kind of dramatic organizational leap. As Hessen (1979) has argued, there is a contractual continuum from partnership to corporation, and this is reflected in eighteenth century English business history.

APPENDIX:
MANAGERIAL EFFICIENCY
IN THE JOINT-STOCK COMPANIES

The early joint-stock companies raise other issues—one concerning an interesting episode in the history of economic thought. Adam Smith—and he was followed in this by many other classical writers—argued that the joint-stock companies were a largely unsuccessful form of business organization, except in certain limited areas such as insurance and banking companies. He believed that they were guilty of charging noncompetitive high prices (owing to their monopoly position), of negligence, profusion, and malversation (Smith 1937, 669–700). In Smith's well-known view, the inefficiency of the joint-stock company was owing to the relation of its management to its owners. In a view of corporate structure close to the modern view held by Berle and Means (1932) and others, Smith saw the divorce between ownership and control—presumably not found in the private co-partnership or in the regulated companies—as creating an incentive structure wherein extreme inefficiency and managerial shirking were predictable. Further, as an example of such inefficiencies, Smith argued that joint-stock companies could seldom successfully compete against interlopers: "It is upon this account that joint stock companies for foreign trade have seldom been able to maintain the competition against private adventurers. They have, accordingly, very seldom succeeded without an exclusive privilege; and frequently have not succeeded with one. Without an exclusive privilege they have commonly mismanaged the trade. With an exclusive privilege they have both mismanaged and confined it" (Smith 1937, 100).

Scott (1951) challenged Smith's argument as biased, however, and presented an opposing view.[27] In Scott's view the control and internal organization of the pre-1720 joint-stock companies was far better than Smith believed, and he cites the early processes of the Royal African and Hudson's Bay companies as evidence. The early chronicles of the East India Company reveal evidence of direct managerial involvement in the company's operations. For example, officers of the company refused honoraria for managerial services, holding that the return on their equities was sufficient to compensate them for services. Scott argues, moreover, that certain controls placed on officers and directors of the company encouraged self-interested participation in matters before the firm: "In the East India company the qualification of a committee was £1,000 stock, of the governor 4,000, in the Royal African company that of an assistant was 2,000—sums which would probably be of sufficient importance to most of the adventurers in the seventeenth century to make them attentive to their duties" (Scott 1951, 1:452).

Further, Scott (1951, 1:452–53) also takes up Smith's comments about "interlopers," arguing, in contrast to Smith, that interlopers (private adventurers, smugglers) were free riders, receiving the benefits of fortifications, political interactions, and other trade infrastructure provided by the companies. Scott also seems to indicate (1951, 1:454) that interlopers were sometimes brought into the cartel, a common practice in contemporary forms of regulated monopoly. Smith's view of the interlopers as competitive entrants seems more generally correct than Scott's characterization of them as free riders. However, this does not mean that the joint-stock firms were inefficient. It means only that it was costly to defend these monopoly rights, a fact inherent to all monopoly trading rights in these times, whether held by regulated or joint-stock firms. The enforcement or policing costs to the monopoly firms were obviously too high to exclude the interlopers completely. (We considered the issue of the interlopers in chapter 6.)

From the point of view of the argument developed in this chapter, Scott was clearly on the right track in defending the efficiency with which the early joint-stock companies were managed. This was precisely the economic reason they were invented. Smith's distaste for the joint-stock company was premised upon the inevitable inefficiencies created by a divorce between owners and managers. However, Smith overstated his case. From an institutional point of view, Smith ignored the possibility of mitigating managerial disincentives by institutional-contractual arrangements. Mill (1965, 138–41), for example, recognized the possibility of such contractual alternatives in his analysis of corporate property-rights arrangements. More recently, and as stressed previously in this volume, Becker and Stigler (1974) have developed an analysis in this tradition, which outlines a general theory of how malfeasance in various institutional settings can be mitigated ("pay them more and they'll steal less"). Thus, the threat of publicity, a high salary, a return as a percentage of profits, stock options, and other contractual arrangements can reduce the problem of separation of ownership from control to minimal proportions. And historically, as Scott shows, accoutrements of these kinds were attached to the managerial contracts in the early joint-stock companies.

In Smith's favor, however, it may be said that managerial shirking may have simply been a red herring in his attack on monopoly. If Smith meant that monopoly chartering of the joint-stock companies by the state led to rent seeking (that is, the dissipation of expected monopoly rents) by agents for these companies, then he may be defended in his analysis of the economic inefficiency of the joint-stock companies. There is some evidence from *The Wealth of Nations* to support this view. Where dealing with "particular branches of commerce," Smith argues: "To establish a joint stock company . . . for any undertaking, merely because such a company might be capable of managing it successfully; or to exempt a particular set of dealers from some of the general laws which take place with regard to all their neighbours, merely because they might be capable of thriving if they had such an exemption, would certainly not be reasonable" (Smith 1937, 714). Thus, while Scott (1951, 1:449–52) argues that profits in early joint-stock companies were indirect evidence of good management, Smith appears to indicate that it is not the level of profits that was important but rather the fact that they were wasted in rent-seeking activity. Rent-seeking activities by domestic cartels and international trading companies flourished throughout the entire mercantile period, as we have argued throughout this book. Viner, for example, discussed the activity of the joint-stock East India Company in the political debate surrounding the commercial clauses in the Treaty of Utrecht in 1713: "The Tories, on the other hand, came to terms with the East India Company, whereby in return for support of the endeavors of the company to preserve its monopoly privileges and to be allowed to import East Indian cloth, the latter gave financial support to the crown through loans, and to its defenders in Parliament through private bribes" (1967, 116). Smith does fail to recognize, however, the simple point that both the regulated companies and the joint-stock companies were state-chartered monopolies, and both were therefore subject to the charge of rent-seeking inefficiencies.

Chapter 8

Conclusion: The Political Economy of Mercantilism

How theoretical study should be carried on in the field
of economic history is a great and difficult question.
—Eli Heckscher

Oh, do not ask, "What is it?"
Let us go and make our visit.
—T. S. Eliot, "The Love Song of J. Alfred Prufrock"

It is now axiomatic that "institutions matter" in both the theoretical and practical realms of economics, especially in the highly dynamic subject of economic development. It is a role of modern economics to explain *how* institutions matter. That is the task of the emerging field of neoinstitutional economics, of which rent-seeking inquiry and property rights theory are two important parts. We have, in this book as in our previous work (1981), attempted to push the analysis of "mercantile" institutions in sixteenth- and seventeenth-century England, France, and Spain forward. Other important researches on this and other periods have been and are being conducted with this same object (for example, Weingast 1995).

All of this work, including our own, has been developed without a *general* theory of institutions, institutional change, and economic development. Many important pieces of the puzzle, including the broad outlines of a cogent and generally applicable theory, are being filled in. The security of property rights is one important key, but the institutional sources of property rights alterations is even more basic to the story. Property rights security is determined by institutional changes and competitions over who got the power to seek rents. These competitions took place under some "stock" of institutions, as in Tudor England, but they also force *changes* in institutions. Institutional change affected property rights security, which altered transactions cost and the volume of exchange, all of which had critical implications for relative economic development in these "mercantile" states. In England, these changes, in some exact manner yet to be determined, produced the "Industrial Revolution." In France and especially in Spain, economic development languished. Just how this might have happened in a tentative analysis of relative institutional developments is the subject of these concluding remarks.

INTERPRETATIONS OF MERCANTILISM

The conventional paradigm for analyzing mercantilism stresses the irrationality of the mercantile social order. The mercantilists are said to have confused power and plenty. We have argued in this study that the essentially normative evaluation of mercantilist theory misses much of the substance of what the mercantilists actually did. From the viewpoint of positive economics, the mercantilists behaved quite rationally in the pursuit of monopoly rents via the economic regulation of internal and external trade. Admittedly, both the conventional and the rent-seeking analyses of mercantilism embody the destruction of wealth as a central concept. In the conventional paradigm wealth destruction occurs through irrational specie accumulation; in the rent-seeking paradigm it takes place through the monopolization of the economy by the state. The primary advantage that the rent-seeking approach possesses vis-à-vis the specie-accumulation paradigm, however, is that normally associated with positive versus normative economics—explanatory value. Positive economics offers a route to understanding the course of economic regulation and economic organization in the mercantile economies, while the conventional paradigm focuses mostly on the stupidity of the mercantile writers.

The normative implications of the rent-seeking model, moreover, concern not the irrationality of the mercantilists but rather the welfare costs of their policies. The positive theory of rent seeking therefore concentrates on the competition for prospective rents facing demanders and suppliers of economic regulation, while the normative theory of rent seeking consists of evaluating costs to the economy of government-sponsored monopolies. Thus, in the case of English mercantilism a major point of the rent-seeking interpretation is that the process—including the enforcement apparatus of local regulations—helped bring about unintended institutional changes that made rent seeking and internal regulation by the central government less feasible. Under the altered institutional structure, liberalism, free trade, and economic growth became viable alternatives. In the case of French mercantilism the rent-seeking interpretation suggests a clear answer to much-debated issues concerning French economic development. That the pattern and rate of economic growth were influenced by regulatory policies of the mercantile administrators and that monopolization of the entire economy would retard innovation and economic growth seem to us incontrovertible. We do not argue that rent seeking was the only force at work in impeding economic growth and industrialization and in pushing the economy toward luxury manufactures at the expense of basic productions. However, if modern studies of the social costs of monopoly and regulation are useful guides (Posner 1975; Cowling and Mueller 1978), it is not unreasonable to suggest that rent seeking is a very strong and heretofore unexplored explanation of the various puzzles of French economic development.

MERCANTILE ENGLAND

The hypothesis of this book is that there were important institutional changes in the rent-seeking economy of mercantilist England that explain the rise of free trade on both internal and external levels. This interpretation is more robust than the standard interpretation of mercantilism in that it explains both the rise and fall of mercantilism with the same model. In the case of mercantile England we have argued that the conventional mercantilist paradigm of power versus plenty offers no conventional means of explaining the decline of state interference. Higher cost owing to uncertainty and growing private returns reduced industry demands for regulation and controls in England. All this strengthened the emergent constitutional democracy, which created conditions making rent-seeking activity on the part of both monarch and merchants more costly. When the locus of power to rent seek shifted from the monarch to Parliament via more stringent controls on the king, the costs of supplying regulation through legislative enactment rose, for reasons suggested by the theory of public choice. Lobbying costs and nondurability of laws passed because of competition within the judiciary contributed to the decline of mercantilism in England.

The competitive nature of legislatively supplied regulation, in contrast to the monarchical monopoly of an earlier period, undoubtedly reduced the net benefits from regulatory supply. A shifting institutional structure between 1540 and 1650 facilitated these developments, which were built, in turn, upon the constraints on the king, institutionalized even earlier. In addition, the inability of the monarch to enforce even simple local regulations resulted from the political structure of England and, as we have seen, from the changing cost-benefit structure to royal representatives charged with enforcement. The monarch could not maintain town guilds, in particular, and industry moved to the countryside, as we argued in chapter 3.

We have not argued that no factors other than rent seeking contributed to the decline of regulation in the post-Restoration and especially in the post-1740 period. Recent research, as noted in chapter 3, has extended this argument. The security of property rights—North and Weingast (1989) and Weingast (1995) argue—led to greater constraints on the behavior of the government and the ability to engage in secure contracting across time and space (allowing impersonal capital markets). These developments and the Glorious Revolution of 1688 led to declining interest rates and the ability of England to defeat the French.[1] Elsewhere North (1989) adopted the principal arguments (see above) of Ekelund and Tollison (1981, 149) regarding the decline of mercantilism in England, but adds that his is a "more complicated" story than ours. In particular, he says, "the embedding of economic and political freedoms in the law, the interests of principals (merchants, etc.) in greater degrees of freedom, and the ideological considerations that swept England in the 17th combined to play a role in institutional change" (1989, 1328) are those complications. Unfortunately, North offers not one jot of evidence that "ideological considerations" had any independent influence on constitutional change, the locus of the power to regulate, or high enforcement costs of guild regulations independent of self-interest coalitions of jurists, merchants, and enforcers of mercantile regulations at the local level.[2] These confusions and problems of interpretation suggest that the neoinstitutional theory relating to the decline of mercantilism is, at least in some of its elements, incomplete.

Interpretive problems—ideological considerations or rent-seeking coalitions—are only one factor in providing a more exact assessment of the decline of mercantilism and the emergent "Industrial Revolution" in England. Other facts call part of North and Weingast's simple outline of falling loan rates—government financing of the Wars with France—into question. Interest rates were falling throughout the seventeenth century, not only after the "security" provided by constitutional changes before and after the Glorious Revolution. More important, the explanation of the occurrence and dating of the Industrial Revolution in England may be far more complex than North and others have suggested. Two factors are of special interest. Internal expansion of English firms before and during the late seventeenth century as the Industrial Revolution progressed in the eighteenth was not financed by banks, which played a minor role, but through self-financed industrial development (Crouzet 1967, 172; Crouzet 1972, 179–94). The "security" of property rights vis-à-vis government loans to fight the French cannot easily be extended to the financing of technological innovations and capital formation.

Of even more importance in assessing relative growth rates between England and France is the matter of resource pressures in England that did not exist in France prior to and during the Industrial Revolution. Crouzet (1967, 168–69) notes that the high price of timber in England relative to France led to the development of methods of using coal, a resource found in England, such as the steam engine. Labor-saving inventions were likewise necessitated in the textile industry because of the limits to the "putting-out" system, limitations that did not exist in France, again according to Crouzet (1967, 170). These relative price differences were clear inducements to technological change and surely had an enormous impact on relative growth rates in mercantile economics. That they occurred within the context of "secure" property rights in England—where the crown's power to tax, regulate, and/or confiscate was very limited—is also significant, but the relative ingredients leading to the (ultimate) dominance of England over France is more complex, demanding a far more elaborate theory of relative growth than provided by North.[3]

Rent-seeking activity leading to property rights structures that limited market exchange and welfare was significantly diminished in England after the seventeenth century in our interpretation, *but it was not eliminated.* The rent-seeking capacity of Parliament (as in the case of the U.S. Congress) underwent an evolution toward a "committee" system, which improved the capacity to extract rents through rule and regulatory changes.[4] The reform agenda for England after 1815 included a scaling down of licensing of monopolies, guild powers, and other feudal artifacts, but other changes were taking place simultaneously. Population growth, industrialization and urbanization, and the almost continuous fiscal difficulties stemming from wars between 1776 and 1815, as well as other factors, may also have been influential in the ultimate demise of the old regulatory technology. After the fiscal turmoil of war, for example, the Bank of England was put back on strict convertibility in 1821, and by 1844 further restrictions cut off the treasury from any automatic access to the bank. The laws of trade and navigation were to be dismantled by William Huskisson at the Board of Trade in 1825, following the Free Trade Letter of the Merchants of London in 1821.

The nature of regulation also changed somewhat in the later period to include bureaucratic and administrative enforcement machinery. Social issues were emphasized, and by mid-nineteenth century a new beginning had been made in Parliament's action in this area. A number of writers (for example, Hartwell 1976) have commented on the origins of a professional bureaucracy and upon its critical importance for the implementation and development of social legislation in nineteenth-century England, although they have not provided a satisfying explanation for the origins of such legislation and its administration. An important exception deals with the origin of the Factory Act of 1833. The first factory act in 1802 concerned the labor of pauper children, and in 1819 Sir Robert Peel sponsored an act in Parliament that regulated hours and conditions of children's employment. Though revised in 1825 and replaced by a substitute in 1831, these acts contained very minimal provisions for enforcement. Finally, Lord Althorp's Factory Act of 1833 was drafted (under the aegis of Royal Commission Chairman Edwin Chadwick) and passed, placing controls on the employment of children in England's huge textile industry. Regarded as a landmark piece of social legislation and as one of the first important interventions into the market system in England, the Factory Act of 1833 has been subjected to both qualitative and quantitative analysis by Marvel. He concludes that his findings "suggest that this innovation in industrial regulation was not enacted and enforced solely out of compassion for the factory children. It was, instead, an early example of a regulated industry controlling its regulators to further its own interests" (Marvel 1977, 402). Marvel thus describes the very same process of rent seeking in representative democracy that we have underscored in the setting of mercantile England. (The Stuart method of administering poor relief described in our chapter 3 is a good example of the effects of the administration of social policy in this era.)

Although Marvel provides evidence for a rent-seeking interpretation of one factory act, other forms of early nineteenth-century social controls have not received such analysis. The mode of the introduction of "neo-mercantilism"—through constitutional constraints inadequate to control socially destructive rent seeking—is thus an important area for future research. We have simply argued that economic incentives in the form of rivalrous rent-seeking forces were at the nexus of the decline in regulation in the sixteenth and seventeenth centuries.

Mercantile France

The pattern of mercantile rent seeking in France until the late eighteenth century was manifestly different. Absolute tax powers and ever more efficient royal enforcement at local levels permitted and supported a system of outright venality administered by an institutionalized aristocratic bureaucracy. Monarchical controls over technology further altered the cost-benefit structure of the demand for monopoly franchises by reducing the returns to production and participation in the private economy. It is easy to understand the persistence and growth of venality in France considering the degree of monopoly in the supply of franchises. Absence of significant representative institutions as a check to crown rent seeking, or rather the conditions that would facilitate their emergence, is sufficient to explain the historical pattern.

As we have demonstrated, Louis XIII and especially Louis XIV were masters at cartel creation and enforcement. The administrative genius of a Colbert, coupled with the vast power of the crown to subdue the *parlements* and to impose absolute authority, are the proximate explanations for the incredibly vast and detailed centralized system of French mercantilism of the seventeenth and early eighteenth centuries. The forms of rent seeking and (attempted) methods of collection in mercantile England and France were quite the same, but the difference consisted in the power to implement and to police the underlying regulations.

Mercantilism underwent a decline in eighteenth-century France, just as it did in England, but that decline was less significant, as Schaeper's research (1983) suggests. English and French growth rates, according to the best evidence from the eighteenth century, were not dissimilar. Colonial trade was an important source of growth for both the French and the English, but French trade with Europe was growing faster than England's with the Continent (Crouzet 1967, 147). But the "physiocratic interlude" supporting freer exchange in the eighteenth century was insufficient to compete with the stable political institutions of England after the French Revolution. Bureaucracy and administrative stultification of the French economy survived the Revolution, as did inadequate constitutional checks on the taxing power of the central government.

Mercantile Spain

The tragic story of Spanish development followed along lines similar to the French case, but with a number of important differences. A case study of the Mesta reveals an overarching problem in the assignment of property rights. The *relative* assignment of rights to a mobile shepherding industry, inspired by the desire of the monarchy to collect rents, had clear and negative implications for the development of sedentary agriculture throughout the medieval-mercantile period. But more, property rights shifts, as a function of the internecine interplay of aristocratic, ecclesiastical, and representative interests, created far more uncertainty in the Spanish than in the French case. The movement of industries to the French countryside and the development of nonprice modes of competition described in chapter 3 did create property rights instability, but in the French case the instability was on the part of the monopoly franchise holders granted by the central government in the face of welfare-enhancing competition. Geographically dispersed urban centers interests, along with endemic separatist tendencies (which still characterize Spain), also help tell the story of insecure property rights. The Spanish economy was far less integrated than the French system, with long-held traditions of regional and local social and economic coalitions.

Property rights instability and uncertainty, again owing to inadequate constitutional checks on the central taxing authority, led to lower long-term investment and a less socially productive capital stock. Broadly speaking, our views concerning the instability of property rights coincide with those of North (1989, 1328–29). An adequate explanation of the course of development, or rather underdevelopment, is probably somewhat more complex than that implied in his several discussions of Spanish development. North, in the case of Spain, has focused on one important exogenous variable—monarchical spending on military adventures in the presence of new and expensive military technology (1981, 151; 1990, 113). The taxation created fiscal crises, bankruptcy, and insecure property rights. We certainly agree, but a story with finer gradations needs to be told. Surely the increased cost of military technology in the sixteenth century was a factor in pressing taxing and regulatory institutions to their limit, but this took place in an institutional milieu that was both evolving and being affected by a number of important "exogenous" forces—international demand for exports including wool, population pressures, unanticipated demands on the fisc as a result of unplanned colonial discoveries, and so forth. The security of property rights was also a function of, as we have argued, the strength of competing interests in agriculture, church, and in local, regional and national politics. These institutions, unchanged from those molded much earlier in Spanish history, were unable to encourage socially productive investments. In other nations, England for instance, similar military technology and desires for empire did not have the same effects. This simply points up the fact that a more formal and detailed *model* of institutional change (and development) is necessary to partition cause and effect in particular cases and in a manner that permits finding answers to important questions.

The ultimate question, of course, which cannot be answered fully here, revolves around the origins of the particular sets of institutions we find in England, France, and Spain in the sixteenth, seventeenth, and eighteenth centuries. That institutions were rapidly changing in both countries over this period is manifest, but it is clear that important checks (respecting taxation power, for example) were imposed upon English monarchs as early as the thirteenth century, whereas such checks were not binding in France until the eighteenth century or even much later in Spain. An obvious point, then, is that crucial constraints upon the power to tax and to enforce economic regulations differed greatly among England, France, and Spain, but upon what ultimate bases were these different institutions established? It has not been our intention in this book to present a broad social theory of why nation-state institutional patterns differed over the mercantilist era. Rather, accepting some "stock" of institutions as given, we have analyzed English, French and Spanish mercantile policies and events in positive-economic terms over a somewhat limited time period. We have shown that modern contributions to the theory of public choice and economic regulation provide us with explanations for episodes historians unsatisfactorily attribute to other causes.[5] Undeniably, the surface of a neoinstitutional approach to economic development over and after the "mercantile" period has only been scratched. A better characterization awaits a more elaborate theory of institutional change.

Mercantile Industrial Organization

Our foray into the study of business organizations in the mercantile era can only serve to show the kinds of insights that may be gained from studying industrial organization during this important formative period. Most useful and relevant in the study of mercantile industrial organization are the relationships that can be observed in this period between firms and the state. In this sense there would seem to be much of value to be learned from the study of economic regulation in the mercantile economies. This is all the more true since mercantilism, conceived of as a broad process of economic regulation, seems to be a perennial state of most societies, and professional economics is just coming to grips with developing testable theories of state intervention in the economy (for example, Stigler 1971b; Peltzman 1976; Pincus 1975). While the old mercantilism may have developed in a different institutional setting from the modern (monarchy versus representative democracy), it is fairly clear that the result of widespread state intervention in the economy is much the same in both cases. The old mercantilism, reinterpreted as a manifestation of man's eternal proclivities toward rent seeking, can thus serve as a useful historical laboratory for the examination of modern developments in the theory of economic regulation and the economic approach to politics. The usefulness of Demsetz's (1968) model of monopoly franchising in explaining the productive efficiency of the English regulated companies is a good example of this point. Moreover, our hypothesis concerning the origin of the corporation illustrates the old maxim that good results often spring from bad intentions. From the idea of operating monopolies more efficiently came the idea of the joint-stock companies.

We devoted considerably more attention here than in our earlier work on mercantilism (1981) to the subject of mercantile industrial organization. The reasons for the renewed emphasis are apparent in the topics discussed. The mercantile companies were, in large part, the sine qua non of the rent-seeking model of mercantilism. These companies were the nexus of the "exchange" between king and rent seekers. They were also far-flung international organizations that faced problems inherent in similar modern organizations. Further the devices they used to address these problems were very modern in their sum and substance. Thus, the study of mercantile industrial organization helped us better to explicate the rent-seeking theory of mercantilism and to illustrate how "modern" the early firms actually were. And, indeed, we were able to articulate as well as hypothesize about why the corporate contract was invented and went on to prosper as an organizational format for business.

HECKSCHER AND THE METHODOLOGY OF ECONOMIC HISTORY

No contemporary consideration of mercantile and preclassical political economy and institutions could ignore the methodological perspective of the greatest researcher of all times on these issues. Inasmuch as some scholars continue to champion Heckscher's method in the study of mercantilism—Coats (1993, 263), for example, looks to "a new Heckscher" for the further study of mercantilism—it is useful to reexamine Heckscher's actual views on the relations between history, theory, and statistics as a part of a conclusion to our own study.

Heckscher, for his part, was far more prescient in his view of (what is now called) neoinstitutional economics than virtually all historiographers and many modern economic historians. In a lecture before the International Historical Congress at Oslo in 1928 Heckscher presented a brilliant defense of the use of general economic theory—that is, *neoclassical* theorizing—in the study of economic history against the onslaught of those (German historians in particular) whose "treatment of social evolution as subject to historical laws has so proved of small value" (1929, 526). The generality of economic theory in *all* epochs of human history and in *all* aspects of human activity is clearly stressed by Heckscher. In a remarkably modern view of economic theory applied to economic development, Heckscher emphasizes the unifying force of economic behavior in producing the gradual evolution of economic institutions from the most primitive to modern times. According to Heckscher (1929, 528):

> [E]ven if it is intended exclusively for modern conditions, theory must not limit itself to one particular set of circumstances. If the theory starts from abstract and consequently unreal conditions, these premises [sic] must in the subsequent study be modified not in one direction and now in another, in order to make them suit actual facts. There is not the slightest reason for giving up this method when the facts of previous ages come to be studied. There may be a difference in degree, but there certainly is none in character, between what is done with regard to modern and what should be done for earlier economic problems.

To imply that some age is "preindustrial" or "precapitalist" (or Cro-Magnon for that matter), and therefore not subject to the same economizing principles of behavior on the part of its inhabitants is simply misguided. From this perspective, many modern historians (Appleby 1978) err in propounding the general irrelevance of economic theory in, say, medieval or ancient settings. Markets, either in pecuniary or nonpecuniary terms, always adjust to the forces of supply and demand, and economizing is always and everywhere the central theme in describing economic development.[6]

But Heckscher, himself a very able theorist, took his argument much further than simply supporting the universal applicability of economic theory throughout history. He also took the Beckerian position that economizing was at the core of *all* behavior. Economic behavior as utility maximization, Heckscher argued, was practically universal. As he noted, "Economics is not a particular branch or department of human life, as is often believed; it is an aspect of almost all human activities, or those activities as regarded from a particular point of view" (1929, 527). The economic problem—maximization of utility under scarcity and other constraints—applies in activities not generally appreciated as "economic."

This view is extended to the role of statistics and quantitative measurement as a complement to economic theory as well. With appropriate caveats concerning data reliability and other problems, Heckscher advocated the same use of the statistical or econometric methods in studying history as that used in "present-day economic life 'in being'" (1939, 168). The only difference, according to Heckscher, was that the study of economic history required the study of (long-period) social and institutional changes in the economy as well. Ironically, Heckscher believed that contemporary theorists would be helped the most. The theorists must understand that society is in constant flux and that "the situation they are studying is no more than a horizontal section of an indivisible whole, conditioned by what went before and leading to something different from the object of their theories" (1939, 168). But in the study of historical and institutional change, methods for ascertaining and choosing the facts must be exactly the same as for contemporary analysis. Heckscher chides historians for "leaving aside the political side of human evolution" and for the exclusion of "the influence of economic conditions upon this" (1939, 169).

That Heckscher came close to understanding the necessary interrelations between interests and policy is undeniable. His defense of statistics included an adjuration to look for the results of policies, doctrines, laws, "ordinances and government regulations," not the intended or stated consequences. Heckscher in fact advances the Stiglerian argument (Stigler and Friedland 1962) that one should inquire whether laws and regulations "represented more than the pious wishes or beliefs of their originators" (1939, 170). "Properly speaking," according to Heckscher, "the existence of . . . documents cannot tell more than one fact with regard to economic conditions, and that is that they were different from the contents of the regulations, since it would otherwise have been unnecessary to issue any regulations" (1939, 170). Should, in other words, chambers of commerce or congressional regulations on trade be taken seriously when they are enacted to "save local businesses" or to "provide essential materials for national defense?"

Finally, Heckscher would not have been surprised at the main lines of our argument—that laissez-faire doctrines and economic theory *followed* rather than led empirical "mercantile" policies. He says as much in an essay (1936) evaluating some of the criticisms of his famous book. Speculations on the *means* of promoting the general welfare led mercantile writers to pave "the way to a theory of economics, in spite of having started from purely practical considerations. It is not . . . a question of a choice between theory and practice, but of *practice leading unintentionally to theory*" (1936, 45; emphasis supplied). Such views reverse and replace the ordinary speculations of historiographers that "more than anything, mercantilism was a literature, a discourse, on trade and economics" (Magnusson 1994, vii). The practice of mercantilism—the passage of regulations, domestic and international—did not arise de novo as Venus arising from the sea. Mercantilism emerged within an evolving institutional framework that included a constitutionally determined political and economic structure. Rent seeking by coalitions of economic interest working through a pliant political structure (within England) and rock-hard mercantile structures in France and Spain were the sources of mercantile "practice." Rent seeking within English constraints brought on the practice of laissez-faire with accompanying institutions such as secure property rights and long-term private investment and (within an entirely different nexus of constraints) the retention of mercantilism for far longer periods in France and Spain. As Heckscher noted, a commercial conception of society was quite common to both mercantilism and laissez-faire. The point was that "mercantilist and *laissez-faire* policies were poles asunder" (1936, 53).

Heckscher's early defense of economic theory and statistics in the study of economic history, including its intertemporal relevance and behavioral generality, brings us full circle to modern-day historicist and other criticisms of neoclassical theorizing in the study of institutions and institutional change. Some writers would have us believe that economic theory qua Marshallian utility maximizing and economizing—even that elegantly recast and reinvigorated with contemporary theories of transaction costs, information cost, and property rights—is insufficient to analyze institutional or evolutionary change (Magnusson 1993b). So-called path dependence and informational problems are depicted as insurmountable barriers to a neoclassical analysis of institutions and/or economic development.[7] The total absence of a coherent, cohesive, and testable alternative theory of any dimensions does not appear to deter these critics. If no theory has been developed, no alternative application has appeared to challenge the interpretation of any particular historical episode. If better explanations for institutional change in preclassical economies exist, especially those that might use new and improved tools, researchers are obliged to bring them forward.

The central issue is that self-interest and neo-Marshallian microeconomic theory may not predict all events, but that is the way to bet until critics of these axioms demonstrate the superiority of other speculations. In some of this literature it is as if we are re-playing the fin de siècle Veblenian, British, and German Historicist criticisms of economic theory. Veblenians argued, in effect, that economic theory was not "modern" and was incapable of handling problems of institutional change. But neither Veblen nor his followers have provided an alternative theory of institutional change. The same criticism applies to modern critics of *contemporary* Marshallian theorizing. It is one thing to maintain that orthodox positive economics does not reach all phenomena of interest. It is quite another to provide a superior theory or to supply "refereed" evidence that rational self-interest does not provide a bountiful harvest of explanations in varied historical settings. No one could put it better than Heckscher (1929, 529) when he noted that "the value of economic theory increases enormously when the work of historians is carried further than the stating of external facts; for its most important use refers to the choice of facts and the explanation of them." Along with Heckscher we would like to make a simple point: A modified neoclassical approach, with special emphasis on the rent-seeking part of that view, is sufficient to provide a rich theory of the behavior of the interests within the mercantile state and, more generally, within all other preclassical economies.

THE "MEANING" OF MERCANTILISM

High on the lists of many historians of thought and historiographically oriented researchers is a "definition" of mercantilism. Unfortunately such enterprise—sufficient to maintain a small army of academics—is of limited value if the central role of the economist is to explain, analyze, and predict the course of economic development and growth. Ideas, of course, *can* have force and power—enormous power in some cases. But ideas must find a market. Ideas become action through market or political forces and competition. Ideology is merely an extension of the concept of an idea to a set of ideas, doctrines, or beliefs that form the basis of some cultural, political, or economic system. The role of ideology, however, is as yet undetermined in explaining "policies," "regulations," and property rights changes within a political context.[8]

The argument of this book, as well as our previous studies, suggests that Hume, Smith, and all the other great free-trade intellectuals were bystanders (albeit important bystanders) in a process having its origins many years before in the changing constraints facing rent seekers in mercantile England. An identical argument holds for "physiocracy" in France, where, as we noted in chapter 4, deregulation in the countryside preceded the formal (but ultimately futile) policies of Turgot and others interested in laissez-faire. In Spain (see chapter 5) adjurations to economic freedom pronounced by Enlightenment practitioners went largely unheeded.

The etymology of economic terms and purely historiographic studies of the works of the "nth" mercantilist do possess limited interest as intellectual exercise, but these approaches to "mercantilism" do not and cannot arrive at a cogent and consistent explanation of why mercantilism significantly declined in England but not in France and Spain. Why? Because mercantilism is not a set of doctrines, it is a *process*. *Mercantilism is a process through which rent seeking alters property rights systems in socially inefficient manners reducing exchange, efficiency, and economic welfare. Mercantilism flowers when political institutions, formed from constitutions, permit rent-seeking redistributions of property rights.* The story of the decline of mercantilism in some particular country or context and the explanation of the reassertion of mercantilism in some other country or context is told with the same set of tools. Political institutions permitting, domestic and international regulations (called "mercantilist") will develop. Again, institutions permitting, a decline in "mercantile" regulations will occur when cost-

benefit configurations make "competition" or laissez-faire more profitable
to interest groups also in a position to dominate the political process. These
factors illustrate the enduring appeal of mercantilism. The desire to redis-
tribute wealth through the political process will occur so long as institutions permit the activity and so long as rent-seeking individuals or coalitions
profit therefrom.[9]

Weingast (1995), correctly in our view, also underlines the essential interrelations between the growth of markets and limited government. A
paradox—first raised by Plato—must be resolved. That paradox is that the
state or government must first be strong enough to protect its citizens'
property rights (from internal and external encroachment) but constrained
from confiscating the wealth of its citizens. Autonomous and hierarchical
government at upper and lower levels, a common market, a "hard" budget
constraint (no money printing or unlimited borrowing power at local level),
and primary regulatory power at the local level—all characteristics of
"market-preserving" federalism—are clearly and accurately emphasized by
Weingast.[10] This federalism was, as we have seen, developed in the local
markets through the ability of firms to escape guild and other regulations
in the "countryside" and because the system gave rise to opportunistic
behavior on the part of the unpaid justices of the peace (the enforcers of
regulation). At the national level, moreover, court competition for the rights
to supply monopoly charters created a redivision of power to regulate between monarch and Parliament and among the crown and common-law
court systems.

We agree with Weingast (1995, 25) that "the political foundations of
markets are as essential to their success as the details and specification of
the market itself" and that self-enforcing restrictions on government are
the essential prerequisites to exchange, reduced transactions costs, and
growth. There is, however, nothing *inevitable* concerning these developments. Federalism grew out of these factors in England because particular
economic factors—high transactions and enforcement costs, insufficient
"slack" in the tax system to finance enforcement of local regulations (the
latter in contrast to France and Spain)—happened to encourage the development of the self-enforcing restrictions of a federal system. Restrictions
(and formal and informal constraints that are credible to the population)
are required, as Weingast maintains, but application of this keen observation requires an understanding of the economic factors that support the
development of the "federalist" constraints.[11]

As such, mercantilism (or what we call mercantilism) cannot be understood outside of a neoinstitutionalist framework. The construction of formal models of institutional change is of ongoing importance because mercantilism as a system of regulatory supply and demand for rent-seeking purposes has never entirely disappeared. The magnitude of controls is perhaps not as interesting as their movement and direction, and here it is interesting to speculate on how exactly economic controls were systematically reduced in the English economy between 1640 and 1914 or how "mercantile" policies were implemented in the domestic U.S. economy between the 1930s and the late 1970s, with some decline thereafter. We believe that a good deal of the answer will come from further analysis of the constraints (formal or informal) put on rent seeking. Under any given institutional framework, we also find individuals, such as Gladstone, whose influence on economic policy spanned the middle two decades of the nineteenth-century in England. His philosophy (put into practice) was one of denying the government access to revenue-raising instruments and, further, of raising taxes only to cover specific items of expenditure, after which tax laws would self-destruct (Baysinger and Tollison 1980a). English fiscal conservatism of a high degree of sophistication fostered by the costs associated with parliamentary rent seeking, then, provides a potential explanation for why and how English mercantilism subsided for so long.

Thus, we have argued that the application of the modern theory of economic regulation to the mercantile period yields new insights into the growth and decline of mercantile restrictions. Surely our argument would not have surprised Adam Smith, and we view it as an extension of Smith's (admittedly) fragmentary analysis of the rent-seeking modes of the period. As noted throughout the present book, however, there is no dearth of arguments concerning the decline of overt mercantile policies, although the reasons for this significant episode of deregulation are largely assumed rather than explored in the literature. Credit is implicitly given to Adam Smith and his "liberal" predecessors, who advocated the advantages of the free and spontaneous coordination of economic activity, for making such a forceful intellectual case for their point of view that it was translated into public policy. Our interpretation of mercantilism as a rent-seeking society does not suggest that intellectual developments will have much impact on public policy. We thus tend to disagree with Keynes, who was certain "that the power of vested interests is vastly exaggerated compared with the gradual encroachment of ideas" (1936, 38).[12]

We again maintain, in short, that commentators on mercantilism, including Heckscher and Viner, have "overscholarized" the period. It is not that these renowned writers have not added greatly to our knowledge but rather that they have implicitly emphasized ideas as primary causal forces of change rather than as (sometimes interesting) rationalizations based upon one's position in the rent-seeking game of income distribution. The motives of mercantile writers, as Smith cunningly indicated, should always be suspect. Heckscher has pointed out, with reference to intellectual arguments, that "there was little mysticism in the arguments of the mercantilists. . . . they did not appeal to sentiment, but were obviously anxious to find reasonable grounds for every position they adopted" (1934, 2:308).

We certainly do not disagree that writers of all persuasions sought reasonable grounds for their arguments, but we argue that these grounds in the main were a veneer over the underlying self-interested forces of the components of society.[13] The Platonic philosopher or "impartial observer," if any existed, could not have been persuasive in the absence of an institutional environment that permitted gain in the manner he supported. It is our thesis, in short, that rent-seeking engendered forces that drastically altered institutions in England, while producing in a milieu of French and Spanish constraints a mercantile rigidity lasting until the nineteenth (and even the twentieth) century. Our view is thus a reassertion of Smith's primitive analysis of mercantilism. It is, moreover, an elaboration of that view, in that it finds, utilizing modern theories of regulatory behavior within a neoinstitutional context, a crucial link between rent-seeking agents, property rights alterations, and fundamental institutional change.

Notes

CHAPTER I

MERCANTILISM, RENT SEEKING, AND INSTITUTIONAL CHANGE

1. This is not meant to imply that important, if particularized, studies did not precede these developments. Two important contributions to our understanding of particular writers and particular institutions under Spanish mercantilism appeared in the pre-Heckscher, pre-Viner period. See Klein (1920) and Castillo (1930). Heckscher's study first appeared in Swedish in 1931.

2. This "absolutist" position has had a number of influential followers, including J. A. Schumpeter and George Stigler. An interesting exploration of Viner's view is offered in Allen (1970). Viner's brilliant study of mercantile trade doctrine first appeared in journal form in 1930 and was reprinted in his *Studies in the Theory of International Trade* in 1937.

3. A brief survey of these "central tendencies" may be found in Ekelund and Hébert (1996, 39–60) or in any standard manual on the history of economic doctrines. The literature concentrating on the so-called mercantile "tool box" is vast and of interest in itself, but we strongly downplay, in this work as in our initial work (1981), the importance of any mercantile theoretical paradigm, however crudely conceived, for the course of economic institutions and development. Much may be learned from this literature, however. In addition to the works of Heckscher and Viner, see Schumpeter (1954, 335–76), Roy (1943), and DeRoover (1944). Some of the most fascinating material of this kind has concerned the philosophical and analytical thought of specific individuals; see for example, Beer (1938), Morris (1957), Dewar (1965), Chalk (1966), and Evans (1967). More recently, essays by Herlitz (1993) and Grampp (1993) should be mentioned as in the lineage of this earlier literature.

4. Keynes (1936, chap. 15) offered a well-known defense of the mercantilists on the grounds that a favorable balance of trade was the only means available to a country at that time of lowering domestic interest rates and increasing home investment and employment. Heckscher argued in rebuttal that unemployment in the mercantilist era was essentially voluntary and insensitive to changes in aggregate demand (1955, 2:340–58).

5. Other important historical treatments of mercantilism are those of Ashley (1923–1925), Cunningham (1968), and Scott (1951).

6. North and Thomas were preceded in this broad approach by Frederic C. Lane (1958, 1979), who investigated organized violence and its effects upon the economic motives and behavior of Renaissance governments in exacting tribute from merchants for protection. Studies exploring the interconnection of economic activity and social institutions have been very uncommon since Lane's pioneering work, however, and cliometrics has dominated the scene in economic history. One other exception is the work of J. R. T. Hughes (1977), who presented a broad and interesting perspective of the impact of U.S. governmental and legal institutions upon social welfare. North's (1979) research on the role of state in economic history should also be mentioned, as must his progressive development of neoinstitutional theory in two later works (1981; 1990).

7. Unappropriable costs and benefits may "build up" under certain institutions creating enough economic incentive for change. Some economists, for example, argue that radical alterations in property rights in the Soviet Union and other communist countries were the result of such unappropriable costs to planned systems.

8. Thus, in North and Thomas's initial story of the rise of the Western world (1973), technological invention (in the form of more expensive technologies to wage war) and population-decimating plague are featured as major factors in altering property rights for greater efficiency and growth in certain parts of western Europe. North's analysis is embellished in a number of later works (1981; 1989; 1990).

9. A survey of the field may be found in Eggertsson (1990) or in the far more informative and concise treatment by Pejovich (1995).

10. As in Marshall's own era, but for other reasons, some modern economists are searching for a new theoretical base to analyze institutions. Some (Williamson 1985) claim that rational choice cannot apply to problems where transactions costs and "bounded rationality" lead to nonmarket solutions. Further, these problems together with the "path dependence" and "rule following" associated with institutional change has led important and informed observers to call for the sacking of traditional microeconomics entirely (Furubotn 1994) and for replacing it with a "new" theory. We here acknowledge these in-progress concerns with the theory of institutional change but believe that the neoinsitutionalist paradigm is sufficient for our *particular* analysis of mercantilism. On the other side, there are those who believe that a neoinstitutional or any theory of institutional change is "excessively schematic," presumably meaning that no theory of institutional change is possible (Rothbard 1995, 516).

11. North (1990, 112) argues for a modification of neoclassical theory, ostensibly to accommodate the problem of path dependence. We argue, however, that the theory of path dependence, if a theory can be said to exist, is an empty concept or at least seriously flawed (see the discussion of path dependence later in this chapter).

12. That gap was pointed out as late as 1980 by a distinguished economic historian who argued that "if we are to understand economic history, we must be able to understand and to explain the behavior of the government sector" (Davis 1980, 3). Davis argued further that a new "polinomic history," blending positive economics and politics, is essential for understanding the central questions relating social and economic structure, in other words, institutional change (Davis 1980, 15). Some (Rashid 1993, 136) argue, precipitously we believe, that the "entire rent-seeking edifice" was carefully discussed and criticized with Charles Wilson's (1968) attack on the "lobby theory of legis-

lation." In reality Wilson's work is irrelevant to the application of a rent-seeking theory of institutional change. Wilson appears to have been totally unaware of the theory and meaning of rent seeking, not to mention the testable propositions that support it. He provides neither understanding nor citations to the literature that existed on the matter in 1968. For example, in reference to Adam Smith and David Hume, Wilson argues that "at the time they were laying and even inscribing the foundation tablets of the new system, there were relatively few businessmen with the foresight to understand the case they were expounding" (1968, 98). Not only did businessmen "understand" the case for favorable restrictions and (to them) the deleterious nature of competition, as we argue in chapter 3, they—through their representatives—attempted to thwart the growing institutional possibilities of free trade more than a century earlier. That they became increasingly unsuccessful (in the English case) had nothing to do with their ability to "understand" the principles of free trade. Smith and Hume may have been "universalists" in their thought, but the course of free trade in England had little if anything to do with that "philosophy," as Wilson staunchly maintains.

13. Note that all theories and practical applications of institutional change must take some set of institutions as given. This was certainly so in our initial treatment of mercantilism as it is in other serious investigations of institutional change (North and Weingast 1989, 804 n. 1).

14. Our depiction of the fate of property rights and political institutions in France was, of course, quite different. There rent-seeking activity was destructive of social product. The same, we argue, applies to the Spanish economy of the mercantile period (see chapter 5).

15. The contretemps between monarch and business-democratic interests over civil powers is actually as old as the medieval wool trade. Our analysis of the role of Coke and other common law jurists as philosophers and rent seekers is extended in the present work (see chapter 3).

16. See our concluding chapter for an evaluation of this argument.

17. Root's treatment of the French guild system and Colbert's role in monopoly creation is a case in point. Root used our argument concerning guild cartels, product differentiation and competition from the "informal sector" (1994, 133), and rent seeking (1994, 116–17 n. 12) as the centerpiece of his analysis, but carries the historical discussion forward to consider guild finance in the eighteenth century (1994, 121–27).

18. Our initial argument concerning mercantilism, or parts thereof, has been developed in relation to a number of other research concerns. The question of the relation between "totalitarianism" and urbanization, for example, is answered in part by our analysis of the failure of guild cartelization by the English crown (Ades and Glaser 1995, 218–19). Problems of "neomercantilism" were also analyzed using our initial analysis (DeSoto 1989).

19. Historians of thought have, by and large and in sharp contrast to economic historians, championed Heckscher's ideational and "doctrinal" treatment. In addition to the literature cited in note 2 above, see B. F. Haley's (1936) laudatory and noncritical discussion of Heckscher's book. Heckscher was preceded in the doctrinal approach by a number of writers, such as Furniss (1965 [1920]), Castillo (1930), and, in a series of interesting papers, E. A. J. Johnson (1931, 1932a, 1932b). Attempts have also been made to relate mercantile writings to economic conditions (Hinton 1955). A doctrinal approach has recently been utilized by Magnusson (1993) and championed in particular and loosely

constructed historiographic essays on the spirit of the "times" (for example, Coats 1993). The fundamental emptiness of most "intellectual approaches" to mercantilism consists precisely in identifying "the mercantilists" or "mercantile policies" apart from self-interested forces propelling institutions and institutional change. In this vein, see the essay by Perrotta (1991), who puts this kind of interpretation forward and even goes beyond, claiming that "the mercantilist concept of international trade perfectly fulfilled the requirements of the national economies of the period," as if "national economies" had "requirements." Self-interested coalitions of interest groups in all countries between the sixteenth and eighteenth centuries determined domestic and international regulatory policies, not "mercantilists" or the requirements of national economies. The consistency or nonconformity of economic opinion (of the "mercantilists") with the imputed goals or requirements of the "national economy" are quite irrelevant for interpreting the mercantile period. Self-interest qua utility maximization, as Stigler observes (1982, 13), means that "as preachers" economists "are well received in the measure that we preach what the society wishes to hear."

20. Root (1995, xv) considers these historiographic interests and methods and is indeed sympathetic to them and to tolerance among neighboring fields. However, he notes, "I do not propose to conduct or interpret research without a conceptual framework" (xv). Interestingly, his principal conclusions, which amplify those we reached in our earlier work on mercantilism, do not appear to depend in any critical way on historiographic or sociological categories.

21. Wolfe (1984, 99) suggested that an early essay by Wilson (1959) in some way indicates that economic interests—rent-seeking interest groups—do not explain mercantile policy. But Wilson himself admits that while theories or principles informed thought and policy over the period, "It is equally fallacious to suppose that thought and policy were distinct activities that can and should be treated separately" (83). But his examination of the ideas of mercantile scribblers such as Mandeville and Defoe leads him to argue that "employment policies" of the mercantilist—"their attitude towards the poor" can in no way be explained in terms of the economic interests or the "alignment of supporters" for such policies. We most certainly do not argue that individual observers necessarily had economic interests in policy change. We *do* argue that much of the scribbling was of the chamber of commerce type—defending trade restrictions on the basis of some stalking horse such as national defense in the modern case, or defending a balance of trade objective as a cover for special interests. Wilson offers no parliamentary evidence other than the testimony of mercantile writers themselves to support his case. This does not mean that scholars, ideas, and ideologies do not sometimes affect policy. It simply means that neoinstitutional economics presents a positive theory of mercantile developments and that, as yet, there are no positive theories of ideology or idea formation to set against an economic approach.

22. To repeat, we do not maintain that ideas exert no influence on policy. As Anderson (1982, 979) suggested, "The American experience with rent seeking most definitely has been influenced by ideas." That may be correct, but it takes coalitions of interests acting through political processes to press ideas into action. Franklin D. Roosevelt's secretary of labor, Frances Perkins, lobbied for years for child labor reform on the basis of "justice" but only achieved it (in 1938) when coalitions of rent seekers finally passed it (as part of a larger bill called the Fair Labor Standards Act). (See Davidson et al. 1995.) Anderson raises a more unsettling question concerning the self interest of intellectuals

when he notes that some kind of contradiction exists between those who discount the importance of ideas but are employed in the idea industry (such as the current authors). Do employees of "think tanks" (e.g., the Hoover Institute, Common Cause, the Heritage Foundation, the Cato Institute, and so on) feel compelled to spout a particular "line" because of self-interest and economic survival instincts? Or do individuals "self select" on the basis of some indigenous philosophical predilections? There are no robust answers to these questions, but we offer two observations: (a) ideas have impact when they can be sold to individuals who have interest and ability to implement them, and (b) there is no good evidence, at least up to this point, that ideas (or ideology) have a direct impact on policy apart from competing coalitions of self-interested groups working through particular political processes and constraints.

23. That external trace regulations and restrictions were the result of blatant rent seeking is hardly in question, especially as regards the colonies (see chapter 3).

24. If such an argument ever worked to explain laissez-faire in England, why did not the presence of very active "Enlightenment economists" in both France and Spain not produce or even nudge a transformation of those economies toward competitive markets?

25. A recent paper suggests as much (Irwin 1991). Irwin, in an interesting contribution, investigates mercantile foreign trade (and colonial and East India Company adventures) in terms of a contemporary model of strategic trade. He showed that the Dutch—engaged in strategic competition with the British—earned profits in greater amounts in the East India trade than would have been expected under standard profit-maximization.

26. In an earlier historical and quasi-Marxian interpretation of mercantilism, Magnusson (1978) emphasizes the exportation to and growth of mercantile trade policies in Sweden. Adopting the Marxian notion of the "merchant capitalist" (113–14), Magnusson explains why mercantile export policies, such as those that characterized other European countries, were so popular in Sweden. An exploitative interpretation of merchant capitalism is not necessary to explain the emergence of mercantile policies of any sort. An analysis of the costs and benefits of regulatory supply and demand is relevant to any mercantile economy. Magnusson's discussions continue (1987) to rest on the soft schools of "ideology" and "vision" as the basis for Swedish mercantile policies and less on identifiable rent-seeking interests. That "Swedish mercantilists shared a view of how to improve and modernize the economy with the help of the state-regulated powers" (1987, 425) is not inconsistent with their desire to effect particular income distributions. His association of rent seeking with a crude Marxian capture argument is also in error. The theory of rent seeking is far more general in application. Coalitions of interest groups (the American Medical Association, Citizens for Democratic Action, labor unions), along with coalitions to oppose particular interests, expend resources to control the political process. Similarities between the theory of rent seeking and Marxian class interests are more apparent than real. In Marx, capital wins and labor loses, always. In the theory of rent seeking, the organized wins at the expense of the unorganized. Coats, Magnusson, and other historiographers do not appear to understand what the rent-seeking argument means.

27. A similar argument holds for physiocracy in France where actual deregulation in the countryside preceded the formal (but ultimately futile) policies of Turgot and others interested in laissez-faire (see Shaeper 1983 for details). In Spain, adjurations to eco-

nomic freedom pronounced by Enlightenment practitioners, undoubtedly influenced by French and English counterparts, went largely unheeded (see chapter 5).

28. Boland (1979, 961) warns, correctly, of the circularity and dangers of explanations running along reductivist lines. Some item in a theory, norm, value, or institution must be exogenous in order for the neoclassical process of economizing to explain change. So-called "path dependent institutions" change at different rates, but the neoclassical apparatus cannot explain infinite regress.

29. The literature on nonexplicit markets and institutions is growing rapidly. Examples include Becker's (1981) analysis of the "family," discussions of the form of religion and "dogma" as being determined by economic or rent-seeking behavior (Ekelund et al. 1996; Iannaccone 1988), or the form of cuisine as a function of economic variables (Ekelund and Watson 1991).

30. One need not denude the role of ideas and ideology to the point that a crude materialism explains historical and institutional evolution in order to analyze critical changes in mercantile institutions. Indeed, ideas conceived of as mechanisms or inventions that reduce transactions cost or reduce unappropriable costs (increase net gains) are central to the economizing process that propels institutional change and economic growth. The trick is to explain, in testable form, how (exactly) ideas and ideology affect economic and political institutional change.

31. Seltzer (1995) claims to have identified an ideological component in a study of voting on the Fair Labor Standards Act of 1938, presenting it as a regression residual and as some evidence against Peltzman's hypothesis (1984) that ideology is, in effect, squeezed out in repeated elections. This "evidence" is not persuasive, however. Economic factors may simply be unidentified (as explaining the residual), or the residual may well be attributed to shirking or boredom. Professor Tyler Cowen proposes the following resolution as the best defense of the claim that ideas matter: In the real world there are multiple possible equilibria, and "ideas" determine which equilibrium "holds." In this regard ideas play a significant role and serve as more than a residual. Yet the explanation does not require that any individual sacrifice his material interest for reasons of ideology.

32. Some critics have claimed to find lacunae in the self-interested theory of institutional change in areas of mercantile policy that have yet to be fully analyzed. Rashid (1993, 135), for example, claims that the rent-seeking paradigm does not apply to certain English colonization policies. He argues that the results of the Corn Bounty and colonization did not maximize returns to monopoly interests after being in effect for more than a century and that this is proof that rent-seeking theories can fail to illuminate history. The chief flaw in this argument is that rent-seeking theory does not predict perfect monopoly profit maximization. The state serves multiple interests, and trade-offs among them are inevitable. The state does not set up perfect cartels, and there are, of course, transactions costs that attend all market functioning, competitive or monopolistic.

33. In Veblen's serious and popular publications, habits and institutions are in fact exogenous, and although he recognized "a specific sociological-anthropological variant of economizing, he failed to identify how the cost-benefit mechanism applied to real wealth or utility maximizing behavior to explain change under conditions of instinctually-determined goals" (Ault and Ekelund 1988, 42). Pecuniary values were not associated with material progress. For example, Veblen *did* argue that "pecuniary behavior" was primarily responsible for creating institutions such as the corporation, common and preferred stock, and corporate finance generally (Raines and Leathers 1993, 256–58), but

he did not believe or understand that these new and evolving institutions produced *real* wealth. This is of course not a general theory of *endogenous* habit formation (as Raines and Leathers themselves point out: 1993, 264), and Veblen did not describe a utility maximizing view of institutional change outside an ill-understood "pecuniary context."

34. There are those who believe that a neoinstitutional or any theory of institutional change is "excessively schematic," presumably meaning that *no* theory of institutional change is possible (Rothbard 1995, 516).

35. Liebowitz and Margolis have summarily exploded the most commonly advanced examples, including the QWERTY typewriter (1990), the adoption of the VHS format (1995a), and the so-called existence of network externalities (1994).

36. The simple observation that some people donate blood does not negate the regularity and predictability that rational self-interest guides events and policies. Do tax deductions for museums increase, decrease, or remain the same when deductibles are gauged at current market value versus original cost? Results (after a change in the law in 1993) unequivocally favor the former. Government placement of property rights have served to discourage the market provision of blood, all in order to benefit the Red Cross and hematologists (Kessel 1974). Increase the market reward by monetary inducements and/or changed liability and more blood would be "donated."

37. Though English population grew significantly over the period, the varying growth rates among subgroups contributed to overall stability. The English peerage grew markedly over the first half of the period, causing social disorders within this class, but, as deVries (1976, 10–11) explains, celibacy, later marriage, reduced fertility, and high mortality after 1675 led to reduced numbers within the aristocracy. The upward mobility and concentration of wealth thus created were powerful forces in promoting a stable English society. Other countries, such as Spain, were not so situated with respect to population (Nadal 1986).

38. Historians seem to be at pains to explain just why the major site of the Industrial Revolution was England rather than the states of the Dutch republic, since the Dutch had established an extremely viable preindustrial economy replete with private property rights and cost-saving inventions, especially in the earlier part of the period from 1600 to 1750. Inventions and their exploitation, especially the type of inventions that led to the Industrial Revolution, are the product of a nurturing economic and social environment. The environment created by the vast social and institutional change in England between 1600 and 1750 brought about the necessary preconditions for the Industrial Revolution. Some of these important institutional changes were created by the rent-seeking environment we analyze in this book.

39. North (1981; 1989; 1990) also discusses, in a broad and sweeping assessment, the product of sixteenth- and seventeenth-century institutional development on the modern age in Latin America and North America.

CHAPTER 2.

RENT-SEEKING THEORY AND ITS APPLICATION TO MERCANTILISM

1. This result assumes a labor market equilibrium in which, for example, a lawyer's wage is an accurate proxy for his opportunity cost as an engineer and in which the lawyer is indifferent at the margin with respect to choice of profession.

2. Keep in mind the above point that rents are not transfers or bribes but must be expended in real resources devoted to regulatory favor seeking.

3. Cowling and Mueller (1978) also make the important point that since many rent-seeking costs are buried in business expenses, there is a bias toward underestimation in the way most studies calculate rents. That is, observed rents will understate the true costs of rent seeking.

4. Magee carries the analysis a step further by looking at the rent-seeking costs of having an additional lawyer in the legislature. He estimates that each additional lawyer in the U.S. Congress costs more than $1 billion. See Rauch (1992, 984).

5. For a similar exercise, see Joseph Phillips in an appendix to Baran and Sweezy (1966), who estimated the "cost" of monopoly capitalism at 56 percent of U.S. GNP.

6. In a mercantile (and in a modern) context, monopoly often means a number of combined producers rather than a single seller-producer. The cartels are simply a formal conglomeration of firms acting as a single monopolist under formal or centralized control. (We shall see in later chapters that French and Spanish producers—especially of luxury goods such as textiles and fine wool—and English foreign-trading companies were organized in this fashion.) In cartels, prices or output share (or both) are ordinarily assigned to the various firms whose behavior is, in some manner, monitored or policed, and entry conditions must, of course, be conscribed. Cartels may be privately or publicly organized, but there is a keen incentive to cheat on cartel price or output when there is no legal sanction to the arrangement, since each firm has an incentive to lower price or sell outside its assigned market. In sum, most privately organized cartels are unstable and tend to break down over time. The acquisition of public regulation, therefore, is a common and low-cost means used by an industry to organize as a cartel, since the regulatory agency supplies the continuous enforcement of the rules. Through regulation, backed up by legal sanctions against "cheaters," the government may attempt to control such items as entry, rates, or profits.

7. However, note the following conundrum (Higgins and Tollison 1988). Consider two types of models. In one, rent-seeking waste is exact and complete. Here, the incentive to create monopoly will be low because there are no excess returns from doing so, but the social cost per instance of realized monopoly will be high. In the alternative model politicians have succeeded in converting rent-seeking costs into transfers. There are thus significant excess returns to monopoly creation; hence, there will be more monopolies in such a society. Returns to politicians are only transfers in this society, but this society will have more monopolies and more Harberger losses than the first society—the social cost per instance of realized monopoly will be low. The dilemma is now clear—which society will be wealthier? There does not appear to be an a priori way to say: one society has less monopoly and more waste per monopoly; the other has more monopoly and less waste per monopoly.

8. A contemporary example is the *nonpecuniary* level of rent seeking at the state level of government. Research reveals that the concentration of restaurants and golf courses in U.S. state capital cities is statistically and significantly greater than matched-state cities, allowing for a number of important characteristics, including income (Mixon, Laband, and Ekelund 1994).

9. For a proof of this proposition with some empirical evidence favorable to it, see McCormick and Tollison (1980).

CHAPTER 3.

ECONOMIC REGULATION AND RENT SEEKING IN MERCANTILE ENGLAND

1. Internal regulation of industry in France and migratory agriculture in Spain, which we discuss in chapters 4 and 5, are sufficiently different from that in England to merit separate analysis. As Heckscher stresses, "On common foundations were erected two edifices which nevertheless were different in England and France; and the differences are as important as the similarities. As an approximate generalization we may say that the resemblances were greater in form than in content, though quite extensive in both" (1934, 1:222).

2. This is not meant to deny that on a number of occasions the general welfare within cities received a voice. For example, in 1690 Elizabeth was entreated by fifty citizens to allow the Dutch bay makers to return to the town of Halstead in Essex County (Tawney and Power 1924, 1:319–20), and earlier, in 1575, the city of Norwich issued a litany of the advantages of having aliens in their city, including urban renewal ("Advantages Received by Norwich from the Strangers," Tawney and Power 1924, 1:135). Contractual accommodations between English producers and aliens within a city were also not uncommon. Evidence that consumer interests influence the pattern of economic regulation is quite consistent with the underlying theory, as Peltzman (1976) has shown in a generalization of Stigler's (1971b) theory of economic regulation.

3. A good deal of paper and ink has been used to try to differentiate the old mercantilism from modern mercantilism ("neo-mercantilism"). The former is seen as a system engineered by a national elite to secure power rather than plenty, and the latter as a system that reflects the increase in the influence of domestic pressure groups in securing policies that have important domestic and international repercussions. We argue that, while there are some important institutional differences between the two mercantilisms, they are basically fueled by the same economic phenomenon—rent seeking. We will have more to say on this matter in chapter 8.

4. It might be asked why violations of exclusion from trades could not be detected and prosecuted by the trade itself. This is because violations had to be brought to trial, and the justices of the peace served as local judges. Rather than waiting for a royal judge to come by the district periodically to conduct trials, the justices of the peace provided an on-the-spot means of prosecuting violations of the monopoly statutes. The benefits of promptly forestalling cheating on cartel arrangements do not need to be belabored.

5. See, for example, "Complaint of the Citizens of London against Aliens, 1571" (Tawney and Power 1924, 1:308–9). Occupational rents were created, of course, by retarding the entry of new practitioners. We should note here that there were some curious aspects of the pattern of occupational regulation in the mercantile economies. See Faith and Tollison (1983) for further discussion and analysis.

6. Notice the parallel between mercantilist and modern economic regulation. Competition from without is retarded by a licensing procedure (apprenticeship) and competition from within is restricted by ensuring that list prices equal transaction prices (wage-fixing).

7. This is indicated in the following excerpt relating to an assessment of wages and other regulations made by the justices of the peace: "Requiring and straytlye charging and commanding in her maiestie name, All mayours, Bayleffs, constables, officers &

ministers, As well within lybertyes as without to se the same executed. And yf eny person or persons shall Refuce to yeld hym selff to thys order, Then the same to be brought to the next Iustice, And to be by hym committed to the gaol, And ther to Remayne for one hooll yere, or els to be send to the cownsell, yf the qualitie of the person do so require. And for the better execution hereoff they ys a governour of Laborers appoyncted in every towne within the iij hyndrythes of Chylterne, Whoo shall sertefye to the Isutices of peace or to the grand Jure every moneth of all suche as he shall fynd obstinate or disobedyent to thees Rate & orders following yf eny be; And that every servand hyred by the weeke or moneth during the tyme of haruist, to take but after the same Rate" (Tawney and Power 1924, 1:334).

8. Section 19 of the memorandum recharged the justices with enforcement duties, noting that enforcement "is a thinge that is not done in most places, And therefore, the Statute remayneth utterly unobserved, as if there were no such law at all" (Tawney and Power 1924, 1:362).

9. In 1561, for example, local justices for Buckinghamshire set out detailed regulations relating to mobility: "Item that no laborer do shyfte his dwelling or departt out of hys hundryth, without Declaration of some reasonable cause to the next Justice of Peace, & ther to Receyve lycens, And yf eny do other wyse departte, then the governor ther, or the constables before his departture yf they can, or els immediately after, to make advertysement thereoff to some Justice of peace, whoo shall award a preceptt to fetche hym agayne And to punisshe hym in example of others" (Tawney and Power 1924, 1:336).

10. Indeed, the memorandum of 1573 permitted the mobility of certain classes of workers upon permission of two justices of the peace, thereby opening up the legal possibility of profitable collusion, though we can find no evidence of such activity. The interest of justices in rural jurisdictions would have been simply to expand the size of the local economy. Since there were no large objects to regulate, expansion of the local economy could be best achieved by keeping labor cheap. Thus, it may have been in the interests of rural justices of the peace to encourage the migration of labor from the cities, an interest that could have been facilitated by collusive arrangements with town justices to regulate wages or to encourage the out-migration of certain types of labor.

11. Town control was somewhat easier in France. The medieval artifact of the walled city applied to many towns in France, which meant that control over movement to the countryside and "smuggling" wares back into the city would have carried a lower cost than in the English case, with implications for the amount of cheating that occurred.

12. These features of our initial argument (1981) concerning enforcement by the unpaid Justices of the Peace have formed the basis for several of subsequent analyses of British mercantilism (e.g., Root 1994, 151–54; also see Weingast 1995, 7–8).

13. Heckscher's discussion (1934, 1:294–325) of the decay of the industrial code thus tends to look for other causes for the demise of local monopolies in England, for example, the treatment of the guilds by the common law courts. We should comment at this point on the Poor Law and on the so-called policy of welfare discussed by Heckscher (1934, 1:256–61). The justices of the peace were also charged with welfare administration. In the main, although there are some bizarre aspects of Stuart welfare policy, this aspect of economic regulation was not directed at poor relief, as Heckscher argues, but again at cartel formation. Witness Heckscher's (1934, 1:259) account of the regulation of the trading of foodstuffs: "The J.P.s were usually responsible for undertaking by themselves or by means of special juries, a complete inventory of the stock of corn in the hands of

producers and dealers and for regulating its sale down to the smallest detail." Pity the poor who were the "recipients" of such poor relief!

14. Heckscher relies, as we have (in part) here, on the "great work of Holdsworth" (Heckscher 1934, 1:278 n. 59) for his discussion of the judiciary. However, as will become apparent, we reach an alternative economic interpretation of the competition between the mercantile legal systems. Although Holdsworth (1966) is a primary source on these matters, the works of Pollock and Maitland (1895), Maitland (1908, 1957), and Maitland and Montague (1915) have also been consulted. Although these authors are less concerned with commercial policy and matters pertaining to grants of monopoly than is Holdsworth, the existence of competing court systems and the existence of a self-interested legal profession (Maitland and Montague 1915, 110, 121–22) are prominent features of their historical accounts.

15. At this time the Court of King's Bench became simply a common law court. Significantly, however, King's Bench retained, in both style and jurisdiction, traces of a royal court. Holdsworth points out that in its wide powers of control over other courts and officials, and in its wide criminal jurisdiction, it retained powers of a quasi-political nature which came to it from the days when the court held coram rege was both King's Bench and Council. In the future, the possession of these powers by a common law court that was allied to Parliament was destined to be a factor of no mean importance in determining the position of the common law in the state, and in settling the shape of the English constitution (1966, 1:211).

16. By the end of the seventeenth century, common law judges had usurped the right to appoint officers of the court, positions of freehold with no duties. Holdsworth reports that these appointments were blatantly venalized by the judges (1966, 1:255).

17. This court competition over fees and jurisdictions is also a major feature of North and Weingast's analysis of the period (1989, esp. 813) as is the role of an independent judiciary in securing rights (817–19). It is also a principal feature of Root's (1994, 145–51) analysis of English mercantilism.

18. Although Coke once argued otherwise (Holdsworth 1966, 4:186–87), Parliament is the supreme legal authority. Common law courts only interpret the law.

19. Indeed, Heckscher argues that the general alternative to monopoly held to be desirable in these times was "balanced oligopoly." Thus, in speaking about the common law interpretation of monopoly, Heckscher (1934, 1:273) argues that "they overlook the whole principle of the system—oligopoly based on a fair standard of living." This concept of competition can be viewed as antimonopoly, as Heckscher sees it, or as an attempt to apply Aristotelian concepts in such a way as to cloak the real economic basis of interest-group activity.

20. Arguments to the effect that the public interest demanded a transfer of control over economic activity from monarch to Parliament must have been very convincing to parliamentary constituencies. In the debate on monopolies in 1601, George Moore, M.P., waxed eloquent: "There be Three Persons; Her Majesty, the Patentee, and the Subject: Her Majesty the Head, the Patentee the Hand, and the Subject the Foot. Now, here is our Case; the Head gives Power to the Hand, the Hand Oppresseth the Foot, the Foot Riseth against the Head" (Tawney and Power 1924, 2:275).

21. Practice before the bar of the common law was highly restricted and, in 1600, there were approximately two thousand barristers (Levack 1973, 3) with common law judges (paid fees in the main) selected from the ranks of barristers. Returns available to

barristers were potentially very high. Most competent barristers could expect to earn at least £300 per year, "an excellent salary in the seventeenth century" (Richardson 1975, 488). Many barristers became extremely wealthy as the result of their legal practices; Coke himself was one of the richest and is described by one historian as having been "fabulously wealthy" (Prest 1986, 155). After his death, Coke left a bequest of ninety-nine separate estates (Malament 1967, 1324).

22. Ephraim Lipson (1956), Eli Heckscher (1934), John Nef (1968), Donald Wagner (1935, 1937), and Bruce Yandle (1993) all argue that Coke was an early advocate of laissez-faire and link his views to the later writings of the classical economists. Although more recent economists agree that Coke was indeed a major force behind the deregulation of the seventeenth-century economy, some of them have treated these claims with greater skepticism. Still, they maintain that Coke was principally motivated by his philosophical commitments to the dominance of the common law.

23. Parliament passed numerous restrictions on foreign trade as well, such as a law that made it a felony to carry leather out of the country; a prohibition on the export of sheepskins and buckskins; a prohibition on the importation of gloves, girdles, knives, daggers, scabbards, and pins; and even a law that made it a crime for a traveler to take his own horse abroad for personal use (Elton 1986: 234, 247–48. 255).

24. The term *monopoly* was used inconsistently by contemporaries, including Coke; by use of the term, he normally meant to refer only to royal grants of exclusive privileges to specific individuals. In the course of debate over the bill to restrain monopolies in 1621, it was apparent that members of the House of Commons meant a variety of different things by the term "monopoly," none of which included the notion of legal entry barriers (White 1979, 129).

25. For example, Hayek (1960, 168) discusses Coke's later account of the *Darcy* case but fails to note that Coke was the lawyer for the monopolist plaintiff.

26. During the Darcy proceedings, Coke asserted that "the customary rights and ordinances of the cities and corporations are legal although they oppose the common law and the liberty of the subject"; and previously, while speaking in Parliament, he said that "If Her Majesty makes a Patent or a Monopoly to any of Her Servants, That we must go and cry out against; But if she grants it to a Number of Burgesses or a Corporation, that must stand; and that, forsooth, is no Monopoly" (quoted in Heckscher 1934, 287).

27. City corporations also granted monopolies to favored individuals, and such monopolies were exempt from the statute. Nominally these monopolies were aimed at securing some public service or on grounds that they would provide employment in the urban area (Thirsk 1978, 66).

28. Corporations were explicitly excluded from the statute so that a grant of monopoly to such an organization was a legal evasion of the law, a device used by the crown later in the century (Gardiner 1965, 71). But such corporations also had parliamentary charters, and Parliament could and did sometimes pull the charters from corporations. Such companies had a powerful incentive to lobby for favors from both the crown and Parliament. As Parliament became more involved with company charters and corporate affairs, company shareholders and officers increasingly sought membership in Parliament, where they would be well situated to defend their company's interests. Several examples are offered by Ruigh (1971, 56). Lobbying costs rose, of course, as this transition became more complete, making monopoly grants more costly and less likely.

29. More "lawyer welfare" was also part of the Statute of Monopolies in that it established that the common law courts were to determine exactly which monopolies were legally valid (Holdsworth 1966, 4:353).

30. He was the chief justice who approved the confirmation of the charters of the East India and the Russia Companies; he settled the Charter of the Virginia Company and was retained as counsel by the Draper's Company, the Cutler's Company, the Cook's Company, and the Stationer's Company. Since all ordinances of all crafts and guilds required the chief justice's signature, he signed off on the ordinances of the Merchant Tailor's, the Salters, and the Saddlers.

31. For a comparable analysis of the English judiciary and Coke, see Leoni (1961). We do, of course, recognize that the standard applied by the Parliament and common law courts in the mercantile period was not the free-trade standard in the modern sense. That is, Parliament and the courts may have regarded the public interest as identical to the removal of patent-granting power from the crown. The unintended consequences of the actions of these two groups, however, brought about an institutional framework wherein free trade, in the modern sense, was made more feasible.

32. Tullock's (1988) position on vested interests of the independent judiciary may be contrasted with the Landes-Posner view. Contrary to jurists' vested interests in enforcing contracts with special interests, juries may not have such incentives. If individuals are assigned as jurors to a case where special interests plead for a rent-seeking (price greater than marginal cost) coalition, they will likely vote in favor of competitive pricing arrangements unless their own special interests are an issue in the proceeding. During the period we are considering, juries were ordinarily composed of twelve of the most prominent citizens (large landholders). Juries were thus automatically rigged against poachers. Most monopolistic activities that were brought before these tribunals were cases in which an outside monopolist would argue that a local industry was violating his monopoly. Here, the jury could easily hold against the outside monopolist, as Tullock predicts they would.

33. Again Power's (1941, 84–85) analysis of the situation is instructive. She notes that "it is—in my view—a mistake to regard parliament and the assembly of merchants as rival bodies competing for survival and each representing a different conception of social orders—the estates of the realm *versus* the estate of merchants. They were essentially the representative assemblies of different economic interests. The assembly of merchants did not represent all the merchants, and parliament did not represent all the estates minus the merchants. They were two economic groups—on the one side wool merchants and on the other side the other interests, including the growers and those merchants who were not wool merchants, that is the great bulk of the burgesses. If finally the separate existence of an assembly of wool merchants came to an end (though, incidentally, it continued to function spasmodically for purposes other than taxation), it was not because the estate of merchants had ceased to exist, but because the separate and united attention of the wool merchants to the one important economic issue, that of taxation, ceased to function. It was no longer separate and certainly no longer united."

34. Here we must emphasize that we are not trying to explain the decline of rent seeking solely in terms of the rise of constitutional democracy, though we argue that it is a major causal factor in explaining mercantile policies. Technological growth and an emergent factory system, a familiar deus ex machina, may have, for example, fostered powerful interests (such as wool buyers or household producers), which arose to com-

pete with the large wool producers and exporters for rents in Parliament, thereby dissipating them. North and Thomas (1973) emphasize still other changes as the grounds of economic development and the emergence of property rights. While their arguments concern somewhat more fundamental causal features of development, they do not emphasize, as we do here, the role of rent seeking in the decline of mercantilism. See, however, North and Weingast (1989).

35. It is interesting that, though Elizabeth claimed regalian rights on grounds of national defense, she stood to gain monetarily by the conditions of the rent split. All unused gunpowder could be sold by her at a profit to both domestic and foreign consumers. Since by law she claimed all of Evlyn's output, a time of peace meant pure profit to Elizabeth.

36. Exceptions granted were for "patents of Invention" and the alum and soap monopolies. The latter were excepted because the patents were soon to expire and, further, because the privy council agreed not to renew them.

37. While some of the more scientifically minded merchants and gentlemen supported the exemption of limited patents for invention in the statute of 1640 in order to encourage inventors (i.e., in permitting internalization of benefits), it is by no means the case that the self-interest of members of Parliament, judges, and magistrates was not a larger factor in this decision. Nef notes, in this connection, that "the increasing industrial investments of the wealthy merchants and the improving landlords, represented in parliament, in the courts, and in the town governments, led them to welcome any invention designed to reduce costs of production and to increase profits. . . . Such industrial adventurers and their political representatives saw in the granting of patents a means of encouraging the search for new inventions with which their prosperity was increasingly bound up" (1968, 119).

38. We must emphasize that in our analysis of British mercantilism—as in the French and Spanish episodes as well—we are considering important factors that others have not emphasized. We do not claim that these largely internal factors are the only or (necessarily) the most important factors explaining the course of mercantilism (see, for example, the discussion of the Spanish economy that concludes chapter 5). International trade and foreign policy most certainly played a crucial role. As Cowen (1986) argues, Britain's divorce from mercantile policies was, at least in part, motivated by the desire militarily to beat France, Spain, and the Netherlands. He argues that since England was an island nation, the gains to winning wars spread to more interest groups than would be the case for a landlocked nation (marine interests, less damage to native soil, concomitant trade advantages with a strong navy, and so on). Mercantilist writers, including Nicholas Barbon, were explicit in emphasizing these reasons for freer trade. We agree that these factors were important in the course of institutional change in England at the time. Their relative importance, however, is yet to be determined.

39. In particular North and Weingast adduce evidence on financial innovations that produced a virtual halving of interest rates from the early 1690s to the end of that decade with falling rates (to about 3 percent in the 1730s). This occurred over a period when the size of loanable funds and the demands of government borrowing were increasing dramatically. They argue that "As the [British] society gained experience with its new institutions, particularly their predictability and commitment to secure rights, expectations over future actions began to reflect the new order" (1989, 823–24).

40. Weingast, in an interesting paper emphasizing the necessity of a coexistence of

market-assisting "federalism" with free exchange (1995)—argues that these preconditions existed in mercantile England and elsewhere for at least limited time periods. See
chapter 8 for a discussion of these matters.

41. As noted previously, many observers incorrectly identify rent seeking (and rent
dissipation) within a political process as a Marxian "capture" argument. The theory of
rent seeking is far more general in application.

42. The American colonists were hampered in trading relations by many factors,
including a legally prescribed lack of money and credit institutions. Ultimately, mercantile laws and regulations forced a high degree of "self-sufficiency" and a huge reduction
in the welfare of the average colonist. Rent-seeking policies benefiting English merchants and the monarchy helped mightily to set the collision course that ended in the
Declaration of Independence.

CHAPTER 4.

VENALITY IN FRENCH MERCANTILE INSTITUTIONS

1. Economic historians concerned with France are not, of course, a monolithic entity. We have relied upon well-known English sources, such as Cole and Heckscher, to
develop our analysis. The interested reader may also wish to consult Nef (1968) and
Cameron (1970) for an excellent collection of essays and sources on French economic
history by French scholars. An analysis that parallels and embellishes upon our initial
argument (1981) may be found in Root (1994, 113–39).

2. As Root (1994, 118) maintains, "the need to establish state-sponsored monopolies
or royal manufactures cannot be understood apart from the rising role of the guilds
during [Colbert's] period." Also see Ekelund and Tollison (1981, 76).

3. The judgment that economic growth in the French economy lagged behind England for most of the eighteenth century may not be sustainable given the research of
Crouzet (1967; 1972 [1965]). Crouzet argues (1967, 145–60), without statistical evidence
but with sound logic, that both English and French growth rates were about the same in
the post-1715 period (up to the Revolution), but that, for a number of reasons, French
economic development was ultimately swamped by England's industrial revolution. These
and other arguments are evaluated in the concluding chapter.

4. These problems were even more grave for the Spanish economy (see chapter 5)
where, at that time, one became a student, monk, beggar, or bureaucrat since there was
nothing else to be (North and Thomas 1973, 131).

5. Crude calculations from Cole (1939, 1:304–9) suggest that the revenue from only
three monopolies (tobacco, coinage, and postage) amounted to one-half of all state
revenues at roughly the midpoint of Colbert's administration (1670).

6. See Cole's enumeration of the nineteen major internal duties and taxes levied
within and without five French provinces between 1304 and Colbert's attempted reform
of 1664 (Cole 1939, 1:420–27).

7. Institution of the Chambre de Justice by edict in 1661 permitted Colbert to try
hundreds of financiers for "abuses" dating back to 1635. In this act, amounting to a legal
exaction of tribute, Colbert raised over 100 million *livres,* some of which was used to buy
back offices that had been sold. In addition, Colbert "revised" the *rentes*—government
bonds and other obligations issued before Louis XIV's majority—by cutting the
government's payment on the obligation by one-third. By decree of the Chambre or by

royal edict, more than 8 million *livres* per year were saved for the state in this manner (Cole 1939, 1:301–3). In spite of these once-and-for-all ministrations to Louis's budget, the demands were well ahead of Colbert's ability to supply funds in this manner. The attempted abolition of the hereditary features of certain offices as well as the farming of certain taxes by open bidding was also of no avail.

8. In our opinion Cole strays wildly off the point when he concludes that Colbert's "most earnest desire was to create a [tax] system of which the keynote should be 'good order'" (1939, 1:303). Surely his "most earnest desire" was to create a lucrative sinecure for himself by providing (in any manner possible) for the greater glory and magnificence of Louis XIV.

9. Naturally static "efficiency" is not guaranteed since such bidding ordinarily takes place under conditions of uncertainty (see chapter 2).

10. Heckscher (1934, 1:146) offers a competing hypothesis that seems generally weaker than ours: "The regulation was certainly intended to make craftsmanship more uniform throughout the country, by giving the craftsmen of more advanced districts the opportunity of propagating their skill in backward regions." See Faith and Tollison (1979) for an economic analysis of the pattern of occupational regulation in mercantile France and England. Mancur Olson argues (1982) that the principles of public choice and the costs of lobbying a political body suggest that regulation and administrative controls are expected to be concentrated at local levels in a large country where towns are geographically dispersed and transaction costs are high. Root (1994, 114–15) notes (and we agree) that the argument might fit the pattern of regulation in medieval Europe and that it might even suggest that one reason for the decline of guilds in England was the ascendance of the national political power of Parliament. The argument, as Root also suggests, does not fit the situation in pre-Revolutionary France. Further, it is perfectly consistent with public choice principles that Parisians masters could gain favorable treatment even in a national system of guild administration.

11. Although there is nothing analogous to an independent judiciary in mercantile France, there were the independent and powerful high courts, the *parlements*. In contrast to the *intendants,* positions in these courts were typically purchased and passed on within a family. We view this process as a means of rent protection; that is, individual monopolists bought these positions as a form of insurance against adverse rulings by the cartel-enforcement agents of the king. We shall have more to say about the competition between the *parlements* and the *intendants* later in the chapter.

12. The "public-spirited" Colbert, despite a relatively low birth in a family of traders, managed to acquire great wealth and massive influence for himself and for members of his family. As agent for the powerful Cardinal Mazarin, Colbert became wealthy and influential, "receiving a growing stream of offices, benefices, and gratifications and asking for more without embarrassment" (Cole 1939, 1:283). In addition to receipt of great wealth over his career, Colbert attempted to build a family dynasty. A first cousin was made intendant of the army in Catalonia and of the government of Brouage; to one brother went the bishopric of Lugon; to another, the command of a company in the Navarre region; and to still another, the ambassadorship to England. Although Colbert's efforts to groom his son, Seignelay, as his successor did not pan out (though Seignelay did a very creditable job in control of the French navy), Colbert's philosophy is revealed with great clarity in one of his instructions to his son. Colbert admonished Seignelay that "as the chief end that he should set himself is to make himself agreeable to the king,

he should work with great industry, during his whole life to know well what might be agreeable to His Majesty" (Cole 1939, 1:291).

13. Root (1994, 131–32) considers the role of "fashion" in the entry of unregulated firms into guild turf. Guild argument was familiar: The public would be exploited and unprotected from low-quality goods. The argument underlies much contemporary regulation in all nations of the world.

14. Punishment was inconsistent, possibly because some local *intendants* were bribed. Though punishment was meted out in varying degrees of severity to offending merchants, printers, and smugglers, there are good reasons to doubt Heckscher's estimate that sixteen thousand people were put to death. Unfortunately, Heckscher is as vague as to the time period he is considering as he is to what constitutes a calico-related death. Huguenot persecution in France between 1680 and 1720, according to one authority (Scoville 1960), resulted in only two hundred deaths related to the production of calicos. The underlying cause of Huguenot persecution appears to have been the desire to rid France of Calvinists (the Edict of Nantes was repealed in 1684). Cole (1943, 173) argues that most sanctions from 1686 to 1759 were monetary, though he does note that there were occasional executions in port cities. Cotton riots occurred in Rouen in 1752, but only fifteen people were killed (Rude 1964, 22). Thus, other sources do not tend to corroborate Heckscher's estimate of sixteen thousand deaths. Even several thousand killed over the matter of calicos is significant, however.

15. Spies of the government, in the words of Cole, were soon "peering into coaches and private houses and reporting that the governess of the marquis de Cormoy had been 'seen at her window clothed in calico of a white background with big red flowers, almost new or that the wife of a lemonadeseller had been seen in her shop in a casaquin of calico,'" (1943, 176).

16. Thomas J. Schaeper's excellent historical study, based in part on Depitre (1912), of the post-Colbertian coalition of monarchy and merchants—the Council of Commerce—provides an interesting story of the *toiles peintes* (printed calicoes) and their role in the quasi-breakdown in mercantilism over the eighteenth century (1983, 175–77). Between 1700 and 1715, dozens of laws (*arrêts*) were aimed at keeping the new cloth out of the country. Despite a draconian stiffening of the law (merchants handling the prohibited fabrics get fines of 3,000 livres and lifelong banishment from the profession with royal officials put in the galleys for nine years for opportunistic behavior), the government could not enforce the prohibition. Schaeper reports (176) that "by the 1750s French workers had pirated from England the secret for using dyes on cotton" leading to the French crown to eliminate all prohibitions in 1759. This episode provides a clear example that regulations are simply pieces of paper when high transaction costs severely limit enforcement and changing demand, cost or technological conditions create unappropriable benefits to "cheating."

17. In March 1671, Colbert had a "general Instruction for the dyeing of wool and manufactures of wool in all colors" prepared and published. The instructions contained 317 articles and were incredibly detailed: "Those [fabrics] that are to be dyed black should be boiled with gall and sumach, and, lacking sumach, with myrtle-leaved sumach [*Rhus myrtifolis*] of *fovic* [a native French plant]; being well galled, they have a color between fallow and gray; and it will be observed that fallow and root color are really the same thing" (example in Cole 1939, 2:408). Instructions such as these are added evidence of an extreme attempt to control quality competition within the textile cartels.

18. Heckscher's example of button making speaks for itself: "Buttonmaking was controlled by various organizations, according to the particular materials that were used, although the most important part of the business belonged to the cord- and button-makers' gild. And so, when tailors and dealers began to produce buttons from the same material as the particular cloth used and even to use woven instead of hand-made buttons, the button-makers raised terrific opposition. The government came to their aid, in the first place because they considered the innovation an outrage against a settled industry of good standing, and secondly, because it adversely affected handicraft (1694–1700). A fine was imposed not only on the production and sale of the new sort of buttons, but also on those who wore them, and the fine was continually increased. The wardens even demanded the right to be allowed to search people's houses and claimed police aid to be able to arrest anybody in the street who wore unlawful buttons. When the otherwise extremely zealous and conscientious chief of the Paris police, de la Reynie, would have denied them this, he received a severe reproof and even had to apologize" (1934, 1:171–72). Cole (1943, 177–79) describes some of the difficulties of enforcement. *Intendants* in the provinces complained that the button makers themselves were willing to make illegal buttons at the tailor's request. In 1698 an *intendant* from Provence complained that he could not enforce the law since news had come to the "people of quality" in his province that illegal buttons were being worn openly at Paris and Versailles.

19. In his doctrinal survey of French mercantile thought before Colbert, Cole traces the strands of early antiluxury sentiment in France primarily to the ethic of Christian humility (1931, 215–16). These views gave way, however, to the "spirit of bullionism" and, chiefly, to the recognition of the profitability of state-enfranchised luxury cartels, so that from the time of Colbert France has supplied a large part of the world with luxury goods.

20. In May 1665, a royal proclamation was issued establishing monopoly privileges for the manufacture of lace in order to prevent "the export of money and to give employment to the people" (Cole 1939, 2:239). In return for rents from lace manufacturers, the state enforced the cartel by precluding anyone other than the franchisees from making lace. In order to discourage smuggling and cheating, more edicts were required—the wearing of foreign lace was prohibited after 1667. More important, fixed places of manufacture had to be established. As Colbert wrote to a lace supervisor: "I beg you to note with care that no girl must be allowed to work at the home of her parents and that you must oblige them all to go to the house of the manufactures" (Cole 1939, 2:248).

21. Monopsony buying from competitively organized suppliers of military equipment seems to have been an entrenched practice under Colbert. Vast quantities of munitions, and especially small arms (pikes, muskets, pistols, swords, and so on), were purchased by the French army and navy in this fashion (see Cole 1939, 2:340, for example). Colbert also "fostered" the competitively organized iron industry in this manner (Cole 1939, 2:328–29).

22. There are more elaborate explanations for the phenomenon we describe in figure 4.1. For example, the transfer-pricing theorem suggests that regulatory profits are higher if collected at the final point in the production chain. By distorting input proportions, "wedges" between price and cost upstream cause profits to be lower than otherwise. A variable-proportions technology model would explain why Colbert would have had an interest in promoting open market conditions in key input industries. Our argu-

ment centers on the lower organization, policing and enforcement costs in the city (versus the countryside), but it is also compatible with other explanations.

23. We want to emphasize, moreover, that it was rent extraction in the system, not monopoly per se, that was the likely culprit in retarding French economic growth.

24. The "disinterest" in deregulation, i.e., entrenched bureaucratic local interests and the interests of guild members, is a partial explanation for the staying power of guilds. The dependence of the crown on organized cartels for taxes is another, and the relative attractiveness of monopoly-cartel creation vis-à-vis the transaction and information costs of direct taxation is yet another. All of these factors naturally had important implications for efficient property rights and economic growth.

25. Other examples of the *parlements'* acting in their own self-interest could be given. The *parlement* attacked the crown during the Fronde because it "would deprive 'officers' of many of their powers, and thus in the long run reduce the value of their posts" (Lough 1969, 129). The crown faced its greatest opposition when it tried to increase the number of *parlementaires* (Moote 1971, 53) and when it tried to "carry out a proper land survey" (Lough 1960, 182) in order to make a more just levying of the land tax, a policy which would have required the *parlementaires* to pay more taxes.

26. Even later, in the eighteenth century, the concept of "the public interest" and "liberty of trade" took on curious definitions. As Schaeper notes (1983, 258), the deputies of the Council of Commerce, following Colbert, regarded "liberty" as a vested privilege or a right. The "public interest," moreover, was interpreted by some as a Colbertian "ordering" of trades and manufactures.

CHAPTER 5.

INTERNAL REGULATION IN THE SPANISH MERCANTILE ECONOMY

1. See, for example, the works of Count Pedro Rodríguez de Compomanes, who, in his *La regalía de Amortización* championed free trade eleven years before Smith's great work. Some of this literature is discussed in the conclusion to this chapter.

2. While no detailed rent-seeking or interest group analysis of the Mesta exists in the literature, it cannot be said that the Mesta has been neglected by economic historians, past or present. The classic and still unparalleled historical study is that of Julius Klein (1920 [1964]), an account that we heavily rely upon, but a number of newer studies are important as well. These include an important set of essays on the history of Spanish transhumance (García Martín and Sánchez Benito, 1986). Following Klein, historians have generally argued that the support of the Mesta by crown interests had deleterious effects on the development of Spanish agriculture and, derivatively, on economic development (see, for example, Cameron 1989, 110). Other economic historians (Enciso and Merino 1979) take a descriptive approach to the medieval-mercantile Spanish economy. Enciso and Merino, who do provide an interesting assessment of the role of the public sector in the Spanish economy, circa 1750, note the incredible complexity of possible explanations for the impetus, or lack thereof, for economic growth. Many of these writers are understandably skeptical of explanations linking institutions with growth and growth prospects. In the words of Enciso and Merino, "it remains doubtful . . . whether the application of modern economic theory can provide a reasonable explanation of the working of an Ancien Regime economy. There does not seem to be a case for support-

ing any particular economic theory" (1979, 554). We argue, in contrast to a rigid interpretation of this position, that the modern theory of neoinstitutional economics, featuring self-interested coalitions within an overall perspective of public choice and property rights theory, can add valuable insights into dynamic historical processes such as those of medieval-mercantile Spain.

3. Pastoral and agricultural land use was regulated by a monarchical "zoning authority," who assigned rights to the highest bidder (Mesta, town agricultural interests, or the Church) in this model presented in the form of a parable. Rights flowed to the highest-valued user revealed in a process of rent seeking. Rent seeking, far from being a competing hypothesis, is a vital complement to the efficient property rights thesis as suggested by Nugent and Sanchez (1989, 279).

4. North correctly emphasizes that the quid pro quo of providing the Mesta exclusive privileges was a means of financing the war with the Moors. But North goes further to argue that "in consequence, the development of efficient property rights in land was thwarted for centuries" (1981, 150). We emphasize that the ability and success of monarchs at rent-seeking through the Mesta was a function of a number of factors, some of them exogenous, that shifted property rights through time.

5. One interesting facet of the Spanish guild system was the maintenance of the ancient custom of "exclusive sales territories" for the different trades by streets, localities, and regions. By the mid-thirteenth century most common trades fell under guild regulations (including stonecutters, butchers, tanners, bakers, silversmiths, and shoemakers).

6. The suppression of competitors by the Church across Europe was especially virulent against "proselytizing religions." Judaism—a nonproselytizing religion—grew alongside the Roman monopoly in *relative* peace outside Spain. In Spain, however, especially in the late middle ages, Jews received serious repression from particular Inquisitorial interests (Peters 1988, 86–104). Torture, confiscation of property, and banishment of both Jews and *conversos* took place with the full support and complicity of the "civil authorities." (See Prescott 1850; Kamen 1968; and Turberville 1968.) That the inquisition constituted blatant rent seeking is beyond doubt: see Netanyahu (1995).

7. A number of questions surround the quest of Ferdinand and Isabella to expel the Jews. Importantly, these Catholic monarchs acceded to a more virulent and socially damaging Inquisition than occurred elsewhere in Europe. In 1482 the pope protested to Ferdinand that "the Inquisition has been moved not by zeal for faith but by lust for wealth, and that many true and faithful Christians have without any legitimate proof been imprisoned, tortured and condemned as heretics" (Kamen 1983, 40). Perhaps it is significant that an enormous amount of property and wealth owned by the Jews was transferred to ecclesiastical and civil authorities. It has been maintained that Ferdinand's objective was national uniformity, that he believed that Jews were a threat to orthodoxy, and that "national security and uniformity" had to be maintained over material concerns of the state. The super-religious Isabella, despite high-level protests and the *noncomplicity* of Pope Innocent VII, went ahead with persecutions and the expulsions on the advice of her confessor, the arch-evil cleric and Grand Inquisitor (1483–1498) Tomás de Torquemada. Vicens-Vives (1969, 297) argued that Ferdinand and Isabella "had the economic factor well in mind, and that in consequence they were sacrificing it for the religious benefit of the country." It is most likely, of course, that interest groups

working through the political and religious frameworks were major factors in the actual decision. The social, cultural, and intellectual damage that the Inquisition caused in Spain is incontestable, and it was only in the nineteenth century (1834) that the Inquisition was finally suppressed. Michener (1968, 453–57), despite some serious flaws in his assessment of Torquemada, provides an interesting and readable account of the impact of the Inquisition on Spanish society. These effects should serve as an apt warning against permitting theocracy to thrive in any time or at any place.

8. An excellent primer on the history and current development of the Merino wool culture is by the Spanish minister of agriculture (Laguna Sanz 1986) for the second world conference on Merino sheep.

9. The wool trade was also the object of monopolization in England, but in sedentary agricultural conditions.

10. Transhumance was not peculiar to Spain but was practiced all over medieval Europe. It is still practiced by dairy farmers in Switzerland (Cameron 1989, 109). The uniqueness of the Spanish practice is in the extent of the migrations, which covered the entire Spanish state from the Bay of Biscay to the Mediterranean, and the imposition of crown control over the practice.

11. As Nugent and Sanchez (1989) have noted, these battles often involved attempted enclosures by town interests with fencing as a costly alternative.

12. The primary royal *cañadas* had a width of about 250 feet and entailed one-way travel of from 150 to 450 miles.

13. Similarities between the geographically-dispersed *entregadores* to Colbert's *intendents des provinces* (see chapter 4)—the enforcers of French mercantile policies in a geographically dispersed setting in the seventeenth century—are striking. While Colbert undoubtedly made inroads into policing and enforcement techniques in industry cartelization and rent-collection techniques, we believe that the official monopolization of sheepherding for rent-seeking purposes by the Spanish crown in the thirteenth century puts the Spanish in the vanguard of these directed and concerted activities in medieval-mercantile Europe. The early functioning of the Mesta as a rent-seeking machine for the crown calls into question the opinion of Smith (1971, 2) that "the economic advisers of the first Bourbons [early eighteenth century] were steeped in French mercantilism; and *Colbertismo*, with some minor exceptions, held sway until after the mid-eighteenth century." The argument might provide a partial explanation for the nature and course of Spanish mercantilism, but features of mercantile rent-collecting devices were extant in late medieval Spain, centuries before Colbert. Indeed, Colbert (and English Tudor monarchs for that matter) might have learned a great deal from observation of the functions and institutions of the Spanish Mesta.

14. Incredibly detailed and complex regulations attended the Mesta monopoly, reminiscent of Colbert's "rules" for the production of French textiles (see chapter 4). Consider the efforts to control the quality of the product and to prevent cheating through the following managerial rules imposed by the *alcaldes* and enforced by *entregadores*. The herdsman's flocks, pack train, horses, cows, and swine were collectively known as his or her *cabaña*. Each *cabaña* was under the general charge of a chief herdsman and was divided into total flocks (*rebaños*) of about a thousand head of sheep each. Smaller flocks existed (and were called *hatos, manadas,* or *pastorías*). The *rebaño* included five rams and twenty-five bellwethers who were each in charge of a herder, with four boys as

assistants and five dogs (Klein 1964, 24). Food allotments were made for dogs and humans; relatively heavy fines were specified for mistreatment of dogs or for possession of illegal dogs, and even salt quotas per sheep were specified.

15. Basas Fernandez (1961) provides important details on wool marketing in Burgos, perhaps the most famous of mercantile trade cities. In Burgos, a number of important commercial innovations (maritime insurance, financing arrangements with sheep owners, and so on) accompanied wool marketing on a massive scale (1961, 41–42, 55–65).

16. Expenditures to *avoid* rent extraction by government monopolization or regulation may also be considered a legitimate social cost.

17. The simplified theory of vertical monopoly is identical to the one applied to the cartelization of "luxury productions" in mercantile France (see chapter 4).

18. Cities also got into the rent-seeking act. In the sixteenth century, the market center of Burgos, for example, levied discriminatory "sack" taxes on wool sold for domestic consumption and that sold to foreigners (Basas Fernández 1961, 60).

19. The incredibly complex underlying mosaic of property rights shifts over the sixteenth through twentieth centuries is the subject of a detailed literature. Vassberg (1983) studies the exchange and sales of common and uncultivated lands in the sixteenth century. Ortega López (1986, 19–33) analyzes the agrarian conflicts and the movement to free trade in agriculture in the eighteenth century. Also of interest is the adumbration of civil and legal codes relating to common property in agriculture in the nineteenth and twentieth centuries (Cuadrado Iglesias 1980).

20. North implies that the Castilian Cortes was in effect the "controlling" representative body after Ferdinand and Isabella—relinquishing at this time control over taxation to the crown (1981, 151). Each of the kingdoms within Spain (Castile, Aragon, Valencia, Catalonia, Navarre) had a Cortes, which represented cities having tax agreements with the crown.

21. That ploy is familiar to anyone who listens to the American Medical Association's propaganda concerning the "quality of physicians" services or to universities (and their input cartel called the National Collegiate Athletic Association) who appeal to the purity of the "scholar athlete" as a rationale for their income-maximizing restrictions.

22. The disposition of the revenues at crown and local levels is also not without interest. Even where fencing was a "high cost" production, enclosures would have been demanded and supplied to some extent at the local levels.

23. In the words of Klein (1964, 267), exemptions were "scattered broadcast by unscrupulous lessees and collectors. Tax receipts were even being sold *firmado en blanco*—'signed in blank'—with the spaces for the amounts left open to be filled in by the purchaser as desired."

24. Note that this is a *mutatis mutandis* (rather than a *ceteris paribus*) result. Our test is analogous to the "final form multiplier" of modern macroeconomics and gives the total long-run effect of taxes. A *ceteris paribus* test might be run (using appropriate denominators), but that would, in our view, pervert the purity of the relationship by introducing factors that we could not account for. The TIME trend in our model should help capture factors exogenous to the relationship we posit.

25. In steady state equilibrium, $SM_t = SM_{t-1} = SM_{t-2} \ldots = SM_{t-n}$, so that $dE(t)/dSM = a_2 = a_3 = a_4 = a_5 + a_6 = .76$. This means that the sum of past experience with crown rent seeking by pressures and alterations of taxes and exactions was very clearly anticipated and acted upon by Mesta managers each year. In addition, Durbin-Watson values indi-

cate that no first-order auto correlation is present in the regressions. A test for Granger causality adds even more strength to these results; taxes and other rent exactions were driving costs, and costs were not causing taxes to change.

26. Lawyers and legal aids to Mesta interests, called *procuradores de Cortes* and *procuradores de cancillería,* were always on call at respective courts to attempt to attain the cartel's goals. Other legal functionaries such as the *procuradores de dehesa* obtained long-term leases for pasturage through effective collective bargaining (Klein 1964, 56).

27. These authors, however, appear to argue that efficiency followed once property rights were secured by the Mesta through crown interventions. All rent transfers may then be regarded as taxing "unearned increment" à la Henry George's single tax. Our exploration raises two potential problems with this line of reasoning. First, static efficiency (with the Mesta as a low-cost alternative) criteria do not make much sense when applied to intertemporal comparisons. Even if correct at some point in time, something like *dynamic* "market failure" may apply to the restriction of sedentary agriculture over the course of Spanish medieval-mercantile history. A second problem is that property rights at various times over the long period of Mesta functioning were most uncertain for both Mesta and local farming interests. Security for either of these two interests depended on the relative power of the crown versus the Cortes and regional powers. When the relative strengths of these interests shifted owing to changes in such factors as wool export demand and population, so did the security and, in some cases, the existence of property rights. Agricultural productivity and the rents generated by the Mesta would be expected to vary with the existence and relative security of property rights to the various interests groups. And, of course, property rights had even more ultimate determinants.

28. Illusory logic was often used to support property rights establishment so that rent seeking could proceed. An example was the strong and convenient arguments that Mesta officials used against intemperance. It so happened that enclosures of vineyards were an obstacle to the grazing areas (Klein 1964, 97).

29. On the matter of sheep exports and the international sheep trade generally, see Bilbao and Fernandez de Pinedo (1986, 343–62).

30. There is evidence that internal restrictions on the grain trade, lifted by the *decretos* of 1765, were a cause of the riots in Madrid and elsewhere (Rodríguez 1973a). Government involvement in grain storage and credit facilities for farmers were also important elements in the protests (Rodríguez 1973b; Anes 1981).

31. Campomanes, who generally sought to improve the efficiency of the Mesta vis-à-vis agricultural interests, prematurely terminated payments of bounty hunters of wolves and to other predation control personnel. Marín Barriguete reports that the result of this action in 1781 was a disastrous increase in the number of wolves and unanticipated losses in *transhumance* and in the animal industry (Marín Barriguete 1990a, 101).

32. It might be argued that "missed opportunities" in the course of Spanish development might, if effected, have dramatically altered institutions. The comunero (Castile) and germnías (Aragon) revolts against Charles V (circa 1520) and his taxes were tragically failed attempts to impose constitutional legal checks on the crown. Such failures presaged the later weakness of the Cortes. A "pseudo-republican" government was advocated, for example, in Catalonia. (We are grateful to Mr. Luis Dopico for this observation).

33. We follow North in emphasizing the impact of the Mesta on property rights in Spain. But other factors applying chiefly to the events of the sixteenth century, as sug-

gested to us by Professor Gordon Tullock, appear to be as critical to the fate of Spanish economic development. The important part of the empire of Phillip II was his overseas possessions. His foreign adventures were disastrous in that maritime trade between Iberia and its overseas possessions were fractured. But, in terms of potential revenue, Spain's holdings on the American continent, in Asia, Italy, and (for a time) the Netherlands dwarfed actual and potential Mesta rents. Phillip, however, was a failure in pressing the former rents in comparison to the real estate he owned. In short, a satisfying explanation of Spanish development requires a more inclusive model. See the comments concerning this matter in the concluding chapter of this book.

34. In his assessment of the practice in Castile between 1552 and 1700, Thompson (1979) notes the difficulties the crown (and their agents in patent sales, the *corregidores*) had in correctly "pricing" the patents. Such patents of nobility or *hidalguías* were apparently not as lucrative or as socially important as those sold in France or England, but tax exemptions did shift some tax burden from rich to poor. There is actual evidence, moreover, of a significant transferral of rents in the state of Castile.

35. North argued that monopoly, high taxation, and confiscation reduced trade and commerce. He observed (1981, 151) that "the only areas safe from the crown were in the church, government services, or the nobility. The widely reported observation that the *hidalgos* had an aversion for trade and commerce and a preference for careers in the church, army, or government suggests that they were rational men."

36. This dangerous intellectual stew was composed of a number of important social scientists and reformers. These included Manuel Rubín de Celis (1743–?), Gaspar Melchor de Jovellanos (1744–1811), Francisco de Cabarrús (1752–1810), Pablo de Olavide (1725–1803) and a number of other writers and reformers. The greatest of these was probably Count Pedro Rodríguez de Campomanes (1723–1802), who is attributed with writing the *Discurso sobre el fomento de la industria popular* in 1774. This work, predating Smith's *Wealth of Nations* by two years, was one of the most influential economic works of eighteenth-century Spain and was widely read in Latin America. The work got high praise from Schumpeter who noted that "in view of the date of Campomanes' *Discurso* (1774) it is not without interest to observe how little, if anything, he stood to learn from the *Wealth of Nations*" (1954, 172–73). We note, however, that the work was not "theoretical" even to the extent of Smith's famous discussion of competition. Important English language sources on this important chapter in the history of thought include Herr (1958; 1989), Urzainqui and Ruiz (1983), Street (1986; 1987; 1991; 1994), and Llombart (1991; 1995). Great insight into economic processes and a proto-Austrian free-market position is ascribed to the Spanish scholastics, particularly the Salamanca "school" of theorists, in interesting contributions by Murray N. Rothbard (1976; 1995). While these views are informative in an ideational sense, it is difficult to reconcile Thomistic and Jesuitical interpretations of natural law and markets with the rationalism and individualism of the Enlightenment. In the scholastic world generally, there are no positive rights of the individual, only the "authority of tradition," that is, the Roman Catholic Church's moral tradition. Individual freedom, upon which modern economic theory is built, takes a back seat in this theocratic conception.

37. Perrotta is in this camp when he argues (concerning Moncada) that he "actually seemed to want to defend the established interests and dominant cultural prejudices that were the true causes of Spain's economic decline" (1993, 39). Perrotta fails to note that it was market, nonmarket, and political economizing through coalitions, interest

groups, and rent seeking that created and changed the institutions affecting property rights that was the "true cause" of the economic tragedy. Of even greater curiosity is Perrotta's comment that rent seeking is not applicable to England and France but only for mercantile Spain. He further notes that "even here, it [rent seeking] does not apply to the mercantilists, who sought in every possible way to combat this tendency [rent seeking]" (1993, 47–48 n. 96). Here the futility of the identification of "mercantilism" with "doctrine" or with a period of time is full blown. First, no one ever argued that all mercantilists themselves represented particular interests or that observers could not accurately pinpoint structural or policy problems that reduced social product. A rent-seeking view, within an overall neoinstitutionalist approach, merely emphasizes that ideas or doctrines cannot be of much impact if self-interested groups and coalitions (working through the political institutions) have interests that do not coincide with those "ideas." Traditional economic historians, including some (but not all) doctrinal historians, simply proceed neither with "evidence" nor with a model to analyze that "evidence." That approach has not been at all fruitful in answering important questions concerning growth or institutional change. But in the case of England and France, rent-seeking and neoinstitutional economic approaches have been fruitful (North and Weingast 1989; Root 1994).

CHAPTER 6.

ECONOMIC ORGANIZATION AND FUNCTIONS
OF THE MERCANTILE CHARTERED COMPANIES

1. A close modern parallel to this practice of stationing cartel monitors in foreign market towns was the practice of the meat-packing industry in the United States from roughly 1910 to 1940. The meat packers effected a market-sharing agreement that was monitored via inspection of input purchases at the Chicago livestock market. See Nichols (1941) for this discussion.

2. Other forms of cheating were proscribed in the details of charters. Thus, in a patent to Sir Nicholas Crisp for the Company of Merchants trading to Guinea (1630), it was provided that no Englishman, save the patentees, was allowed to import any merchandise produced in Africa. The reason for the provision was to end indirect importation of such commodities through European countries (Scott 1951, 2:14).

3. The genuine mystery is why markets for production rights within cartels do not generally emerge. Such a market would facilitate trade in production rights between low- and high-cost firms, and cartel profitability would be enhanced as a result. See Maloney and McCormick (1982) for an instructive analysis of this problem.

4. This is not to say, of course, that the efficiency and profitability of these cartels was not constantly challenged by the activities of illegal competitors or interlopers. "Smuggling," then and now, is a predictable response to protected markets. A number of patentees, such as Sir Nicholas Crisp, who founded a company for the Africa trade in 1630, got their franchises by successfully challenging the privileges of preceding companies. When it was in the crown's interest, moreover, interlopers received support from the monarchy itself. Such was the case when James I—irritated at having been refused a "loan" of £10,000 from the London East India Company—supported a rival association (Courten's Association) for his own profit (see Scott 1951, 2:112–16).

5. There are a number of problems in the practical implementation of this plan; for a discussion of some of these issues, see Williamson (1976) and Crain and Ekelund (1976).

6. This method of auctioning off monopoly rights to maximize state returns may have played an important role in the colonizing and exploratory adventures of England, as well as in the fishery and mineral exploitations of the crown. There is evidence that a similar plan was instituted by Cromwell in 1653 for the provision of postal services (see Priest 1975, 36–37 and n. 24).

7. This does not imply, of course, that these companies were not organized by governments (at least initially) for some particular purpose or purposes. The Dutch West India Company was chartered in 1621, and the Royal Company of Adventurers for the importation of Negroes was formed in 1662 (Royal African Company). These companies allowed for independent decision making by colonial powers when distance was a factor (see Thornton 1994, 31–34).

8. There is circumstantial evidence that Smith was influenced by Tucker on this point. Mizuta (1967) lists a total of eleven separate works by Tucker as present in Smith's personal library, including the work (*The elements of commerce and theory of taxes*, 1759) in which Tucker discussed questions involving forts and other supposed necessary infrastructure for foreign trade.

9. An even earlier critic worth mentioning is George White, who published a pamphlet entitled, *An account of the trade to the East Indies together with the state of the present company* (1691), a broadside aimed at the monopoly charter of the London East India Company. Ridiculing the company's argument that the high costs of the trade rendered a monopoly charter necessary, he writes: "Another thing was, the great Expence in making Interest at Court to procure a Power to destroy both Fellow-Subjects and foreigners: For besides the several Ten Thousand Guineas to the two late Kings, there was a far greater amount to the Ministers and Favorites" (1691, 6). White was criticizing the company apologists' line regarding the public-goods character of military investments overseas.

10. Admittedly, there is an evident confusion in the reasoning of the early pamphleteers who wrote regarding these matters. Specifically, there was confusion with respect to the provision of defense against the aggressive activities of foreign powers, and "defense" against the peaceful trading activities of foreign and unlicensed domestic competitors. The defenders of the chartered companies usually implied that the former was a crucial function of the companies' forts and garrisons and represented an important aspect of the public-goods problem. That this was not exclusively the case and that the military arm of the companies was also employed against the peaceful trading activities of both foreign and unlicensed domestic firms is documented below.

11. The garrisons were usually no more formidable than the forts. The English garrison at Calcutta in 1756, which was apparently extraordinarily large by the standards of the time, was composed of 264 soldiers, most of whom were natives. This was at wartime strength (Fuller 1955, 2:221).

12. Apparently, another significant function of forts was providing secure places to protect trade goods from pilferage which in some areas was a serious problem. See Wilson (1963, 112), for an account of this problem in Delhi.

13. Interestingly, the importance of forts and garrisons as tools for interfering with the trading activities of other national trading companies declined in the later 1600s. The foreign-trading companies began operating together in a cartel-like manner. By 1677 the

King of England was permitting the Royal African Company to "treat with the Dutch East India Company for the restraining of interlopers" (Payne 1930, 41). In India by 1697 "the pirate problem became so great that by a mutual agreement the English, French and Dutch eventually agreed to an arrangement for policing the Eastern seas for the purpose of destroying their common foe. Thus the English looked after the southern Indian Ocean, the Dutch were responsible for the Red Sea, and the French for the Persian Gulf" (Chatterton 1971, 253–54). Fuller (1955, 2:223) notes that the French and English East India companies were unwilling participants in warfare instigated by the governments of France and England; repeatedly, they unsuccessfully attempted to remain neutral. Despite this pressure, the companies maintained what effectively amounted to an international cartel in India intermittently after 1700, its heyday being the period between 1748 and 1756, during which time the territorial boundaries of national spheres of influence were well defined and respected (Blum, Cameron, and Barnes 1970, 393).

CHAPTER 7.

THE ENGLISH EAST INDIA COMPANY AND
THE MERCANTILE ORIGINS OF THE MODERN CORPORATION

1. We do not argue that the East India Company was necessarily the *first* firm to be organized in this fashion. Indeed, the medieval Roman Catholic Church displayed similar characteristics (see Ekelund et al. 1996, chap. 2).

2. In addition to the references mentioned throughout this chapter, see the interesting anecdotal survey of the company by Keay (1991).

3. In the eighteenth century the Court of Committees began to be commonly called the Court of Directors, although there was no formal change of title or alteration of functions.

4. The Court of Directors under ordinary circumstances would give secret instructions to the commanders of the company's ships as to the course they were to follow on the voyage to and from India and China. This appears to have been a security precaution taken against the threat of piracy (Philips 1940, 9). During time of war, this function was usually delegated to the Secret Committee.

5. As a further example of autonomy, the company's organization in India sometimes took out local loans in order to adjust the sequence of purchasing and financing import goods in accordance with the requirements of the shipping schedules determined by the Court of Committees (Chaudhuri 1978, 66).

6. As early as 1614, for example, a factor named Caesarian David wrote to the company office in London from Bantam accusing by name a half dozen East India Company employees of "purloining the Company's goods, deceiving private men, insolent behavior . . . and great wealth they have suddenly gathered together" (Chaudhuri 1968, 87).

7. These various details of the company's organization can be found in Chaudhuri (1968, chaps. 1 and 2).

8. There is a further reason that, even in the absence of a monopoly charter, the company may have been expected to have developed in a complex, vertically integrated form during the seventeenth century. During this period, the Asian markets in which the company conducted its trading activities were characterized by extraordinarily high communication and transportation costs. This was caused in part by the nonexistence of

an inland road network and in part by governmental institutions that provided a poor framework for the development of efficient markets (the arbitrary, unpredictable, and frequently anticapitalist tendencies of domestic governments in India was noted by Smith [1976, 30, 80]). As the result of these and other institutional problems, "[extreme] fragmentation, multiplicity of markets, and unstable prices were the main features of Asian trade," according to Chaudhuri (1978, 136). Under these conditions extensive "contracting out" by English traders would typically have been not only inefficient but generally infeasible. Given the relatively inefficient markets in Asia (at least insofar as the early history of the trade is concerned), the establishment of factories in Asia, that is, internalizing a high proportion of trading operations on the part of the firm, might have represented an efficient response by the company even in the absence of legal entry restrictions imposed by the English government. However, even in this case, what seems more likely is something like today's trade association, with compulsory dues for financing these services.

9. The allowance for privilege trade was only a partial solution to the problem, however, in that it sometimes gave rise to perverse incentive effects. Captains would sometimes divert the return voyage of an East Indiaman from, say, Bengal to a port in Western India or Persia, before continuing their voyage to England if some momentary profit opportunity so prescribed. Such diversions created delays, which could involve significant cost to the company. The manner in which this problem was addressed illustrates the specialization in strategic and operational decision making by the London office and the presidencies. Periodically, the Court of Directors offered programs of gratuities for captains who made their return voyages in a sufficiently timely fashion (Datta 1958, 134). The directors reserved the right to fire captains who failed to respond to these gratuities. However, monitoring, enforcement, and decisions regarding particular cases were entirely relegated to the presidencies.

10. As late as 1626, the company considered the possibility of vertically disintegrating, abolishing the factory system, and sending out "only ad hoc voyages." See Chaudhuri (1968, 68).

11. We recognize that franchise contracts and vertically integrated firms cannot be sharply distinguished; the franchisee may not, as is typically assumed, receive all the profits of the enterprise. If the franchisor receives a share of the proceeds, this motivates him to be efficient in those aspects of the contractual relationship that require his ongoing performance. Typical examples are maintenance of a supply network and product advertising.

12. Moreover, in the context of the emerging capital markets of the time, the company may have had recourse to vertical and horizontal integration as a risk-pooling strategy. That is, there was diversifiable risk in voyages that could not be efficiently eliminated through portfolio adjustments. Hence, licensing and franchising were not likely to have been least-cost organizational forms in this case.

13. Perhaps the force of opportunistic behavior was symmetric. It is plausible that the company faced a quality-control problem with respect to the goods it sold in England that was not confronted by domestic chartered monopolists. With import licenses or franchising there may have been a problem of controlling the flow of inferior goods to the market that could not subsequently be traced to an individual seller. By integrating forward and controlling the final sale of goods in London, the company internalized this quality control problem into the demand curve it faced for its products.

14. Another example of the cost of contracting argument relates to the defense and diplomatic services provided by the company. It is well known that the company, in the course of developing its trade in Asia, also evolved the means to defend this trade and the international relations activity that greased the trade. While these services could have been sold to franchisors as a part of the fee that they paid for the privilege, there would have been clear incentive problems on the company's part in providing these services if the franchise fee were paid up front. On the other hand, if the fee were paid periodically, the cost of contracting could have swamped the gains from such arrangements. Perhaps for these reasons the company was large, vertically integrated, and provided its own defense and diplomatic services.

15. We have emphasized the importance of decentralized property rights in the company's operations. However, malfeasance on the part of the company employees remained a persistent problem, which could be controlled but never actually eliminated. The company's attempts to establish a mutuality of interests with its servants in Asia were remarkably successful, all things considered, even if they never functioned perfectly. A fundamental change occurred after 1757, which magnified the monitoring and control problem the company faced. The trading operations of the company became subordinate to its governmental functions in India, and the main source of its revenues shifted from trade to extortionate taxation. Huge fortunes became available to company servants in India associated with the exercise of force. The incentives for malfeasance were greatly increased, while the costs to malfeasors decreased owing to the effect of corruption in the Court of Proprietors. But until the unique circumstances in Indian affairs produced this aberrant situation, malfeasance and shirking by company factors was a manageable problem. See Anderson and Tollison (1982, 1249–54) for a discussion of these developments in the company's history after 1757.

16. A general point seems relevant here: a very basic reason for any "firm"—partnership or joint-stock company—to emerge in a rent-seeking world is that lobbying costs are thereby reduced. Coalescence for production, i.e., establishment of a "firm," reduces the potential for free-riding on the firm's lobbying expenditures. The cost of procuring government protection from the firm's viewpoint is thus reduced.

17. Transferable property rights play a central role in the explanation of the evolution and dissipation of peasant society in England. For a consideration of the origins of transferable property rights in this broad setting see Macfarlane (1978).

18. That is to say, nepotism is sometimes an efficient form of behavior. We hypothesize that in early companies such behavior derived from monopoly positions that were not easily marketable. In a modern setting we might expect disproportionate numbers of the children of doctors, lawyers, politicians, and local businessmen to remain in the family firm for quite similar reasons.

19. As the joint-stock form grew, institutions facilitating the floating of new issues and the trading of shares began to emerge. While the formal founding of the London Stock Exchange was not until 1773, stockbrokers and jobbers began to assemble where rich men gathered as early as the sixteenth century. Coffeehouses and commodity exchanges such as the Royal Exchange (1571) or the Amsterdam Borse (1611) were popular sites (Clough and Rapp 1975, 155; Blum, Cameron, and Barnes 1966, 666). Door-to-door selling of stock shares was not unknown over the early period, as bankers had strong economic incentives to seek buyers. The institutions of stockjobbing and stock exchanges did not, of course, proceed smoothly. The South Sea Bubble of John Law burst in 1720,

setting back these institutions somewhat, and the French appear to have restricted early share-trading institutions (Freedeman 1979, 6).

20. The debate generated by this legislation among professional economists over this period was both heated and protracted, with (for example) N. W. Senior in favor, J. R. McCulloch vehemently opposed, and Alfred Marshall reservedly supportive of limited-liability legislation (see Amsler, Bartlett, and Bolton, 1981).

21. There are testable implications of our analysis, moreover, which, with sufficient data, could be pursued. For example, corporate primogeniture should have declined over the joint-stock era, and the cost of capital to the regulated and early joint-stock companies should have been roughly equivalent.

22. See DuBois (1971, 269). Most older writers regarded the Bubble Act as the legislative response to the popular hysteria surrounding joint-stock enterprise at the time, and based on a misunderstanding of these business organizations by legislators. See, for example, Holdsworth, (1966, 219). However, Hessen, (1979, 29), mentions that the act was actually passed at the urging of the (chartered) South Sea Company, which "resented the competition for investor's capital."

23. DuBois notes: "There is surprisingly little discussion in the records of the period of the liability of a corporation for its acts or the acts of its agents to persons who are not members of the corporation" (1971, 118). On occasion injured third parties presented petitions for relief to the directors of a company; when compensation was granted, "the directors' attitude was frequently that of persons distributing largesse" (119). Lawsuits were practically unheard of, and the granting of compensation seems to have been an investment in goodwill by the firm.

24. Cited by DuBois, (1971, 222). In America between 1775 and about 1840, complete shareholder liability was accepted as a matter of course in the dealings of widespread unincorporated joint-stock firms.

25. This line of reasoning also allows us to explain an apparent anomaly: why was it unusual for partnerships to offer limited liability features to their members by means of contract? There was no technical reason that partnerships in this period could not make contractual provisions to limit partners' liability to assets contributed to the partnership. In fact, some partnerships did offer effective limited liability by means of specific contractual clauses by the early nineteenth century (see Hunt 1935a, 16 n. 23).

26. We note that the literature arguing for the crucial importance of limited liability to the corporation consistently neglects to apply simple economics on another level as well. The dichotomy usually posed between limited and unlimited liability is false because the latter is an economic unicorn. Shareholder liability will always be limited by information, transaction, and litigation costs confronting the creditors of the firm, even in the absence of express limited liability protection. Shareholders may invest resources in the concealment of their wealth in a defense in court against creditors' actions. The creditor's collection of a debt from shareholders in the event of default by the firm is not costless. The paucity of creditors' suits in the eighteenth century may reflect the economic feasibility of shareholder debt collection under ordinary circumstances. The transaction costs associated even with simple credit checks were often prohibitively high. Many joint-stock firms with express limited liability features by charter dealt extensively with government (for example, the East India Company); this may have reflected the greater efficiency of governmental actions against shareholders owing to the coercive

measures at their disposal. In other cases—such as unincorporated firms that utilized limited liability clauses by contract—these features may have simply functioned as a kind of marketing device designed to appeal to potential investors unfamiliar with customary investment practices or to individuals whose wealth holdings had a high community visibility and hence were more vulnerable to creditor actions. The important point is that what mattered was the amount of collateral available to the firm; limited liability was generally of dubious significance.

27. Scott, in fact, accuses Smith not only of almost exclusive reliance upon Anderson's *Historical and Chronological Deduction of Commerce* for his account of the joint-stock companies but also of biased selection of examples from that work. Smith may also have utilized the very critical "Monopolies and Exclusive companies How Pernicious to Trade" (from Cato's *Letter, or Essays on Liberty, Civil and Religious,* 1733) to develop his comments on the joint-stock argument (see the discussion in Scott 1951, 1:448–49). See, however, Anderson and Tollison (1982).

CHAPTER 8.

CONCLUSION: THE POLITICAL ECONOMY OF MERCANTILISM

1. It goes without saying that stable property rights and low loan rates were unable to provide the English secure control over their North American colonies later in the eighteenth century.

2. As our digression on Sir Edward Coke suggests (chapter 3), the embedding of economic (and possibly political) freedoms in the law may well have been far less "ideological" than North and others appear to suggest.

3. North and Weingast (1989, 830), following Crouzet, note that French growth rates (at least what we know about them) actually paralleled English growth in the post-1715 period. As we noted in chapter 4 and in our initial discussions of French mercantilism, this development was likely fostered by the inability of French autocrats to enforce guild cartels (textile and other) in the face of rural productions and the introduction of differentiated products.

4. This fact calls into question the view put forward by one political scientist that "democratic and autocratic societies extract similar levels of rents but distribute them over greater and smaller sets of groups, respectively" (Lake 1992, 34 n. 15). Constitutional constraints put limits on rent seeking in democracies, both in particular markets and overall, and such constraints may be of greater or lesser effectiveness. No comparison of rent extraction is possible with identifying *particular* societies.

5. Thus, Cole pinpoints the motive for protective regulations in the desire to encourage new industry and, indeed, utilizes the "infant-industries" argument for tariff protection as support for argument (1939, 1:349). We would simply point out that a policy of regulating only new industries (which did not develop in mercantile France) was a convenient method of expanding the scope of a rent-seeking society. In addition, we find no evidence of significant deregulation of infant industries once they were cartelized.

6. Heckscher's discussion of wage controls after the Great Plague and the adjustment of feudal land rents is revealing in that he clearly understood how market activity

worked around and changed institutions. Implicit price adjustments resulting from economizing activity rather than the invocation of "custom" or regulation had primary explanatory power in treating institutional change (1929, 533).

7. It is noteworthy that some of those who make this argument (e.g., North 1990, chap. 3) go right ahead using modern "Marshallian" tools melded with Armen Alchian's analysis of property rights to analyze institutions, such as those of seventeenth- and eighteenth-century England (North and Weingast 1989; Weingast 1995). While there is no integration of path dependence or advanced informational theory with neo-Marshallian economics in the latter, those such methods are denigrated in the former. Perhaps there are important differences between "theoretical discourse" on this subject and nuts and bolts analysis of particular questions.

8. There has been recent research in this regard, however. In addition to the literature cited in chapter 1, see Hinich and Munger (1994).

9. Thus North and other observers (DeSoto 1989) are correct to find parallels between the forms of rent-seeking in the "old" mercantile age and in neomercantile economies of, for example, Latin America. The evolving economies of eastern Europe are also highly suitable for analysis utilizing a backdrop of the insights of rent-seeking and neoinstitutional analysis of mercantilism.

10. We do not do justice to the whole of Weingast's argument. He develops a two-person game theoretic model featuring the opposing and complementary interests of a sovereign and his constituents, explaining stability or revolution as a coordination problem. Further, he explains the (at least temporary) durability of federalism in England and the United States (along with Chinese-style federalism).

11. Credible restrictions on government based on some majoritarian "norms" that accept or repel government incursions on property rights are themselves driven by economic forces. These "norms" supported limited government with two major exceptions or "breakdowns" as Weingast calls them (1995, 26–27)—the matter of slavery and the breakdown that occurred during the Great Depression. It is important to note that these new "norms"—rejection of the *delegata* rule, acceptance of federal regulation in economic markets, and so forth—and the new political majority they supported after the Depression in the United States did not appear from nowhere and were themselves determined by *economic calculation*. However, the lifting of constitutional constraints on government incursions on property rights may have created (and, indeed, may be engendering) new constraints that will elicit new "norms" of resistance to upper federal authority. All this is to say that there are important limits to static analysis.

12. Other types of explanations are as unlikely as the intellectual history one. For example, within the context of our rent-seeking model, the movement to free enterprise might be explained by the relative costs facing certain political interests. No matter how fine an academic scribbler Adam Smith was, we suspect that the roles of special interests and ideas were reversed in the ascension of free enterprise over mercantilism. Certainly, Smith himself characterized mercantilism correctly as a system built entirely upon self-interest. The inefficiencies concomitant to monopoly organization offer a range of mutually beneficial gains from exchange. Presumably consumers would offer to buy out monopolists to the net benefit of both parties. The difficulty with such a solution is the existence of prohibitively high transaction costs to consumers, which implies that monopoly and regulation will persist despite the potential social gains of ending them. Moreover, perhaps there were fewer consumers in mercantilist times, and more such

Pareto-superior bargains could be struck. If this were operationally so, the movement to free enterprise from the monopolistic policies of mercantilism would be susceptible to rational explanation. This is, however, an extremely unlikely explanation of the decline of mercantilism, since the mathematics of transaction costs imply that the number of transactors must be very small before meaningful reductions in transaction costs obtain. It is therefore very likely that in mercantilist times the organizing costs to consumers would have dominated the returns from abolishing monopoly and regulation via Pareto-superior moves.

13. In a provocative paper published at the end of the nineteenth century Sir W. S. Ashley (1897) assessed the then-growing literature on free-trade "precursors" of Adam Smith. Specifically, Ashley identified the origins of the free-trade sentiments of Sir Dudley North, Sir Josiah Child, William Davenant, and Nicholas Barbon with their membership in and support of the Tory party in the late seventeenth and early eighteenth centuries. Noting a "natural connection" over the whole period, 1673–1713, between advocacy of a free-trade policy and the Tory party, Ashley argued that "it is clear that Tory writers on trade, however sensible we may suppose them, could hardly fail to have a partisan bias in favor of liberty of commerce, and that, however clear-sighted they may have been, they were likely to have their insight sharpened by party prejudice. McCulloch's explanation of North's enlightenment, that on questions of trade party interests were not directly affected; is the very opposite of truth" (1897, 338). Ashley proceeds, cleverly, to develop this idea and to document Tory advocacy of free trade (especially with France) as opposed to the Whig party's support of tariffs. Thus, Ashley was able to document party (i.e., rent-seeking) interests as dominant in the movement to free trade after the Restoration. Allied self-interested components of society (through political parties) may therefore provide the raison d'etre for the views of the "modern mercantilists" of the period. Thus, we may explain why, as Ashley reports, Josiah Child turned Tory in 1680 in order to save the privileges of the East India Company, why Barbon was one of the projectors of the Tory Land Bank, and why North eagerly served Charles II as sheriff of London during the Tory reaction (1897, 337). The designation of writers as "mercantile" or "liberal" based upon immediate individual interest (if, indeed, that is identifiable) must be supplemented by a study of major tenets of party platforms and intraparty interactions of special-interest groups. In mercantile context such a study would be very complex, but we believe that the general proposition raised by Ashley demands closer scrutiny.

References

Ades, A. F., and E. L. Glaser. 1995. "Trade and Circuses: Explaining Urban Giants." *Quarterly Journal of Economics* 110:195–227.

Alchian, A. 1975. "Corporate Management and Property Rights." In *The Economics of Legal Relationships,* ed. H. Manne, 499–510. St. Paul, Minn.: West Publishing.

Alchian, A., and H. Demsetz. 1972. "Production, Information Costs, and Economic Organization." *American Economic Review* 62:777–95.

Allen, W. R. 1970. "Modern Defenders of Mercantilist Theory." *History of Political Economy* 2:381–97.

———. 1973. "The Interpretation of Mercantilist Economics: Some Historiographical Problems: A Rearguard Response." *History of Political Economy* 5:496–98.

Amsler, C. E., R. L. Bartlett, and C. J. Bolton. 1981. "Thoughts of Some British Economists on Early Limited Liability and Corporate Legislation." *History of Political Economy* 13:774–93.

Anderson, G., and R. D. Tollison. 1982. "Adam Smith's Analysis of Joint Stock Companies." *Journal of Political Economy* 90:1237–56.

———. 1984. "A Rent-Seeking Explanation of the British Factory Acts." In *Neoclassical Political Economy,* ed. D. Colander, 187–201. Cambridge: Ballinger.

Anderson, G. M., W. F. Shughart II, and R. D. Tollison. 1985. "Adam Smith in the Customhouse." *Journal of Political Economy* 93:740–59.

Anderson, T. L. 1982. "Review of *Mercantilism as a Rent-Seeking Society.*" *Journal of Economic History* 42:978–79.

Anes, G. 1981. *Economia e Illustración en la España del Siglo XVIII.* Barcelona.

Appleby, J. O. 1978. *Economic Thought and Ideology in Seventeenth-Century England.* Princeton: Princeton University Press.

Arthur, W. B. 1989. "Competing Technologies, Increasing Returns, and Lock-In by Historical Events." *Economic Journal* 99:116–31.

Ashley, W. J. 1923–1925 [1906]. *Introduction to English Economic History and Theory.* 2 vols. London: Longmans, Green.

———. 1897. "The Tory Origins of Free Trade Policy." *Quarterly Journal of Economics* 2:335–71.

Ault, R. W., and R. B. Ekelund Jr. 1988. "Habits in Economic Analysis: Veblen and the Neoclassicals." *History of Political Economy* 20:431–45.

Azzi, C., and R. Ehrenberg. 1975. "Household Allocation of Time and Church Attendance." *Journal of Political Economy* 84:27–56.

Baran, P., and P. Sweezy. 1966. *Monopoly Capital.* New York: Monthly Review Press.

Barber, W. J. 1975. *British Economic Thought and India, 1600–1858.* Oxford: Oxford University Press.

Basas Fernández, M. 1961. "Burgos en el Comercio Lanero del Siglo XVI." *Moneda y Crédito* 77:37–68.

Baysinger, B., and R. D. Tollison. 1980a. "Chaining Leviathan: The Case of Gladstonian Finance." *History of Political Economy* 12:206–13.

———. 1980b. "Evaluating the Social Costs of Monopoly and Regulation." *Atlantic Economic Journal* 8:22–26.

Bean, R. N. 1984. "Review of *Mercantilism as a Rent-Seeking Society.*" *Public Choice* 1:110–12.

Becker, G. S. 1976. "Comment." *Journal of Law and Economics* 19:245–48.

———. 1981. *A Treatise on the Family.* Cambridge: Harvard University Press.

———. 1983. "A Theory of Competition Among Pressure Groups for Political Influence." *Quarterly Journal of Economics* 97:371–400.

Becker, G. S., and G. J. Stigler. 1974. "Law Enforcement, Malfeasance, and Compensation of Enforcers." *Journal of Legal Studies* 3:1–18.

Beer, M. 1938. *Early British Economists.* London: George Allen and Unwin.

Bensen, B. L. 1984. "Rent Seeking for a Property Rights Perspective." *Southern Economic Journal* 51:388–400.

Berle, A. A., and G. Means. 1932. *The Modern Corporation and Private Property.* New York: Macmillan.

Bilbao, L. M., and E. Fernández de Pinedo. 1986. "Exportación de lanas, trashumancia y ocupación del espacio en Castilla durante los siglos XVI, XVII y XVIII." In *Contribución a la historia de la Transhumancia en España,* ed. P. García Martín and J. M. Sánchez Benito. Madrid: Ministerio de Agricultura.

Blum, J., R. Cameron, and T. J. Barnes. 1966. *The European World: A History.* Boston: Little, Brown.

———. 1970. *The European World: A History.* 2d ed. Boston: Little Brown.

Boland, L. A. 1979. "Knowledge and the Role of Institutions in Economic Theory." *Journal of Economic Issues* 13:957–72.

Boulenger, J. 1967. *The National History of France: The Seventeenth Century,* vol. 4. Ed. F. Funk-Brentano. New York: AMS Press.

Browley, M. R. 1995. "Political Leadership and Liberal Economic Subsystems: The Constraints of Structural Assumptions." *Canadian Journal of Political Science* 28:85–103.

Buchanan, J. M. 1980a. "Reform in the Rent-Seeking Society." In *Toward a Theory of the Rent-Seeking Society,* ed. J. M. Buchanan, R. D. Tollison, and G. Tullock, 359–67. College Station: Texas A&M University Press.

———. 1980b. "Rent Seeking and Profit Seeking." In *Toward a Theory of the Rent-Seeking Society,* ed. J. M. Buchanan, R. D. Tollison, and G. Tullock, 3–15. College Station: Texas A&M University Press.

———. 1983. "Rent-Seeking, Noncompensated Transfers, and Laws of Succession." *Journal of Law and Economics* 26:71–86.

Buchanan, J. M., and G. Tullock. 1962. *The Calculus of Consent*. Ann Arbor: University of Michigan Press.

Buchanan, J. M., R. D. Tollison, and G. Tullock, eds. 1980. *Toward a Theory of the Rent-Seeking Society*. College Station: Texas A&M University Press.

Buchanan, J., and R. Wagner. 1977. *Deficits and Democracy*. New York: Academic Press.

Cameron, R., ed. 1970. *Essays in French Economic History*. Homewood, Ill.: Irwin.

Cameron, R. 1989. *A Concise Economic History of the World: From Paleolithic Times to the Present*. New York: Oxford University Press.

Campbell, R. M. 1967. "The Law and the Joint-Stock Company in Scotland." In *Studies in Scottish Business History*, ed. R. M. Campbell. New York: A. M. Kelley.

Castillo, A. V. 1980 [1930]. *Spanish Mercantilism: Gerónimo de Uztáriz—Economist*. Philadelphia: Porcupine Press.

Cawston, G., and A. H. Keane. 1968. *The Early Chartered Companies, A.D. 1296–1858*. New York: B. Franklin.

Chadwick, E. 1843. *Report on the Sanitary Conditions of the Labouring Population of Great Britain: A Supplementary Report on the Results of a Special Inquiry into the Practice of Interment in Towns*. London: W. Clowes and Sons.

Chalk, A. F. 1951. "Natural Law and the Rise of Economic Individualism in England." *Journal of Political Economy* 59:330–47.

———. 1966. "Mandeville's *Fable of the Bees*: A Reappraisal." *Southern Economic Journal* 23:1–16.

Chambers, M., et al. 1974. *The Western Experience*. Vol. 2: *The Early Modern Period*. New York: Knopf.

Chandler, A. D., Jr. 1966 [1962]. *Strategy and Structure*. New York: Doubleday.

———. 1977. *The Visible Hand: The Managerial Revolution in American Business*. Cambridge: Belknap.

Chatterton, E. K. 1971. *The Old East Indiamen*. London: Conway Maritime Press.

Chaudhuri, K. N. 1968. *The English East India Company*. London: Augustus M. Kelly.

———. 1978. *The Trading World of Asia and the English East India Company 1660–1760*. London: Cambridge University Press.

Cipolla, C. M. 1965. *Guns, Sails, and Empires*. New York: Pantheon.

Clicquot-Blervache, S. de. [1758]. *Considerations sur les Compagnies, sociétés et maitrises*. A Londres, La présente Année.

Clough, S. B., and R. T. Rapp. 1975. *European Economic History*. New York: McGraw-Hill.

Coase, R. H. 1974. "The Lighthouse in Economics." *Journal of Law and Economics* 17:357–76.

Coats, A. W. 1957. "In Defense of Heckscher and His Idea of Mercantilism." *Scandinavian Economic History Review* 5:173–87.

———. 1973. "The Interpretation of Mercantilist Economics: Some Historiographical Problems." *History of Political Economy* 5:449–84.

———. 1985. "Mercantilism, Yet Again!" In *Gli economisti e la politica economica*, ed. P. Roggi. Naples: Ediizione Scientifiche Italiane.

———. 1992. *On the History of Economic Thought: British and American Economic Essays*, vol. 1. London: Routledge.

———. 1993. "Concluding Reflections." In *Mercantilist Economics*, ed. L. Magnusson. Boston: Kluwer Academic Publishers.

Cole, C. W. 1931. *French Mercantilist Doctrines Before Colbert.* New York: Octagon.

———. 1939. *Colbert and a Century of French Mercantilism.* 2 vols. New York: Columbia University Press.

———. 1943. *French Mercantilism, 1683–1700.* New York: Columbia University Press.

Coleman, D. C. 1957. "Eli Heckscher and the Idea of Mercantilism." *Scandinavian Economic History Review* 5:3–25.

———. 1969. *Revisions in Mercantilism.* London: Methuen.

———. 1982. "Review of *Mercantilism as a Rent-Seeking Society.*" *Business History* 24: 321–22.

———. 1988. "Adam Smith, Businessmen, and the Mercantile System in England." *History of European Ideas* 9:161–70.

Comanor, W. S., and R. H. Smiley. 1975. "Monopoly and the Distribution of Wealth." *Quarterly Journal of Economics* 89:177–94.

Congleton, R. D. 1988. "Evaluating Rent-Seeking Losses: Do the Welfare Gains of Lobbyists Count?" *Public Choice* 56:181–84.

Cooper, R. A. 1983. "Review of *Mercantilism as a Rent-Seeking Society.*" *Libertarian Forum* 17:11–12.

Corbbett, W. 1966 [1806]. *Parliamentary History of England,* vol. 1. London: R. Bagshaw.

Corcoran, W. J. 1984. "Long-run Equilibrium and Total Expenditures in Rent-Seeking." *Public Choice* 43:89–94.

Cowen, T. 1986. "Nicholas Barbon and the Origins of Economic Liberalism." *Research in the History of Economic Theory and Method* 4:67–83.

Cowling, K., and D. C. Mueller. 1978. "The Social Costs of Monopoly Power." *Economic Journal* 88:727–48.

Crain, W. M., and R. B. Ekelund Jr. 1976. "Chadwick and Demsetz on Competition and Regulation." *Journal of Law and Economics* 19:149–62.

Crouzet, F. 1967. "England and France in the Eighteenth Century: A Comparative Analysis of Two Economic Growths." In *The Causes of the Industrial Revolution in England,* ed. R. M. Hartwell. London: Methuen.

———. 1972. "Capital Formation in Great Britain During the Industrial Revolution." In *Capital Formation in the Industrial Revolution,* ed. F. Crouzet. Longon: Methuen. (Essay originally published as "La Formation du Capital en Grande-Bretagne Pendant la Revolution Industrielle," *Deuxieme conference internationale d'histoire économique. Aix-en-Provence. 1962,* vol. 2. Paris and the Hague, 1965.)

Cuadrado Iglesias, M. 1980. *Aprovechamiento en Común de Pastos y Leñas.* Madrid: Ministerio de Agricultura.

Cunningham, W. 1968 [1896–1903]. *Growth of English Industry and Commerce.* 2 vols. New York: A. M. Kelley.

Datta, K. K., ed. 1958. *Fort-William-India House Correspondence: Vol. 1: 1748–1756.* Delhi: National Archives of India.

Davidson, A. B., E. Davis, and R. B. Ekelund Jr. 1995. "Political Choice and the Child Labor Statute of 1938: Public Interest or Interest Group Legislation?" *Public Choice* 82:85–106.

Davies, D. 1971. "The Efficiency of Private versus Public Firms: The Case of Australia's Two Airlines." *Journal of Law and Economics* 14:149–66.

Davies, K. G. 1975. *The Royal African Company.* New York: Octagon.

Davis, L. E. 1980. "It's a Long Road to Tipperary, or Reflections on Organized Violence, Protection Rates, and Related Topics: The New Political History." *Journal of Economic History* 40:1–16.

Demsetz, H. 1967. "Towards a Theory of Property Rights." *American Economic Review* 57:347–59.

———. 1968. "Why Regulate Utilities?" *Journal of Law and Economics* 11:55–66.

Depitre, E. 1912. *La Toile Peinte en France aux XVIIe et XVIIIe Siècles*. Paris: Marcel Riviere.

DeRoover, R. 1944. "What Is Dry Exchange? A Contribution to the Study of English Mercantilism." *Journal of Political Economy* 52:250–66.

De Soto, H. 1989. *The Other Path*. New York: Harper and Row.

deVries, J. 1976. *The Economy of Europe in an Age of Crisis, 1600–1750*. Cambridge: Cambridge University Press.

Dewar, M. 1965. "The Memorandum 'For the Understanding of the Exchange': Its Authorship and Dating." *Economic History Review* (Ser. 2): 18:476–87.

Donald, M. B. 1961. *Elizabethan Monopolies: The History of the Company of Mineral and Battery Works from 1565 to 1604*. Edinburgh: Oliver and Boyd.

Dougan, W. R., and J. M. Snyder. 1993. "Are Rents Fully Dissipated?" *Public Choice* 77:793–813.

Douglas, G. W., and J. C. Miller. 1974. *Economic Regulation of Domestic Air Transport*. Washington: Brookings Institute.

DuBois, A. 1971. *The English Business Company After the Bubble Act, 1720–1800*. New York: Octagon.

Dutt, R. C. 1969. *The Economic History of India Under Early British Rule*. New York: A. M. Kelley.

Eames, J. B. 1974. *The English in China*. London: Curzon Press.

Ehrlich, I., and R. A. Posner. 1974. "An Economic Analysis of Legal Rule Making." *Journal of Legal Studies* 3:257–86.

Eggertsson, T. 1990. *Economic Behavior and Institutions*. Cambridge: Cambridge University Press.

Ekelund, R. B., Jr., and R. F. Hébert. 1996. *A History of Economic Theory and Method*. New York: McGraw-Hill.

———. 1981. "A Proto History of Franchise Bidding." *Southern Economic Journal* 48:464–74.

Ekelund, R. B., Jr., et al. 1996. *Sacred Trust: The Medieval Church as an Economic Firm*. New York: Oxford University Press.

Ekelund, R. B., Jr., D. R. Street, and A. B. Davidson. 1996. "Marriage, Divorce, and Prostitution: Economic Sociology in Medieval England and Enlightenment Spain." *European Journal of the History of Economic Thought* 3:183–99.

Ekelund, R. B., Jr., and R. D. Tollison. 1981. *Mercantilism as a Rent-Seeking Society: Economic Regulation in Historical Perspective*. College Station: Texas A&M University Press.

Ekelund, R. B., Jr., and J. K. Watson. 1991. "Restaurant Cuisine, Fast Food and Ethnic Edibles: An Empirical Note on Household Meal Production." *Kyklos* 44:613–27.

Elliott, J. H. 1961. "The Decline of Spain." *Past and Present* 20.

Elton, G. R. 1966. *The Tudor Revolution in Government: Administrative Changes in the Reign of Henry VIII*. Cambridge: Cambridge University Press.

Elton, G. R. 1986. *The Parliament of England, 1559–1581*. Cambridge: Cambridge University Press.

Enciso, A. G., and J. P. Merino. 1979. "The Public Sector and Economic Growth in Eighteenth Century Spain." *Journal of European Economic History* 8:553–92.

Evans, G. H. 1936. *British Corporation Finance, 1775–1850.* Baltimore: Johns Hopkins Press.

———. 1967. "The Law of Demand: The Roles of Gregory King and Charles Davenant." *Quarterly Journal of Economics* 81:483–92.

Faith, R. L., and R. D. Tollison. 1983. "The Supply of Occupational Regulation." *Economic Inquiry* 21:232–48.

Fay, C. R. 1934. "Adam Smith, America, and the Doctrinal Defeat of the Mercantile System." *Quarterly Journal of Economics* 48:304–16.

Fisher, F. M. 1985. "The Social Costs of Monopoly and Regulation: Posner Reconsidered." *Journal of Political Economy* 93:410–16.

Fortescue, J. W. 1899. *A History of the British Army.* Vol. 2: *To the Close of the Seven Years' War.* London: Macmillan.

Foster, W. 1924. *The East India House: Its History and Associations.* London: P. S. King.

Frank, R. H. 1986. *Choosing the Right Pond.* Oxford: Oxford University Press.

Freedeman, C. E. 1979. *Joint-Stock Enterprise in France, 1807–1867.* Chapel Hill: University of North Carolina Press.

Fuller, J. F. C. 1955. *A Military History of the Western World,* vol. 2. New York: DaCapo.

Furber, H. 1970. *John Company at War.* New York: Octagon.

———. 1976. *Rival Empires of Trade in the Orient, 1600–1800.* Minneapolis: University of Minnesota Press.

Furniss, E. S. 1965 [1920]. *The Position of the Laborer in a System of Nationalism.* New York: A. M. Kelley.

Furubotn, E. G. 1994. *Future Development of the New Institutional Economics: Extension of the Neoclassical Model or New Construct?* Jena: Max-Planck-Institute for Research into Economic Systems.

García Martín, P. 1988. *La Ganadería Mesteña en la España Borbónica, 1700–1836.* Madrid: Ministerio de Agricultura.

García Martín, P., and J. M. Sánchez Benito. 1986. *Contribución a la historia de la Transhumancia en España.* Madrid: Ministerio de Agricultura.

Gardiner, S. R. 1965. *History of England from the Accession of James I to the Outbreak of the Civil War, 1603–1642,* vol. 8. New York: AMS Press.

Gardner, Brian. 1972. *The East India Company: A History.* New York: McCall.

Gay, D. E. R. 1982. "Review of *Mercantilism as a Rent-Seeking Society.*" *Kyklos* 35:732–33.

Gerbert, M-C. 1982. "La Orden de San Jeronimo y la Ganaderia en el Reino de Castilla desde su Fundacion a Principios del Siglo XVI." *Boletín de la Real Academia de la Historia* 179:219–93.

Goff, B., and G. Anderson. 1994. "The Political Economy of Prohibition in the United States, 1919–1933." *Social Science Quarterly* 75:270–83.

Grampp, W. D. 1952. "The Liberal Element in English Mercantilism." *Quarterly Journal of Economics* 66:465–501.

———. 1993. "An Appreciation of Mercantilism." In *Mercantilist Economics,* ed. L. Magnusson. Boston: Kluwer Academic Publishers.

Haley, B. F. 1936. "Heckscher, Mercantilism." *Quarterly Journal of Economics* 50:347–54.

Hamilton, E. J. 1947. *War and Prices in Spain, 1651–1800*. Cambridge: Harvard University Press.

Hanbury, H. G. 1960. *English Courts of Law*. London: Oxford University Press.

Hartwell, R. M. 1976. "Capitalism and the Historians." In *Essays on Hayek*, ed. Fritz Machlup. New York: New York University Press.

Harberger, A. C. 1954. "Monopoly and Resource Allocation." *American Economic Review* 44:77–87.

Hayek, F. A. 1960. *The Constitution of Liberty*. Chicago: University of Chicago Press.

Heaton, C. H. 1937. "Heckscher on Mercantilism." *Journal of Political Economy* 45:370–93.

Heckscher, E. F. 1929. "A Plea for Theory in Economic History." *Economic History* 1:525–34.

———. 1934 [1931]. *Mercantilism*. Trans. M. Shapiro. 2 vols. London: George Allen and Unwin.

———. 1936. "Mercantilism." *Economic History Review* 6:44–54.

———. 1939. "Quantitative Measurement in Economic History." *Quarterly Journal of Economics* 53:167–93.

———. 1955. *Mercantilism*. 2d ed. Trans. M. Shapiro. Ed. E. G. Soderlund. 2 vols. London: George Allen and Unwin.

Herlitz, L. 1964. "The Concept of Mercantilism." *Scandinavian Economic History Review* 12:101–20.

———. 1993. "Conceptions of History and Society in Mercantilism, 1650–1730." In *Mercantilist Economics*, ed. L. Magnusson. Boston: Kluwer Academic Publishers.

Herr, R. 1958. *The Eighteenth Century Revolution in Spain*. Princeton: Princeton University Press.

———. 1989. *Rural Change and Royal Finances in Spain at the End of the Old Regime*. Berkeley and Los Angeles: University of California Press.

Hessen, R. 1979. *In Defense of the Corporation*. Stanford: Hoover Institution Press.

Higgins, R., W. F. Shughart, and R. D. Tollison. 1985. "Free Entry and Efficient Rent-Seeking." *Public Choice* 46:247–58.

Higgins, R., and R. D. Tollison. 1988. "Life among the Triangles and Trapezoids." In *The Political Economy of Rent Seeking*, ed. C. K. Rowley, R. D. Tollison, and G. Tullock, 147–57. Boston: Kluwer Academic Publishers.

High, J., ed. 1991. *Regulation: Economic Theory and History*. Ann Arbor: University of Michigan Press.

Hill, L. E. 1983. "Review of *Mercantilism as a Rent-Seeking Society*." *Social Science Quarterly* 64:682–83.

Hillman, A. L., and E. Katz. 1984. "Risk-Averse Rent-Seekers and the Social Cost of Monopoly Power." *Economic Journal* 94:104–10.

Hinich, M. J., and M. C. Munger. 1994. *Ideology and the Theory of Political Choice*. Ann Arbor: University of Michigan Press.

Hinton, R. W. K. 1955. "The Mercantile System in the Time of Thomas Mun." *Economic History Review* 7:277–90.

Holcombe, R. G. 1980. "Contractarian Model of the Decline in Classical Liberalism." *Public Choice* 35:277–86.

Holdsworth, W. 1966 [1903]. *A History of English Law*, vols. 1, 4, and 8. London: Methuen and Co.

Hoselitz, B. F. 1960. "The Early History of Entrepreneurial Theory." Reprinted in *Essays in Economic Thought: Aristotle to Marshall*, ed. J. J. Spengler and W. R. Allen. Chicago: Rand McNally.

Hughes, J. R. T. 1977. *The Governmental Habit: Economic Control from Colonial Times to the Present*. New York: Basic Books.

Hunt, B. C. 1935a. "The Joint-Stock Company in England: 1800–1825." *Journal of Political Economy* 43:1–33.

———. 1935b. "The Joint-Stock Company in England: 1830–1844." *Journal of Political Economy* 43:331–64.

Hurd, Archibald. 1921. *The Sea Traders*. London and New York: Cassell and Co.

Iannaccone, L. R. 1988. "A Formal Model of Church and Sect." *American Journal of Sociology* 94:S241–68.

———. 1995. "Risk, Rationality, and Religious Portfolios." *Economic Inquiry* 38:285–95.

Irwin, D. A. 1991. "Mercantilism as Strategic Trade Policy: The Anglo-Dutch Rivalry for the East India Trade." *Journal of Political Economy* 99:1296–1314.

Jensen, M. C., and W. M. Meckling. 1976. "Theory of the Firm: Managerial Behavior, Agency Costs and Ownership Structure." *Journal of Financial Economics* 3:305–60.

Johnson, E. A. J. 1931. "The Mercantilist Concept of 'Art' and 'Ingenious Labour'." *Economic History* 2:234–53.

———. 1932a. "British Mercantilist Doctrines Concerning the 'Exportation of Work' and 'Foreign-Paid Incomes'." *Journal of Political Economy* 40:750–70.

———. 1932b. "Unemployment and Consumption: The Mercantilist View." *Quarterly Journal of Economics* 46:698–719.

Kalt, J. P., and M. Zupan. 1984. "Capture and Ideology in the Economic Theory of Politics." *American Economic Review* 74:279–300.

Kamen, H. 1968. *The Spanish Inquisition*. New York: New American Library.

———. 1983. *Spain, 1469–1714*. New York: Longman House.

Kau, J., and P. H. Rubin. 1979. "Self-Interest, Ideology and Log Rolling in Congressional Voting." *Journal of Law and Economics* 22:365–84.

Keay, J. 1991. *The Honourable Company: A History of the English East India Company*. New York: Macmillan.

Kessel, R. 1974. "Transfused Blood, Serum Hepatitis, and the Coase Theorem." *Journal of Law and Economics* 17:265–89.

Keynes, J. M. 1936. *General Theory of Employment, Interest and Money*. New York: Harcourt, Brace and World.

Kindleberger, C. P. 1975. "The Rise of Free Trade in Western Europe." *Journal of Economic History* 35:20–55.

Klein, B., R. G. Crawford, and A. A. Alchian. 1978. "Vertical Integration, Appropriable Rents, and the Competitive Contracting Process." *Journal of Law and Economics* 21:297–326.

Klein, J. 1964 [1920]. *The Mesta: A Study in Spanish Economic History, 1273–1836*. Port Washington, N.Y.: Kennikat Press.

Koot, G. 1993. "Historical Economics and the Revival of Mercantilism Thought in Britain, 1870–1920." In *Mercantilist Economics*, ed. L. Magnusson. Boston: Kluwer Academic Publishers.

Kreuger, A. O. 1974. "The Political Economy of the Rent-Seeking Society." *American Economic Review* 64:291–303.

Laband, D. W., and J. P. Sophocleus. 1988. "The Social Cost of Rent Seeking: First Estimates." *Public Choice* 58:269–75.

———. 1992. "An Estimate of Resource Expenditures on Transfer Activity in the United States." *Quarterly Journal of Economics* 107:959–84.

Laguna Sanz, E. 1986. *Historia del Merino*. Madrid: Ministerio de Agricultura.

Lake, D. A. 1992. "Powerful Pacifists: Democratic States and War." *American Political Science Review* 86:24–37.

Landes, W. M., and R. A. Posner. 1975. "The Independent Judiciary in an Interest-Group Perspective." *Journal of Law and Economics* 18:875–901.

Lane, F. C. 1958. "The Economic Consequences of Organized Violence." *Journal of Economic History* 18:401–17.

———. 1979. *Profits from Power: Readings in Protection Rent and Violence Controlling Enterprises*. Albany: State University of New York Press.

Lefebvre, G. 1947. *The Coming of the French Revolution*. Princeton: Princeton University Press.

Le Flem, J. P. 1972. "Las Cuentas de la Mesta (1510–1709)." *Moneda y Crédito* 121:23–104.

Leoni, B. 1961. *Freedom and the Law*. Princeton: D. Van Nostrand Company.

Levack, B. P. 1973. *Civil Lawyers in England, 1603–1641: A Political Study*. Oxford: Clarendon Press.

Lewis, P. S. 1968. *Later Medieval France*. New York: St. Martin's.

Lewis, R. A. 1952. *Edwin Chadwick and the Public Health Movement, 1832–1854*. London: Longmans, Green and Company.

Liebowitz, S. J., and S. E. Margolis. 1990. "The Fable of the Keys." *Journal of Law and Economics* 33:1–26.

———. 1994. "Network Externality: An Uncommon Tragedy." *Journal of Economic Perspectives* 8:133–50.

———. 1995a. "Path Dependence: From QWERTY to Windows 95." *Regulation* 18:33–41.

———. 1995b. "Path Dependence, Lock-In, and History." *Journal of Law, Economics, and Organization* 11:205–26.

Lipson, E. 1956. *The Economic History of England*. Vol. 3: *The Age of Mercantilism*. 6th ed. London: Adam and Charles Black.

Llombart, V. 1991. "The Discurso sobre el modo de fomentar la industria popular and the Discurso sobre el fomento de la industrial popular, Two Editions of the Same Work by Campomanes: A Reply to D. R. Street." *History of Political Economy* 23:527–31.

———. 1995. "Market for Ideas and Reception of Physiocracy in Spain: Some Analytical and Historical Suggestions." *European Journal of the History of Economic Thought* 2:29–51.

Lott, J., and S. G. Bronars. 1993. "Time Series Evidence on Shirking in the U.S. House of Representatives." *Public Choice* 76:125–50.

Lough, J. 1960. *An Introduction to Eighteenth Century France*. London: Longmans, Green.

———. 1969. *An Introduction to Seventeenth Century France*. New York: David McKay.

Lowry, S. T., ed. 1987. *Pre-Classical Economic Thought: From the Greeks to the Scottish Enlightenment*. Boston: Kluwer Academic Publishers.

Macfarlane, A. 1978. *The Origins of English Individualism: The Family, Property and Social Transition*. New York: Cambridge University Press.

Magee, S. P., W. A. Brock, and L. Young. 1989. *Black Hole Tariffs and Endogenous Policy Theory*. Cambridge: Cambridge University Press.

Magnusson, L. 1978. "Eli Heckscher, Mercantilism, and the Favorable Balance of Trade." *Scandinavian Economic History Review* 26:103–27.

———. 1987. "Mercantilism and 'Reform' Mercantilism: The Rise of Economic Discourse in Sweden During the Eighteenth Century." *History of Political Economy* 19:415–33.

———, ed. 1993a. *Mercantilist Economics*. Boston: Kluwer Academic Publishers.

———, ed. 1993b. *Evolutionary and Neo-Schumpeterian Approaches to Economics*. Boston: Kluwer Academic Publishers.

———. 1994. *Mercantilism: The Shaping of an Economic Language*. London and New York: Routledge.

Maitland, F. W. 1908. *Constitutional History of England*. Cambridge: Cambridge University Press.

———. 1957. *Selected Historical Essays of F. W. Maitland*, ed. Helen M. Cam. Cambridge: Cambridge University Press.

Maitland, F. W., and F. C. Montague. 1915. *A Sketch of English Constitutional History*. New York: G. O. Putnam's Sons.

Malament, B. 1967. "The 'Economic Liberalism' of Sir Edward Coke." *Yale Law Journal* 76:1321–58.

Maloney, M. T., and R. E. McCormick. 1982. "A Positive Theory of Environmental Quality Regulation." *Journal of Law and Economics* 25:99–124.

Marín Barriguete, F. 1990a. "Campomanes, Presidente de la Mesta." In *Actas del Congreso Internacional Sobre Carlos III y su Siglo*, 93–114. Madrid: Universidad Complutense.

———. 1990b. "Reformismo y Ganadería: el Honrado Concejo de la Mesta en el Reinado de Carlos III." In *Actas del Congreso Internacional Sobre Carlos III y su Siglo*, 569–86. Madrid: Universidad Complutense.

Marris, R., and D. C. Mueller. 1980. "The Corporation and Competition." *Journal of Economic Literature* 18:32–63.

Marshall, P. J. 1976. *East India Fortunes: The British in Bengal in the Eighteenth Century*. Oxford: Oxford University Press.

Marshall, T. H. 1935. "Review of Heckscher's *Mercantilism*." *Economic Journal* 14:716–19.

Marvel, H. P. 1977. "Factory Regulation: A Reinterpretation of Early English Experience." *Journal of Law and Economics* 20:379–402.

Masselman, G. 1963. *The Cradle of Colonialism*. New Haven: Yale University Press.

McChesney, F. 1987. "Rent Extraction and Rent Creation in the Economic Theory of Regulation." *Journal of Legal Studies* 16:101–18.

McCord, N. 1983. "Review of Mercantilism as a Rent-Seeking Society." *International Review of Law and Economics* 3:94–95.

McCormick, R. E., and R. D. Tollison. 1980. "Wealth Transfers in a Representative Democracy." In *Toward a Theory of the Rent-Seeking Society*, ed. J. M. Buchanan, R. D. Tollison, and G. Tullock, 293–313. College Station: Texas A&M University Press.

———. 1981. *Politicians, Legislation and the Economy: An Inquiry into the Interest-Group Theory of Government*. Boston: Martinus Nijhoff.

McCulloch, J. R. 1970. *Early English Tracts on Commerce*. London: Cambridge University Press.

Meiners, R. E., J. S. Mofsky, and R. D. Tollison. 1979. "Piercing the Veil of Limited Liability." *Delaware Journal of Corporation Law* 4:351–67.

Mettam, R. 1977. *Government and Society in Louis XIV's France.* London: Macmillan.

Michener, J. A. 1968. *Iberia: Spanish Travels and Reflections.* New York: Random House.

Mill, J. S. 1965 [1848]. *Principles of Political Economy,* ed. W. Ashley. New York: A. M. Kelley.

Mixon, F., D. N. Laband, and R. B. Ekelund, Jr. 1994. "Rent Seeking and Hidden Resource Distortion: Some Empirical Evidence." *Public Choice* 78:171–85.

Mizuta, H. 1967. *Adam Smith's Library: A Supplement with a Checklist of the Whole Library.* Cambridge: Cambridge University Press.

Mohammed, S., and J. Whalley. 1984. "Rent Seeking in India: Its Costs and Policy Significance." *Kyklos* 37:387–413.

Moote, A. L. 1971. *The Revolt of the Judges.* Princeton: Princeton University Press.

Morris, C. T. 1957. "Some Neglected Aspects of Sixteenth Century Economic Thought." *Explorations in Entrepreneurial History* 9:160–71.

Morris, R. B., ed. 1961. *Encyclopedia of American History.* New York: Harper and Brothers.

Moss, L. 1983. "Review of *Mercantilism as a Rent-Seeking Society.*" *Southern Economic Journal* 49:901–2.

Mundell, R. A. 1962. "Review of L. H. Janssen: Free Trade, Protection and Customs Unions." *American Economic Review* 52:622.

Murphy, K. M., A. Schleifer, and R. W. Vishny. 1991. "The Allocation of Talent: Implications for Growth." *Quarterly Journal of Economics* 106:503–31.

Myint, H. 1983. "Review of Mercantilism as a Rent-Seeking Society." *Economica* 50: 99–100.

Nadal, J. 1986. *La Población Española (Siglos XVI a XX).* Barcelona: Editorial.

Nef, J. U. 1968 [1940]. *Industry and Government in France and England, 1540–1640.* New York: Russell and Russell.

Netanyahu, B. 1995. *The Origins of the Inquisition in Fifteenth Century Spain.* New York: Random House.

Nichols, W. M. 1941. *Imperfect Competition within the Agricultural Industries.* Ames: Iowa State College Press.

Nieto, A. 1986. "La Posesión." In P. García Martín and J. M. Sánchez Benito, *Contribución a la historia de la Transhumancia en España.* Madrid: Ministerio de Agricultura.

Niskanen, W. A. 1971. *Bureaucracy and Representative Government.* Chicago: Aldine-Atherton Press.

North, D. C. 1978. "Structure and Performance: The Task of Economic History." *Journal of Economic Literature* 16:963–78.

———. 1979. "A Framework for Analyzing the State in Economic History." *Explorations in Economic History* 16:249–59.

———. 1981. *Structure and Change in Economic History.* New York: Norton.

———. 1989. "Institutions and Economic Growth: An Historical Introduction." *World Development* 17:1319–32.

———. 1990. *Institutions, Institutional Change and Economic Performance.* Cambridge: Cambridge University Press.

North, D. C., and R. P. Thomas. 1973. *The Rise of the Western World.* Cambridge: Cambridge University Press.

North, D. C., and B. R. Weingast. 1989. "Constitutions and Commitment: The Evolution of Institutions Governing Public Choice in Seventeenth-Century England." *Journal of Economic History* 49:803–32.

Nugent, J. B., and N. Sanchez. 1989. "The Efficiency of the Mesta: A Parable." *Explorations in Economic History* 26:261–84.

Olson, M. 1982. *The Rise and Decline of Nations*. New Haven: Yale University Press.

Ortega López, M. 1986. *La Lucha por la Tierra en la Corona de Castilla al Final de Antiguo Régimen*. Madrid: Ministerio de Agricultura.

Papillon, T. 1696. *A Treatise Concerning the East India Trade*. London: Privately Published.

Pastor de Togneiri, R. 1970. "La Lana en Castilla y León antes de la Organización de la Mesta." *Moneda y Crédito* 112:47–70.

Payne, A. N. 1930. "The Relation of the English Commercial Companies to the Government, 1660–1715." Ph.D. diss., University of Illinois.

Pejovich, S. 1995. *Economic Analysis of Institutions and Systems*. Dordrecht: Kluwer Academic Publishers.

Peltzman, S. 1976. "Toward a More General Theory of Regulation." *Journal of Law and Economics* 2:211–40.

———. 1984. "Constituent Interest and Congressional Voting." *Journal of Law and Economics* 27:181–210.

Perrotta, C. 1991. "Is the Mercantilist Theory of the Favorable Balance of Trade Really Erroneous?" *History of Political Economy* 23:301–36.

———. 1993. "Early Spanish Mercantilism: The First Analysis of Underdevelopment." In *Mercantilist Economics*, ed. L. Magnusson. Boston: Kluwer Academic Publishers.

Peters, E. 1988. *Inquisition*. New York: Free Press.

Philips, C. H. 1940. *The East India Company, 1784–1834*. Manchester: University of Manchester Press.

Phillips, C. R. 1979. *Ciudad Real, 1500–1750: Growth, Crisis, and Readjustment in the Spanish Economy*. Cambridge: Harvard University Press.

———. 1982. "The Spanish Wool Trade, 1500–1780." *Journal of Economic History* 42: 775–95.

———. 1987. "Time and Duration: A Model for the Economy of Early Modern Spain." *American Historical Review* 92:531–62.

Phillips, C. R., and W. D. Phillips, Jr. 1977. "The Castilian Fairs in Burgos, 1601–1604." *Journal of European Economic History* 6:413–29.

Pinus, J. J. 1975. "Pressure Groups and the Pattern of Tariffs." *Journal of Political Economy* 83:757–78.

Plucknett, T. F. 1948. *A Concise History of the Common Law*. London: Butterworth.

Pollock, F., and F. W. Maitland. 1895. *The History of English Law before the Time of Edward I*, vols. 1 and 2. Cambridge: Cambridge University Press.

Posner, R. A. 1971. "Taxation by Regulation." *Bell Journal of Economics and Management Science* 2:22–50.

———. 1974. "Theories of Economic Regulation." *Bell Journal of Economics and Management Science* 5:335–58.

———. 1975. "The Social Costs of Monopoly and Regulation." *Journal of Political Economy* 83:807–27.

Pound, R., and Plucknett, T. F. T. 1927. *Readings on the History and System of the Common Law*. 3d ed. Rochester, N.Y.: Lawyers Co-operative Publishing Company.

Power, E. 1941. *The Wool Trade in English Medieval History*. London: Oxford University Press.

Prescott, W. H. 1850. *History of the Reign of Ferdinand and Isabella the Catholic*. New York: Harper and Brothers.

Prest, W. R. 1986. *The Rise of the Barristers: A Social History of the English Bar, 1590–1640*. Oxford: Clarendon Press.

Priest, G. L. 1975. "The History of the Postal Monopoly in the United States." *Journal of Law and Economics* 18:33–80.

Raines, J. P., and C. G. Leathers. 1993. "Evolving Financial Institutions in Veblen's Business Enterprise System." *Journal of the History of Economic Thought* 15:249–64.

Rashid, S. 1986. "Lord Townshend and the Influence of Moral Philosophy on *Laissez Faire*." *Journal of Libertarian Studies* 8:69–74.

———. 1993. "Mercantilism: A Rent-Seeking Society?" In *Mercantilist Economics*, ed. L. Magnusson. Boston: Kluwer Academic Publishers.

Rausch, J. 1922. "The Parasite Economy." *National Journal* 24:980–95.

Reid, J. D. 1973. "Sharecropping as an Understandable Market Response: The Post-Bellum South." *Journal of Economic History* 33:106–30.

Rider, C. 1995. *An Introduction to Economic History*. Cincinnati: South-Western College Publishing.

Richardson, W. C. 1975. *A History of the Inns of Court: With Special Reference to the Period of the Renaissance*. Baton Rouge, La.: Claitors Publishing Division.

Rider, C. 1995. *An Introduction to Economic History*. Cincinnati: South-Western College Publishing.

Ringrose, D. R. 1970. *Madrid and the Spanish Economy*. Durham: Duke University Press.

Robertson, D. 1957. *Lectures on Economic Principles*, vol. 1. London: Staples Press.

Rodríguez, L. 1973a. "El Motín de Madrid de 1766." *Revista de Occidente* 121:24–49.

———. 1973b. "Los Motines de 1766 en Provincias." *Revista de Occidente* 122:183–207.

Roehl, R. 1976. "French Industrialization: A Reconsideration." *Explorations in Economic History* 13:233–81.

Rogerson, W. P. 1982. "The Social Costs of Monopoly and Regulation: A Game-Theoretic Analysis." *Bell Journal of Economics* 13:391–401.

Root, H. L. 1994. *The Fountain of Privilege: Political Foundations of Markets in Old Regime France and England*. Berkeley and Los Angeles: University of California Press.

Ross, V. B. 1984. "Rent-Seeking in LDC Import Regimes: The Case of Kenya." Discussion Papers in International Economics: No. 8408. Geneva: Graduate Institute of International Studies.

Rothbard, M. N. 1976. "New Light on the Pre-history of the Austrian School." In *The Foundations of Modern Austrian Economics*, ed. E. Dolan. Kansas City: Sheed and Ward.

Rothbard, M. N. 1995. *Economic Thought before Adam Smith: An Austrian Perspective on the History of Economic Thought*, vol. 1. London: Edward Elgar.

Roy, P. 1943. "The Mercantilist View of Money in Relation to Public Finance." *Indian Journal of Economics* 23:257–70.

Rubin, Paul H. 1978. "The Theory of the Firm and the Structure of the Franchise Contract." *Journal of Law and Economics* 21:223–34.

Rude, G. F. 1964. *The Crowd in History: A Study of Popular Disturbances in France and England, 1730–1848.* New York: John Wiley.

Ruigh, R. E. 1971. *The Parliament of 1624: Politics and Foreign Policy.* Cambridge: Harvard University Press.

Ruiz Martín, F. 1974. "Pastos y Ganaderos en Castilla: La Mesta (1450–1600)." In *Atti della Prima Settimana de Studio,* 271–85.

Rutherford, M. 1994. *Institutions in Economics: The Old and the New Institutionalism.* Cambridge: Cambridge University Press.

Schaeper, T. J. 1983. *The French Council of Commerce, 1700–1715: A Study of Mercantilism after Colbert.* Columbus: Ohio State University Press.

Schmoller, G. 1897. *The Mercantile System and Its Historical Significance.* New York: Macmillan.

Schumpeter, J. A. 1954. *History of Economic Analysis.* New York: Oxford University Press.

Schuyler, Robert L., ed. 1931. *Josiah Tucker: A Selection From His Economic and Political Writings.* New York: Columbia University Press.

Schwier, A. 1984. "Review of *Mercantilism as a Rent-Seeking Society.*" *Review of Social Economy* 42:64–65.

Scott, W. R. 1951 [1912]. *The Constitution and Finance of English, Scottish, and Irish Joint-Stock Companies to 1720.* 2 vols. New York: Peter Smith.

Scoville, W. C. 1960. *The Persecution of Huguenots and French Economic Development, 1680–1720.* Berkeley and Los Angeles: University of California Press.

See, H. 1927. *Economic and Social Conditions in France during the Eighteenth Century.* New York: Knopf.

Seltzer, A. 1995. "The Political Economy of the Fair Labor Standards Act of 1938." *Journal of Political Economy* 103:1302–42.

Shannon, H. A. 1931. "The Coming of General Limited Liability." *Economic History* 2:267–91.

Smith, A. 1976 [1776]. *An Inquiry Into the Nature and Causes of the Wealth of Nations.* Oxford: Clarendon Press.

Smith, A. 1937 [1776]. *The Wealth of Nations,* ed. E. Cannan. New York: Random House.

Smith, R. S. 1971. "Spanish Mercantilism: A Hardy Perennial." *Southern Economic Journal* 37:1–11.

Staley, C. E. 1983. "Review of *Mercantilism as a Rent-Seeking Society.*" *History of Political Economy* 15:141–42.

Stevens, H. 1967. *The Dawn of British Trade to the East Indies.* London: Frank Cues.

Stigler, G. J. 1951. "The Division of Labor Is Limited by the Extent of the Market." *Journal of Political Economy* 59:185–93.

———. 1964. "A Theory of Oligopoly." *Journal of Political Economy* 72:44–61.

———. 1968. "Price and Non-Price Competition." *Journal of Political Economy* 76: 149–54.

———. 1971a. "Smith's Travels on the Ship of State." *History of Political Economy* 3:265–77.

———. 1971b. "The Theory of Economic Regulation." *Bell Journal of Economics and Management Science* 2:3–21.

———. 1982. *The Economist as Preacher and Other Essays.* Chicago: University of Chicago Press.

Stigler, G. J., and C. Friedland. 1962. "What Can Regulators Regulate? The Case of Electricity." *Journal of Law and Economics* 5:1–23.

Stoetzer, M. W. 1988. "Review of *Mercantilism as a Rent-Seeking Society.*" *Kyklos* 41: 672–74.

Street, D. R. 1986. "The Authorship of Campomanes' *Discurso sobre el fomento de la industria popular:* A Note." *History of Political Economy* 18:655–60.

———. 1987. "The Economic Societies: Springboard to the Spanish Enlightenment." *Journal of European Economic History* 16:469–585.

———. 1988. "Jovellanos, An Antecedent to Modern Human Capital Theory." *History of Political Economy* 20:191–206.

———. 1991. "The Authorship of Campomanes' Discurso sobre el fomento de la industrial popular: A Reply." *History of Political Economy* 23:533–36.

———. 1994. "Spanish Enlightenment Economics." SECOLAS Annals, 30–42. Statesboro: Georgia Southern University.

Tawney, R. H., ed. 1958. *Studies in Economic History: The Collected Papers of George Unwin.* London: Royal Economic Society Reprint.

Tawney, R. H., and E. Power. 1924. *Tudor Economic Documents,* vols. 1, 2, and 3. London: Longmans, Green.

Taylor, H. 1898. *The Origin and Growth of the English Constitution.* Part 2. Boston: Houghton, Mifflin.

Thirsk, J. 1978. *Economic Policy and Projects: The Development of a Consumer Society in Early Modern England.* Oxford: Clarendon Press.

Thompson, I. A. 1979. "The Purchase of Nobility in Castile, 1552–1700." *Journal of European Economic History* 8:313–60.

Thornton, M. 1991. *The Economics of Prohibition.* Salt Lake City: University of Utah Press.

———. 1994. "Slavery, Profitability, and the Market Process." *Review of Austrian Economics* 7:21–47.

Tollison, R. D. 1978. "An Historical Note on Regulatory Reform." *Regulation* 2:46–49.

———. 1982. "Rent Seeking: A Survey." *Kyklos* 35:575–602.

———. 1987. "Is the Theory of Rent Seeking Here to Stay?" In *Democracy and Public Choice,* ed. C. K. Rowley, 143–57. London: Blackwell.

Tollison, R. D., and R. E. Wagner. 1991. "Romance, Reality, and Economic Reform." *Kyklos* 44:57–70.

Tullock, G. 1967. "The Welfare Costs of Tariffs, Monopolies, and Theft." *Western Economic Journal* 5:224–32.

———. 1980a. "Efficient Rent-Seeking." In *Toward a Theory of the Rent-Seeking Society,* ed. J. M. Buchanan, R. D. Tollison, and G. Tullock, 97–112. College Station: Texas A&M University Press.

———. 1980b. "Rent-Seeking as a Negative-Sum Game." In *Toward a Theory of the Rent-Seeking Society,* ed. J. M. Buchanan, R. D. Tollison, and G. Tullock, 16–36. College Station: Texas A&M University Press.

———. 1985. "Back to the Bog." *Public Choice* 46:259–64.

———. 1988. "Why Did the Industrial Revolution Occur in England?" In *The Political Economy of Rent Seeking,* C. K. Rowley, R. D. Tollison, and G. Tullock, 409–19. Boston: Luwer.

Tuma, E. H. 1971. *European Economic History.* New York: Harper and Row.

Turberville, A. S. 1968. *The Spanish Inquisition.* New York: Archon.

Urzainqui, I., and A. Ruiz 1983. *Periodismo e illustración en Manuel Rubín de Celis.* Oviedo.

Vassberg, D. E. 1983. *La Venta de Tierras Baldías. El Comunitarismo Agrario y la Corona de Castilla Durante el Siglo XVI.* Madrid: Ministerio de Agricultura.

———. 1986 [1984]. *Tierra y Sociedad en Castilla.* Trans. J. Vicuña Gutiérrez y M. Ortuño. Barcelona: Editorial Crítica.

Vicens-Vives, J. 1969. *An Economic History of Spain.* Princeton: Princeton University Press.

Viner, J. 1930. "English Theories of Foreign Trade Before Adam Smith." Parts 1 and 2. *Journal of Political Economy* 38:249–301, 404–57.

———. 1967 [1937]. *Studies in the Theory of International Trade.* New York: A. M. Kelley.

Wagner, D. O. 1935. "Coke and the Rise of Economic Liberalism." *Economic History Review* 6:30–44.

———. 1937. "The Common Law and Free Enterprise: An Early Case of Monopoly." *Economic History Review* (1st series): 217–20.

Walker, D. A. 1993. "Virginian Tobacco During the Reign of the Early Stuarts: A Case Study of Mercantilist Theories, Policies, and Results." In *Mercantilist Economics,* ed. L. Magnusson. Boston: Kluwer Academic Publishers.

Watts, R. L., and J. L. Zimmerman. 1981. "The Markets for Independence and Independent Auditors," Graduate School of Management, University of Rochester, Working paper series, no. GPB 80–10.

Weingast, B. R. 1995. "The Economic Role of Political Institutions: Market-Preserving Federalism and Economic Development." *Journal of Law, Economics and Organization* 11:1–31.

West, E. G. 1977. "Adam Smith's Public Economics: A Re-evaluation." *Canadian Journal of Economics* 10:1–18.

White, G. 1691. *An Account of the Trade to the East Indies Together With the State of the Present.* London: Privately Printed.

White, S. D. 1979. *Sir Edward Coke and the 'The Grievances of the Commonwealth,' 1621–1628.* Chapel Hill: University of North Carolina Press.

Wilbur, M. E. 1970. *The East India Company and the British Empire in the Far East.* New York: R. R. Smith.

Wiles, R. C. 1987. "The Development of Mercantilist Economic Thought." In *Pre-Classical Economic Thought,* ed. S. T. Lowry. Boston: Kluwer Academic Publishers.

Willan, T. J. 1968a [1959]. *Studies in Elizabethan Foreign Trade.* New York: A. M. Kelley.

———. 1968b [1956]. *The Early History of the Russia Company, 1553–1603.* New York: A. M. Kelley.

Williamson, O. E. 1975. *Markets and Hierarchies: Analysis and Antitrust Implications.* New York: Free Press.

———. 1976. "Franchise Bidding for Natural Monopolies—In General and with Respect to CATV." *Bell Journal of Economics* 7:73–104.

Wilson, C. 1959. "The Other Face of Mercantilism." *Transactions of the Royal Historical Society* 9:81–103.

Wilson, C. 1963. *Mercantilism.* London: Routledge and Kegan Paul.

Wilson, C. 1968. "Government Policy and Private Interest in Modern English History." In *Historical Studies,* ed. T. W. Moody. New York: Barnes and Noble.

Wilson, C. R. 1963. *The Early Annals of the English in Bengal.* Vol. 2, part 2: *The Surman Embassy.* New Delhi: Bimla Publishing House.

Wolfe, M. 1972. *The Fiscal System of Renaissance France.* New Haven: Yale University Press.

Wolfe, M. 1984. "Review of *Mercantilism as a Rent-Seeking Society.*" *Journal of European Economic History* 13:672–74.

Woodruff, W. 1983. "Review of *Mercantilism as a Rent-Seeking Society.*" *American Historical Review* 88:81–83.

Yandle, B. 1993. "Sir Edward Coke and the Struggle for a New Constitutional Order." *Constitutional Political Economy* 4:263–85.

Index